Biomedicine and Beatitude

CATHOLIC MORAL THOUGHT

General Editor: Romanus Cessario, O.P.

Biomedicine and Beatitude

An Introduction to Catholic Bioethics

Nicanor Pier Giorgio Austriaco, O.P.

The Catholic University of America Press
Washington, D.C.

Imprimi Potest:
Very Reverend D. Domonic Izzo, O.P.
Prior Provincial
Province of Saint Joseph

Nihil Obstat:
Reverend Basil Cole, O.P.
Censor Deputatus

Imprimatur:
Most Reverend Barry C. Knestout
Auxiliary Bishop of Washington
Archdiocese of Washington
July 26, 2010

The *nihil obstat* and *imprimatur* are official declarations that a book or
pamphlet is free of doctrinal or moral error. There is no implication
that those who have granted the *nihil obstat* and the *imprimatur* agree
with the content, opinions, or statements expressed therein.

Library of Congress Cataloging-in-Publication Data
Austriaco, Nicanor Pier Giorgio.
Biomedicine and beatitude : an introduction to Catholic bioethics /
Nicanor Pier Giorgio Austriaco.
p. cm. — (Catholic moral thought)
Includes bibliographical references (p.   ) and index.
ISBN 978-0-8132-1881-6 (cloth : alk. paper) — ISBN 978-0-8132-1882-3
(pbk. : alk. paper)
1. Bioethics—Religious aspects—Catholic Church.   I. Title.
QH332.A97 2012
241'.64957—dc23
2011014813

To my parents

Contents

Abbreviations

Acad Med	Academic Medicine
Adv Contracept	Advances in Contraception
Am Fam Physician	American Family Physician
Am J Bioeth	The American Journal of Bioethics
Am J Epidemiol	American Journal of Epidemiology
Am J Hosp Palliat Care	The American Journal of Hospice and Palliative Care
Am J Kidney Dis	American Journal of Kidney Diseases
Am J Obstet Gynecol	American Journal of Obstetrics and Gynecology
Am J Prev Med	American Journal of Preventive Medicine
Am J Psychiatry	The American Journal of Psychiatry
Am J Transplant	American Journal of Transplantation
Ann Intern Med	Annals of Internal Medicine
Ann N Y Acad Sci	Annals of the New York Academy of Sciences
Ann Oncol	Annals of Oncology
Arch Fam Med	Archives of Family Medicine
Arch Intern Med	Archives of Internal Medicine
Arch Neurol	Archives of Neurology
Arch Phys Med Rehabil	Archives of Physical Medicine and Rehabilitation
BMC Med	BMC Medicine
BMJ	BMJ (Clinical Research Ed., British Medical Journal)
Brain Inj	Brain Injury
Br J Psychiatry	The British Journal of Psychiatry
Christ Bioeth	Christian Bioethics
Clin Geriatr Med	Clinics in Geriatric Medicine

Clin J Am Soc Nephrol	Clinical Journal of the American Society of Nephrology
Clin Res	Clinical Research
Cloning Stem Cells	Cloning and Stem Cells
CMAJ	Canadian Medical Association Journal
C R Biol	Comptes Rendus Biologies
Crit Care Med	Critical Care Medicine
Curr Anthropol	Current Anthropology
Curr Opin Biotech	Current Opinion in Biotechnology
Curr Opin Gastroenterol	Current Opinion in Gastroenterology
Curr Opin Neurol	Current Opinion in Neurology
Curr Opin Organ Transplant	Current Opinion in Organ Transplantation
Curr Opin Pharmacol	Current Opinion in Pharmacology
Curr Opin Support Palliat Care	Current Opinion in Supportive and Palliative Care
Emerg Med Clin North Am	Emergency Medicine Clinics of North America
Ethics Medics	Ethics and Medics
Fertil Steril	Fertility and Sterility
Hastings Cent Rep	The Hastings Center Report
Health Prog	Health Progress
Hum Reprod	Human Reproduction
Immunol Allergy Clin North Am	Immunology and Allergy Clinics of North America
Int J Cancer	International Journal of Cancer
Int J Ment Health Addict	International Journal of Mental Health and Addiction
Issues Law Med	Issues in Law and Medicine
JAMA	The Journal of the American Medical Association
J Acquir Immune Defic Syndr	Journal of Acquired Immune Deficiency Syndromes
J Clin Invest	The Journal of Clinical Investigation
J Clin Oncol	Journal of Clinical Oncology
J Gen Intern Med	Journal of General Internal Medicine
J Health Care Poor Underserved	Journal of Health Care for the Poor and Underserved

J Law Med Ethics	*The Journal of Law, Medicine, and Ethics*
J Leg Med	*The Journal of Legal Medicine*
J Med Ethics	*Journal of Medical Ethics*
J Med Philos	*The Journal of Medicine and Philosophy*
J Neurol Sci	*Journal of the Neurological Sciences*
J Pain Symptom Manage	*Journal of Pain and Symptom Management*
J Pathol	*The Journal of Pathology*
J Psychosom Obstet Gynaecol	*Journal of Psychosomatic Obstetrics and Gynaecology*
J R Coll Physicians Edinb	*The Journal of the Royal College of Physicians of Edinburgh*
J Relig Health	*Journal of Religion and Health*
Kennedy Inst Ethics J	*Kennedy Institute of Ethics Journal*
Kidney Int	*Kidney International*
Lancet Oncol	*The Lancet Oncology*
Linacre Q	*The Linacre Quarterly*
Mayo Clin Proc	*Mayo Clinic Proceedings*
Milbank Mem Fund Q Health Soc	*The Milbank Memorial Fund Quarterly. Health and Society*
Mol Ecol	*Molecular Ecology*
Nat Biotechnol	*Nature Biotechnology*
Natl Cathol Bioeth Q	*National Catholic Bioethics Quarterly*
N Engl J Med	*New England Journal of Medicine*
Palliat Med	*Palliative Medicine*
Perspect Sex Reprod Health	*Perspectives on Sexual and Reproductive Health*
Philos Ethics Humanit Med	*Philosophy, Ethics, and Humanities in Medicine*
PLoS Med	*PLoS Medicine*
Proc Nutr Soc	*The Proceedings of the Nutrition Society*
Prog Brain Res	*Progress in Brain Research*
Q JM	*Q JM: Monthly Journal of the Association of Physicians*
Regen Med	*Regenerative Medicine*

Reprod BioMed Online Reproductive Biomedicine Online

Rev Neurol Dis Reviews in Neurological Diseases

Semin Neurol Seminars in Neurology

Semin Perinatol Seminars in Perinatology

Semin Reprod Med Seminars in Reproductive Medicine

ST Summa Theologiae

Stud Fam Plann Studies in Family Planning

Stud Hastings Cent Studies—Hastings Center

Theor Med Bioeth Theoretical Medicine and Bioethics

Transpl Int Transplant International

Trends Genet Trends in Genetics

Yale J Health Policy Law Ethics Yale Journal of Health Policy, Law, and Ethics

Acknowledgments

"In all circumstances give thanks, for this is the will of God for you in Christ Jesus" (1 Thes 5:18). I have been writing this book for some time now, and many persons have contributed to this project over the years.

First, I would like to thank David McGonagle of the Catholic University of America Press, and Romanus Cessario, O.P., the general editor of this series in moral theology, for their invitation to contribute to this project. My students at Providence College, especially my undergraduate research students in the Dead Yeast Society, were always supportive during the writing of this book. Many of them asked penetrating questions that challenged me to articulate better the issues raised in its pages. Special thanks go to Yi Cao, James Cebulski, Shawn Davidson, Erik Gravel, Kevin Murphy, James Ritch, and Jared Sheehan, for our late-night conversations. Erik also read an early draft of the manuscript and gave me a student's perspective on the text. Robert Pfunder was a terrific research assistant—my first ever—who helped me track down more than a single citation. I am grateful to him for his exacting work. Professor William E. May read sections of the manuscript for me. I benefited much from his insights and his generous criticism. Finally, I also thank Joseph J. Piccione and Alfred Cioffi for their expert comments, and Denise Carlson and Carol Kennedy, for their expert assistance in the final production of this book.

Next, I would like to thank my Dominican brothers for their support. Jonathan Kalisch, O.P., and Edward Gorman, O.P., encouraged me to write weekly contributions on bioethical topics of interest for our parishioners at St. Catherine of Siena Parish in New York City. These columns became the basis for many of the sections of this text. Romanus Cessario, O.P., Paul Conner, O.P., Christopher Saliga, O.P., and Ezra Sullivan, O.P., each read chapter drafts and sent me numerous helpful comments. Finally, I am extraordinarily indebted to Basil Cole, O.P., not only for reading every single word of the manuscript several times over, but also for giving me his unfailing encouragement and love.

Last but not least, on a personal note, I especially thank my Dominican brothers Basil Cole, O.P., and Ezra Sullivan, O.P., for their friendship; my Dominican sisters, Sr. Mary of the Sacred Heart, O.P., and Sr. Mary Catherine of the Divine Mercy, O.P., nuns of the Order of Preachers, for their relentless prayers, my Hawthorne Dominican sisters, especially Mother Mary Francis Lepore, O.P., for their tireless and inspiring witness to the inherent dignity of the human person; my parents for their unwavering love that has sustained my siblings and me through the many joys and sorrows of life; and most especially, I thank the triune God, Father, Son, and Holy Spirit, for everything. *Non nisi te, Domine.*

Providence, Rhode Island
February 2, 2011
Feast of the Presentation of the Lord

Biomedicine and Beatitude

Introduction

On November 21, 1964, Pope Paul VI solemnly promulgated the Second Vatican Council's Dogmatic Constitution on the Church, *Lumen gentium*, which articulated the Church's self-understanding about her nature and her universal mission. In essence, according to the Council Fathers, the Church is a sacrament of unity, "a sign and instrument, that is, of unity of communion with God and of unity among all men."[1] A community of faith, hope, and charity, she, as the Apostles' Creed proclaims, is one, holy, catholic, and apostolic. The Church's primary vocation, the Council proclaimed, is to call her sons and daughters to holiness, because the commandment of charity is addressed to all without distinction: "It is therefore quite clear that all Christians in any state or walk of life are called to the fullness of Christian life and to the perfection of love, and by this holiness a more human manner of life is fostered also in earthly society."[2] Ultimately, as sacred Scripture reveals and the Council affirms, the Christian is called to become a saint.

In response to the Second Vatican Council's universal call to holiness, this book narrates a bioethics that emphasizes the pursuit of beatitude in the lives of those who are confronted by the moral questions raised by the biomedical and the other life sciences, and the dynamic interplay of faith and reason that characterizes the Catholic tradition. In this brief introduction, I begin with a synopsis of the themes and the topics that we will discuss in the pages to come.

In chapter 1, I open with an overview of the Catholic moral vision that

---

1. Dogmatic Constitution on the Church, *Lumen Gentium*, no. 1. This citation is from Austin Flannery, O.P., ed., *Vatican Council II: The Conciliar and Post Conciliar Documents* (Northport, N.Y.: Costello Publishing Company, 1975), 350. Subsequent references to Council documents will be to this edition.

2. Ibid., no. 40; 397. For insightful commentary on the universal call of holiness proclaimed in *Lumen Gentium*, see Benôit-Dominique de La Soujeole, O.P., "The Universal Call to Holiness," in *Vatican II: Renewal Within Tradition*, edited by Matthew L. Lamb and Matthew Levering, 37–53 (Oxford: Oxford University Press, 2008).

places bioethics within the context of each individual's striving to imitate the Lord Jesus Christ, particularly in the practice of charity. It is a moral vision that strives to remain faithful to the moral life described by the Lord in His Sermon on the Mount by bringing together faith and reason. As Pope John Paul II taught in his moral encyclical, *Veritatis splendor,* we imitate Christ by seeking, with God's grace, to perfect ourselves through our actions and the virtues they engender. Much emphasis is placed upon how individual acts affect the acting person because it is through these acts that the human agent attains beatitude. In this way, Catholic bioethics differs from other contemporary approaches to bioethics that focus upon either the outcomes of human acts or the procedures that protect the autonomy of the human agent.

In the next chapter, I move to the moral questions at the beginning-of-life. I begin with a discussion of the dignity of the human person, the bedrock foundation for Catholic bioethics, followed by a summary of the Catholic Church's teaching on abortion. The two-thousand-year-old Christian tradition is clear: abortion is a grave moral evil. I then explore and respond to the four arguments that are often used to justify abortions in our free and democratic society, before concluding with a question that often arises in Catholic discussions surrounding the beginning of life: when is the human being ensouled?

Then, in chapter 3, I confront the moral questions raised by scientific developments that impact human procreation—scientific advances that can help a couple prevent or assist the conception of their child. How do we determine if these practices can help the acting person to virtuously respond to the universal call of holiness? Briefly, as Pope John Paul II, confirming the consistent teaching of the Catholic tradition, explained in his theology of the body, authentic conjugal acts have to be open to the transmission of life. This criterion can be used to judge the morality of the different methods available to regulate birth. Natural family planning methods to regulate birth meet this standard because they respect the structure and meaning of human sexuality, and as such are morally upright. In contrast, contraceptive methods to regulate births do not pass this test, that they respect the inseparability principle, the moral principle that affirms that it is necessary that each and every marriage act of sexual intercourse remain ordered per se to the procreation of human life. They distort the structure and meaning of human sexuality and as such are morally reprehensible. Finally, to end chapter 3, I deal with questions that arise from infertility and the technologies that seek to address the sufferings of an infertile couple, including in vitro fertilization, other forms of assisted reproductive technologies, and the emerging possibility of human cloning.

Next, in chapter 4, I deal with several issues surrounding the decision-making process of the patient and his physician, as they are understood within the tradition of Catholic bioethics. We begin with a discussion of the identities of the patient and of the health care professional in the clinical encounter. How are we to understand their particular roles in the struggle with illness? I then move both to the professional-patient relationship that forms the context for many of the healthcare decisions entrusted to the patient, and to the question of confidentiality, an essential ingredient that protects the integrity of this relationship. I conclude with a discussion of informed consent, the process that allows a patient to become a prudent participant in all decision making regarding his health care.

In chapter 5, I move to the moral issues that surround death and the dying process. The chapter opens with a theological account of death and then turns to the two most common scenarios in the clinical setting that raise troubling moral questions at the end of life. The first deals with the management of intense pain that risks hastening the patient's death, while the second deals with the refusal or the discontinuation of medical treatment. I then consider the moral debates surrounding euthanasia, physician-assisted suicide, and the care of individuals in the persistent vegetative state (PVS), the minimally conscious state (MCS), and other disorders of consciousness. In recognition of the truth that life, though inviolable, is not an absolute good, the Catholic moral tradition teaches that we are not morally obligated to use extraordinary means to maintain our lives. This is the principle of elective extraordinary means that should govern the actions of persons seeking to die virtuously.

Chapter 6 deals with the ethics of organ transplantation. I begin with the moral framework that is used to justify the practice of organ donation and exchange: organ donation is an act of self-giving that should be motivated by charity. Because of this, proposals that legitimate the sale and purchase of human organs are illicit. Next, as Pope Benedict XVI reminded the Church and the world in a speech to an international congress on organ transplants, vital organs can be taken only from a person who has been declared dead: "It is helpful to remember, however, that the individual vital organs cannot be extracted except *ex cadavere*."[3] It is not surprising, therefore, that Catholic and other bioethicists continue to try to answer the following question accurately and truthfully: how do we know that someone is dead? Thus, I end this chapter with a critical survey of the debate surrounding the definition of death and the neurological criteria that equate brain death with death, concluding that the available evidence indicates that brain-dead patients are *not* dead.

In chapter 7, I turn to the moral questions raised by biomedical research, beginning with those concerns raised by experimentation with human subjects. The Catholic Church has endorsed the ethical principles summarized both in the Nuremberg Code, written in 1947 in response to the atrocities carried out by Nazi scientists on vulnerable subjects, and in the Declaration of Helsinki, first adopted in 1964 by the World Medical Association. I continue with a parallel discussion of the morality of animal testing: how can one justify the routine, and sometimes lethal, experiments that are done with monkeys, rabbits, and mice, in laboratories throughout the world? In principle, the Catholic Church is supportive of animal research. She teaches that God entrusted the animals to the stewardship of those whom he created in his own image and likeness, and that animals do not and cannot have the dignity ascribed to human beings. Hence it is legitimate to use animals for food, for clothing, and for biomedical research "if it remains within reasonable limits and contributes to caring for or saving human lives."[4] Finally, I close this chapter with a discussion of the moral controversy surrounding stem cell research and the emerging field of regenerative medicine. A moral consensus exists applauding and encouraging the development of cell-replacement therapies that arise from human adult stem cell research. However, embryonic stem cell research as it is done today is gravely immoral because it leads to the killing of embryonic human beings. To be faithful to his vocation, the virtuous scientist has to respect the moral law, especially the moral imperative to respect and to protect the dignity of the human person.

To conclude the book, in chapter 8, I confront the realities faced by a

3. Benedict XVI, "Address of His Holiness Benedict XVI to Participants at an International Congress Organized by the Pontifical Academy of Life." Available at http://www.vatican.va/holy_father/benedict_xvi/speeches/2008/november/documents/hf_ben-xvi_spe_20081107_acdlife_en.html.

4. *Catechism of the Catholic Church*, 2nd ed. (Vatican City: Libreria Editrice Vaticana, 1997), no. 2417.

citizen of faith living in a free and democratic society and deal with the complex moral issue of cooperation in evil. Basically, the Catholic citizen striving for virtue needs to understand that he is living in a society that is at the same time, postmodern, secular, and liberal. It is a society that will inherently oppose his efforts to faithfully live out his moral convictions, and to fulfill the Christ-given mandate to evangelize and transform the world. Therefore, he is being called to speak using the method of tradition-constituted inquiry described by the philosopher Alasdair MacIntyre, and to live the truths of the gospel of life with courage and joy as a witness to the transforming power of grace.

Finally, to end this introduction, I should acknowledge one peculiarity of bioethics. By its nature, bioethics is a moral theology of crises. In other words, it is a branch of moral theology that responds to scenarios where an individual is confronted by a particular life crisis, including, among others, an unexpected pregnancy, a dying spouse, or a morally suspect cure to a chronic illness, that threatens his physical or spiritual well-being. Often, these scenarios cannot be resolved by acquiring virtues because they require that the human agent act within a relatively short period of time. Therefore, in contrast to the other branches of moral theology, which can emphasize the development of virtue, bioethics needs to highlight those virtues already present in the individual, maybe even only in germ, that can dispose him to act well here and now. Consequently, I will conclude each chapter that follows with a discussion of a particular virtue that could help the human agent confront specific moral crises that raise bioethical questions. As St. Thomas Aquinas acknowledged, and our human experience confirms, however, the virtues, especially the moral virtues, are interconnected because it is not the single virtue in isolation but the charitable and prudent person in his integrity who is acting.[5] Thus, a fearful individual lacking fortitude would not be prudent when he is confronted with danger. His excessive desire for safety would prevent him from facing situations that it would actually be good to face. Moreover, as prudence requires moral virtue, however, so, too, moral vir-

5. "We might also say that it refers to the measure of sanctifying grace, by reason of which one man has all the virtues in greater abundance than another man, on account of his greater abundance of prudence, or also of charity, in which all the infused virtues are connected." *ST*, IIa-IIae 66.2. Unless otherwise noted, all citations from the *Summa* (henceforth, *ST*) are taken from the translation of the Fathers of the English Dominican Province: *Summa Theologica* (New York: Benziger Brothers, 1947).

tue requires prudence: a courageous person would need prudence to judge correctly which dangers would be good to face. The same holds for the role of the virtues in Catholic bioethics. Thus, despite our emphasis on individual virtues and their role in bioethics, we need to affirm that these virtues can be properly understood and exercised only within the context of a prudent individual.

CHAPTER ONE

Bioethics and the Pursuit of Beatitude

According to a widely used textbook in the tradition of secular bioethics, the field of bioethics has a recent provenance. The textbook traces the founding of the field to an influential article authored by Dan Callahan in 1974 entitled "Bioethics as a Discipline."[1] As contemporary histories of bioethics often do, however, the text fails to acknowledge the long tradition of bioethical reflection in the history of the Catholic Church, from the early condemnation of abortion in the *Didache*, written in the first century, to the recent papal pronouncement on euthanasia in *Evangelium vitae*, written during the twentieth. Rooted both in faith and in reason, Catholic bioethics is a rich tradition informed by scriptural exegesis, by theological reflection, and by philosophical argument, a tradition that counts St. Augustine, St. Thomas Aquinas, and St. Alphonsus Ligouri among its most distinguished contributors. Today, Catholic bioethics has become a distinctive and mature field of inquiry—there are now several scholarly journals devoted primarily to Catholic bioethics, including the *National Catholic Bioethics Quarterly* and the *Linacre Quarterly*, that strive to apply the principles of Christian morality to the profound and deeply human questions regarding the meaning of life, its beginning, its continuation, and its end, that are raised by the life sciences.[2]

In this chapter, where I summarize the foundational principles of Catholic moral theology, we begin with an overview of the Catholic moral vision that places bioethics within the context of each individual's pursuit of beatitude. It is a moral vision that strives to remain faithful to

1. Nancy S. Jecker, Albert R. Jonsen, and Robert A. Pearlman, *Bioethics: An Introduction to the History, Methods, and Practice,* 2nd ed. (Boston: Jones and Bartlett, 2007), 3, citing Daniel Callahan, "Bioethics as a Discipline," *Stud Hastings Cent* 1 (1973): 66–73.

2. For a history of recent developments in Catholic bioethics, see Charles E. Curran, "The Catholic Moral Tradition in Bioethics," in *The Story of Bioethics,* ed. Jennifer K. Walter and Eran P. Klein, 113–130 (Washington, D.C.: Georgetown University Press, 2003).

the moral life described by the Lord Jesus Christ in His Sermon on the Mount. Since the pursuit of beatitude is governed by the actions that shape our moral character, we then move to a moral analysis of human action that answers several questions: What is a human act? How do we judge the morality of human acts? How do we distinguish good acts from evil ones? Then I will discuss the moral principles that are used to make sound moral judgments according to right judgment, not only in bioethics but also in every sphere of human activity. At the same time, I discuss four dimensions of moral agency and society—the governing role of the virtues, the power of prayer, the experience of suffering, and the teaching charism of the Church—that can and often do shape our actions. Finally, I turn to the principle of double effect, a principle that will help us to act well when we are confronted with choosing acts that have both good and evil effects.

The Pursuit of Beatitude

Bioethics and the Catholic Moral Vision

On August 6, 1993, the Feast of the Transfiguration of the Lord, Blessed John Paul II signed *Veritatis splendor*, his moral encyclical addressed to the bishops of the Catholic Church.[3] It remains an eloquent articulation and defense of the Catholic moral vision. In this encyclical, which calls for a renewal in Catholic moral theology, the pope reminds the Church and the world of three constitutive elements of Christian morality.

First, Blessed John Paul II teaches that the Catholic moral vision begins with and ends in the person of Jesus Christ.[4] Since Christ is the Way, the Truth, and the Life, the decisive answer to every human being's questions, his religious and moral questions in particular, is given

3. John Paul II, *Veritatis splendor*, Encyclical Letter addressed by the Supreme Pontiff Pope John Paul II to all the Bishops of the Catholic Church Regarding Certain Fundamental Questions of the Church's Moral Teaching (Vatican City: Libreria Editrice Vaticana, 1993). A concise summary of the moral vision presented in this encyclical can be found in Servais Pinckaers, O.P., "An Encyclical for the Future: *Veritatis splendor*," in *Veritatis Splendor and the Renewal of Moral Theology*, ed. J. Augustine DiNoia, O.P., and Romanus Cessario, O.P., 11–71 (Huntington, Ind.: Our Sunday Visitor Press, 1999). Also see the essay by Joseph Cardinal Ratzinger (now Pope Benedict XVI), "The Renewal of Moral Theology: Perspectives of Vatican II and *Veritatis splendor*," *Communio* 32 (2005): 357–368.

4. John Paul II, *Veritatis splendor*, no. 2. All citations from the encyclical are taken from the official Vatican translation.

by Jesus Christ, or rather, is Jesus Christ Himself. Jesus opens up sacred Scripture, teaches us the truth about moral action by fully revealing the Father's will, and then gives us the grace to pursue and to live that truth.[5] He is also the one who reveals the authentic meaning of freedom by living it fully in the total gift of Himself and shows us how obedience to universal and unchanging moral norms can respect the uniqueness and individuality of the human being without threatening his freedom and dignity. In all of this, the Lord remains the beginning and the end of an authentic Christian morality.

Next, the pope explained that the human being attains a happy life, what the classical authors called beatitude, only in the following of Christ along the path of perfection.[6] Here, happiness, or beatitude, is understood to signify the fulfillment of every human yearning, spiritual, moral, and emotional. It goes beyond the modern-day notion of happiness as either the emotional wellness or the positive affective mood of the individual. Rather, beatitude is the perfection of the human being as the kind of creature that he is. By focusing on beatitude, Blessed John Paul II places Catholic moral theology within the moral tradition that emphasizes the happiness and the perfection of the human agent as the goal of the moral life. It is a tradition that challenges the human agent to live in such a way as to attain the perfective ends that define a good life. This tradition traces its origins to the ancient Greeks and counts St. Thomas Aquinas as one of its proponents.[7]

As Blessed John Paul II narrates in the encyclical, in response to the rich young man's question—Teacher, what good must I do to gain eternal life? (Mt 19:16)[8]—the Lord Jesus Christ invites the young man, as He invites every human being, to seek God "who alone is goodness, fullness of life, the final end of human activity, and perfect happiness."[9] In doing so, Christ reveals that the young man's moral question is really a religious

5. Ibid., no. 8.
6. Ibid., nos. 19–20.
7. For an insightful discussion of St. Thomas's understanding of beatitude, see Servais Pinckaers, O.P., "Aquinas's Pursuit of Beatitude: From the *Commentary on the Sentences* to the *Summa Theologiae*," in *The Pinckaers Reader*, ed. John Berkman and Craig Steven Titus, 93–114 (Washington, D.C.: The Catholic University of America Press, 2005).
8. Unless otherwise noted, all scriptural translations are taken from the New American Bible translation with the revised New Testament: D. Senior et al., eds., *The Catholic Study Bible* (New York: Oxford University Press, 1990).
9. John Paul II, *Veritatis splendor*, no. 9.

question. In seeking what is good, in seeking beatitude, the human being is seeking God. According to the encyclical, the Lord also reveals that
the desire for God that is at the root of the rich young man's question is
implanted in every human heart, reminding us that, created by God and
for God, we are called to communion with our Creator. Moreover, as the
pope notes, it is a desire that can be assuaged only by accepting Jesus'
challenge in the Sermon on the Mount to follow Him on the path of perfection: "If you wish to be perfect, go, sell what you have and give to [the]
poor, and you will have treasure in heaven. Then come, follow me" (Mt
19:21).[10] Thus, Christian morality is not a list of commands, obligations,
or prohibitions. Rather, it "involves *holding fast to the very person of Jesus*, par-
taking of his life and his destiny, sharing in his free and loving obedience
to the will of the Father."[11] The imitation of Christ, particularly in the
practice of charity, constitutes the moral rule of the Christian life and remains the essential and primordial foundation of Christian morality.[12] It
is the only authentic path to the happy life.

Third, the pope teaches that we imitate Christ by seeking, with God's
grace, to perfect ourselves through our actions and the virtues they engender. Created by God as rational and free creatures, human beings perfect themselves and establish their identities as moral creatures through
their free choices. We make ourselves the kinds of persons we are, in and
through the actions we freely choose to do. As the pope put it in the encyclical, "It is precisely through his acts that man attains perfection as
man, as one who is called to seek his Creator of his own accord and freely
to arrive at full and blessed perfection by cleaving to him."[13] Our freely
chosen acts, the pope continues, "do not produce a change merely in the
state of affairs outside of man but, to the extent that there are deliberate
choices, they give moral definition to the very person who performs them,
determining his *profound spiritual traits*."[14] As Jesus Christ reveals, "man,
made in the image of the Creator, redeemed by the Blood of Christ and
made holy by the presence of the Holy Spirit, has as the *ultimate purpose of
his life to live 'for the praise of God's glory'* (cf. Eph 1:12), striving to make each of
his actions reflect the splendor of that glory."[15] This is the reason why the
pope and the Catholic moral tradition put much emphasis on the morality of individual human acts and of the virtues they engender. They are

10. Ibid., nos. 17–18.   11. Ibid., no. 19.
12. Ibid., nos. 19–20.   13. Ibid., no. 71.
14. Ibid.   15. Ibid., no. 10.

our proximate means toward growing in perfection and toward attaining of beatitude. By highlighting the importance of human action and virtue in the moral life, Blessed John Paul II associates Catholic morality with other moral theories that emphasize the virtues, or moral character, of the human agent, in contrast to those theories that emphasize either duties or rights (deontological theories) or to those theories that emphasize the consequences of actions (utilitarian theories).[16]

Finally, given the vision of the moral life outlined above, it should not be surprising that Catholic bioethics focuses upon the acts of the individual patient, clinician, or scientist in order to evaluate their morality: Which ones would respect the dignity of the person and promote his well-being and ultimate beatitude? Which ones would be detrimental to the perfection of his nature? Thus, when the Catholic bioethicist asks whether it is morally permissible to do experiments with human embryos, he does so by reflecting upon how this type of research would contribute to the personal and spiritual development of the scientist. Much emphasis is placed upon how individual acts affect the acting person because it is through these acts that the human agent attains beatitude. In this way, Catholic bioethics differs from other contemporary approaches to bioethics, several of which will be described in chapter 8, which focus upon either the outcomes of human acts or the procedures that protect the autonomy of the human agent.

Natural Inclinations and the Structure of Human Acts

Created by God and for God, we are called to communion with our Creator. Therefore, it is not surprising that in His providence, God has imprinted natural inclinations within our hearts that move us to our beatitude in Him. Preexisting elicited desire, these inclinations direct us to those ends that are constitutive of the human good. They help us to understand our perfection precisely as human beings. Not unexpectedly, developmental psychologists have identified these inclinations, which direct us to our self-preservation, to true and certain knowledge of the world, to life in society, and to God, even in newborn infants and young toddlers.[17]

---

16. For insightful discussion that places the Catholic moral tradition's understanding of virtue, especially St. Thomas Aquinas's account of virtue, in conversation with contemporary moral philosophy, see the following monographs: Jean Porter, *The Recovery of Virtue* (Louisville: Westminster/John Knox Press, 1990); and Thomas S. Hibbs, *Virtue's Splendor* (New York: Fordham University Press, 2001).

17. For more discussion, see my essay, "The Soul and Its Inclinations: Recovering a

Our natural inclinations provide the ground and ultimate intelligibility for our actions. They move and motivate us to act. As Blessed John Paul II explained in *Veritatis splendor*, the moral challenge is to use our reason, with the help of grace, to order our actions in accordance with these natural inclinations so that together they can achieve our authentic good and the good of our society. Actions are at the heart of the moral life. Thus, I begin our exposition of Catholic bioethics by reflecting upon the structure of human acts to answer the following questions: What is a human act? What exactly are we doing when we act? How do acting persons act? This analysis of moral agency will form the backdrop for our later discussion of the morality of human action.

For St. Thomas Aquinas, the process of human action can be distinguished into three basic stages, three moments, of the human act: intention, decision, and execution.[18] There is also an optional stage involving deliberation that is required when an acting person has to select one means among several alternative means to attain his purpose. Each of the stages is made up of two components, one involving the intellect and another involving the will, though it is important to emphasize the interpenetration of the two basic capacities of the human agent at each moment of the human act. It is neither the intellect nor the will separately, but the whole human being, who is acting.

Intention, the first stage, is the aiming of an action toward something. Here the acting person not only apprehends something that becomes the purpose of his action but also desires it.[19] Thus, a young lacrosse player

---

Metaphysical Biology with the Systems Perspective," in *The Human Animal: Procreation, Education, and the Foundations of Society*, Proceedings of the X Plenary Session of the Pontifical Academy of St. Thomas Aquinas, June 18–20, 2010, "The Human Animal: Procreation, Education, and the Foundations of Society," (48–63 Vatican City: Pontifical Academy of St. Thomas Aquinas, 2011).

18. For this discussion, I am indebted to the insightful analysis of Daniel Westberg, who defends a three-stage Thomistic model for human action. For discussion, see his *Right Practical Reason: Aristotle, Action, and Prudence in Aquinas* (Oxford: Clarendon Press, 1994). In contrast, scholars in the Thomistic commentatorial tradition identify twelve partial acts or successive stages in a single human action. For a summary presentation, see Romanus Cessario, O.P., *Introduction to Moral Theology* (Washington, D.C.: The Catholic University of America Press, 2001), 118–122.

19. Human purposes are the reasons that we have when we act. They emerge from the interaction between our intellect and both our natural inclinations and our elicited desires. They move us to act. Ends, by contrast, belong to things and to organisms apart from elicited desires. Human ends are established by our natural inclinations that are

who wakes up hungry is motivated by the good of a satiated body that he not only apprehends but also desires as the purpose of his acting. This is the intention behind his act to eat. The next stage of human action, called *decision,* is a process of practical reasoning, again involving both the intellect and the will, whereby the acting person chooses to realize a particular means to achieve the desired purpose. In our example, our hungry lacrosse player sees a box of Kellogg's Rice Krispies on the kitchen table and decides that he will have a bowl of cereal here and now in order to attain the purpose of a satiated body. He understands that eating this bowl of cereal is a means that will allow him to attain that purpose, and thus, he chooses it. The last stage of human action is *execution.* It follows decision and is the actual carrying out of the decision into action. After deciding to eat the bowl of cereal, our athlete actually executes his act. He pours the cereal into a bowl and begins to consume it. His act is complete. Finally, there is an additional stage, a fourth stage called *deliberation,* which is not a necessary part of human action. It becomes a moment in the human act when the acting person is not sure if he should choose one particular means or another to achieve his purpose. When this happens, deliberation follows intention and precedes decision. It is a process of practical reasoning from purpose to means that leads the acting person to choose the best of many possible means to achieve the purpose of his action. In our example, our athlete would have to deliberate when he is confronted with two different boxes of cereal on the kitchen table. He would have to figure out if attaining the good of a satiated body is best achieved from eating either the Kellogg's Rice Krispies or the General Mills Lucky Charms. Once he picks one as the better of the two means, eating the Rice Krispies, in our example, the young man would then have to decide to choose to eat the cereal, and then to execute his act.

The Role of the Virtues

In health care and in scientific research, as in all other areas of the moral life, acting persons often struggle to act well. Obstacles to human action often arise because of ignorance in the intellect, weakness in the will, or disorder in our desires. They can arise at any moment of the human

---

rooted in human nature. For further discussion, see Robert Sokolowski, "What Is Natural Law? Human Purposes and Natural Ends," *Thomist* 68 (2004): 507–529; and Francis Slade, "Ends and Purposes," in *Final Causality in Nature and Human Affairs,* ed. Richard Hassing, 83–85 (Washington, D.C.: The Catholic University of America Press, 1997).

act. Some individuals find it easy to intend ends—for example, they find
it easy to make New Year's resolutions—but then find it difficult to execute their acts to accomplish their purposes. In contrast, others may become incapacitated when they are faced with a plethora of possible means.
Deliberation is difficult for them, and they simply cannot decide. Finally,
others may not be able to even motivate themselves to intend purposes for
their acts. They lack the drive to pursue goals in their life, and therefore,
they are unable to act.

Given the common difficulties that prevent the acting person from acting well, the moral life in general, and moral reasoning in bioethics in
particular, require the virtues—stable dispositions in the human agent
that enable him to know, to desire, and to do the good—to help us to act
well.[20] Classically, the virtues can be divided into three categories: the intellectual, the moral, and the theological virtues.

First, the intellectual virtues allow the human agent to perfect his
scientific, artistic, and technical abilities. Particularly important in bioethics, the three virtues of understanding, sure knowledge, and wisdom
perfect the intellect so that the human person can know truth well.[21] Understanding or intuitive insight, *intellectus* in Latin, allows the person to
grasp the necessary truths expressed in first principles, such as the whole
is greater than its parts. Sure knowledge, *scientia* in Latin, perfects the
speculative intellect so that the human agent can reason well. Finally, wisdom, *sapientia* in Latin, disposes the human being so that he can understand reality from the divine perspective. These virtues would allow the
bioethicist and the patient to know the truths that are necessary prereq-
uisites for moral judgment, and would enable the scientist to excel at his
task to understand the world. Last, the intellectual virtues of art, *ars* in
Latin, and of prudence, *prudentia* in Latin, perfect the intellect and predispose the human agent to produce works of skill that are done well—including, for the physician, a healed patient, or for the scientist, an elegant

20. For a concise summary of the morality of the virtues, see *Catechism of the Catholic Church*, nos. 1803–1845. Also see the following: David Beauregard, O.M.V., "Virtue in
Bioethics," in *Catholic Health Care Ethics: A Manual for Practitioners*, 2nd ed., ed. Peter J. Cataldo and Albert S. Moraczewski, O.P., 27–29 (Boston, Mass.: National Catholic Bioethics Center, 2009); and Edmund D. Pellegrino and David C. Thomasma, *The Christian Virtues in Medical Practice* (Washington, D.C.: Georgetown University Press, 1996).

21. For discussion, see Gregory M. Reichberg, "The Intellectual Virtues (Ia IIae,
qq. 57–58)," in *The Ethics of Aquinas*, ed. Stephen J. Pope, 131–150 (Washington, D.C.: Georgetown University Press, 2002).

experiment—and to act well, respectively. As we will see below, prudence is a unique virtue because it is numbered among both the intellectual and the moral virtues, because a prudent individual needs not only to know the true good, but also to act in order to attain it.

Next, the moral virtues order our desires so that we routinely desire the good and then act to attain it. They can be acquired by human effort and are the fruit of repeated morally good acts.[22] The ancients emphasized that these virtues could become like a second nature after long conditioning and constant practice. However, for St. Thomas Aquinas, these natural virtues still require God's grace for them to function well. Significantly, he also proposed that there are infused virtues that correspond to the acquired moral virtues and that elevate the human being so he can perform supernatural acts that transcend reason and duty in light of the Cross. As Michael Sherwin, O.P., has convincingly argued, the infused cardinal virtues must exist because they explain well the experience of those acting persons, especially former addicts, who struggle with the lingering effects of their acquired vices.[23] By definition, these infused virtues are gifts that can be received only from God along with sanctifying grace. They order the human agent toward his ultimate beatitude, which is the life of the Triune God.

The moral virtues are also important because they help the acting person to regulate his emotions, those bodily movements the classical tradition called the passions of the soul.[24] As Etienne Gilson, the distinguished medievalist, observed: "When the moralist comes to discuss concrete cases, he comes up against the fundamental fact that man is moved by his passions. The study of the passions, therefore, must precede

---

22. For a discussion of the moral virtues, see Josef Pieper, *Four Cardinal Virtues* (South Bend, Ind.: University of Notre Dame Press, 1990); and Romanus Cessario, O.P., *The Moral Virtues and Theological Ethics*, 2nd ed. (South Bend, Ind.: University of Notre Dame Press, 2009). Also see the essays by James F. Keenan, S.J., Jean Porter, Martin Rhonheimer, R. E. Houser, and Diana Fritz Cates, on the moral virtues, in *The Ethics of Aquinas*, ed. Stephen J. Pope (Washington, D.C.: Georgetown University Press, 2002), 259–339.

23. For details, see his "Infused Virtue and the Effects of Acquired Vice: A Test Case for the Thomistic Theory of Infused Cardinal Virtues," *Thomist* 73 (2009): 29–52.

24. For an extensive discussion of the nature of the passions in the Thomist tradition, see Robert Miner, *Thomas Aquinas on the Passions: A Study of Summa Theologiae, 1a2ae 22–48* (Cambridge: Cambridge University Press, 2009); and Nicholas E. Lombardo, O.P., *The Logic of Desire: Aquinas on Emotion* (Washington, D.C.: The Catholic University of America Press, 2011).

any discussion of moral problems."[25] In themselves, these passions—and they could include love, pleasure, hatred, fear, despair, or anger, among others—are morally neither good nor evil.[26] However, when they contribute to good action, they are morally good, and when they contribute to evil action, they are morally evil. For example, fear, in one case, fear of cancer, may incline an individual to give up an unhealthy habit like smoking, while fear, in another case, fear of prolonged pain, may incline another patient to ask his physician to kill him. The former passion would be morally good, while the latter passion would be morally evil. Not surprisingly, therefore, the acting person is called to order his passions so that they are directed toward his authentic good.

A handful of the moral virtues, prudence, justice, fortitude, and temperance, are called cardinal virtues because they are those principal virtues upon which the moral life pivots. Prudence is the virtue that disposes the individual not only to discern the true good in every circumstance, but also to choose the right means of achieving it. It is the virtue that facilitates good human acts. It allows the acting person to intend, to deliberate, to decide, and to execute this particular act well, here and now, with his and his community's authentic good in mind. Prudence would be the virtue that disposes a patient not only to properly weigh the medical opinions of his doctors, the desires of his loved ones, the financial exigencies of his particular situation, and his own authentic good before making a morally upright decision with regard to his health care, but also to carry it out.[27] It would also be the virtue that disposes the scientist to properly weigh all the scientific, financial, and moral factors that impact every research program before choosing a morally upright experiment to test a hypothesis.

25. Etienne Gilson, *The Christian Philosophy of St. Thomas Aquinas,* trans. L. K. Shook, C.S.B. (New York: Random House, 1956), 271.

26. For a concise summary of the morality of the passions, see the *Catechism of the Catholic Church,* 2nd ed. (Vatican City: Libreria Editrice Vaticana, 1997), nos. 1762–1775. According to St. Thomas Aquinas, the passions can lead a weak individual to commit evil acts by obscuring those considerations that are relevant to right practical reasoning. For discussion, see Steven J. Jensen, "The Error of the Passions," *Thomist* 73 (2009): 349–379; and the essay by Paul Gondreau, "The Passions and the Moral Life: Appreciating the Originality of Aquinas," *Thomist* 71 (2007): 419–450.

27. For an insightful discussion on how prudence can influence bioethical reasoning, see the essay, Charles W. Henry, O.S.B., "The Place of Prudence in Medical Decision Making," *J Relig Health* 32 (1993): 27–37.

Next, justice is the virtue that disposes the individual to give to God and to neighbor that which is properly due to both of them. It allows the human being to properly see that his own well-being cannot be separated from the well-being of others. As we will see in chapter 6, justice is the virtue that would dispose an individual or a transplantation team to properly allocate transplantable organs to those patients who are most in need of them.

Fortitude is the virtue that disposes the individual to remain firm in the face of difficulty and to remain constant in the pursuit of good. Also called courage, it moderates the passion of fear, allowing the individual to act in a morally upright manner even when he is frightened. Fortitude strengthens his resolve to do the good even in the face of temptations or of strong emotions that may dispose him to do otherwise. It is the virtue that disposes the patient to conquer fear, even fear of death, so that he does not seek physician-assisted suicide. It is also be the virtue that disposes the scientist to avoid experiments that involve the destruction of human embryos, even in the face of pressure from editorial review boards, tenure committees, or grant-funding agencies to do otherwise.

Fourth and finally, temperance is the virtue that disposes the individual to moderate the attraction of bodily pleasures. It steels his will, allowing him to master his instincts and to keep his elicited desires within the limits of what is reasonable and honorable. An important moral virtue associated with the cardinal virtue of temperance is the virtue of chastity, the virtue that moderates the individual's desire for sexual pleasure so that it is properly ordered according to right reason and faith. As we will discuss in chapter 3, chastity is the chief virtue that disposes a married couple to choose only natural family planning methods rather than contraception when they choose to exercise responsible parenting.

Finally, the theological virtues, faith, hope, and charity, unite the human being to God, making him capable of acting as God acts. In contrast to the moral virtues, these virtues cannot be acquired by human effort because they can only be received as divine gifts.[28] Faith is the virtue by which we believe in God and believe all that He has said and revealed

28. For a discussion of the theological virtues, see Josef Pieper, *Faith, Hope, Love* (San Francisco: Ignatius Press, 1997). Also see the essays by Stephen F. Brown, Romanus Cessario, O.P., and Eberhard Schockenhoff, on the theological virtues of faith, hope, and charity, in *The Ethics of Aquinas*, ed. Stephen J. Pope (Washington, D.C.: Georgetown University Press, 2002), 221–258.

to us. Hope is the virtue by which we desire heaven and eternal life as our happiness, placing our trust in God's infinite power and mercy and His promises that He will save us. Charity is the virtue by which we love God above all things for His own sake and our neighbor as ourselves for the love of God. These virtues capacitate the human agent to know, to will, and to love, as God knows, wills, and loves. In bioethics, these virtues dispose the individual to choose the authentic good in light of the mystery of the Cross. Faith, hope, and charity are the virtues that allow a terminally ill patient to unite his sufferings with the sufferings of Jesus Christ for the redemption of the world. They would also enable him to reject any temptation he may have to take his life by reassuring him of the reality of the resurrection. These virtues would also dispose the nurse to care for his patients in a heroic and self-sacrificial manner, moving him in certain cases to visit them even when he is not on call.

The Role of Prayer and the Gifts of the Holy Spirit

The moral life is our response to Christ's call to perfection and beatitude. Thus, bioethics involves more than determining what is permitted or forbidden in a particular clinical or experimental scenario. The minimum obligation is not enough. Instead, both the Catholic bioethicist and the acting person who is being confronted by a bioethical dilemma are called to seek excellence, that perfection of a human action in a particular situation that would contribute to the sanctification and transformation of the human being, his community, and his world.

In light of this, prayer has an integral role in Catholic bioethics. Through prayer—defined by the *Catechism of the Catholic Church* as the raising of one's mind and heart to God or the requesting of good things from God[29]—we grow in knowledge of and love for God. It is this God, especially in the person of the Holy Spirit, who is the source and giver of all beatitude.[30] It is the Holy Spirit who illumines our intellects and enflames our hearts so that we can truly see and desire what is good and holy in light of the mystery of the Cross. He also gives us His gifts to guide us to beatitude so that we may intend, deliberate, decide, and execute our acts well, according to right reason and to faith.

In the Catholic tradition, the gifts are seven abiding spiritual powers by which the individual is perfected to readily obey the promptings of the

---

29. *Catechism of the Catholic Church*, no. 2590.
30. Ibid., no. 749.

Holy Spirit, especially in situations that demand heroic action.[31] The gifts of the Holy Spirit are to the soul as the sail is to the boat. They help the individual to respond to the inspirations of the Holy Spirit in the same way that the sail catches the wind so that the boat skims rapidly along to its destination without any effort from the oarsman. Sacred Scripture enumerates seven distinct gifts of the Holy Spirit: wisdom, understanding, knowledge, counsel, piety, fortitude, and fear of the Lord (cf. Is 11:2–3). These gifts often play an essential role in bioethical decision making. For instance, the gift of counsel assists the intellect and perfects the virtue of prudence by enlightening the patient and his physician so that they can decide, and then execute, the difficult decisions that they need to make. This gift can help us to properly comprehend the moral complexities that are present in many bioethical dilemmas. As Jesus Christ promised His disciples: "When he comes, the Spirit of truth, he will guide you to all truth" (Jn 16:13). In another example, the gift of fortitude empowers the patient to undertake arduous tasks, as well as to endure long and trying difficulties for the glory of God. The gift secures strength to triumph over the difficult obstacles that stand in the way of the authentic good. This is especially true in those cases, common in bioethics, where acting to attain the good can often involve much hardship and extended suffering.

Finally, it is often true that the moral dilemmas that rise in bioethics are complex and confusing. Prayer is a necessary ingredient for discerning these moral dilemmas, especially prayer for the gifts of the Holy Spirit. As St. Alphonsus Liguori taught: "To actually do good, to overcome temptation, to exercise virtue, entirely to keep the divine precepts, it is not enough to receive lights and make reflections and resolutions. We still need the actual help of God. And the Lord does not grant this actual aid except to one who prays and prays with perseverance."[32] Catholics too have recourse to the saints, who can intercede to God on their behalf. It should not be uncommon for both Catholic bioethicists and patients to invoke either St. Jude Thaddeus during seemingly impossible crises, St. Joseph at the end of life, or the Blessed Virgin Mary at all times and places. The best Catholic bioethics is done on one's knees.

31. Ibid., no. 1831; St. Thomas Aquinas, *ST*, Ia-IIae, 68.3. For a discussion of the proper role of the gifts of the Holy Spirit in Catholic moral theology, see Charles E. Bouchard, O.P., "Recovering the Gifts of the Holy Spirit in Moral Theology," *Theological Studies* 63 (2002): 539–558.

32. St. Alphonsus Liguori, *Opere Ascetiche* (Turin: Marietti, 1845), 2:576. Cited by the *Catechism of the Catholic Church*, no. 2744.

The Role of Suffering

Not surprisingly, the alleviation of suffering is often used to justify many medical interventions and scientific research programs. Therefore, it is important to properly grasp the meaning of suffering, because how one values or does not value suffering can influence how one acts well in a clinical or research environment, especially when one is suffering.

In his apostolic letter on suffering, Blessed John Paul II describes suffering this way: "Man suffers on account of evil, which is a certain lack, limitation or distortion of good. We could say that man suffers because of a good in which he does not share, from which in a certain sense he is cut off, or of which he has deprived himself. He particularly suffers when he ought—in the normal order of things—to have a share in this good and does not have it."[33] In other words, suffering is the human experience of evil. We suffer because we know that we are lacking something, some good—for instance, love, health, friendship, or financial security—that we think we should have. This can often lead to an existential crisis. Eric Cassell, author of *The Nature of Suffering*, describes suffering as "the distress brought about by the actual or perceived impending threat to the integrity or continued existence of the whole person."[34] Suffering can lead to a sense of isolation and abandonment, because by its nature, the distress of suffering is necessarily private and highly individualized.

Numerous cultures and religious traditions have struggled to respond to the mystery of suffering. However, for many in contemporary society, suffering has no meaning. It is pointless and absurd. In fact, for these individuals, suffering is a great evil in itself, because it appears to undermine the dignity of the human being by robbing him of his independence and self-respect. Thus, for many, suffering is something to be absolutely avoided, and when encountered, something to be aggressively eradicated no matter the moral cost. This is often the argument to justify the so-called mercy killing of terminally ill patients.

In contrast, for Christians, sacred Scripture reveals that suffering, though an evil in itself, is suffused with profound meaning that can radi-

33. John Paul II, *Salvifici doloris*, Apostolic Letter of the Supreme Pontiff John Paul II to the Bishops, to the Priests, to the Religious Families and to the Faithful of the Catholic Church on the Christian Meaning of Human Suffering. (Vatican City: Libreria Editrice Vaticana, 1984), no. 7. This citation from the apostolic letter is taken from the official Vatican translation.

34. Eric Cassell, *The Nature of Suffering* (New York: Oxford University Press, 1991), 31.

cally transform and redeem it. In the Old Testament, we learn that suffering is a result of original sin and the introduction of evil into the order of creation. Pain, strife, toil, and death were not part of God's original plan. They entered the world as punishment for sin (cf. Gn 3:16–19). However, we also learn, especially from the Book of Job, that while it is true that suffering is sometimes a punishment when it is connected with a fault, this is not always the case.[35] Job is aware that he does not deserve the suffering he has had to endure and challenges God to explain it. In the end, God reveals that Job's suffering is the suffering of someone who is innocent. Nonetheless, it must be accepted as a mystery, which the innocent individual cannot completely comprehend.

The Book of Job, however, is not the last word on suffering. In the New Testament, sacred Scripture reveals that our Lord Jesus Christ has redeemed suffering. He has transformed it into sacrifice by linking it to love. Thus, after the Cross, any human suffering can be fruitful—it can be redemptive—when it is united to the suffering of Christ. For this reason St. Paul could write: "Now I rejoice in my sufferings for your sake" (Col 1:24). The Apostle's joy comes from his discovery that suffering has meaning. It comes from his realization that through his suffering, he can contribute to the salvation of the world.

As I mentioned earlier, the alleviation of suffering is a common justification for many medical interventions and scientific research programs. With regard to medical care, we should use all morally permissible means to alleviate human suffering.[36] This is an authentic good. Alleviating human suffering can be an act of heroic charity. However, despite our best efforts, we often still suffer, for pain is an unavoidable part of a fallen world. At this point, the Gospel reveals that Christians are given a choice. Either they can choose immoral means to attempt to alleviate their suffering in the short term, or they can choose, with God's grace, to bear their suffering with courage, offering it up for the salvation of those they love. In doing so, they unite themselves with the Lord Jesus, echoing the words of St. Paul, "In my flesh I am filling up what is lacking in the afflictions of Christ on behalf of his body, which is the church" (Col 1:24).

35. See John Paul II, *Salvifici doloris*, no. 11.

36. For a scholarly exchange that explores the role of suffering in a Catholic understanding of medical ethics, see Jorge L. A. Garcia, "Sin and Suffering in a Catholic Understanding of Medical Ethics," *Christ Bioeth* 12 (2006): 165–186; and David Albert Jones, "Sin, Suffering, and the Need for the Theological Virtues," *Christ Bioeth* 12 (2006): 187–198.

The Role of the Church

As the Son of God, Jesus Christ is the Way, the Truth, and the Life. He promised that His Church would teach the truth and that this truth would set us free (cf. Jn 8:32). As the Apostle Paul well understood, the Church is "the pillar and foundation of the truth" (1 Tim 3:15). Thus, Catholics believe that "in order to preserve the Church in the purity of the faith handed on by the apostles, Christ who is the Truth willed to confer on her a share in his own infallibility."[37] In other words, Catholics believe that Christ loved His people so much that He gave them His Church to guide them to the truth: "The Church puts herself always and only at the *service of conscience* . . . helping it not to swerve from the truth about the good of man, but rather, especially in more difficult questions, to obtain the truth with certainty and to abide in it."[38]

All the baptized belong to the Church. However, the Lord's authority to teach in His name was given to only a few. Jesus founded His Church upon St. Peter, giving him alone both the keys to the Kingdom of Heaven and the office of shepherd of the whole flock (see Mt 16:18–19; Jn 21:15–17). The Lord also made St. Peter head of the apostles, all of whom were given the authority of loosing and binding. This pastoral office, this charism to speak and teach in the name of Christ, continues today through the ministry of the college of bishops, the successors to the apostles, under the primacy of the pope who, as the bishop of Rome, is successor to St. Peter.[39]

It is important to recognize that the charism that protects the Magisterium, or teaching office, of the Catholic Church from error applies only to her definitive teachings regarding matters of faith and morals.[40] Thus, though members of the Church have made mistakes—Blessed John Paul II has acknowledged that there have been times in history when grievous sin was committed in the name of the Church[41]—the Church itself has never erred in those definitive teachings regarding faith and morals. This is God's promise. It is guaranteed by His gift of the Holy Spirit, who would guide the apostles and their successors into all truth. Hence, the Second Vatican Council teaches that when we accept and live accord-

37. *Catechism of the Catholic Church*, no. 889.
38. John Paul II, *Veritatis splendor*, no. 64.
39. *Catechism of the Catholic Church*, nos. 880–887.
40. Ibid., nos. 888–892.
41. Luigi Accattoli, *When a Pope Asks for Forgiveness*, translated by Jordan Aumann, O.P. (Boston: Pauline Books and Media, 1998).

ing to the teachings of the pope and the bishops, we are receiving "not the mere word of men, but truly the word of God."[42]

In recent years, the Catholic Church has made several definitive statements regarding different bioethical issues. Key texts include Pope Paul VI's 1968 encyclical, *Humanae vitae*, which restated the Christian tradition's constant condemnation of contraception, and Blessed John Paul II's 1995 encyclical, *Evangelium vitae*, which repeated the tradition's condemnation of abortion and euthanasia. Documents focusing on bioethics published by the Congregation for the Doctrine of the Faith (CDF), the papal office responsible for protecting the integrity and fidelity of the Catholic faith, include the *Declaration on Procured Abortion* (1974), the *Declaration on Euthanasia* (1980), *Donum vitae* (1987), and *Dignitas personae* (2008). The third and fourth texts are a response to current questions regarding artificial reproductive technologies and embryo research. This corpus of magisterial teachings is a sure guide for the proper formation of the moral conscience in bioethics.[43] The teaching of the Catholic Church can help the acting person to intend, to deliberate, to decide, and to execute his acts so that they promote his authentic good and the good of his community according to right reason and faith.

42. Vatican II, *Lumen gentium*, Dogmatic Constitution on the Church, no. 12. This citation is from *Vatican Council II: The Conciliar and Post Conciliar Documents*, 363.

43. In recent decades, there has been much discussion regarding the authoritative nature of the different kinds of documents issued by the Magisterium of the Catholic Church. In 1990, the Congregation of the Doctrine of the Faith issued a statement called *Donum veritatis* in regard to the acceptance of Church teaching. This instruction outlined four different forms of magisterial teaching that call for four different levels of assent from the Catholic faithful (*Donum veritatis*, nos. 23–24). First, there are infallible pronouncements that call for the assent of theological faith. Second, there are pronouncements made by the Magisterium "in a definitive way," which even if not divinely revealed, are nevertheless strictly and intimately connected with revelation. These must be firmly accepted and held. Third, there are "non-definitive" pronouncements made by the Magisterium that lead to a better understanding of divine revelation in matters of faith and morals and to moral directives derived from such teaching. These call for a response of religious submission of intellect and will (*obsequium intellectus et voluntatis*). Finally, there are pronouncements made by the Magisterium in order to warn against dangerous opinions that could lead to error. This last category of Church teachings, which often contain certain contingent and conjectural elements, call for a response of prudential assent in the sure knowledge that magisterial decisions, even if they are not guaranteed by the charism of infallibility, are not without divine assistance and call for the adherence of the faithful. For details, see "*Donum Veritatis*: Instruction on the Ecclesial Vocation of the Theologian," *Origins* 20 (1990): 117–126. Also see the comprehensive text by Avery Cardinal Dulles, S.J., *Magisterium: Teacher and Guardian of the Faith* (Naples, Fla.: Sapientia Press, 2007).

The Morality of Human Action

Specifying the Human Act

We now turn to another dimension of moral agency: how does one determine if human acts are good or evil? For the Catholic moral tradition, the morality of human acts depends upon several factors.[44] Most importantly, the acts have to be freely chosen. Acts that arise from either compulsive addiction or subconscious reflex—for example, the automatic scratching of an itch—because they are not deliberately and voluntarily chosen, are not subject to moral analysis. We are morally accountable only for those acts that we elect to do, since it is these acts and only these freely chosen acts that shape and mold us as human beings. Once freely chosen, however, every human act is either good or evil. Its being good or evil depends upon the three sources of morality that the Catholic moral tradition calls the *object*, the *intention*, and the *circumstances* of the act.[45]

The *object* of the act specifies the act. For St. Thomas Aquinas, the object is what the act is about relative to reason. It is the answer to the questions: What is being done? What proximate good, real or apparent, is being desired by the acting person? The object is intimately related to the means chosen by the human agent during the decision stage of his act. Note that here we are dealing with the moral order. Thus, when we speak about the object of an act, we are speaking about the *moral* object and not merely the physical object of that act. To put it in the words of Blessed John Paul II: "*The object of the act of willing is in fact a freely chosen kind of behavior. . . .* By the object of a given moral act, then, one cannot mean a process or an event of the merely physical order, to be assessed on the basis of its ability to bring about a given state of affairs in the outside world. Rather, that object is the proximate end of a deliberate decision which

---

44. Specifying or describing human action is an essential—and controversial—task in contemporary moral theology. For further discussion of the moral structure of human acts, see Ralph McInerny, *Aquinas on Human Action* (Washington, D.C.: The Catholic University of America Press, 1992); Steven A. Long, *The Teleological Grammar of the Moral Act* (Naples, Fla.: Sapientia Press, 2007); Joseph Pilsner, *The Specification of Human Actions in St. Thomas Aquinas* (Oxford: Oxford University Press, 2006); and Steven J. Jensen, *Good and Evil Actions* (Washington, D.C.: The Catholic University of America Press, 2010). Also see the *Catechism of the Catholic Church*, nos. 1749–1761.

45. On finding goodness in objects, intentions, and circumstances, see Cessario, *Introduction to Moral Theology*, 149–191; and Ralph McInerny, *Ethica Thomistica*, rev. ed. (Washington, D.C.: The Catholic University of America Press, 1997), 77–89.

determines the act of willing on the part of the acting person."[46] Thus the object of an act is the specific kind of action chosen by the acting individual, described in morally significant terms.[47] Therefore, if someone chooses to shoot an assailant, the object is not the physical act of shooting itself. Rather, the moral object can either be the shooting to incapacitate an unjust aggressor or the shooting to maliciously kill the attack-

46. John Paul II, *Veritatis splendor,* no. 78 (original emphasis). Much of the controversy in contemporary Catholic moral theology can be traced to disagreements regarding the proper description of the objects of human acts. Richard McCormick, S.J., and other revisionist moral theologians who have used a proportionalist approach to moral analysis have concluded that talking about the "objects" of moral action is not helpful and should be abandoned. They argue that it is impossible to distinguish the object of an action from further intentions for the sake of which the acting person is choosing to act. In response, Martin Rhonheimer, quoting *Veritatis splendor,* has pointed out that we can distinguish the object of an act from the intention of the acting person. Properly speaking, the object of an act is a kind of behavior *insofar as it is an object of choice.* It is the specific kind of action chosen by the acting individual described in morally significant terms. It is precisely what the acting person is choosing to do here and now. Therefore, when a man engages in sexual intercourse with a woman with whom he is not married, the object of his action is not simply sexual intercourse, but sexual intercourse with a woman who is not his spouse. This is what the man is choosing to do. This is the object of the act we call fornication or, if he is married, adultery. For further discussion, see Martin Rhonheimer, "Intentional Actions and the Meaning of Object: A Reply to Richard McCormick," in *Veritatis Splendor and the Renewal of Moral Theology,* ed. J. Augustine Di Noia, O.P., and Romanus Cessario, O.P., 241–268 (Huntington, Ind.: Our Sunday Visitor Press, 1999). Rhonheimer's essay was written in response to the essay by Richard McCormick, S.J.: "Some Early Reactions to *Veritatis splendor,*" *Theological Studies* 55 (1994): 481–506. Also see the insightful essay by Servais Pinckaers, O.P.: "Revisionist Understandings of Actions in the Wake of Vatican II," in *The Pinckaers Reader,* ed. John Berkman and Craig Steven Titus, 236–270 (Washington, D.C.: The Catholic University of America Press, 2005).

47. Catholic moralists have also proposed that objects of acts correspond not to freely chosen behaviors, but to physical things, *res* in Latin. For instance, as St. Thomas Aquinas explained, there are actions whose objects are "things" beyond counting. The object of simony is the spiritual thing that is bought and sold (*ST,* IIa-IIae, 100.1) while the object of teaching is twofold: the subject matter and the students (*ST,* IIa-IIae, 181.3). However, as Stephen Brock has convincingly argued, both formulations of what constitutes the object of a human act are reasonable and are not mutually exclusive. In certain cases, some actions will involve moral objects that are things, while others will have objects involving behaviors by which the things are either made or used or changed. It is clear, for example, that an act of choosing a tie could also be specified by a moral object that involves choosing to wear a tie. Both objects adequately specify the action. For discussion, see Stephen L. Brock, "*Veritatis Splendor* §78, St. Thomas, and (Not Merely) Physical Objects of Moral Acts," *Nova et Vetera* 6 (2008): 1–62.

er. These are the two alternatives that the acting person could choose to specify the physical act of shooting a gun at another human being.[48] In

48. It is important to emphasize the nonarbitrary relationship between the human act as it is specified by the moral object chosen from the perspective of the acting person and the physical structure of that act as it is, in itself, in the world. Our everyday human experience reveals that certain physical acts cannot be specified by a particular moral object: someone who claimed that he was maliciously killing a person when he was clapping his hands would be unintelligible, because the physical act of clapping one's hands is in itself not ordered toward the death of a person, the purpose that is sought by the human agent. Clapping one's hands does not routinely kill people. (We do not consider here the possibility that the hand clapping could be a signal for an assassin to shoot his target.) In contrast, our moral experience also confirms that other physical acts must include a particular moral object for the acting person to remain intelligible. Consider the naughty child who claimed that she did not intend to burst her brother's balloon when she pricked it with her mother's sewing needle. Pricking balloons with sharp objects routinely leads to their destruction. Therefore, as all reasonable individuals would acknowledge, bursting the balloon must be included in the child's description of her actions if she is to remain intelligible and coherent.

How are we to formally describe the relationship between the moral and physical dimensions of the human act? As St. Thomas Aquinas taught, the moral object is constituted both by the choice of the acting person and the physical structure of the act in the same way that form and matter constitute a substantial being. It is this composite whole that is deliberately chosen by the will. Thus, the physical act limits the moral objects that can be legitimately chosen to specify it in the same way that matter limits form. To put it another way, the teleological ordering of the physical act constrains the legitimate moral objects that can be chosen to specify it from the perspective of the acting person in the same way that matter limits form. (One cannot sculpt Michelangelo's David from toothpaste!) This description of human action explains well our everyday experience of acting. It would explain why the act of clapping one's hands cannot be specified by a moral object involving the intentional killing of a human being: the act of clapping is in itself not ordered toward a human being's death. It also explains our intuition that the naughty girl who claimed that she did not intend to burst her brother's balloon when she pricked it with the needle is lying. The act of pricking a balloon with a needle is, by its nature, ordered toward the destruction of that balloon. By their nature, physical acts rule out and rule in particular moral objects that can be legitimately chosen to specify that act.

Therefore, it is unintelligible and erroneous to claim, as Catholic moralists Germain Grisez, John Finnis, and Joseph Boyle Jr., have done, that the physician who crushes the skull of an unborn child in an operation known as a craniotomy is not killing an innocent human being but is merely redesigning the circumference of the child's skull. According to their flawed account, the death of the child would only be a side effect of changing the dimensions of the skull. Since crushing an infant's skull necessarily leads to his death—in the same way that pricking a balloon necessarily leads to its destruction—the killing of the child needs to be included in the moral object chosen by the surgeon as he describes his action, if he is to remain intelligible and morally coherent.

the former case, the act would be an act of self-defense, while in the latter scenario, the act would be an act of murder. Another example of an object of a human action is the taking of an item that belongs to another in the absence of a grave need. This is the object that specifies the act we call theft.

The *intention* of the act is the reason for which the agent chooses to do something. It is the purpose apprehended and desired by the acting person. It is the answer to the question: why is this being done here and now? For example, a benefactor could give money to a beggar, either because he wishes to care for the individual's needs or because he wishes to be seen and admired by his associates. In the former case, the intention motivating the act of almsgiving is charity, while in the latter scenario, the intention motivating the act is vanity.

Third, the *circumstances* of the act specify the manner in which the act is carried out. They are the conditions surrounding an action that can contribute to increasing or diminishing its goodness or evil and the degree of our responsibility for it. Among others, these conditions include answers to the questions: Who? What? Where? By which means? How? and When? For instance, stealing ten dollars from a panhandler is a more grievous evil than stealing the same amount from a millionaire. Also, note that circumstances can and often do change the moral status of an act. For instance, they can transform a good act into an evil one. (As we explain below, however, the converse is not true. Circumstances cannot transform an evil act into a good one because for an act to be good, it has to be good in its entirety.) Take the following example. If a married couple chooses to have sexual intercourse, it would be a good act that unites them and realizes their one-flesh union. However, if they also choose to engage in the conjugal act in a city park in plain view of the public, this

---

Moral objects specify physical acts, but physical acts constrain legitimate moral objects.

For extensive discussion on the controversy surrounding the relationship between the moral object and the physical structure of the human act, see Long, *The Teleological Grammar of the Moral Act.* Also see the critical comments on this monograph by William F. Murphy, Jr., "Developments in Thomistic Action Theory: Progress toward a Greater Consensus," *Natl Cathol Bioeth Q* 8 (2008): 505–528; and the author's response: Steven A. Long, "The False Theory Undergirding Condomitic Exceptionalism: A Response to William F. Murphy Jr. and Rev. Martin Rhonheimer," *Natl Cathol Bioeth Q* 8 (2008): 709–732. For Grisez, Finnis, and Boyle on craniotomies, see "'Direct' and 'Indirect': A Reply to Critics of Our Action Theory," *Thomist* 65 (2001): 1–44. Finally, for a discussion of the intelligibility of human action, see my essay, "On Reshaping Skulls and Unintelligible Intentions," *Nova et Vetera* 3 (2005): 81–99.

circumstance would change the moral quality of the act, making it morally reprehensible. It would become an act of public exhibitionism that
undermines the common good. Finally, some circumstances can also add
another moral object to an act. For an example, if a person steals an item
and the item is a consecrated chalice, the person's action is now both an
act of theft and an act of sacrilege. Not surprisingly, therefore, judging
the morality of any given act requires that one familiarize oneself with all
the pertinent dimensions of the act involved.

Perfecting the Acting Person

After we have properly specified a human act by identifying its object,
its intention, and its circumstances, how then do we determine whether
it is good or evil? For instance, what makes almsgiving good, or murder
evil?

First, for an act to be good, every moral source of that act—the object, the intention, and the circumstances—has to be good. Each moral
source is chosen by the will so each must be good if the will itself is to
remain properly ordered toward the authentic good. The scholastic axi-
om—*malum ex quocumque defectu*, or evil comes from a single defect—en-
capsulates this moral truth that the whole act is evil if even one of the
moral sources of an act is not in accord with right reason.[49] In an analogous way, defacing one panel of an altar's triptych mars the beauty of
the whole masterpiece. It is not uncommon for an acting person to seek
to justify his immoral action by appealing to the good intentions or the
good circumstances involved. For instance, a doctor may justify his freely
choosing to end the life of a terminally ill patient by arguing that his act
is a merciful act that alleviates the pain of the patient. However, it is not
enough that the individual intended to alleviate the pain of the terminally ill patient. The object of his act—the killing of an innocent person—
makes this act an act of murder, which cannot be morally justified by the
good intention to alleviate the pain of a patient who is suffering. As we
will discuss below, the killing of an innocent human being is inherently
unjust and therefore is intrinsically evil.

Next, for the Catholic moral tradition, acts are good if they are in accordance to right reason, which is ultimately measured by the eternal law
and the natural law that flows from it. In other words, human acts are

---

49. *Catechism of the Catholic Church*, nos. 1755–1756, citing St. Thomas Aquinas, *ST*, Ia-IIae,
18.4, ad 3; 19.6, ad 1.

good if they are directed to those purposes that are in harmony with our ultimate end of happiness in God. Such acts are virtuous and lead to the moral perfection of the human agent as an individual and as a member of a moral community. They make us good persons by fulfilling those perfective ends identified by reason as it reflects upon the natural inclinations that emerge from our common human nature. Evil acts, on the other hand, are not in accordance with right reason and therefore detract us from our ultimate end in God. They make us less than the creatures we were made to be.[50]

50. There has been much debate among moral theologians working within the Catholic tradition regarding the ontological and epistemological relationship between the human good and human nature. Following in the tradition of British philosophers David Hume and G. E. Moore, Catholic moralists Germain Grisez, John Finnis, and their collaborators have argued that one cannot come to know the human good from facts about human nature because this conceptual move would constitute a logical fallacy. They propose that this naturalistic fallacy, sometimes called the fact-value distinction, is committed whenever a moral theologian attempts to prove a claim about what ought to be, nature-as-normative, by appealing to what is, nature-as-normal.

In response, as other moralists have similarly argued, I suggest that the account described here escapes the naturalistic fallacy because it presupposes a Thomistic anthropology that rejects the distinction between "facts" and "values" that is implicitly invoked by Moore and his successors. For St. Thomas Aquinas, the human person is a dynamic being that has an intrinsic tendency and natural inclinations to the perfection of his nature. In this way, the human creature is like all other living beings.

Within this metaphysical framework that acknowledges the teleological ordering of nature, an "ought" statement is a statement of fact rather than a statement of value. Take the example of a Hovawart puppy named Cleo. To say that Cleo ought to eat meat and ought not to eat wood chips is to say that eating meat is more perfective for the puppy than eating wood chips. It is a statement of fact in the same way that the statement "the number 'two' is greater than the number 'one'" is a statement of fact rather than a statement of value. In a similar manner, to say that a human being ought to preserve his life and ought not to seek physician-assisted suicide is to make a normative claim that preserving human life is more perfective for a human being than ending that life. Within the teleological anthropology presupposed here, the movement from the "is" to the "ought" is a movement from a factual statement to another factual statement. There is no fallacious move from a fact to a value statement.

For further discussion of the so-called naturalistic fallacy and its impact on Catholic moral theology, contrast the following essays: John Finnis, "Natural Inclinations and Natural Rights: Deriving 'Ought' from 'Is' According to Aquinas," in *Lex et Libertas: Freedom and Law According to St. Thomas Aquinas*, ed. Leo Elders and Klaus Hedwig, 43–55 (Rome: Vatican Press, 1987); and Steven Long, "Natural Law or Autonomous Practical Reason: Problems for the New Natural Law Theory," in *St. Thomas Aquinas and the Natural Law Tradition: Contemporary Perspectives*, ed. John Goyette, Mark S. Latkovic, and Richard S. Myers, 165–194 (Washington, D.C.: The Catholic University of America Press, 2004).

Not surprisingly, therefore, moral theology emerges from an anthropological account of the ends that perfect the human agent. Reflecting upon the order of nature and the order of grace, St. Thomas Aquinas proposed that human beings have two ultimate ends that make us happy, one in an imperfect and another in a perfect manner.[51] First, he taught that there is our ultimate end that defines the human species, that of knowing the truth and of desiring the good, especially the truth that God exists and that He has created the world. Attaining this connatural end would contribute to an earthly but imperfect happiness. However, this natural ultimate end is distinct from, inferior to, but ordered toward, our supernatural ultimate end, that of knowing the very essence of God in the intimate communion with the Triune God, Father, Son, and Holy Spirit, called the beatific vision. Attaining this supernatural end in the friendship of God would lead to our glorification and our perfect happiness. Furthermore, according to Aquinas, reason discovers four subordinate ends, life, procreation, community, and truth, either from immediate experience or from reasoned reflection upon the connatural inclinations imprinted within the human heart, which are required to attain our ultimate perfection.[52] These goods—these perfective ends—are interrelated

---

Also see the comprehensive analysis by Piotr Lichacz, O.P., *Did Aquinas Justify the Transition from "Is" to "Ought"?* (Warsaw: Instytut Tomistyczny, 2010). For a novel and an original defense of the moral account described here written by a contemporary philosopher in the analytic tradition, see Phillippa Foot, *Natural Goodness* (Oxford: Oxford University Press, 2003).

51. There is much debate among contemporary Thomists regarding the nature of the human end, or *telos*. In contrast to the account described here, some scholars have proposed that the human being has only one true ultimate end, that of supernatural beatitude, which perfects him and completes his nature. This position, however, appears to deny the gratuity of grace and of the beatific vision. For discussion, compare the following texts: Denis J. M. Bradley, *Aquinas on the Twofold Human Good* (Washington, D.C.: The Catholic University of America Press, 1997); and Lawrence Feingold, *The Natural Desire to See God according to St. Thomas Aquinas and His Interpreters,* 2nd ed. (Naples, Fla.: Sapientia Press, 2010).

52. St. Thomas Aquinas, *ST,* Ia-IIae, 94.2. Other authors have proposed more elaborate lists of human ends. For example, Germain Grisez has suggested that human beings have seven categories of human goods that perfect persons and contribute to their fulfillment both as individuals and as communities: self-integration, practical reasonableness and authenticity, justice and friendship, religion, life and health, knowledge of truth and appreciation of beauty, and satisfaction in playful activities and skillful performances. For details, see his book, *The Way of the Lord Jesus: Christian Moral Principles* (Quincy, Ill.: Franciscan Press, 1983), 115–140. John Finnis proposes a similar list of basic

and mutually support each other. First, we need life to strive for our goals and for our perfection. This is the most basic end necessary to achieve all our other natural ends. Next, we need to procreate to preserve the human community. Third, we need the human community because as social creatures, we can attain our perfection only in communion with others. Finally, we need to know truth because it is truth that gives our lives meaning and purpose. Ultimately, of course, we need to know the truth about God, who is the cause of all that exists, in order to attain, with the help of his grace, the happiness that is friendship with him. Together, these ends structure human action. In our earlier example with the hungry lacrosse player who eats the Kellogg's Rice Krispies for breakfast, in choosing to eat the cereal, he is acting to attain the subordinate end of life that he would need in order to attain not only the earthly happiness that comes from knowing the truth and possessing the good, but also, with the help of grace, the perfect happiness of the beatific vision.

Human acts whose objects are in conformity with right reason are good for the human being, because they help him to attain both his natural and his supernatural perfections. They express the rational order of good and evil impressed into creation. Thus, almsgiving is good because it perfects the almsgiver. In providing for the needs of his neighbor, the individual grows in charity and promotes both his own well-being and the well-being of his neighbor and their human community. In doing so, he perfects his nature and fulfills the commandment to love God and his neighbor. In contrast, there are acts whose objects are not in conformity with right reason and the moral order. These acts are intrinsically evil because their moral objects are "by their very nature 'incapable of being ordered' to God, because they radically contradict the good of the person made in his image."[53] In other words, these acts are evil because they do not promote the perfection of the individual human being, who is made in the image and likeness of God. For instance, murder is evil because it is an act of injustice. The murderer deprives another individual of the

_____

human goods. See his *Natural Law and Natural Rights*, Corrected ed. (Oxford: Clarendon Press, 1982), 85–92.

53. John Paul II, *Veritatis splendor*, no. 80. For a history and summary of the contemporary debate and a defense of moral absolutes and intrinsically evil acts, see the following texts: John Finnis, *Moral Absolutes* (Washington, D.C.: The Catholic University of America Press, 1991); and Servais Pinckaers, O.P., "A Historical Perspective on Intrinsically Evil Acts," in *The Pinckaers Reader*, ed. John Berkman and Craig Steven Titus, 185–235 (Washington, D.C.: The Catholic University of America Press, 2005).

life that is rightfully his. In doing so, the murderer makes himself unjust, thus contradicting his vocation to become perfectly just as his Heavenly Father is perfectly just (cf. Mt 5:48). Clearly, an act of murder—an act that takes the life of an innocent person—is incompatible with the pursuit of beatitude. Thus, the *Catechism of the Catholic Church* teaches: "There are acts which, in and of themselves, independently of circumstances and intentions, are always gravely illicit by reason of their object; such as blasphemy and perjury, murder and adultery."[54] These moral absolutes, usually articulated in the form of commandments, are ordered toward the realization of human excellence and beatitude. They are guides that help us to live fulfilling and holy lives.

The Role of the Common Good

Human acts in accordance with right reason are good, leading to the perfection of the individual human being and to the attainment of those ends that define a good life. However, as a social creature, the human being lives in a community. Thus, his perfection cannot be separated from the good of his community and the common goods that comprise it. A common good is a good in which many persons can share at the same time without in any way lessening or splitting it. For instance, the peace of the state is a common good, provided it is a genuine peace of the whole from which no one is excluded. When I share peace, I do not lessen the peace that can be experienced by others. *The* common good is the sum total of all the common goods necessary for individuals to attain their ultimate end more easily. The *Catechism of the Catholic Church* defines it as "the sum total of social conditions which allow people, either as groups or as individuals, to reach their fulfillment more fully and more easily."[55] Today, these social conditions—these common goods—include, among others, the availability of transportation, health care, justice and law enforcement systems, a healthy economy, and an educational system that forms morally upright and virtuous citizens. All of these are societal goods that are necessary for the perfection of the human being.[56]

Within the commonweal, the government is given the authority to

54. *Catechism of the Catholic Church*, no. 1756.

55. Vatican II, *Gaudium et spes*, Pastoral Constitution on the Church in the Modern World, no. 26. The citation is from *Vatican Council II: The Conciliar and Post Conciliar Documents*, 927. Quoted in *Catechism of the Catholic Church*, no. 1906.

56. For more discussion on the nature of the common good, see Charles De Koninck, "On the Primacy of the Common Good against the Personalists," *Aquinas Review* 4

care for the common good. This is its primary responsibility. However, individuals too have a duty to preserve and protect the common good, because attaining those perfective ends necessary for human excellence and the good life requires the assistance of other persons who bring their skills and talents to the common effort. For example, the preservation of life and health requires hospitals, medical schools, and the expertise of health-care professionals. Likewise, the pursuit of truth, another basic human endeavor in accordance with right reason, requires an educational system, libraries, and the scholarly community. Thus, the perfection of the individual that comes with the attainment of his perfective ends cannot be divorced from the perfection of his community. We become saints together. Therefore, as we shall see in chapter 4, in certain clinical scenarios, the individual may have to surrender some of his personal privileges in charity and in justice in order to protect the common good.

The Role of the Ecological Good

As a social creature, a human being is a member of a community. However, as one creature living within a creation of incredible diversity and beauty, he is also an integral part of the environment. Thus the perfection of each individual cannot be separated from the good of his environment, a good that can be called the ecological good. As Pope Benedict XVI explained in his social encyclical, *Caritas in veritate*, "the way humanity treats the environment influences the way it treats itself, and vice versa."[57] This ecological good is composed of those conditions necessary for the integrity and well-being of the environment. It includes the sustainable use of our natural resources, the preservation of our diverse ecosystem, and the conservation of the environment, among other goods. Therefore, to live out a virtue ethic, we have to ask if our actions—every action—promote not only our personal good and the common good but the ecological good as well.

How do we respect the ecological good? Many of our contemporaries

---

(1997): 1–71; and Michael Waldstein, "The Common Good in St. Thomas and John Paul II," *Nova et Vetera*, 3 (2005): 569–578.

57. Benedict XVI, *Caritas in veritate*, Encyclical Letter of the Supreme Pontiff Benedict XVI to All the Bishops, Priests, and Deacons, Men and Women Religious, the Lay Faithful, and All People of Good Will on Integral Human Development in Charity and Truth (Vatican City: Libreria Editrice Vaticana, 2009), no. 51. For a summary of Pope Benedict XVI's teaching on creation and environmental responsibility, see Woodeene Koenig-Bricker, *Ten Commandments for the Environment: Pope Benedict XVI Speaks Out for Creation and Justice* (Notre Dame, Ind.: Ave Maria Press, 2009).

assume that the solution to the global ecological crisis lies in a worldwide and sustained effort to reduce each individual's carbon footprint, a measure of the impact that our activities have on the environment, which relates to the amount of greenhouse gases produced in our day-to-day lives. However, simply reducing our carbon footprints will not be enough because the ecological crisis calls for much personal and communal sacrifice, sacrificial demands that will not easily be embraced in our self-indulgent society. This became clear during the 2009 United Nations Climate Change Conference held in Copenhagen, when both rich and poor countries haggled over the cost of embracing climate-friendly social and industrial policies. None of the nations were willing to make the necessary sacrifices for the sake of the common and the ecological good. Thus, it is not surprising that as a response to the global ecological crisis, Pope Benedict XVI has called for a radical conversion to virtue: "What is needed is an effective shift in mentality which can lead to the adoption of new lifestyles 'in which the quest for truth, beauty, goodness, and communion with others for the sake of common growth are the factors which determine consumer choices, savings, and investments.'"[58] We are called to become virtuous individuals who are willing to give up some of the conveniences of life for the sake of both the common and the ecological good.

Finally, according to the Holy Father, this ecological conversion must include a recovery of a culture that respects life. Only a society that properly respects the dignity of every human being at every stage of life can properly respect the environment:

In order to protect nature, it is not enough to intervene with economic incentives or deterrents; not even an apposite education is sufficient. These are important steps, but the decisive issue is the overall moral tenor of society. If there is a lack of respect for the right to life and to a natural death, if human conception, gestation and birth are made artificial, if human embryos are sacrificed to research, the conscience of society ends up losing the concept of human ecology and, along with it, that of environmental ecology.[59]

For the pope, environmental ethics is inherently linked to bioethics and vice versa. To be pro-environment, one must be pro-life. To be pro-life, one must be pro-environment.

58. Benedict XVI, *Caritas in veritate*, no. 51, quoting John Paul II, *Centisumus Annus*, no. 36.
59. Ibid.

The Role of Conscience

Much emphasis is placed upon how individual acts shape the acting person because it is through these acts that the human being attains beatitude in imitation of our Lord Jesus Christ. Since our choices manifested in our actions transform us and make us into either saints or sinners, it is important that we choose well in all areas of our lives. Choosing to act in health care and in scientific research is no different. Here as well, we are called to choose perfection and beatitude and to act in conformity with right reason. Not surprisingly, however, moral decision making in bioethics, in particular, as it is in life in general, is not always easy. As the *Catechism of the Catholic Church* teaches, "Man is sometimes confronted by situations that make moral judgments less assured and decision difficult. But he must always seek what is right and good and discern the will of God expressed in divine law."[60] Nevertheless, with the help of grace, we should always strive to choose the authentic good, those ends, which perfect us. In these difficult moral decisions, our consciences play a key role.

What is the moral conscience?[61] The *Catechism of the Catholic Church* defines it this way: "Conscience is a judgment of reason by which the human person recognizes the moral quality of a concrete act."[62] It is an individual's interior guide to morality. In the words of Blessed John Paul II, "conscience is *the witness of God himself*, whose voice and judgment penetrate the depths of man's soul, calling him ... to obedience."[63] More specifically, conscience is the human intellect, inasmuch as it discerns right and wrong conduct.

Conscience is exercised in three steps: First, the individual grasps the principles of morality impressed in the order of creation by God. He understands the law of nature that has been stamped on his heart. As St. Paul wrote: "When the Gentiles who do not have the law by nature observe the prescriptions of the law, they are a law for themselves even

60. *Catechism of the Catholic Church*, no 1787.
61. For an extensive discussion on the nature of the moral conscience, see the essays in Russell E. Smith, ed., *Catholic Conscience: Foundation and Formation* (Braintree, Mass.: Pope John XXIII Center, 1991). For a history of the Christian teaching on moral conscience, see Servais Pinckaers, O.P., "Conscience and Christian Tradition," in *The Pinckaers Reader*, ed. John Berkman and Craig Steven Titus, 321–341 (Washington, D.C.: The Catholic University of America Press, 2005).
62. *Catechism of the Catholic Church*, no. 1796.
63. John Paul II, *Veritatis splendor*, no. 58.

though they do not have the law. They show that the demands of the law are written in their hearts" (Rom 2:14–15). In bioethics, these moral truths include the truths about the sanctity of life and the dignity of human procreation. Next, the acting person applies these moral principles to a particular situation and given circumstances in a process St. Thomas Aquinas called practical reasoning. He decides which principles are pertinent here and now and which ones are not. This step is aided by the virtue of prudence. As we shall see in chapter 4, in the clinical encounter, this exercise of conscience presupposes informed consent. Finally, the acting person makes a moral judgment about his concrete act, yet to be performed or already performed. In other words, he judges his act to be either good or evil.

Once he has made a judgment of conscience, the human being has the right, all things considered, to act in conscience and in freedom to make moral decisions.[64] As the Second Vatican Council taught: "[The human person] must not be forced to act contrary to his conscience. Nor must he be prevented from acting according to his conscience."[65] This right to act according to one's conscience arises from the dignity of the human being, who is created to seek the truth in freedom. Thus, as we will discuss in chapter 8, society has an obligation to protect the right of an individual to choose not to cooperate with immoral acts that violate his conscience.

However, everyone also has a duty to inform and educate his conscience so that it can make judgments according to right reason and the moral order willed by the wisdom of the Creator. In other words, an individual conscience is not free to invent right and wrong. This is especially true because as a result of original sin, human beings are prone to sin and to self-deception: "In the judgments of our conscience, the possibility of error is always present. Conscience *is not an infallible judge*; it can make mistakes."[66] Thus, an individual's conscience could make an erroneous moral judgment. For instance, Adolf Hitler and his Nazi associates believed with sure conviction that their actions, some involving the murder of millions of innocent people, were good. Their consciences were wrong.

64. On the relationship between conscience, truth, and freedom, see John Paul II, *Veritatis splendor*, nos. 54–64. Also see the essays by then Joseph Cardinal Ratzinger, now Pope Benedict XVI, in the book *On Conscience: Two Essays* (San Francisco: Ignatius Press, 2006).

65. Vatican II, *Dignitatis humanae*, Declaration on Religious Liberty, no. 3. The citation is from *Vatican Council II: The Conciliar and Post Concilliar Documents*, 801–802.

66. John Paul II, *Veritatis splendor*, no. 62.

Often an erroneous conscience can be traced to ignorance of the moral order, the order of right and wrong. If the ignorance can be attributed to personal irresponsibility—in other words the individual should have known what he did not know—then the acting person is culpable for the evil he commits. On the other hand, if the human being is not responsible for the ignorance leading to his erroneous judgment—for instance because he was either misinformed or enslaved by his emotions—then the evil of his action cannot be ascribed to him. However, the act in itself remains no less an evil act. Accordingly, there is a moral duty on everyone to continually strive to form and to educate their consciences. As Blessed John Henry Cardinal Newman, the great defender of the rights of conscience, put it: "Conscience has rights because it has duties."[67] This would apply too to individuals making decisions in bioethics. For example, a married couple struggling with the cross of infertility has an obligation to seek and to understand the Church's teachings regarding artificial reproductive technologies. Only this way could they be certain that they were making a decision that seeks to embrace God's will for them in their lives.

The Principle of Double Effect

Often in life, human actions can lead to both good and bad effects simultaneously. For instance, a mother who disinfects her young son's wounded knee with an antiseptic both cleans his injury and causes him pain. How are we to evaluate the morality of such acts? Or to put it more specifically, how do we morally evaluate the action of the injured child's mother? Is she performing a good or an evil act?

In the Catholic moral tradition, the principle of double effect is used to morally evaluate human actions that have both good and bad effects.[68] To understand the moral reasoning behind the principle of double effect, recall that human beings determine themselves and establish their identities as moral creatures through their freely chosen actions. Therefore, to morally evaluate actions that have multiple effects, both good and evil, we

67. John Henry Cardinal Newman, *A Letter Addressed to His Grace the Duke of Norfolk: Certain Difficulties Felt by Anglicans in Catholic Teaching* (London: Longman, Green, and Company, 1868–1881), 2:250, quoted in John Paul II, *Veritatis splendor,* no. 34.

68. For a history of the principle of double effect, see Joseph T. Mangan, S.J., "An Historical Analysis of the Principle of Double Effect," *Theological Studies* 10 (1949): 41–61. For more philosophical analysis, see the essays in P. A. Woodward, ed., *The Doctrine of Double Effect* (Notre Dame, Ind.: University of Notre Dame Press, 2001).

need to ask the acting person what he is choosing to do in this particular act. In other words, we need to determine the moral object of his act as he describes it. Clearly, however, we can sometimes mislead ourselves or lie to others about our choices and intentions. The acting person could claim that he is choosing to do one thing while he is in fact choosing to do something else. Therefore, to help us evaluate the moral choices of an agent whose acts lead to multiple effects, both good and bad, the principle of double effect lists four conditions that need to be met in order to reasonably conclude that the acting person is indeed choosing to perform a good act.

First, the object of the act must be morally good or at least morally indifferent or neutral. Or to put it another way, the act to be performed must be morally good in itself or at least morally indifferent or neutral. It must not detract the agent from his perfect and integral fulfillment in Christ. In our example of the mother applying an antiseptic on her child's wounded knee, disinfecting a wound is a morally good act in itself. Her action makes her a good mother.

Second, the intention of the agent must be directed toward realizing the beneficial effect and avoiding the foreseen harmful effect of his actions. In other words, the agent must not choose or desire the evil effect. In our example, for her act to be good, the mother must not will or choose to cause her child pain. She must not desire her son's suffering. To do so would make her action evil because it would be an act that makes her an abusive mother.

Third, the beneficial effect must not come about as a result of the harmful effect. Or to put it another way, the bad effect cannot *cause* the good effect. To understand this condition, note that when we act, we act in order to attain a purpose. When we act, we decide what we want, and then we figure out how to get it. Thus, practical decision making necessarily involves choosing both a purpose and the means that would achieve that purpose. Therefore, it would be unreasonable for an acting person to claim that he was neither choosing nor desiring a harmful effect if he knew that the harmful effect brought about the beneficial effect. This is simply not possible. In our example, the pain experienced by the child does not cause the disinfection of the wound. Rather, the disinfection comes about from the use of the antiseptic. Hence, it is reasonable for the woman to claim that she did not intend or choose to cause pain to her child.

Finally, the beneficial effect must be equal to or greater than the fore-seen harmful effects. To put it another way, in the moral order the good effect must be proportionate to the bad effect. Unless this condition is met, it would be difficult to conclude that the acting person was choos-ing only the good effect of his action and did truly not desire the evil out-come. For instance, if a man used the principle of double effect to absolve himself of the death of his wife by claiming that her death was a foreseen but unfortunate effect of his efforts to save the life of their cat, we would justly question his motives. Given the disproportion between the death of his wife and the death of his cat, we would ask him: "Are you sure that you were not *really* desiring the death of your wife?" In our example of the mother, however, in the moral order, the good effect of preventing infec-tion far outweighs the evil effect of the antiseptic's sting. Thus, our moth-er's action passes the test of this fourth condition of the principle of dou-ble effect.

In sum, the principle of double effect confirms that our mother's ac-tion would be an act of healing—and thus would be morally commend-able—if she told us that the disinfection of her son's wound was her cho-sen outcome, the direct effect, of her action. She only wanted to care for her child. Thus, her child's experience of pain was only an unintend-ed but foreseen outcome of her action of healing—what classical moral theologians would call a *praeter intentionem* effect—that does not specify ei-ther the moral object or the morality of the act. This example is a rela-tively straightforward application of the principle of double effect. As we shall see later, the principle of double effect becomes more difficult to ap-ply in more serious bioethical scenarios, especially those involving a grave moral evil.

A Common Objection: The Principle of Double Effect Is Morally Insignificant

The primary objection to the principle of double effect is that it is based upon a distinction that lacks moral significance.[69] In other words,

69. For representative critiques of the principle of double effect, see Timothy Quill, Rebecca Dresser, and Dan Brock, "The Rule of Double Effect—A Critique of Its Role in End-of-Life Decision Making," *N Engl J Med* 337 (1997): 1768–1771; and Jonathan Ben-nett, "Foreseen Side Effects versus Intended Consequences," in *The Doctrine of Double Effect*, ed. P. A. Woodward, 85–118 (Notre Dame, Ind.: University of Notre Dame Press, 2001).

for the objector, there is no morally significant difference between choosing an evil and accepting one as a foreseen but unintended side effect. According to this alternative moral hypothesis, we are responsible for all the outcomes of our acts because we cause them. Thus, the morality of an act depends not upon the choice of the acting person, but upon a moral calculation that compares the relative weights of the good and bad outcomes that are caused by the act. A good act is one where the good effects outweigh the bad effects.

In response, the primary flaw with this objection is that it fails to acknowledge the morally significant difference between apparently identical physical actions that involve a morally good choice and those that involve a bad one. Take the example we discussed above, the example of the mother disinfecting her son's wounded knee with a painful antiseptic. Most reasonable individuals would agree that there is a morally significant difference between the act of this mother who intends to care for her wounded child and only foresees his suffering and the act of another mother who admits that she intended to cause her son pain with the antiseptic. "I wanted to make him cry," this second mother says; "I didn't really care if the antiseptic disinfected the wound." Externally, both actions appear to be identical—in both cases, one observes a mother swabbing the wound of her whimpering son, and in both cases, the good and the bad outcomes are identical—but most reasonable individuals would recognize that these are morally different actions.

In classical terminology, the acts of the two mothers have different moral objects that specify apparently identical physical acts.[70] Thus, they are different, and the difference is morally significant, precisely because they involve different choices that shape and determine the moral character of the mothers. The first mother's action is commendable. In contrast, the second mother's action would be a morally deplorable act comparable to that of a third mother who causes her child pain by burning her daughter with a lit cigarette. Both these women, the second with the antiseptic and the third with the cigarette, intentionally choose to inflict their children with pain. Both make themselves abusers. In the end, what an agent *chooses* to do is of paramount importance in moral analysis. This

70. As I emphasized above, human agents are not free to arbitrarily choose random moral objects to specify their acts. However, there are cases—and this is one of them—where a physical act, by its very teleological ordering, can be specified by alternative objects in a legitimate manner.

is the warrant for making the distinction between choosing an evil and accepting one as a foreseen, but unintended, side effect.

Highlighting the Role of Virtue in Bioethics

Contemporary bioethics tends to stress rules, duties, and obligations. A renewal of bioethics in light of the moral vision articulated in *Veritatis splendor* will need to recover the proper role of the virtues in bioethical decision making as they order and shape our inclinations and our actions. They—and the virtue of prudence, in particular—are especially important to consider when one is applying bioethical conclusions drawn from an abstract moral analysis to a particular and concrete scenario involving either this ninety-three-year-old patient who is considering having her ventilator removed, or that thirty-nine-year-old scientist who is considering using cells taken from an aborted fetus for his research program examining cell senescence, or this married couple who are considering using their life savings to undergo fertility treatment in a Manhattan IVF clinic.

Moral theologian William E. May questions the central importance of the virtue of prudence in bioethical reasoning:

I think that Ashley, like Hall, is mistaken in claiming that only the virtue of prudence shows the truth of specific moral norms. First of all, prudent persons can themselves disagree over ethical issues, and their disagreements can be contradictory.... There are no objective reasons for holding one person more prudent (virtuous) than the other. Thus the virtue of prudence will not settle the dispute; rather, appeal to relevant moral principles and to the *arguments* and evidence marshaled by the virtuous persons can alone show who is correct.[71]

For May, prudence cannot adequately settle moral disputes.

In response, I believe that May misunderstands the role of the virtues in Catholic bioethics. Bioethics, as a practical science, is ordered toward a particular action done here and now by a particular human agent. Thus, it is not enough for a Catholic bioethicist to argue that having an abor-

---

71. See his essay, "Contemporary Perspectives on Thomistic Natural Law," in *St. Thomas Aquinas and the Natural Law Tradition: Contemporary Perspectives,* ed. John Goyette, Mark S. Latkovic, and Richard S. Myers, 113–156 (Washington, D.C.: The Catholic University of America Press, 2004), 129 (original emphasis).

tion is intrinsically evil. The Catholic bioethicist also needs to be able to convince a seventeen-year-old teenager living in Overland Park, Kansas, who is scared of disappointing her mother and of angering her boyfriend, of the truth of this teaching so that she will not have an abortion. This is an integral part of Catholic bioethics. Here, the virtues of the bioethicist and, more significantly, of the young woman are crucial. Prudence especially would enable one to see things rightly so as to act well. One of its functions is to enable one to grasp rightly the relative importance of different purposes in one's life. It would guide the bioethicist to choose the right words as he strives to guide the teenager, and it would predispose the teenager to choose the good in spite of all the obstacles she faces in life. In the end, the virtues, especially prudence, help the individual as he decides how to act here and now, by applying the conclusions and teachings of the Catholic moral tradition to his particular moral and bioethical situation.

CHAPTER TWO

Bioethics at the Beginning of Life

In March of 1970, an unmarried pregnant woman, Norma L. McCorvey, then using the fictitious name "Jane Roe," sued the State of Texas to challenge a state law that prohibited abortions except in those cases where the mother's life is in danger. Three years later, the United States Supreme Court overturned the Texan law in its landmark decision, *Roe v. Wade*, and ruled in favor of Roe's right to an abortion.[1] Appealing to a right of privacy broad enough to encompass a woman's decision whether or not to end her pregnancy, a majority of the justices held that the government may not prevent a mother from having an abortion for any reason, up to and until the point at which the fetus becomes viable. The Court also held that abortion after viability must be permitted when needed to protect a woman's health, which the Court defined broadly, in the companion case of *Doe v. Bolton*, to include all factors—physical, emotional, psychological, familial, and the woman's age—relevant to the well-being of the mother.[2] Since that time, over 40 million abortions have been performed in the United States.[3] Every year, about 2 percent of women aged 15–44 have an abortion.[4] Sadly, 47 percent of these mothers have had at least one previous abortion.[5] Nonetheless, a heated debate continues over legalized

1. *Roe v. Wade*, 410 U.S. 113 (1973). For a documentary history of the abortion jurisprudence of the U.S. Supreme Court, including a summary of the text of *Roe v. Wade* and dissenting opinions, see Ian Shapiro, ed., *Abortion: The Supreme Court Decisions* (Indianapolis: Hackett, 2007). For a commentary from a Catholic perspective on the historical and legal invention of the right to privacy, see Janet E. Smith, *The Right to Privacy* (San Francisco: Ignatius Press, 2008).

2. *Doe v. Bolton*, 410 U.S. 179 (1973).

3. Janna C. Merrick and Robert H. Blank, *Contemporary World Issues: Reproductive Issues in America* (Santa Barbara, Calif.: ABC-CLIO, 2003), 137.

4. R. K. Jones, J. E. Darroch, and S. K. Henshaw, "Patterns in the Socioeconomic Characteristics of Women Obtaining Abortions in 2000–2001," *Perspect Sex Reprod Health* 34 (2002): 226–235.

5. Ibid.

abortion, with polls showing that in 2009, more Americans are calling themselves pro-life (51%) than pro-choice (42%) for the first time since the Gallup Poll began asking this question in the mid-1990s.[6]

The morality of abortion remains one of the most controversial ethical disputes of our day. In this chapter devoted to moral questions at the beginning of life, I begin with a discussion of the dignity of the human person, the bedrock foundation for Catholic bioethics, followed by a summary of the Catholic Church's teaching on abortion. I then explore and respond to the four arguments that are often used to justify abortions. Next, I will move to moral questions surrounding abortion in those circumstances involving rape, ectopic pregnancies, and prenatal testing. Finally, I will close with a question that often arises in Catholic discussions surrounding the beginning of life: when is the human being ensouled?

Human Dignity and the Sanctity of Human Life

To understand the Catholic Church's teaching on abortion—in fact, to understand all of the Church's moral teachings regarding the human being—we need to begin with a discussion of the dignity of the human being. To affirm that a human being has dignity is to affirm that there is something worthwhile about each and every human being such that certain things ought not to be done to any human being and that certain other things ought to be done for every human being.[7] Beyond this basic formulation, however, there is controversy over the precise meaning of human dignity. Ruth Macklin, a prominent secular bioethicist, has even argued that appeals to human dignity are useless because they are either restatements of the principle of respect for autonomy or mere slogans whose meaning remains hopelessly vague.[8] In the tradition of Catholic bioethics, however, the truth of the dignity of the human being is a

6. "More Americans 'Pro-Life' Than 'Pro-Choice' for First Time," at http://www.gallup.com/poll/118399/More-Americans-Pro-Life-Than-Pro-Choice-First-Time.aspx.

7. I am indebted to Michael J. Perry for this notion of human dignity, which I take with some modification from his book, *The Idea of Human Rights* (Oxford: Oxford University Press, 1993), 13.

8. Ruth Macklin, "Dignity Is a Useless Concept," *BMJ* 327 (2003): 1419–1420. For insightful discussion on the meaning of human dignity from a variety of perspectives, see the essays commissioned by the President's Council on Bioethics: *Human Dignity and Bioethics* (Washington, D.C.: President's Council on Bioethics, 2008); and Gilbert Meilaender, *Neither Beast Nor God: The Dignity of the Human Person* (New York: Encounter Books, 2009).

bedrock principle that necessarily emerges from and is justified by other truths regarding his relationship with his Creator. It is the cornerstone of a moral vision of the human person that properly acknowledges his exalted place in the universe.

For the Judeo-Christian tradition, the human being is unique in all creation for he is made in the image and likeness of God: "God created man in his image; in the divine image he created him; male and female he created them" (Gn 1:27). He is able to think and to choose, and as such is the only visible creature that can know and love his Creator. To put it another way, the human being is a *person*, a moral agent, who is capable of self-knowledge, of self-possession, and of freely giving himself and entering into communion with other persons.[9] Moreover, the human being is the only creature on Earth that God has chosen for its own sake. He alone is called to share, by knowledge and by love, in God's own inner Trinitarian life. This transcendent and eternal destiny is the fundamental reason for the human being's dignity, a personal dignity that is independent of human society's recognition.[10]

From this account of the dignity of the human being, we can conclude four essential truths. First, human dignity is intrinsic. According to the *Oxford English Dictionary*, to call something *intrinsic* is to affirm that it is something "belonging to the thing in itself or by its very nature."[11] It is a quality that is inherent, essential, and proper to the thing. Thus, to affirm that human dignity is intrinsic is to claim that this dignity is constitutive of human identity itself. In other words, to affirm that human beings have intrinsic dignity is to claim that they are worthwhile because of the kind of things that they are. This type of dignity is not conferred or earned. It is a dignity that is simply recognized and attributed to every human being regardless of any other considerations or claims. It is also a dignity that can be possessed only in an absolute sense—one either has it completely or does not have it at all—since one is either a human being or not one at all. There is no such thing as partial human dignity since there is no such thing as a partial human being.[12]

9. *Catechism of the Catholic Church*, no. 357.

10. Ibid., no. 356.

11. *Oxford English Dictionary*, 2nd ed. (New York: Oxford University Press, 1989).

12. As we will discuss in chapter 5, a fundamental disagreement exists in our pluralistic society between those who acknowledge that human dignity is intrinsic to the human person because it is constitutive of human identity and those who think that it is

Next, because human beings have dignity, human life is sacred. It is worthy of respect and has to be protected from all unjust attack. As Blessed John Paul II clearly explained: "The inviolability of the person, which is a reflection of the absolute inviolability of God, finds its primary and fundamental expression in the inviolability of human life."[13] Human life is inviolable because it is a gift from God. He alone is the Lord of life from its beginning until its end. Thus, no one can, in any circumstance, claim for himself the right directly to destroy an innocent human being.[14] Sacred Scripture expresses this truth in the divine commandment: "You shall not kill" (Ex 20:13; Dt 5:17).

Third, because of their dignity, human beings can never be treated as objects. In other words, as persons, they can never be treated purely as a means to an end or be used merely as tools to attain a goal. Instead, they have to be respected as free moral agents capable of self-knowledge and self-determination in all the actions involving them. As Blessed John Paul II forcefully declared: "The human individual cannot be subordinated as a pure means or a pure instrument either to the species or to society; he has value *per se*. He is a person. With his intellect and his will, he is capable of forming a relationship of communion, solidarity and self-giving with his peers."[15] We know this truth from our own experience. Individuals who discover that they have been manipulated often feel violated and diminished, because they intuit that they are persons who have a dignity that is attacked when they are used merely as objects.

Finally, because of their common dignity, all human beings are equal.

---

only extrinsic to the human person, because it is rooted in the individual's autonomy, which can be gained or lost. However, as we will see in chapter 8, an intrinsic account of human dignity is also the only account that can coherently sustain a liberal society. Therefore, by the standards of liberalism itself, the account of dignity articulated here is superior to its rivals.

13. John Paul II, *Christifideles laici*, Post-Synodal Apostolic Exhortation of His Holiness John Paul II on the Vocation and the Mission of the Lay Faithful in the Church and in the World (Vatican City: Libreria Editrice Vaticana, 1998), no. 38.

14. See the Congregation for the Doctrine of the Faith's *Donum vitae*, Instruction on Respect for Human Life in its Origin and on the Dignity of Procreation, Replies to Certain Questions of the Day (Vatican City: Libreria Editrice Vaticana, 1987), Introduction, no. 5.

15. John Paul II, "Address to the Plenary Session on the Subject 'The Origins and Early Evolution of Life', October 22, 1996," in Pontifical Academy of Sciences, *Papal Addresses to the Pontifical Academy of Sciences 1917–2002 and to the Pontifical Academy of Social Sciences 1994–2002*, Scripta Varia 100, 370–374 (Vatican City: Pontifical Academy of Sciences, 2003), 373.

Despite any real differences in their physical or cognitive or spiritual capacities, all human beings, as persons made in the image and likeness of God, have an inestimable and thus equal worth. As the Second Vatican Council taught: "Every form of social or cultural discrimination in fundamental personal rights on the grounds of sex, race, color, social conditions, language, or religion must be curbed and eradicated as incompatible with God's design."[16] Social discrimination is unjust precisely because it attacks the intrinsic and equal dignity of human beings.

This profound appreciation for the dignity of the human being and the sanctity of every human life is the bedrock of Catholic bioethics. It is often used as the primary justification for most of the Church's moral teachings in bioethics.

The Catholic Church's Teaching on Abortion

As defined in *Evangelium vitae*, John Paul II's encyclical on the inviolability of human life, abortion is "the deliberate and direct killing, by whatever means it is carried out, of a human being in the initial phase of his or her existence, extending from conception to birth."[17] Since the first century, the Church has affirmed the moral evil of every procured abortion. The *Didache*, the most ancient nonbiblical Christian text dating to around AD 80, already condemned abortion, declaring: "You will not murder offspring by means of abortion, (and) you will not kill [him/her] having been born."[18] The First Council of Mainz in AD 847 decided that the most rigorous penance would be imposed "on women who procure the elimination of the fruit conceived in their womb."[19] In the thirteenth century, St. Thomas Aquinas taught that abortion is a grave sin against the natural law: "He that strikes a woman with child does something unlawful: wherefore if there results the death either of the woman or the animated fetus, he will not be excused from homicide, especially seeing that

16. Vatican II, *Gaudium et spes*, no. 29.

17. John Paul II, *Evangelium vitae*, Encyclical Letter Addressed by the Supreme Pontiff John Paul II to the Bishops, Priests and Deacons, Men and Women Religious, Lay Faithful, and All People of Good Will on the Value and Inviolability of Human Life (Vatican City: Libreria Editrice Vaticana, 1995), no. 58.

18. Aaron Milavec, *The Didache: Text, Translation, Analysis, and Commentary* (Collegeville, Minn.: Liturgical Press, 2003), 5.

19. Canon 21 (Mansi, 14, 909). Cited in Congregation for the Doctrine of the Faith, *Declaration on Procured Abortion* (Vatican City: Libreria Editrice Vaticana, 1974), no. 7.

death is the natural result of such a blow."[20] Finally, seven centuries later, the Second Vatican Council would describe abortion, together with infanticide, as an "unspeakable crime."[21] In light of this evidence, John Connery, S.J., concluded his definitive work on the history of the Catholic Church's teaching on abortion as follows:

> The Christian tradition from the earliest days reveals a firm antiabortion attitude. . . . The condemnation of abortion did not depend on and was not limited in any way by theories regarding the time of fetal animation. Even during the many centuries when Church penal and penitential practice was based the theory of delayed animation, the condemnation of abortion was never affected by it. Whatever one would want to hold about the time of animation, or when the fetus became a human being in the strict sense of the term, abortion from the time of conception was considered wrong, and the time of animation was never looked on as a moral dividing line between permissible and impermissible abortion.[22]

The two-thousand-year-old Christian tradition is clear: abortion is a grave moral evil.

As Blessed John Paul II taught in *Evangelium vitae*, the moral gravity of procured abortion is real because it is an act that involves the murder of an absolutely innocent human being at the very beginning of his life.[23] The Holy Father continues by noting that "it is true that the decision to have an abortion is often tragic and painful for the mother, insofar as the decision to rid herself of the fruit of conception is not made for purely selfish reasons or out of convenience, but out of a desire to protect certain important values such as her own health or a decent standard of living for the other members of the family." Nevertheless, in the same encyclical, the pope concludes, "these reasons and others like them, however serious

20. *ST*, IIa-IIa, 65.8. As we will discuss later in this chapter, inadequate theories about embryology during the Middle Ages led some theologians, including St. Thomas Aquinas, to speculate that a developing human being capable of receiving a rational soul may not exist until several weeks after the beginning of pregnancy. While these theories positing delayed hominization—none of which were explicitly endorsed by the Magisterium of the Catholic Church—led to a distinction in penalties between very early and later abortions in canon law, the Church's moral teaching never justified or permitted abortion at any stage of development.

21. Vatican II, *Gaudium et spes*, no. 50.

22. John R. Connery, S.J., *Abortion: The Development of the Roman Catholic Perspective* (Chicago: Loyola University Press, 1977), 304.

23. John Paul II, *Evangelium vitae*, no. 58.

and tragic, can never justify the deliberate killing of an innocent human being." Thus, the United States Conference of Catholic Bishops (USC-CB), in its *Ethical and Religious Directives for Catholic Health Care Services*, concludes: "Abortion (that is, the directly intended termination of pregnancy before viability or the directly intended destruction of a viable fetus) is never permitted. . . . Catholic health care institutions are not to provide abortion services, even based upon the principle of material cooperation. In this context, Catholic health care institutions need to be concerned about the danger of scandal in any association with abortion providers."[24]

Abortion is also evil because it harms the mother of the child. Numerous studies have documented the detrimental effects, medical, psychological, and spiritual, of abortions on women. For example, there is research that reveals that the suicide rate following abortion is six times greater than that following childbirth, and three times the general suicide rate.[25] This is only one strand of the overall evidence that suggests that some women who have had abortions, and in some cases the fathers of the unborn children, suffer from post-abortion stress syndrome (PAS or PASS), with symptoms including, among others, depression, self-destructive behavior, sleep disorders, sexual dysfunction, chronic problems with relationships, anxiety attacks, difficulty grieving, chronic crying, flashbacks, and difficulty bonding with later children.[26] In many cases, symptoms do

---

24. United States Conference of Catholic Bishops, *Ethical and Religious Directives for Catholic Health Care Services*, 5th ed. (Washington, D.C.: USCCB, 2009), no. 45.

25. Mika Gissler, Elina Hemminki, and Jouko Lonnvist, "Suicides After Pregnancy in Finland, 1987–94: Register Linkage Study," *BMJ* 313 (1996): 1431–1434. For a comprehensive analysis and summary of the evidence that documents the psychological and medical difficulties associated with abortion, see Elizabeth Ring-Cassidy and Ian Gentles, *Women's Health after Abortion: The Medical and Psychological Evidence*, 2nd ed. (Toronto: De-Veber Institute, 2003).

26. For representative studies that link induced abortions and mental distress, see David M. Fergusson, L. John Horwood, and Joseph M. Boden, "Abortion and Mental Health Disorders: Evidence from a 30-year Longitudinal Study," *Br J Psychiatry* 193 (2008): 444–451; and Anne N. Broen, Torbjorn Moum, Anne Sejersted Bodtker, and Oivind Ekeberg, "The Course of Mental Health after Miscarriage and Induced Abortion: A Longitudinal, Five-Year Follow-Up Study," *BMC Med* 3 (2005): 18. For studies that are critical of the published evidence, see Vignetta E. Charles, Chelsea B. Polis, Srinivas K. Sridhara, and Robert W. Blum, "Abortion and Long-Term Mental Health Outcomes: A Systematic Review of the Evidence," *Contraception* 78 (2008): 436–450; and Trine Munk-Olsen, Thomas Munk Laursen, Carsten B. Pedersen, Ojvind Lidegaard, and Preben Bo Mortensen, "Induced First-Trimester Abortion and Risk of Mental Disorder," *N Engl J Med* 364 (2011): 332–339. The Munk-Olsen study is flawed because it lim-

not manifest themselves immediately after the abortion. Instead, numbness follows the procedure, only to be replaced months or even years later by mental and emotional distress. Post-abortion syndrome is often compared to post-traumatic stress disorder, which can affect military veterans, rape victims, or any other individual who has experienced an overwhelming personal shock or injury.

To women who have had abortions, Blessed John Paul II had this to say:

> The Church is aware of the many factors which may have influenced your decision, and she does not doubt that in many cases it was a painful and even shattering decision. The wound in your heart may not yet have healed. Certainly what happened was and remains terribly wrong. But do not give in to discouragement and do not lose hope. Try rather to understand what happened and face it honestly. . . . The Father of mercies is ready to give you his forgiveness and his peace in the Sacrament of Reconciliation. You will come to understand that nothing is definitively lost and you will also be able to ask forgiveness from your child, who is now living in the Lord.[27]

The decision to choose an abortion is often made in tragic circumstances. It is a time of great anxiety and stress, with pressure from parents, from the father of the child, and from the grief of lost dreams. The so-called choice that ends in tragedy is rarely free. And yet, as the Holy Father reveals, we should never forget that God is a Father of Mercies, who is always waiting to forgive, twenty, thirty, or even fifty years after an abortion. The path to healing is always open to those who seek mercy and love.

Common Objections

The Post-Conception Beginning of Life Argument

Four arguments are commonly used to justify the morality of procured abortions. The simplest argument is that the life of the human be-

---

ited its analysis of the incidence of mental distress in women to the year immediately following the abortion. As noted in the text, post-abortion stress syndrome often manifests itself years after the procedure. For a study of the effects of abortion on men, see Arthur B. Shostak, Gary McLouth, and Lynn Seng, *Men and Abortion: Lessons, Losses, and Love* (Westport, Conn.: Praeger Publishers, 1984). Project Rachel is the name of the Catholic Church's healing ministry to those who have been involved in abortion and who suffer from post-abortion stress syndrome. For more information, see their website, www.hopeafterabortion.com.

27. John Paul II, *Evangelium vitae*, no. 99.

ing does not begin at fertilization but at some point post-conception. Thus, it is argued that abortions, especially at the beginning of pregnancy, do not involve the destruction of a human being. Instead, it is comparable to a surgical procedure that removes a lump of tissue from a patient. Therefore it is important to begin with the basic question: when does the life of the human being begin?[28]

In response, the most recent biological research has demonstrated that the origin of the individual human being can be traced back to the union of sperm and egg, the biological event called either conception or fertilization. There are two lines of evidence that support this biological argument.

First, from the moment of conception, the human embryo is a unique human organism, a unique human being. The human embryo is unique because fertilization brings together a unique combination of forty-six chromosomes in the embryo; twenty-three chromosomes come from the father and twenty-three from the mother. This unique combination of genes distinguishes the embryo from any other cell either in his[29] mother or in his father. Next, the human embryo is human because his forty-six chromosomes is the defining genetic feature of the human species. Finally, the human embryo is an organism because his molecular organization gives him the active and intrinsic self-driven disposition to use his genetic information to develop himself into a mature human being, the telltale characteristic of a human organism. Therefore, as the Congregation for the Doctrine of Faith put it:

From the time that the ovum is fertilized, a life is begun which is neither that of the father nor of the mother; it is rather the life of a new human being with his own growth. It would never be made human if it were not human already. . . . [M]odern genetic science brings valuable confirmation [to this]. It has demonstrated that, from the first instant, there is established the program

28. For example, the former governor of the state of New York, Mario Cuomo, argued in an opinion piece published in the *New York Times* that the crucial moral issue at the center of the debate surrounding the destruction of human embryos is whether "human life starts at conception." Cuomo proposed that answering this question is a matter not of science but of faith. See his "Not on Faith Alone," *New York Times,* June 20, 2005, at A15.

29. Properly speaking, since the sex of the human being is determined at the moment of fertilization when a sperm carrying either an X or a Y chromosome unites with an egg with its own X chromosome, the human embryo from its very beginning is already either male or female.

of what this living being will be: a man, this individual man with his charac-teristic aspects already well determined. Right from fertilization is begun the adventure of a human life, and each of its great capacities requires time—a rather lengthy time—to find its place and to be in a position to act.[30]

Therefore, it is incorrect to say that the human embryo is a potential hu-man being. Rather, he is an actual human being with great potential.

One major objection has been raised to this line of evidence. In re-cent years, some bioethicists have questioned the claim that fertilization is that moment that properly marks the beginning of the human organ-ism, because scientists often define fertilization as a complex sequence of coordinated events that begins with sperm penetration and ends some hours or days later with the union of the pronuclei of the sperm and of the egg.[31]

In response, it is important to note that the developmental process that begins with the fertilization of the human egg and that can end with the death of the human organism a century later is a single and integral whole. Thus, the distinctions between sperm penetration, union of pro-nuclei, and any of the later events in embryogenesis and development are conventional and arbitrary designations of points within a single contin-uum of developmental change that continues for decades. Fertilization, therefore, is properly that moment when the whole chain of developmen-tal events is set in motion, when the organism comes to be. It can be com-pared to the toppling over of the first domino that begins the collapse of a branching chain of ten million dominoes. If one had to pick a biologi-cal event to correspond to this falling first domino, it is properly the en-try of the sperm that leads to the explosion of intracellular calcium lev-els that triggers the reorganization of the egg. Prior to sperm penetration, the egg is a cell in stasis that only has a lifespan of about twenty-four hours. After fertilization, however, the embryo is an organism undergo-ing change, change that can continue unhindered for a hundred years.[32]

30. Congregation for the Doctrine of the Faith, *Declaration on Procured Abortion*, nos. 12–13.

31. For an extended discussion of this view, see Ronald M. Green, *The Human Embryo Research Debates* (Oxford: Oxford University Press, 2001), 25–30. A similar argument is made by Thomas A. Shannon and Allan B. Wolter in their "Reflections on the Moral Status of the Pre-embryo," *Theological Studies* 51 (1990): 603–626; 606–608; and more spe-cifically, by Shannon in his "Cloning, Uniqueness, and Individuality," *Louvain Studies* 19 (1994): 283–306.

32. Secular bioethicist Ronald Green has correctly noted that the egg emits chemoat-

Second, from the moment of conception, the zygote is an *individual* human organism. Biologically, individuality is defined by the presence of body axes, the coordinate system that tells the body where are up and down, left and right, front and back. All multicellular organisms have at least one of these axes. Most have all three. Body axes are significant because they establish the blueprint for the organism's body plan and manifest the intrinsic biological organization that makes an organism an integrated whole. Significantly, experimental work from two independent laboratories in the United Kingdom has demonstrated that the embryonic axes are already present in the one-celled mammalian zygote, though this developmental pattern is not rigidly determined.[33] The same research group has also shown that the axes of the zygote establish the axes of later stages of embryonic development, including the fetus, suggesting that an organismal continuity exists between the one-cell embryo, the fetus, and, therefore, the newborn. Thus, the scientific evidence is conclusive: the life of the human being begins at conception.

But what about twinning? For many, the objection most threatening to the position that accords the early human embryo the moral status of a person from the moment of fertilization is the proposal that scientists have shown that the early embryo is not an individual. Norman Ford, S.D.B., an Australian theologian, has formulated the challenge this way: "[W]hen the zygote divides during normal development to form two cells, do we have a two-celled individual, or simply two individu-

---

tractants, chemical signals that attract the sperm even before the sperm enters the fallopian tubes. This, he speculates, may therefore be the proper beginning of fertilization because here the sperm and egg come into "contact." See Green, *Human Embryo*, 27. Green's speculation is incorrect. Yes, interaction with the chemoattractants of the egg changes the behavior of the sperm, but fertilization properly marks the cell-to-organism transition that alters the systems dynamics of the molecules not in the sperm but in the *egg*. The egg is the critical gamete here because it is the egg that in itself bears the molecular components necessary for axes specification, an essential component in the cell-to-organism transition. As cloning technology has demonstrated, the sperm is not necessary for this. For further discussion, see my essay, "On Static Eggs and Dynamic Embryos: A Systems Perspective," *Natl Cathol Bioeth Q* 2 (2002): 659–683; and Maureen Condic, "When Does Life Begin? A Scientific Perspective," *Natl Cathol Bioeth Q* 9 (2009): 129–149.

33. For a summary of the scientific evidence, see M. Zernicka-Goetz, "Cells of the Early Mouse Embryo Follow Biased and Yet Flexible Development," in *The Human Embryo Before Implantation: Scientific Aspects and Bioethical Considerations*, ed. Elio Sgreccia and Jean Laffitte, 30–36 (Vatican City: Libreria Editrice Vaticana, 2007). For discussion, see my essay, "The Pre-implantation Embryo Revisited: Two-Celled Individual or Two Individual Cells?" *Linacre Q* 70 (2003): 121–126.

al cells?"[34] He and others have asserted that the totipotency of the cells of the early embryo, that is, their ability to give rise to several individual adult organisms if they are disaggregated into separate cells, suggests that no individual is present early in development. To put their argument another way: if one sign of the individuality of an adult human being is that he cannot be split into twins, then an early human embryo cannot be an individual since he can give rise to twins. Thus, the argument continues, individuality arises only with the appearance of the primitive streak, when the human embryo no longer has the potential for twinning. This objection has been widely used in support of proposals that would lead to the destruction of early human embryos since the lack of individuality would suggest that no single entity—no person—is present who would merit moral status.

In response, as we discussed above, recent work on the appearance of organization within mammalian embryos provides compelling evidence that the embryo, even during his earliest stages of development, is an integral whole specified by his body axes. To reply to Ford, we can now say with scientific certainty that the two-celled mammalian embryo is indeed a two-celled individual. Moreover, one can argue that the developmental plasticity of the human embryo that makes twinning possible does not necessarily preclude individuality. Take the planarian, a flatworm found in many freshwater lakes throughout the world. It can be divided into nearly three hundred pieces, including brain, tail, and gut fragments, each of which has the potential to regenerate a complete organism, and yet no one would doubt the individuality of the original intact invertebrate.[35] In the same way, twinning can be explained by proposing that the early human embryo, though already an individual, manifests a developmental plasticity that allows each totipotent cell to give rise to an intact organism if the embryo is disrupted. Note, however, that this would interrupt the normal developmental process of the human embryo. Not surprisingly, therefore, it is significant that twinning is associated with an increased incidence of birth defects in humans.[36] This is just another reminder that twinning is the exception and not the rule in mammalian embryonic development.

34. Norman Ford, S.D.B., "The Human Embryo as Person in Catholic Teaching," *Natl Cathol Bioeth Q* 1 (2001): 155–160, 160.

35. For details, see the scientific review by A. Sanchez Alvarado, "Planarian Regeneration: Its End Is Its Beginning," *Cell* 124 (2006): 241–245.

36. For details and citations to the scientific literature, see the review by J. G. Hall, "Twinning," *Lancet* 362 (2003): 735–743.

The Non-Personhood Argument

Next, to support their convictions, proponents of abortion often make the distinction between human beings and human persons. Appealing to a high standard of personhood, they concede that human embryos are human beings in the genetic or biological sense, but then contend that they are not human persons because they are incapable either of sensing or of feeling or of thinking.[37] Consequently, according to this non-personhood argument, human embryos, as nonpersons, do not have the moral status accorded to adult human beings and as such cannot claim any basic human rights, including the most basic right to life, until the moment when they acquire the capacity for mental acts.[38] Some defenders of abortion argue that this decisive moment occurs after birth, while others argue that the unborn human being gradually becomes a person as it develops and acquires different mental capacities.

In response, the fundamental flaw of this non-personhood argument is that it confuses being with function. The argument posits a *functional* definition of personhood that equates a person with an entity that functions in a particular way. Therefore, abortion advocates conclude that a human fetus is not a person because he cannot sense or think or desire. However, this functional definition is problematic because it would also exclude the unconscious, the sleeping, and the temporarily comatose, from personhood, since individuals in these states, like the human fetus, are not able to sense or to think or to desire. As Francis Beckwith concludes, "it seems more consistent with our moral intuitions to say that a person

37. As Ruth Macklin has noted, authors writing on the notion of personhood fall into two camps: "low standard" and "high standard." Low-standard personhood corresponds to those who believe that the embryo is a person quite aside from brain function. High-standard personhood corresponds to those who believe that some form of self-consciousness is necessary to achieve personhood. According to this latter view, persons are beings with the capacity for higher mental functions. See her "Personhood in the Bioethics Literature," *Milbank Mem Fund Q Health Soc* 61 (1983): 35–57.

38. For examples of pro-abortion scholars who advocate a high standard of personhood that distinguishes human beings from human persons, see Bonnie Steinbock, *Life before Birth: The Moral and Legal Status of Embryos and Fetuses* (Oxford: Oxford University Press, 1992), and David Boonin, *A Defense of Abortion* (Cambridge: Cambridge University Press, 2003). For excellent responses to this objection and other pro-abortion arguments that deny the personhood of the embryo, see Christopher Kaczor, *The Ethics of Abortion* (New York: Routledge, 2011); Patrick Lee, *Abortion and Unborn Human Life*, 2nd ed. (Washington, D.C.: The Catholic University of America Press, 2010), and Robert P. George and Christopher Tollefsen, *Embryo: A Defense of Human Life* (New York: Doubleday, 2008).

functions as a person because she is a person, not that she is a person because she functions as a person."[39] Consequently, it is more reasonable to posit an *essential* definition of personhood that equates a person with an entity that is a particular kind of being that is able to function in a particular kind of way. In other words, as the ancients understood well, an adult human male is a person not because he can think or feel or desire right now, but because he is a kind of being, a human being, who has a nature that includes the capacities to function in these particular ways. In the same way, the human embryo is a person not because he can sense or think or desire, but because he too is a human being with a nature that includes the capacities to perform these acts.

Now, the abortion advocate could retort by claiming that the response given above is itself flawed because it does not properly recognize that the sleeping, the unconscious, and the comatose differ from the unborn in a morally significant way: Sleeping, unconscious, and comatose individuals were once persons who were once able to think and to feel and to desire, while the unborn never were. Moreover, it is likely that these individuals will function as persons again once they awake. Thus, the proponent of abortion could argue that sleeping, unconscious, and comatose individuals, in contrast to unborn human beings, are persons because one is a person if one once functioned as a person, and will probably function as a person again in the future.

In response, the abortion advocate does not realize that to claim that one can be functional as a person, then become nonfunctional as a person, and then become functional again as a person is to implicitly presuppose that the person has a stable underlying nature that perdures through sleep, unconsciousness, or coma, a nature that is the source of his ability to function in a particular way. In other words, with this retort, the proponent of the non-personhood argument actually presupposes the truth of the essential definition of personhood that he is attempting to deny. He affirms that a stable human nature exists that is the source of human function and the ground for moral status, a human nature that, according to developmental biology, originates at fertilization when the human organism comes into being.

Finally, as numerous scholars have pointed out, the non-personhood argument leads to an implicit endorsement of substance dualism, the er-

39. Francis J. Beckwith, *Politically Correct Death: Answering Arguments for Abortion Rights* (Grand Rapids, Mich.: Baker Books, 1993), 108.

roneous proposition that posits that the human person understood as a conscious being, called either the soul or the mind, is substantially distinct from the human being understood as a biological organism, called the body.[40] Dualism—and therefore, the non-personhood argument—is flawed because it forgets that human persons are not just conscious minds. We are embodied beings, human beings that the Aristotelian-Thomistic tradition describes as integrated and unified substances composed of two complementary spiritual and material principles. Our commonsense experience confirms this: when we are sick with the flu, we do not say, "My body has the flu." Rather, we say, "*I* have the flu." When someone hits us, we do not say, "Don't hit my body." Instead we say, "Don't hit *me!*" Our identity, and thus, our personhood, has a bodily dimension. Moreover, as Maurice Merleau-Ponty has convincingly argued, even our acts of perceiving the world are not purely mental events.[41] Rather, they arise from the agent's interaction, as a body-subject, with his world. Therefore, a proper understanding of personhood has to appreciate that as embodied persons, *wherever* our bodies are, there we are. More important for our purposes, however, a proper understanding of personhood would acknowledge that *whenever* our bodies were, there we were as well. And if there is anything that developmental biology has shown us over the last few decades, it is that our bodies have their origins at fertilization, when the body plan is established. Thus, a five-day-old human embryo is a person because he is the same embodied being he will be when he is a forty-one-year-old adult.

The Bodily Rights Argument

Third, some pro-abortion proponents have argued that the unborn baby, regardless of whether he is a human person who has a full right to life, cannot use the body of another individual, his mother, against her will.[42] A woman, the argument continues, cannot be forced to use

40. For examples of this critique, see both Germain Grisez, "When Do People Begin?" *Proceedings of the American Catholic Philosophical Association* 63 (1989): 27–47; and Helen Watt, "The Origin of Persons," in *The Identity and Status of the Human Embryo*, ed. Juan de Dios Vial Correa and Elio Sgreccia, 343–364 (Vatican City: Libreria Editrice Vaticana, 1999). Also see the comprehensive text by Patrick Lee and Robert George, *Body-Self Dualism in Contemporary Ethics and Politics* (Cambridge: Cambridge University Press, 2007).

41. Maurice Merleau-Ponty, *The Phenomenology of Perception*, trans. Colin Smith (New York: Routledge, 1962).

42. For a well-known example of this argument, see Judith Jarvis Thomson, "A De-

her organs to sustain another person's life. Just as one does not have the right to use another person's liver if one's liver has failed, the unborn baby does not have the right to use his mother's organs to sustain his own life. Thus, the woman has a right to deny her baby the use of her organs. She has a right to an abortion.

The objection is flawed for several reasons.[43] Three will be discussed here. First, it assumes that moral obligations must be voluntarily accepted in order to have moral force. However, it is possible for someone to become responsible for another person without his having chosen that responsibility. Imagine a woman who discovers an abandoned baby behind her home one frigid winter night. Is she not morally obligated to take the child indoors, feed it, and care for it until such a time as someone else can take over? In the same way, a woman who finds herself with child, even unexpectedly, is morally obligated to bring him to term to preserve his life.

Second, it overlooks the fact that preserving the life of another human being is a higher good than simply preserving the free use of one's body. For example, if a woman breastfeeds or bottle-feeds her child, she is using her body to do this. Few of us would say that she therefore has a right to refuse this kind of support if the child would die without it. Or take this other scenario: suppose that a woman returns home to discover an abandoned child at her doorstep. For the sake of argument, let us also suppose that there is no one else who can take care of this child for nine months. (After that time, a couple has offered to adopt the baby.) Imagine further that the presence of the child in the woman's home would cause her bouts of morning sickness, cramps, and other minor discomfort. Would the woman have the right to let the baby starve in its crib simply because she did not want to use her body to feed him? Both our commonsense moral intuitions and the law say no.

Finally, the bodily rights argument fails to acknowledge that abortion, in most cases, is an act of killing and not merely an act that withholds life support. It involves an attack on the body of the unborn child that can include the burning, the crushing, and the dismembering of the fetus. Thus, just as it would be wrong to attack the woman's body, it is wrong

---

fense of Abortion," in *The Problem of Abortion*, 2nd ed., ed. Joel Feinberg, 173–187 (Belmont, Calif.: Wadsworth, 1984). This essay was originally published in *Philosophy and Public Affairs* 1 (1971): 47–66.

43. For a more extensive discussion of the rebuttals to this objection, see Beckwith, *Politically Correct Death*, 123–135.

to attack the body of the fetus. Whatever rights a woman has, they do not include a right to a bodily attack on her own unborn child.

The Delayed Hominization Argument

Finally, unlike the three other objections just considered, the argument for delayed hominization has a uniquely Catholic provenance. Appealing to the thought of Aristotle and St. Thomas Aquinas, several Catholic philosophers and theologians, the more influential of whom include Joseph Donceel, S.J., Thomas A. Shannon, Allan Wolter, O.F.M., and Jean Porter, have argued that the earliest human embryo is not a human being because his body is capable only of biological and not of rational action.[44] According to the theory of delayed hominization, the embryo passes through stages of vegetative and animal ensoulment before arriving at a human stage when the body is sufficiently organized and developed for the infusion of the rational soul by the immediate action of the Creator. For the ancients, this moment occurred forty days after conception. In like manner, modern proponents of this theory hold that the developing human being is not truly human until it has developed a nervous system that makes it apt to receive a properly rational soul.

In response, it is important to note that the theory of delayed hominization was based upon two biological assumptions that we now know are false. First, Aristotle and the ancients thought that the human embryo was formed into a human being from the mother's menstrual blood, which was homogenous and therefore needed to be formed in a series of progressive steps by some external agent. Second, they thought that this external agent was the father's semen, which remained in the womb, separate from the menstrual blood, forming it first as a vegetative body, and

44. For details, see the following essays: Joseph F. Donceel, S.J., "Immediate Animation and Delayed Hominization," *Theological Studies* 31 (1970): 76–105; Shannon and Wolter, "Reflections on the Moral Status of the Pre-Embryo"; and Jean Porter, "Is the Embryo a Person? Arguing with the Catholic Traditions," *Commonweal*, February 8, 2002, 8–10. For responses to these essays, see the following: Benedict Ashley, O.P., "A Critique of the Theory of Delayed Hominization," in *An Ethical Evaluation of Fetal Experimentation: An Interdisciplinary Study*, ed. Donald McCarthy, 113–133 (St. Louis: Pope John XXIII Medical-Moral Research Center, 1976); Mark Jordan, "Delayed Hominization: Reflections on Some Recent Catholic Claims for Delayed Hominization," *Theological Studies* 56 (1995): 743–763; and my essay, "Immediate Hominization from the Systems Perspective," *Natl Cathol Bioeth Q* 4 (2004): 719–738. For a comprehensive historical overview of the Christian tradition's reflections on the ontological and moral status of the human embryo, see David Albert Jones, *The Soul of the Embryo* (London: Continuum, 2004).

then as an animal body, and finally as a human body, which could then be ensouled by a human soul because it had a human heart. Thus, based on their flawed biology, the ancients believed that hominization could be completed only after a period of time after fertilization, when the human organism came into being from the gradual action of the father's semen on the mother's menstrual blood.

In light of recent biological discoveries, however, we now know that the human organism is present once fertilization begins when the sperm and the egg physically interact.[45] Thus, calling the human organism an embryo, fetus, infant, teenager, or adult is to arbitrarily label and distinguish certain segments of a continuous chain of developmental events that do not differ in kind. Each is a different manifestation of the same human organism, the same living system, at a later stage of change. Once human development begins at fertilization, there simply is no place in the developmental process for the series of substantial changes envisioned by delayed hominization. Substantial change can occur only at the onset of development because the organization of the molecules that drives development and specifies the identity of the human organism is established then. All change after this point can only be accidental change that does not involve the change of a being's nature. Thus, the same sound philosophy that led the ancients to affirm a theory of delayed hominization now leads us to affirm that hominization is complete at fertilization when the human organism comes into being.

The Immorality of Abortion after Rape

Rape, the forcible violation of the sexual intimacy of another person, is a brutal crime of violence that does injury to justice and charity. As the *Catechism of the Catholic Church* teaches, rape "deeply wounds the respect, freedom and physical and moral integrity to which every person has a right. It causes grave damage that can mark the victim for life. It is always an intrinsically evil act."[46] In those situations when the victim becomes pregnant, some have argued that abortion should be permitted to help the woman heal from and move beyond the trauma of rape.[47]

45. For a detailed discussion of the scientific evidence, see my essay, "On Static Eggs and Dynamic Embryos"; and Condic, "When Does Life Begin?"

46. *Catechism of the Catholic Church*, no. 2356.

47. For one example of this proposal, see Felicia H. Stewart and James Trussell,

In response, the circumstances surrounding the sexual act have no bearing on the dignity of the child who is conceived. The unborn child remains a human being, a person of immeasurable worth, who has a rightful claim to life. Thus, a sexual violation, no matter how despicable, cannot justify the killing of the innocent child who was conceived during that act. It would be a further act of grave injustice to punish a child for the sins of his father.

But does the pregnancy not compound the psychological problems that arise from rape? How can we force a woman to carry her pregnancy to term when it is a constant reminder of her sexual violation? Certainly this is a complex issue. It is a natural human reaction to try to eradicate all traces of a traumatic experience. However, should our response to a trauma be equally traumatic? Significantly, one early study of pregnant rape victims published less than a decade after *Roe v. Wade* found that 75 percent of these women (28 of 37 victims) chose *against* abortion.[48] Some of the reasons given by the victims for their choice are illuminating. First, some believed that abortion would just be another act of violence perpetrated against them and their children. As such, they believed that abortion was immoral. Others thought that their child's life may have some intrinsic meaning or purpose that they did not yet understand. They hoped that perhaps good could come out of evil. Finally, a few felt that they would suffer more mental anguish from taking the life of the unborn child than carrying the child to term. Intriguingly, when asked what conditions or situations made it most difficult for the victim to continue her pregnancy, the most frequent response was social pressure—the opinions, attitudes, and beliefs of others about the rape and pregnancy. In sum, the testimonies of these women are evidence that encouraging abortion as a panacea for rape pregnancy may in fact be counterproductive since this may prevent the healing that can come about from carrying the unborn baby to term.

"Prevention of Pregnancy Resulting from Rape: A Neglected Preventive Health Measure," *Am J Prev Med* 19 (2000): 228–229.

48. Sandra Mahkorn, "Pregnancy and Sexual Assault," in *The Psychological Aspects of Abortion*, ed. D. Mall and W. F. Watts, 53–72 (Washington, D.C.: University Publications of America, 1979). For an insightful discussion about rape pregnancies, including those pregnancies that arise from incest, see David C. Reardon, *Aborted Women: Silent No More* (Chicago: Loyola University Press, 1987), 188–218.

Distinguishing Direct and Indirect Abortions

As we defined above, a direct abortion is the directly intended kill-ing of an unborn child. This is gravely evil. An indirect abortion, on the other hand, is the foreseen but unintended loss of a baby as a result of a medical procedure necessary for the preservation of the life of his mother. The classic example involves the pregnant woman who discovers that she has cancer of the uterus. The doctor tells her that the uterus must be re-moved immediately in order to save her life. Can she morally consent to this procedure even if she knows that her developmentally immature baby would not be able to survive outside her body? The Catholic moral tradi-tion appealing to the principle of double effect says that she can do this as long as she and her surgeon do not intend the death of her child.[49]

Recall from chapter 1 that for the principle of double effect to apply, four conditions have to be met. These conditions ensure that the agent's act is a good one. First, the act has to be morally good or at least morally neutral. Here, in this surgical procedure, the removal of a cancerous or-gan is in itself a good act. It preserves the health and life of the patient. Second, the agent must desire and choose the good effect and not desire the evil outcome. Thus, for the surgical procedure to be morally com-mendable, the mother and her surgeon must only desire the saving of her life. The death of the baby would be a foreseen but unintended side ef-fect of the surgical procedure. Third, the beneficial effect must not come about as a result of the harmful effect. Or to put it another way, the bad effect cannot *cause* the good effect. Here, the saving of the mother's life is a direct result of the removal of the cancerous uterus and not a result of the baby's death. In support of this, note that the exact same surgical pro-cedure performed on a mother with a fetus who is at least twenty-four weeks old could save her life without necessarily leading to the death of her child because of technological advances in neonatal intensive care.

49. For instance, Pope Pius XII referred to the distinction between a direct and an indirect abortion in his "Allocution to Large Families, November 26, 1951," in *The Hu-man Body: Papal Teaching*, selected and arranged by the Monks of Solesmes, 180–182 (Bos-ton: St. Paul Editions, 1960), 182: "Because if, for example, the saving of the life of the future mother, independently of her pregnant condition, should urgently require a sur-gical act or other therapeutic treatment which would have as an accessory consequence, in no way desired or intended, but inevitable, the death of the foetus, such an act could no longer be called a direct attempt on an innocent life. Under these conditions the op-eration can be lawful."

Thus, the surgical procedure saves the life of the mother independently of the death of the baby. Finally, for the principle of double effect to apply, the beneficial effect must be of equal or greater moral gravity than the foreseen harmful effect. In our example, saving of the mother's life is of proportionate moral gravity as permitting the baby's death. In sum, in the case of the surgical removal of a cancerous and gravid uterus, the principle of double effect would morally justify the actions of the mother and of the surgeon as long as they do not desire or choose the death of her child. Thus, indirect abortions are morally justifiable. As the *Ethical and Religious Directives* of the United States Conference of Catholic Bishops puts it: "Operations, treatments, and medications that have as their direct purpose the cure of a proportionately serious pathological condition of a pregnant woman are permitted when they cannot be safely postponed until the newborn child is viable, even if they will result in the death of the unborn child."[50]

Finally, we need to distinguish an indirect from a therapeutic abortion, which is defined as the termination of pregnancy before fetal viability in order to preserve maternal health. In most cases, the abortion is performed—the baby is killed—precisely to preserve either the health or the life of the mother. In other words, the saving of the mother's life is a direct result of the baby's death. Thus, a therapeutic abortion is in fact an instance of a direct abortion. As Blessed John Paul II reminds us, a direct abortion includes every act tending to destroy human life in the womb "whether such destruction is intended as an *end* or only as a *means* to an end."[51] This moral argument also applies to so-called selective reduction procedures that are used to kill one or more fetuses when a mother becomes pregnant with multiple babies after infertility treatment.[52] As the Congregation for the Doctrine of the Faith explained: "From the ethical point of view, *embryo reduction is an intentional selective abortion.* It is in fact the deliberate and direct elimination of one or more innocent human beings in the initial phase of their existence and as such it always constitutes a grave moral disorder."[53] Direct abortions, regardless of the further ends for which they are done, are always intrinsically evil.

50. *Ethical and Religious Directives for Catholic Health Care Services,* 5th ed., no. 47.

51. John Paul II, *Evangelium vitae,* no. 62.

52. For commentary, see Mark I. Evans and David W. Britt, "Fetal Reduction," *Semin Perinatol* 29 (2005): 321–329.

53. Congregation for the Doctrine of the Faith, *Dignitas personae,* Instruction on Certain Bioethical Questions (Vatican City: Libreria Editrice Vaticana, 2008), no. 21.

Disputed Questions

The Management of Ectopic Pregnancies

An ectopic pregnancy occurs when the developing embryo implants himself outside the uterus where he normally belongs.[54] Instead, he implants either in the fallopian tube, or in rare cases, in the ovary, in the cervix, or elsewhere in the abdomen. Such pregnancies can threaten the life of the mother because of the danger of bleeding. There are four general approaches to managing ectopic pregnancies.

First, there is "expectant" therapy. Here, one simply waits for the tubal pregnancy to resolve itself by spontaneous abortion or miscarriage.[55] Numerous studies have shown that between 47 percent and 82 percent of ectopic pregnancies resolve themselves in this way. Second, there are surgical procedures to remove that part of the mother affected by the extrauterine pregnancy.[56] This could involve the removal of the cervix, the ovary, the entire fallopian tube, or even that portion of the tube containing the ectopic pregnancy. The removal of the fallopian tube is called a salpingectomy. Third, there is a surgical procedure, called a salpingostomy, where an incision is made in the affected part of the fallopian tube so that the developing embryo can be extracted by the use of forceps or other instruments. Finally, there is drug therapy involving the use of methotrexate (MTX).[57] MTX resolves ectopic pregnancies by attacking and killing the trophoblast, the outer layer of cells of the embryo that eventually develops into the placenta.

The Catholic Church has not yet made a definitive moral judgment regarding the management of ectopic pregnancies. The *Ethical and Religious Directives* of the United States Conference of Catholic Bishops only state

---

54. For recent reviews of the medical literature, see David Della-Giustina and Mark Denny, "Ectopic Pregnancy," *Emerg Med Clin North Am* 21 (2003): 565–584; and Anne-Marie Lozeau and Beth Potter, "Diagnosis and Management of Ectopic Pregnancy," *Am Fam Physician* 72 (2005): 1707–1714.

55. For discussion, see D. Trio et al., "Prognostic Factors for Successful Expectant Management of Ectopic Pregnancy," *Fertil Steril* 63 (1995): 469–472; and E. Shalev et al., "Spontaneous Resolution of Ectopic Tubal Pregnancy: Natural History," *Fertil Steril* 63 (1995): 15–19.

56. For a review of the medical literature, see Mohammed Al-Sunaidi and Togas Tulandi, "Surgical Treatment of Ectopic Pregnancy," *Semin Reprod Med* 25 (2007): 117–122.

57. For a review of the literature, see Gary H. Lipscomb, "Medical Therapy for Ectopic Pregnancy," *Semin Reprod Med* 25 (2007): 93–98.

that in cases of extrauterine pregnancies, "no intervention is morally licit which constitutes a direct abortion."[58] We should note however that expert theological opinion does exist regarding the four procedures discussed above. First, expectant therapy is not morally problematic since no medical intervention occurs here. Second, with either the salpingectomy or the removal of other affected organs in the woman's body, there is a consensus among Catholic bioethicists that this type of surgical procedure is an indirect abortion morally analogous to the removal of the cancerous uterus of a pregnant woman. Here the death of the immature baby would be the foreseen but unintended side effect of a surgical procedure that preserves the life of his mother. Thus this procedure would be morally permissible under the principle of double effect. In contrast, there is no consensus regarding the liceity of either the salpingostomy or MTX. Some Catholic moralists—and I count myself among them—argue that the use of both of these approaches constitutes a direct abortion because these procedures involve direct and lethal attacks on the unborn child. Other moralists disagree. These theologians argue that both the salpingostomy and MTX use are only indirect abortions. In the case of MTX use, for example, they suggest that the surgeon simply seeks to remove the trophoblastic tissue that is damaging the fallopian tube. Thus, the death of the embryo is only a foreseen but unintended side effect of the procedures. What these moral theologians overlook is that the trophoblast is an essential organ of the developing embryo. He uses it to receive nourishment from his mother. Therefore, destroying the trophoblast of an embryo is comparable to destroying the heart of an adult human being. How can these acts be anything but direct attacks on the life of the person?[59]

Prenatal Testing and the Premature Induction of Labor

In the past thirty years, prenatal tests have been developed that allow physicians to evaluate the health and overall well-being of unborn children. These tests raise grave moral concerns since they can be used either to promote a safe pregnancy and birth or to detect fetal abnormalities in

58. *Ethical and Religious Directives for Catholic Health Care Services*, 5th ed., no. 48.

59. For more discussion, see the following essays: Patrick A. Clark, S.J., "Methotrexate and Tubal Pregnancies: Direct or Indirect Abortion?" *Linacre Q* 67 (2000): 7–24; Christopher Kaczor, "Moral Absolutism and Ectopic Pregnancy," *J Med Philos* 26 (2001): 61–74; and Eugene F. Diamond, "The Licit Use of Methotrexate," *Ethics Medics* 31.3 (2006): 3.

order to avoid the birth of a disabled child. In addition, tests that are invasive carry a risk of losing or damaging the unborn child.

The Catholic Church teaches that with the informed consent of the parents, prenatal testing is morally permissible "if prenatal diagnosis respects the life and integrity of the embryo and the human foetus and is directed towards its safeguarding or healing as an individual."[60] In other words, tests that promote the health of the mother and her unborn baby—for instance, those blood tests routinely used in prenatal care to determine both blood type and Rhesus (*Rh*) factor compatibility between mother and unborn child—are morally commendable. Ultrasound used to assess the best time and mode of delivery of the child would also fall under this category.

In contrast, tests that are undertaken simply to detect a fetal abnormality so that an abortion can be performed are morally ruled out. In most clinical scenarios, these include blood tests to measure either alpha-fetoprotein (AFP) or human chorionic gonadotropin (hCG) levels. Both tests are routinely used to detect either neural tube defects or Down syndrome so that an abortion can be offered to the mother. The same thing can be said about amniocentesis and chorionic villus sampling. In both these invasive tests, cells are obtained either from the amniotic fluid surrounding the unborn child or from the chorionic tissue surrounding the unborn baby in order to detect a growing number of chromosomal abnormalities. Significantly, both procedures are associated with an increased risk for miscarriage. For instance, according to the U.S. Centers for Disease Control (CDC), the risk for miscarriage associated with amniocentesis is about one in two hundred pregnancies (0.5%).[61] Again, both of these procedures are used to routinely advise mothers to avoid the birth of children with disabilities. In such cases, they are morally reprehensible. It is not surprising that disability rights advocates have criticized selective prenatal testing for promoting a eugenic mindset that devalues disabled persons.[62] Thus, these are the kinds of test that the

60. Congregation for the Doctrine of the Faith, *Donum vitae*, para. I.2.

61. For details, see the Centers for Disease Control and Prevention Report entitled "Chorionic Villus Sampling and Amniocentesis: Recommendations for Prenatal Counseling," *Morbidity and Mortality Weekly Report: Recommendations and Reports* 44, no. RR-9 (July 21, 1995), at http://www.cdc.gov/mmwr/preview/mmwrhtml/00038393.htm.

62. Erik Parens and Adrienne Asch, "The Disability Rights Critique of Prenatal Genetic Testing: Reflections and Recommendations," in *Prenatal Testing and Disability Rights,* ed. Erik Parens and Adrienne Asch, 3–43 (Washington, D.C.: Georgetown University Press, 2000).

pregnant mother should refuse since they do not promote either her or her unborn child's health. Finally, we should acknowledge that there is also a growing movement to use prenatal testing to detect neural tube defects so that corrective prenatal pediatric neurosurgery can be done, or to give families advance warning of a disease or disabling condition so that they can make adequate preparations for the care of their child. This is morally laudable and should be encouraged. The *Ethical and Religious Directives* of the United States Conference of Catholic Bishops state that prenatal diagnosis is permitted "when the procedure does not threaten the life or physical integrity of the unborn child or the mother and does not subject them to disproportionate risks; when the diagnosis can provide information to guide preventative care for the mother or pre- or postnatal care for the child; and when the parents, or at least the mother, give free and informed consent."[63]

Next, as we noted above, with the advent of prenatal testing, congenital defects can now be diagnosed and repaired weeks or even months before the unborn baby reaches full term. However, some of these congenital abnormalities are inevitably fatal. For instance, most newborns lacking the cerebral hemispheres of their brain, a lethal defect called anencephaly, die soon after birth. Given these tragic circumstances, some doctors have counseled mothers carrying anencephalics to prematurely induce labor. Is this moral? Catholic moral theologians are divided on this issue.

Within the Catholic moral tradition, two things are not disputed. First, anencephalic babies remain human persons regardless of the degree of severity of their congenital deformity. They are persons whose brains have failed to complete embryonic development. Thus, anencephalics have to be treated with the inestimable and inherent dignity that is properly theirs. As persons, they have just as much of a right to life as their healthy siblings. Second, there is an important distinction between the premature induction of labor before the viability of the unborn child and induction after viability. For most, if not all, Catholic moral theologians, premature delivery of the anencephalic child *before viability* would constitute a direct abortion. Here, the death of the child would be a direct result of its premature delivery. It would be intrinsically evil.

In contrast, some Catholic theologians have suggested that the premature induction of labor for an anencephalic baby *after viability* would be morally licit. Norman Ford, S.D.B., has suggested that after a gestational

63. *Ethical and Religious Directives for Catholic Health Care Services*, 5th ed., no. 50.

age of thirty-three weeks—at this age, healthy newborns have a two out of three chance of survival even without neonatal intensive care—anencephalic babies can be delivered prematurely to alleviate the psychological burden on the mother as well as to minimize her potential health risks from obstetrical complications.[64] In addition, pointing to epidemiological data from Australia that indicate that a significant number of anencephalic fetuses (73%) die just before or during labor at full-term, Ford notes that this early induction of labor would minimize the possible fetal trauma experienced by the anencephalic child during the final weeks of pregnancy. In this scenario, Ford argues that the anencephalic newborn dies from the lethal defect and not from prematurity. Thus, he concludes that this would not constitute a direct abortion.

In response, Catholic physician Eugene Diamond and other Catholic moralists have argued that the early induction of labor of an anencephalic is always unjustified because the purpose of the procedure is unavoidably the earlier death of the anencephalic child who dies two months earlier than if allowed to go to term.[65] Thus, it would be an instance of a direct abortion. Furthermore, Diamond points out that this procedure leads to the societal devaluation of handicapped children. Clearly, however, Diamond's argument overlooks the epidemiological statistics that suggest that premature induction can preclude the trauma experienced by an anencephalic child during the final weeks of pregnancy. These data suggest that the premature induction of labor, as Ford proposes, could also be a medical intervention that tries to minimize the stress of birth experienced by the anencephalic child. If so, then the death of the newborn would be an unintended but foreseen side effect of an act undertaken to protect the unborn child from the unnecessary suffering associated with the trauma of birth at full term. Significantly, the *Ethical and Religious Directives* of the United States Conference of Catholic Bishops state: "For a proportionate reason, labor may be induced after a fetus is viable."[66]

Finally, we should add that regardless of the time of delivery, comfort

64. Norman Ford, S.D.B., "Early Delivery of a Fetus with Anencephaly," *Ethics Medics* 28.7 (2003): 1–4.

65. Eugene F. Diamond, "Anencephaly and Early Delivery: Can There Ever Be Justification?" *Ethics Medics* 28.10 (2003): 2–3. Also see the essays: Kevin O'Rourke, O.P., "Ethical Opinions in Regard to the Question of Early Delivery of Anencephalic Infants," *Linacre Q* 63 (1996): 55–59; and Nancy Valko, "The Case against Premature Induction," *Ethics Medics* 29.5 (2004): 1–3.

66. *Ethical and Religious Directives for Catholic Health Care Services*, 5th ed., no. 49.

care and nursing care, including hydration and nutrition according to the needs of the newborn, even a newborn with a fatal condition, should always be provided. Furthermore, all effort should be taken to provide for the emotional, psychological, and spiritual needs of the parents of the child.[67]

The Question of Ensoulment

The term "soul" signifies the spiritual principle of the human being.[68] The *Catechism of the Catholic Church* describes it this way: "It is because of its spiritual soul that the body made of matter becomes a living, human body."[69] The Catholic Church also teaches that God immediately creates every spiritual soul. In other words, while the human parents, each in his or her own way, contribute to the making of their child, it is God who directly infuses the soul into the individual. Furthermore, the spiritual soul is immortal and does not perish when it separates from the body at death. It will be reunited with its body at the final resurrection.[70]

When is the spiritual soul infused into the person? The Catholic Church has not yet definitively answered this philosophical question. However, in its *Declaration on Procured Abortion*, the Congregation for the Doctrine of the Faith, acknowledging the discoveries of the biomedical sciences, concluded the following: "From the time that the ovum is fertilized, a life is begun which is neither that of the father nor of the mother; it is rather the life of a new human being with his own growth. It would never be made human if it were not human already."[71] Given the scientific facts outlined earlier in this chapter, the CDF then argued that "it suffices that this presence of the soul be probable (and one can never prove the contrary) in order that the taking of life involve accepting the risk of killing a man, not only waiting for, but already in possession of his soul."[72]

---

67. In recent years, perinatal hospices have been established to provide a program of structured interdisciplinary care for the families of children prenatally diagnosed with a lethal congenital anomaly. For discussion, see Mary-Joan Marron-Corwin and Andrew D. Corwin, "When Tenderness Should Replace Technology: The Role of Perinatal Hospice," *NeoReviews* 9 (2008): e348–e352.

68. For a philosophical defense of the immateriality of the soul, see Richard Swinburne, *The Evolution of the Soul*, rev. ed. (Oxford: Oxford University Press, 1997).

69. *Catechism of the Catholic Church*, no. 365.

70. Ibid., no. 366.

71. Congregation for the Doctrine of the Faith, *Declaration on Procured Abortion*, no. 12.

72. Ibid., n. 19.

Thus, the CDF in a subsequent document, *Dignitas personae,* declared the following:

> Although the presence of the spiritual soul cannot be observed experimental-
> ly, the conclusions of science regarding the human embryo give "a valuable in-
> dication for discerning by the use of reason a personal presence at the moment
> of the first appearance of human life: how could a human individual not be a
> human person?" Indeed the reality of the human being for the entire span of
> life, both before and after birth, does not allow us to posit either a change in
> nature or a gradation in moral value, since it possesses *full anthropological and ethi-
> cal status.* The human embryo has, therefore, from the very beginning, the dig-
> nity proper to a person.[73]

In sum, prudentially, we need to treat human embryos as human persons
even if we are not metaphysically certain if they have been ensouled—a
conclusion that is beyond the reach of empirical verification because of
the immateriality of the soul, though science can demonstrate that the
human embryo is already a human individual—because of the grave moral harm that we could do to these embryonic human beings and to ourselves if we treated them otherwise.

Highlighting the Role of Virtue in Bioethics

As we noted in chapter 1, a renewal of bioethics in light of the moral
vision articulated in *Veritatis splendor* will need to recover the proper role of
the virtues in bioethical decision making. How should one do this when
one is confronted with a moral crisis involving the beginning of life, especially a crisis that could potentially lead to the abortion of an unborn
child?

Studies published by the Guttmacher Institute in New York, a non-
profit organization that has played a leading role in advancing abortion
practices worldwide, have revealed that the two most common reasons
that women in the United States give for seeking an abortion are that
having a baby would lead to unwanted changes in her life and that having
a baby would cause financial distress.[74] More specifically, these women re-

73. Congregation for the Doctrine of the Faith, *Dignitas personae,* no. 5, citing the Congregation's earlier instruction, *Donum vitae,* para. I.1.

74. For discussion, see Lawrence B. Finer, Lori F. Frohwirth, Lindsay A. Dauphinee,
Susheela Singh, and Ann M. Moore, "Reasons U.S. Women Have Abortions: Quantita-
tive and Qualitative Perspectives," *Perspect Sex Reprod Health* 37 (2005): 110–118.

port that they believe that having their child would interfere with their education, their careers, or their families.

In light of this study and others like it, it is important to highlight the importance of the virtue of fortitude, among others, during moral crises at the beginning of life.[75] Women seek abortions because they fear the changes that would accompany a new child in their lives, and fortitude, which is synonymous with courage, would moderate this emotion, allowing the individual to act in a morally upright manner even when she is frightened and anxious.[76] Catholic bioethicists, priests, and counselors have to be prepared to give a woman reasons that would strengthen her fortitude. They would need to help her understand that there are certain goods in life, in this case, the life of her child and the happiness that this child could bring, either to her and to her family or to a childless couple, that outweigh important but lesser goods, like the physical comfort and well-being that she would have to surrender for the duration of her pregnancy. They also would need to encourage her to seek not only financial but also emotional and moral support from those around her, including members of her family, her parish, and pro-life organizations. It is not surprising that one study has shown that in fragile families the most important factors in determining a women's choice to abort a second pregnancy were those associated with the father's inability or unwillingness to provide assistance in rearing their first child.[77] A woman in crisis—indeed, anyone in a crisis—needs to know that she has the support she needs to suffer hardship well. Courage is enabled by love.

Finally, it is fitting to conclude this chapter by recalling the memory of St. Gianna Beretta Molla (1922–1962), an Italian pediatrician, wife, and mother, who refused an abortion and a hysterectomy when a uterine tumor was discovered during her pregnancy with her fourth child.[78] On

75. For a classical overview of the virtue of fortitude, see Josef Pieper, *Fortitude and Temperance,* trans. Daniel F. Coogan (New York: Pantheon Books, 1954), 9–43.

76. For an insightful discussion of the virtue of fortitude that places it in conversation with modern psychosocial theory and research on human resilience and vulnerability, see Craig Steven Titus, *Resilience and the Virtue of Fortitude* (Washington, D.C.: The Catholic University of America Press, 2006).

77. Priscilla K. Coleman, Charles D. Maxey, Maria Spence, and Charisse L. Nixon, "Predictors and Correlates of Abortion in the Fragile Families and Well-Being Study: Paternal Behavior, Substance Use, and Partner Violence," *Int J Ment Health Addict* 7 (2009): 405–422.

78. For more details on the inspiring life of this saint, see Pietro Molla, Elio Guerriero, and James G. Colbert, *Saint Gianna Molla: Wife, Mother, Doctor* (San Francisco: Igna-

April 21, 1962, which was Good Friday of that year, Gianna was admitted to the hospital, where her fourth child, Gianna Emanuela, was delivered by cesarean section. The saint, however, continued to experience severe pain, dying of an infection seven days after the birth. She was canonized by Blessed John Paul II at the Vatican on May 16, 2004, with her husband, Pietro, and their youngest child, Gianna, in attendance. The miracle attributed to her intercession by the Church involved a mother, Elizabeth Comparini, who sustained a tear in her placenta that had drained her womb of amniotic fluid when she was sixteen weeks pregnant. She was told that the baby had no chance of survival. After asking St. Gianna to intercede on her behalf, Comparini delivered a healthy baby, who, in a medically inexplicable manner, grew to term in the absence of amniotic fluid. St. Gianna Beretta Molla and Elizabeth Comparini illustrate well the virtue of fortitude during crises at the beginning of life. They are model exemplars, and with St. Gianna Molla, an intercessor, for women who are struggling with an unexpected or difficult pregnancy.

tius Press, 2004); and Gianna Beretta Molla, *Love Letters to My Husband,* ed. Elio Guerriero (Boston: Pauline Books and Media, 2002).

CHAPTER THREE

Bioethics and Human Procreation

It has been more than thirty years since Louise Joy Brown, the world's first baby conceived by in vitro fertilization (IVF) in a laboratory, was born in England on July 25, 1978. Since then, IVF and the other assisted reproductive technologies (ART) have radically changed the procreative landscape of contemporary society.[1] Today, a postmenopausal sixty-year-old woman can still become a mother by carrying a child conceived using her husband's sperm and the egg of a young Ivy League graduate purchased for fifty thousand dollars from an Internet egg bank. Also today, two men in a same-sex relationship can father children by employing a woman who will act as a surrogate mother who will carry to term embryos conceived with their sperm. Finally, today, a woman carrying six babies conceived by ART can choose to selectively "reduce" her pregnancy to increase the chances that some of her children will survive to birth. Technology has changed the way that our society begets and brings children into the world.

In this chapter, which explores the moral questions raised by scientific developments that impact human procreation—scientific advances that can help a couple assist or prevent the conception of their child—I will begin with an overview of the Catholic Church's understanding of human sexuality and the inherent link between the unitive and procreative meanings of authentic conjugal acts. I will then move to those moral questions surrounding the regulation of births, focusing on the moral difference between natural family planning methods and contraception. Basically, couples who use NFP do not inhibit their fertility but keep it intact and work within it. Contraceptive couples, on the other hand, distort the

1. For a comprehensive overview of the reproductive landscape made possible by ART, see Liza Mundy, *Everything Conceivable: How Assisted Reproduction Is Changing Men, Women, and the World* (New York: Alfred A. Knopf, 2007). ART has also generated a million-dollar industry. For details, see Debora L. Spar, *The Baby Business: How Money, Science, and Politics Drive the Commerce of Conception* (Cambridge, Mass.: Harvard Business School Press, 2006).

structure and meaning of human sexuality and as such are morally reprehensible. Next, I turn to those moral questions that arise when women use contraceptive pills either to treat an existing medical condition or to prevent conception after rape. Both of these practices can be morally justified under certain circumstances. Finally, I deal with questions that arise from infertility and the technologies that seek to address the sufferings of an infertile couple, including IVF, other forms of ART, and the emerging possibility of human cloning. I close with a consideration of the moral dispute occasioned by proposals to promote the adoption of abandoned human IVF embryos who are destined for destruction.

The Meaning of Human Sexuality and the Theology of the Body

The unitive and procreative meanings of our sexual acts have a profound theological and personal significance that are inextricably linked. This is the truth at the heart of the Catholic Church's teaching on the morality of human procreation. Therefore, to understand the Church's answers to the bioethical questions raised by technological advances that impact human procreation, we need to begin with a sketch of the Church's magnificent yet often misunderstood vision of human sexuality.[2] Here, we will focus especially on Blessed John Paul II's theology of the body, a series of weekly catecheses delivered early in his pontificate on the meaning of human sexuality and on the morality of our sexual acts.[3] These catecheses remain an eloquent account of the Catholic Church's understanding of human sexuality and a persuasive argument for its claim that there is a

2. For an introduction to the Catholic tradition's understanding of human sexuality, see John S. Grabowski, *Sex and Virtue: An Introduction to Sexual Ethics* (Washington, D.C.: The Catholic University of America Press, 2003).

3. John Paul II, *Man and Woman He Created Them: A Theology of the Body* (Boston: Pauline Books and Media, 2006). For an introduction to John Paul II's theology of the body, see the excellent books by Christopher West, *Theology of the Body Explained: A Commentary on John Paul II's "Gospel of the Body,"* rev. ed. (Boston: Pauline Books, 2007); and by Mary Shivanadan, *Crossing the Threshold of Love: A New Vision of Marriage in Light of John Paul II's Anthropology* (Washington, D.C.: The Catholic University of America Press, 1999). For a critical appraisal of John Paul II's moral vision, see Charles Curran, *The Moral Theology of Pope John Paul II* (Washington, D.C.: Georgetown University Press, 2005), 160ff. For a comprehensive and an incisive response to Curran, see E. Christian Brugger and William E. May, "John Paul II's Moral Theology on Trial: A Reply to Charles E. Curran," *Thomist* 69 (2005): 279–312.

necessary link between the unitive and procreative dimensions of human sexuality.

To recognize the truth about the profound meaning of human sexuality, the pope begins his catecheses by reminding us that each of us is fundamentally incomplete. Each of us is alone. Citing the creation narratives in Genesis, Blessed John Paul II observes that this alone-ness is a constitutive and an ontological dimension of the human condition that was already present in the beginning as the original solitude of Adam: "Man is alone because he is 'different' from the visible world, from the world of living beings."[4] If we are honest with ourselves, the pope continues, we discover that this alone-ness generates a profound yearning within each one of us to be made complete, to be made whole, through and with another person. This yearning—what Blessed John Paul II calls the sexual urge—moves us to seek another in a communion of persons.[5] As the pope explains: "[S]olitude is the way that leads to the unity that we can define, following Vatican II, as *communio personarum* [a communion of persons]."[6] To understand human sexuality as the Catholic tradition understands it, therefore, one must realize that it emerges from a natural inclination within human persons to enter into communion with one another.

But how do we achieve communion? How are we made complete? The key to answering these questions and others like them, according to the pope, is the law of the gift that is revealed by the human body: created either as male or as female, we discover that we are made for a communion of persons—ultimately, of course, for communion with the Triune God, Father, Son, and Holy Spirit—where each of us freely gives himself to another in love and receives another in love in return. Properly understood, therefore, our bodies have a spousal meaning, which John Paul II defines as the body's "power to express love: precisely that love in which the human person becomes a gift and—through this gift—fulfills the very meaning of his being and existence."[7] Self-giving and love are synonymous in the mind of the pope. All of us, the Holy Father proclaims, are called to give ourselves away in love to another. In this disinterested gift of ourselves, we form a communion with the other, and in doing so, we

4. John Paul II, *Man and Woman He Created Them*, 150.

5. For discussion of the relationship between the person and the sexual urge, see Karol Wojtyla (Pope John Paul II), *Love and Responsibility*, trans. H. T. Willetts (New York: Farrar, Straus and Giroux, Inc., 1981), 21–69.

6. John Paul II, *Man and Woman He Created Them*, 162.

7. Ibid., 185–186.

find ourselves. According to the pope, this invitation to union, this call to spousal love revealed by the reality of our sexual difference, is "the fundamental component of human existence in the world."[8]

Next, in his theology of the body, the pope reveals that the communion that comes from self-giving presupposes mutual acts of giving and accepting: "These two functions of the mutual exchange are deeply connected in the whole process of the 'gift of self': giving and accepting the gift interpenetrate in such a way that the very act of giving becomes acceptance, and acceptance transforms itself into giving."[9] Our ordinary everyday experience confirms this basic insight of the theology of the body. When a child is small, he gives his mother a drawing he has made to put on the refrigerator door. This drawing is a gift that is meant to be a part of him. It is an expression of his love precisely because it is something personal. It is something that belongs to him. Through his drawing, the child gives himself to his mother, and when she accepts it, she forms a union with her son, the union we call the love between a mother and her son. As the child matures, he continues to give himself away in different ways. Often, he shares his secrets, his hopes, and his dreams with his closest friends. These again are expressions of his love precisely because they are things that are part of him. They are profoundly his, and they are part of who he is. By sharing them with his friends, he gives himself to them, and when they reciprocate in kind, they form a union with him, the union we call friendship. These vignettes illustrate that to realize any union, there must be a mutual giving and accepting of persons. This is the essence of the love that creates and nurtures communions of persons.

According to Blessed John Paul II, though many types of unions are possible throughout our lives, the most radical and intimate form of human communion is the sexual union of a man and a woman in the covenant of marriage. It is radical because this union and this union alone can involve a *total* self-gift where the spouses are able to give themselves to each other with and through their bodies. The Holy Father has described this total self-donation and fidelity communicated by sexual intimacy within marriage as one dimension of the "language of the body."[10] In sexual union, a married couple, with and through their bodies, can speak a language of love. They can tell each other, "I give myself totally to you. I also receive you totally." However, they can do this only when

8. Ibid., 189.   9. Ibid., 196.
10. Cf. ibid., 531–544.

their sexual acts involve a total and mutual exchange of persons. This only happens, according to the pope, when their sexual acts are conjugal acts that include the giving and accepting of each spouse's fertility. Anything less than this, any sexual act that involves the intentional withholding of either spouse's fertility, would not be a total self-gift, and as such, would not be unitive.

In light of his phenomenological analysis, the pope proposes that the human body reveals the hidden mystery of God from all eternity: "The body, in fact, and only the body, is capable of making visible what is invisible: the spiritual and the divine. It has been created to transfer into the visible reality of the world the mystery hidden from eternity in God, and thus to be a sign of it."[11] First, in their loving, the married couple images the unity of God, for in their union, they make visible the unity of the Creator who as Father, Son, and Holy Spirit is in Himself a life-giving communion of persons. Second, in their loving, the spouses image the fruitfulness of God, for in their union, they make visible the power of the Creator who in His providence can cause their radical self-gift to generate a new person, a child: "The *union of man and woman* in marriage is a way of imitating in the flesh the Creator's generosity and fecundity."[12] Finally, the mystery of the one-flesh communion between man and woman foreshadows the mystery of Christ's communion with His Church (cf. Eph 5:31–32). Human sexuality and procreation are deeply meaningful because they allow two human beings in a communion of persons to image the mystery of the Most Holy Trinity.

In sum, the unitive and procreative dimensions of human sexuality are inextricably linked for two reasons. First, from the perspective of reason, they are linked because the total and mutual exchange of persons that unites the two spouses in their conjugal acts necessarily involves the mutual exchange of the gift of their fertility. To put it another way, in order to be unitive, conjugal love must also be open to the procreative. Next, from the perspective of faith, they are linked because conjugal acts can make God, who is both one and life-giving, visible in the world only when they are simultaneously ordered toward the union of the spouses and the transmission of life: love by its very nature is a participation in the God who is love. The Catholic Church's teaching on the morality of procreation flows from these truths.

11. Ibid., 203.
12. *Catechism of the Catholic Church*, no. 2335.

Regulating Birth

The Vocation of the Parent

Since conjugal love is ordered toward the union of two persons, it is ordained by its very nature toward the establishment of a family. To put it another way, a married couple by the nature of their vocations as husband and wife are called to be parents, a *telos* that necessarily includes the desire for the begetting and educating of children, the supreme gift of marriage.[13] As the Second Vatican Council taught: "Married couples should regard as their proper mission to transmit human life and to educate their children; they should realize that they are thereby cooperating with the love of God the Creator and are, in a certain sense, its interpreters."[14] However, every married couple is also called to the responsible exercise of parenthood. As Blessed John Paul II affirms: "In its true meaning, responsible procreation requires couples to be obedient to the Lord's call and to act as faithful interpreters of his plan. This happens when the family is generously open to new lives and when couples maintain an attitude of openness and service to life even if, for serious reasons and in respect for the moral law, they choose to avoid a new birth for the time being or indefinitely."[15] Thus, a couple is not obliged to have as many children as they could physically have.

But which reasons are serious enough to justify the regulation of birth? To guide the couple making decisions regarding family size, the Second Vatican Council taught that a husband and a wife

should regard it as their proper mission to transmit human life and to educate their children; they should realize that they are thereby cooperating with the love of God the Creator and are, in a certain sense, its interpreters. This involves the fulfillment of their role with a sense of human and Christian responsibility and the formation of correct judgments through docile respect for God and common reflection and effort; it also involves a consideration of their own good and the good of their children already born or yet to come, an ability to read the signs of the times and of their own situation on the mate-

---

13. For a summary of the Catholic Church's teaching on marriage, see Ramon Garcia de Haro, *Marriage and the Family in the Documents of the Magisterium*, trans. William E. May (San Francisco: Ignatius Press, 1993).

14. Vatican II, *Gaudium et spes*, no. 50.

15. John Paul II, *Evangelium vitae*, no. 97.

rial and spiritual level, and, finally, an estimation of the good of the family, of society, and of the Church.[16]

In other words, the decision to regulate the size of one's family is one that will depend upon the particular circumstances of each family evaluated against at least five criteria: (1) the good of the marriage, including the health of both husband and wife; (2) the good of the children, those born and those perhaps to come; (3) the financial welfare of the family; (4) the spiritual development of all involved; and (5) the good of the Church and of society. This decision needs to be discerned by each married couple with the help of both prayer and prudence.

There could be many reasons that might convince a couple to limit the size of their family. However, they have to be careful not to base their decisions on materialistic factors alone. Life is a gift to be shared, and Christian couples are called to be as generous in the service of life as their circumstances permit. Putting it another way, having another child is more valuable and life-giving than either having a swimming pool in the backyard or providing an Ivy League education for one's children. Children in large families receive benefits from being raised with numerous siblings.[17] Thus, Blessed John Paul II reminds couples:

Decisions about the number of children and the sacrifices to be made for them must not be taken only with a view to adding to comfort and preserving a peaceful existence. Reflecting upon this matter before God, with the graces drawn from the Sacrament, and guided by the teaching of the Church, parents will remind themselves that it is certainly less serious to deny their children certain comforts or material advantages than to deprive them of the presence of brothers or sisters, who could help them to grow in humanity and to realize the beauty of life at all its ages and in all its variety.[18]

Once a couple has discerned in prayer that for serious and responsible reasons, they are being called to avoid a new birth for the time being or indefinitely, they may regulate their births with chaste methods that respect the dignity of the human person and the profound meaning of conjugal love.

16. Vatican II, *Gaudium et spes*, no. 50.

17. For discussion, see Eugene Diamond, *The Large Family: A Blessing and a Challenge* (San Francisco: Ignatius Press, 1996); and Chris Jeub and Wendy Jeub, *Love in the House* (Monument, Colo.: Monument Publishing, 2007).

18. John Paul II, "Homily at Capitol Mall," *L'Osservatore Romano*, October 7, 1979, 7.

Finally, we should add that the call to responsible parenthood may involve a call to a couple not to decrease but to *increase* their family size. It may involve "the willingness to welcome a greater number of children."[19] This is because of the good that children bring not only to their immediate families but also to society, to the Church, and to the human family as a whole.

The Teaching of the Catholic Church

Recall from chapter 1 that human acts are good if they are rightly directed to those purposes that are in harmony with our ultimate end of happiness in God. In accordance with this basic moral principle, our sexual acts are good if they are ordered toward the end of marriage in both of its complementary dimensions, the unitive dimension and the procreative dimension.[20] This can happen, however, only when sexual acts involve a total and mutual exchange of persons, which can happen only when they are conjugal acts that are open to the transmission of life. Thus, the Catholic Church teaches, "it is necessary that each and every marriage act remain ordered *per se* to the procreation of human life."[21] This teaching—called the inseparability principle—is "based on the inseparable connection, established by God, which man on his own initiative may not break, between the unitive significance and the procreative significance which are both inherent to the marriage act."[22]

As a corollary to this truth, any attempt to sterilize the sexual act either through contraception or through direct sterilization undermines the integrity of the gift of self, for here, the husband not only withholds his fertility from his wife but also refuses to accept her fertility and vice versa.[23] A couple who engages in a sterilized sexual act, that is, a sexual act without the total giving and accepting of persons that it should signify, falsifies the language of the body. In the end, despite their best intentions, spouses who actively frustrate their fertility inevitably treat one

19. John Paul II, *Man and Woman He Created Them*, 637.

20. For an insightful discussion of the integrated nature of the end of marriage, understood from a hylomorphic perspective, see Paul Gondreau, "The 'Inseparable Connection' between Procreation and Unitive Love (*Humanae vitae*, §12) and Thomistic Hylemorphic Anthropology," *Nova et Vetera* 6 (2008): 731–764.

21. Paul VI, *Humanae vitae*, Encyclical Letter of the Supreme Pontiff Paul VI on the Regulation of Birth (Vatican City: Libreria Editrice Vaticana, 1968), no. 11.

22. Ibid., no. 12.

23. Cf. John Paul II, *Man and Woman He Created Them*, 617–630.

another as objects to be used rather than as persons to be loved and mysteries to be contemplated.

Natural Family Planning and Contraception

Authentic conjugal acts have to be open to the transmission of life. This criterion can be used to judge the morality of the different methods available to regulate birth, methods that can be divided into two categories, natural family planning (NFP) methods and contraceptive methods. Methods involving natural family planning use the natural rhythms of the woman's body to determine when sexual relations may or may not lead to pregnancy. With the two most common NFP methods, the Billings Ovulation Method and the sympto-thermal method, couples observe changes in the woman's cervical mucus, in her bodily temperature, and/or in other bodily signs to determine her fertile period.[24] Since both cervical mucus and bodily temperature are responsive to the hormonal changes that regulate fertility, NFP couples are able to accurately determine when they are fertile and when they are not. Thus, NFP is very effective both for achieving and for avoiding pregnancy. It is not to be confused with the older and less effective rhythm or calendar method, which estimated the couple's fertile and non-fertile periods by observing when these periods occurred in previous cycles.[25]

Contraceptive methods of birth control consist of "any action which either before, at the moment of, or after sexual intercourse, is specifically intended to prevent procreation—whether as an end or as a means."[26] In other words, contraception involves any action that is intentionally undertaken to sterilize a couple's love, either temporarily or permanently. There are three basic kinds of contraceptive methods.[27] Chemical contra-

24. For descriptions of different types of natural family planning, see the following books: John F. Kippley and Sheila K. Kippley, *The Art of Natural Family Planning*, 4th ed. (Cincinnati: Couple to Couple League International, 1996); Evelyn Billings and Ann Westmore, *The Billings Method: Controlling Fertility without Drugs or Devices* (New York: Random House, 1980); and Toni Weschler, *Taking Charge of Your Fertility, 10th Anniversary Edition: The Definitive Guide to Natural Birth Control, Pregnancy Achievement, and Reproductive Health* (New York: Harper Collins, 2006).

25. For a scientific discussion of the efficacy of the rhythm method, see R. T. Kambic and V. Lamprecht, "Calendar Rhythm Efficacy: A Review," *Adv Contracept* 12 (1996): 123–128.

26. Paul VI, *Humanae vitae*, no. 14.

27. For guides to different contraceptive methods, see Leon Speroff and Philip D. Darney, *A Clinical Guide to Contraception* (Philadelphia: Lippincott Williams and Wilkins,

ceptives include oral contraceptives such as the Pill, hormonal injections such as Depo-Provera, and hormonal implants such as Norplant. Barrier methods include condoms and diaphragms that prevent fertilization by impeding the union of sperm and egg. These are usually used with a spermicidal or chemical agent to enhance their effectiveness. Surgical procedures include tubal ligations, vasectomies, and even hysterectomies that are performed to sterilize an individual.

Finally, we should note that several studies have demonstrated that NFP methods are just as effective as commonly used contraceptive methods for the prevention of pregnancy. For instance, the percentage of American women experiencing an unintended pregnancy within the first year of perfect use of the sympto-thermal method of NFP is just over 2 percent.[28] This is in comparison with a failure rate of approximately 2 percent for the condom and under 1 percent for the Pill.[29]

Judging the Morality of NFP and Contraception

The criterion that authentic conjugal acts have to be open to the transmission of life can be used to judge the morality of the different methods available to regulate births. Natural family planning methods to regulate birth meet this standard because they respect the structure and meaning of human sexuality and as such are morally upright. Couples who use NFP do not inhibit their fertility but keep it intact and work within it. If they have a just reason to avoid pregnancy, they choose to abstain from intercourse during their fertile period. During their infertile period, however, they could choose to engage in the conjugal act. Their lovemaking during this time would still involve a complete, total, and mutual exchange of selves. The spouses still do not hold anything back. The man still gives his wife all that he has, while she in return still gives her husband everything that she has. Because of the way she is created, however, a wife's total self-gift during her infertile period does not include the capacity to conceive a child. In the end, therefore, the fact that a pregnancy usually does not result from those marital acts performed during a cou-

2005); and Steven T. Nakamima, *Contemporary Guide to Contraception* (Newtown, Pa.: Handbooks in Health Care, 2006).

28. See the study by Margaret P. Howard and Joseph B. Stanford, "Pregnancy Probabilities during Use of the Creighton Model Fertility Care System," *Arch Fam Med* 8 (1999): 391–401.

29. Robert A. Hatcher, James Trussell, Anita L. Nelson, Willard Cates Jr., and Felicia Stewart, *Contraceptive Technology*, 19th rev. ed. (New York: Ardent Media, 2007), 24.

ple's infertile period is not the couple's doing but a consequence of God's design. The couple remains open to both the unitive and procreative dimensions of the marital act. Indeed, couples using NFP who are seeking to live out the vision of authentic human sexuality proposed by the Catholic tradition should be willing to accept a child in the unlikely event that the wife does become pregnant.

Not surprisingly, given that it respects the dignity of the spouses, NFP promotes communication between the spouses—the spouses need to keep talking to each other about intimate matters in order for them to share responsibility for their combined fertility—and encourages tenderness between them. The couple is encouraged to grow in the virtue of chastity and to develop an authentic human freedom that liberates them from the sometimes overwhelming power of lust. This may explain why the divorce rate among NFP couples in the 1990s was between ⅒ and 1/25 of the overall divorce rate in the United States.[30] The virtuous use of NFP can strengthen a marriage by increasing marital peace, decreasing spousal selfishness, and increasing the parents' appreciation of their children.

In contrast, contraceptive methods to regulate births do not pass the test that they respect the inseparability principle. They distort the structure and meaning of human sexuality and as such are morally reprehensible. Couples who use contraception withhold their fertility. They withhold part of themselves from each other. With their bodies, they say to each other, "I give you everything *except* my power to give life. You can have all of me *except* my gift to make you a parent, a father or a mother, of our child. This, I do not give you." Couples who engage in contraceptive sex are lying to each other with their bodies—they are telling each other that they love each other without giving each other the total self-gift that is the sign of authentic love. Moreover, sex that is not a total self-gift to the other can easily become self-directed and selfish, reducing it to a means of self-indulgence and physical gratification. It can do much damage to marriage. Thus, it is not surprising that couples who engage in contraceptive sex can often feel used, for implicit in their action is a mutual rejection of the other. In recent years, sociological research, including the work of Nobel Prize–winning economist George Akerlof, has argued persuasively that contraceptive practices have undermined marriage

30. Mercedes Arzu Wilson, "The Practice of Natural Family Planning versus the Use of Artificial Birth Control: Family, Sexual, and Moral Issues," *Catholic Social Science Review* 7 (2002): 1–20.

by discouraging men both to marry and to live with their children, lead-ing to numerous social ills.[31] They have especially exacerbated the already difficult lives of the poor. Thus, the *Ethical and Religious Directives* of the United States Conference of Catholic Bishops make clear that "Catholic health institutions may not promote or condone contraceptive practices but should provide, for married couples and the medical staff who coun-sel them, instruction both about the Church's teaching on responsible parenthood and in methods of natural family planning."[32]

Common Objections to the Teaching of the Catholic Church

On July 25, 1968, Pope Paul VI published his landmark encyclical, *Hu-manae vitae*, which reiterated the constant tradition of the Church with re-gard to the immorality of contraception.[33] The encyclical reaffirmed the necessary link between the unitive and procreative dimensions of human sexuality, concluding that "it is necessary that each and every marriage act remain ordered *per se* to the procreation of human life."[34] This teach-ing has been confirmed by both Blessed John Paul II and Pope Bene-dict XVI.[35] More decisively, after consultation with all the bishops of

31. For details see George Akerlof, Janet L. Yellen, and Michael L. Katz, "An Anal-ysis of Out-of-Wedlock Childbearing in the United States," *Quarterly Journal of Econom-ics* 111 (1996): 277–317; and George Akerlof, "Men without Children," *Economic Journal* 108 (1998): 287–309. For discussion, see W. Bradford Wilcox, "The Facts of Life & Mar-riage: Social Science and the Vindication of Christian Moral Teaching," *Touchstone* 18 (2005): 38–44.

32. *Ethical and Religious Directives for Catholic Health Care Services*, 5th ed., no. 52.

33. For nearly two millennia, the Christian churches and ecclesial communities unanimously condemned contraception because they understood that the practice was contrary to the Creator's design for human sexuality and that it was detrimental to the welfare not only of the family specifically, but also of society more generally. The Anglican Communion broke this consensus at the Lambeth Conference in 1930 when it sanctioned contraception for married couples in some limited circumstances. For comprehensive histories of the Catholic doctrine on contraception, see John Gallagher, "Magisterial Teaching from 1918 to the Present," in Pope John XXIII Medical-Moral Research and Education Center, *Human Sexuality and Personhood: Proceedings of the Workshop for the Hierarchies of the United States and Canada*, 191–210 (St. Louis, Mo.: Pope John XXIII Center, 1981); and John T. Noonan Jr., *Contraception: A History of Its Treatment by the Catholic Theologians and Canonists*, enlarged ed. (Cambridge, Mass: Harvard University Press, 1986).

34. Paul VI, *Humanae vitae*, no. 11.

35. Blessed John Paul II condemned the contraceptive mentality that has infected nu-merous contemporary societies and developed the teaching found in *Humanae vitae* in his apostolic exhortation on the family. See his *Familiaris consortio*, Apostolic Exhortation of

the Catholic Church, it has been reaffirmed in the *Catechism of the Catholic Church*,[36] suggesting that it is a definitive teaching of the ordinary Magisterium, or teaching authority of the Church, requiring "obedience of intellect and will" from all Catholics.[37]

At the time of its publication, *Humanae vitae* generated a firestorm of protest and led to the publication of numerous treatises challenging its teaching.[38] Here we will concentrate on the four most common objections raised by those who still dissent from the Church's teaching.[39]

First, some have argued that it is contradictory to affirm the morality of NFP while condemning contraception since both involve the same intention to avoid pregnancy. As David F. Kelly puts it: "The only difference between the permitted method and other forbidden methods, such as condoms, would have to be found in the act itself. Surely the couple's intention is the same in both procedures: to have sex and avoid having children. Thus, *both* procedures would seem equally to 'separate the unitive and the procreative aspects of married sexuality,' which recent doc-

---

Pope John Paul II to the Episcopate, to the Clergy, and to the Faithful of the Whole Catholic Church on the Role of the Christian Family in the Modern World (Vatican City: Libreria Editrice Vaticana, 1981), nos. 28–32. In a speech to mark the 40th anniversary of the publication of *Humanae vitae* at the Lateran University, Pope Benedict XVI affirmed: "The truth expressed in *Humanae vitae* does not change; on the contrary, precisely in the light of the new scientific discoveries, its teaching becomes more timely and elicits reflection on the intrinsic values it possesses." See his "Address of His Holiness Benedict XVI to Participants in the International Congress Organized by the Pontifical Lateran University on the 40th Anniversary of the Encyclical 'Humanae Vitae,'" at http://www.vatican.va/holy_father/benedict_xvi/speeches/2008/may/documents/hf_ben-xvi_spe_20080510_humanae-vitae_en.html.

36. *Catechism of the Catholic Church*, no. 2369–2371.

37. Vatican II, *Lumen gentium*, no. 25. Theologians John C. Ford and Germain Grisez have argued that the teaching found in *Humanae vitae* is infallible since it pertains to the ordinary and universal Magisterium that Vatican I and Vatican II declared to be infallible and unchangeable. See their essay, "Contraception and the Infallibility of the Ordinary Magisterium," *Theological Studies* 39 (1978): 258–312. Their argument has been criticized by Francis Sullivan, S.J., in his *Magisterium: Teaching Authority in the Catholic Church* (Dublin: Gill and Macmillan, 1983), 143ff. Also see the discussion in Germain Grisez, "Infallibility and Specific Norms: A Review Discussion," *Thomist* 49 (1985): 248–287.

38. For a comprehensive overview of the reactions to *Humanae vitae*, see William H. Shannon, *The Lively Debate: Response to Humanae vitae* (New York: Sheed & Ward, 1970).

39. For an overview of recent arguments in support of *Humanae vitae* forty years after the publication of the encyclical, see William F. Murphy, Jr., "Forty Years Later: Arguments in Support of *Humanae vitae* in Light of *Veritatis splendor*," *Josephinum Journal of Theology* 14 (2007): 122–167.

uments forbid and propose as the basis for the condemnation of direct contraception."[40]

In response, as I already explained above, it is important to affirm that using NFP to exercise responsible parenthood radically differs from using contraception to achieve the same end because in the former the spouses seek to achieve a good end by a means that is consonant with human nature and beatitude, while in the latter the couple seeks to achieve the same end by a means contrary to their good. More specifically, the NFP couple does not intend to render a fertile act infertile—a means that is contrary to human excellence and perfection—while the contraceptive couple does precisely this. Therefore, in the former case, the spouses are still causing the total self-gift that is integral to authentic human sexuality, while in the latter case, the husband and the wife are not capable of the same. As Blessed John Paul II taught, NFP and contraception are different because in the former,

the couple respect the inseparable connection between the unitive and procreative meanings of human sexuality, . . . acting as "ministers" of God's plan and they "benefit from" their sexuality according to the original dynamism of "total" self-giving, without manipulation or alteration, [while in the latter, the couple] separate[s] these two meanings that God the creator has inscribed in the being of man and woman [acting] as "arbiters" of the divine plan . . . manipulat[ing] and degrad[ing] human sexuality and with it themselves and their married partner by altering its value of "total" self-giving.[41]

The use of NFP and that of contraception are radically different kinds of human acts.

Next, critics contend that the teaching of the Church on contraception is erroneous because of its emphasis on the immorality of a single contraceptive act even when this act is performed within a lifetime of sexual acts, most of which are open to children by a married couple who only want to achieve responsible parenthood. As Paul Lauritzen has argued, "the inseparability principle, as it is formulated in *Humanae vitae* . . . is badly flawed because it focuses on the physiological integrity of the act of sexual intercourse at the expense of responsible parenthood."[42] In sup-

40. See his *Contemporary Catholic Health Care Ethics* (Washington, D.C.: Georgetown University Press, 2004), 105.

41. John Paul II, *Familiaris consortio*, no. 32.

42. Paul Lauritzen, *Pursuing Parenthood: Ethical Issues in Assisted Reproduction* (Bloomington: Indiana University Press, 1993), 11.

port of his argument, he cites the majority report of the Papal Commission on Birth Control with added emphasis: "The morality of sexual acts between married people takes it meaning first of all and specifically from the ordering of their responsible, generous and prudent parenthood. *It does not then depend upon the direct fecundity of each and every particular act.*"[43]

In response, as I already explained above, individual human acts are morally significant in themselves because they are our proximate means toward growing in perfection and attaining the beatitude for which we yearn. Furthermore, single acts matter because single acts not only shape but also reveal the acting person. We know others and ourselves through our individual acts. Our commonsense experience confirms this truth. A single act of adultery, even after decades of marital fidelity, can irreparably damage a marriage. A single lie can undermine a trusted friendship. In the same way, a single contraceptive act, in itself, because it distorts the structure and meaning of human sexuality, hinders the spouses from attaining the beatitude that comes from the practice of chaste sexual acts. Therefore, it is morally defective.

Third, critics argue that the Church's opposition to contraception is based upon an outdated and flawed methodology that emphasizes the biological or physical aspects of the sexual act without any concern for the personal or human dimensions of the act in its circumstances. Instead of this antiquated "physicalist" methodology, David F. Kelly and other revisionist theologians suggest a more contemporary "personalist" approach that would look at the human, social, spiritual, physical, and psychological consequences of the contraceptive act, revealing that "it is not valid to make an absolute moral rule against such a [contraceptive] practice because often the human and personal growth, the holiness if you will, of the people demands or at least permits the use of contraceptives."[44]

In response, as Gustave Martelet, S.J., has persuasively shown, the teaching of *Humanae vitae* based its argument not only upon the physical structure of but also upon the human *meaning* of the sexual act.[45] Com-

---

43. "The Theological Report of the Papal Commission on Birth Control," in *Love and Sexuality*, compiled by Odile M. Liebard (Wilmington, N.C.: Consortium Books, 1978), 302–303, cited in Lauritzen, *Pursuing Parenthood*, 11.

44. Kelly, *Contemporary Catholic Health Care Ethics*, 95.

45. See the discussion in Gustave Martelet, S.J., "A Prophetic Text under Challenge: The Message of *Humanae vitae*," in *Natural Family Planning: Nature's Way/God's Way*, ed. Anthony Zimmerman, S.V.D., 153–167 (Collegeville, Minn: De Rance Inc. and Human Life Center, 1981).

menting on the teaching of the encyclical, Martelet writes: "The inseparability of meanings in 'every marriage act' does not, then, rest primarily
on a biological structure which in fact separates them; on the contrary,
it rests on a decision: that of maintaining in the conjugal act its 'sense
of mutual and true love,' no less than its 'ordination to the exalted vocation of man to parenthood.'"[46] Thus, it is erroneous to argue that the
Church's teaching that is opposed to contraception is based on a so-
called physicalist methodology that ignores the human person. Rather, as
Blessed John Paul II's theology of the body reveals, an authentic personal-
ism makes the Church's teaching on the immorality of contraception and
its detrimental effect on human and personal growth even more apparent.
As such it can never be reconciled with the universal call to holiness.

Finally, critics of the Church's condemnation of contraception argue that the teaching must be erroneous because a significant number of
Catholics, even those otherwise devout, have rejected it, suggesting that
this teaching is not from the Holy Spirit, who guides all Christians. For
example, in a recent pamphlet, a group of dissenting Catholics has concluded that the Vatican should change the Church's position on the birth
control in light of the rejection of this teaching by many of its lay members: "It is also clear that the Catholic church cannot move forward until
it honestly confronts the paradox of *Humanae vitae:* that most Catholics use
modern contraceptives, believe it is a moral choice to do so, and consider
themselves Catholics in good standing."[47]

In response, we must begin by distinguishing between appeals to the
sense of the faithful, what theologians have called the *sensus fidelium,* or
more properly, the *sensus fidei,* and to popular opinion within the Church.
As the Second Vatican Council taught, the former is a theological source
attributable to the Holy Spirit: "The whole body of the faithful who have
an anointing that comes from the holy one (cf. 1 Jn 2:20 and 27) cannot
err in matters of belief. This characteristic is shown in the supernatural appreciation of the faith (*sensus fidei*) of the whole people, when, 'from
the bishops to the last of the faithful' they manifest a universal consent
in matters of faith and morals."[48] In contrast, the latter is merely a sociological fact. As Avery Cardinal Dulles, S.J., has observed, "Public opinion

46. Ibid., 158–159.
47. Catholics for Choice, *Truth and Consequence: A Look behind the Vatican's Ban on Contraception* (Washington, D.C.: Catholics for Choice, 2008), 18.
48. Vatican II, *Lumen gentium,* no. 12.

may be correct, but it often reflects the tendencies of our fallen human nature, the trends of the times, and the pressures of the public media."[49] How then are we to evaluate the theological significance of the often-cited statistic that a majority of Catholics have rejected the Church's teaching on contraception? Is it of God? There is probably no better test than the one proposed by the Lord Jesus Christ Himself, that we judge a tree by its fruit: "You will know them by their fruits. Are grapes gathered from thorns, or figs from thistles? So, every sound tree bears good fruit, but the bad tree bears evil fruit" (Matt 7:16–17). And, as I already noted above, sociological research has demonstrated that contraceptive practices have undermined marriage by discouraging men to marry and to live with their children, leading to numerous and serious social ills. It is clear that the fruit of contraception has not been good. It is not of God.

Distinguishing Direct and Indirect Contraception

Contraception—more precisely, direct contraception—consists of every action that seeks, whether as an end or as a means, to render a person sterile or infertile, either permanently or temporarily, for whatever reason. This is immoral because it does violence to the dignity of the human person and undermines the meaning of human sexuality. Putting it bluntly in the language of the body, contraceptive intercourse turns lovers into liars.

Indirect "contraception," on the other hand, involves actions that bring about the foreseen but unintended infertility or sterility of a person as a result of a medical procedure directed at the treatment of some present pathology. For instance, in women, the birth control pill sometimes is prescribed to treat endometriosis, a painful condition that occurs when the tissue that lines the uterus grows elsewhere in the abdomen.[50] In another example, in men, both testicles may be removed in order to cure patients from testicular cancer. These medical procedures render the patients infertile or even sterile, but the Catholic moral tradition, appealing to the

49. Dulles, *Magisterium*, 45.

50. For a study that shows the efficacy of low doses of the oral contraceptive pill in treating the pain associated with endometriosis, see Tasuku Harada, Mikio Momoeda, Yuji Taketani, Hiroshi Hoshiai, and Naoki Terakawa, "Low-Dose Oral Contraceptive Pill for Dysmenorrhea Associated with Endometriosis: A Placebo-Controlled, Double-Blind, Randomized Trial," *Fertil Steril* 90 (2008): 1583–1588.

principle of double effect, reasons that they are morally permissible because the patients do not intend their infertility or sterility. These patients simply want to be treated either for the endometriosis or for the testicular cancer, and their infertility or sterility is a foreseen but unintended side effect of the treatment. Note that this moral analysis presupposes that no simpler therapy is available and that the medical procedure is done only for a proportionately grave reason. These two premises ensure that the patients are truly choosing the medical procedure as a treatment for the pathology rather than as a method of contraception. The analysis here parallels the reasoning outlined in chapter 2 for the morality of indirect abortions. Thus, the *Ethical and Religious Directives* of the United States Conference of Catholic Bishops explains: "Direct sterilization of either men or women, whether permanent or temporary, is not permitted in a Catholic health care institution. [However,] procedures that induce sterility are permitted when their direct effect is the cure or alleviation of a present and serious pathology and a simpler treatment is not available."[51]

Finally, we should emphasize that the distinction between direct and indirect contraception applies only to medical procedures that treat a present pathology. The moral analysis made here cannot be used to justify procedures that sterilize a patient in order to prevent a future pathology that may arise from a future pregnancy. For instance, a doctor may suggest performing either a tubal ligation or a hysterectomy on a woman who might not be able to carry a future pregnancy without medical risk. In these cases, however, neither the fallopian tubes nor the uterus, in and of themselves, pose a pathological problem for the woman at the present time. Thus, the Catholic Church rules out these procedures because here, "the end of avoiding risks to the mother, deriving from a possible pregnancy, is . . . pursued by means of a direct sterilization, in itself always morally illicit, while other ways, which are morally licit [e.g., complete or periodic abstinence] remain open to free choice."[52] In other words, these procedures are effective only because they sterilize the individuals. Sterilization is not incidental to the efficacy of the treatment. Thus, in these procedures intended to prevent the harms of a future pregnancy, sterilization cannot but be directly intended and chosen by the patients and their doctors. As such, it is morally disordered.

51. *Ethical and Religious Directives for Catholic Health Care Services*, 5th ed., no. 53.

52. Congregation for the Doctrine of the Faith, *Responses to Questions Proposed Concerning "Uterine Isolation" and Related Matters* (Vatican City: Libreria Editrice Vaticana, 1993).

A Disputed Question: The Use of Condoms to
Prevent the Transmission of HIV/AIDS

In an article entitled, "The Truth about Condoms," Martin Rhon-heimer, a priest of Opus Dei and a professor at the Pontifical University of the Holy Cross in Rome, proposed that an HIV-infected spouse may use a condom to protect his wife from an infection.[53] Rhonheimer argues that condom use to prevent the transmission of HIV would not consti-tute an act of contraception because, properly speaking, the moral object of such an act is not to prevent conception—the moral object of a con-traceptive act—but to prevent infection.[54] Moreover, he suggests that the use of a condom to prevent transmission of HIV is compatible with the Church's teaching that conjugal acts must be open to the transmission of life because, in his opinion, "the required 'openness' of the marital act to the transmission of life must be of an intentional kind: Nothing must be done to use the gift of sexuality in a way incompatible with a will to serve the transmission of human life."[55]

In contrast, other Catholic moralists have argued that any act in which insemination is impeded cannot be called a marital act because it is not an act of a generative kind.[56] Thus, according to these theologians, by its very nature, condomistic sex is contraceptive. To put it another way, they propose that a couple that uses a condom to prevent the transmission of HIV necessarily intends to alter the finality of their sexual act, thus sev-ering the unitive meaning of their act from its procreative meaning. As such it is contraceptive and therefore intrinsically evil.

Rhonheimer has replied to his interlocutors by proposing that he and his critics disagree because they believe that the decisive point in the case

53. Martin Rhonheimer, "The Truth about Condoms," *Tablet* (July 10, 2004): 10–11.

54. For discussion, see the exchange between Benedict Guevin, O.S.B., and Martin Rhonheimer, "On the Use of Condoms to Prevent Acquired Immune Deficiency Syn-drome," *Natl Cathol Bioeth Q* 5 (2005): 37–48.

55. Ibid., 46.

56. For example, see William E. May, "Using Condoms to Prevent HIV," *Natl Cathol Bioeth Q* 4 (2004): 667–668; Germain Grisez, *The Way of the Lord Jesus*, vol. 2: *Living a Chris-tian Life* (Quincy, Ill.: Franciscan Press, 1993), 636; Luke Gormally, "Marriage and the Prophylactic Use of Condoms," *Natl Cathol Bioeth Q* 5 (2005): 735–749; and Christopher Oleson, "Nature, 'Naturalism,' and the Immorality of Contraception: A Critique of Fr. Rhonheimer on Condom Use and Contraceptive Intent," *Natl Cathol Bioeth Q* 6 (2006): 719–730.

of contraception is a determinate behavioral pattern that essentially includes the deposition of the man's semen into the woman's vagina.[57] Thus, condomistic sex is necessarily contraceptive sex. He, on the other hand, contends that impeding insemination actually is contraception, but only provided that it is done for the sake of impeding the natural purpose of insemination, which is to conceive new human life. Therefore, condomistic sex done for the sake of preventing infection rather than for the sake of preventing conception is not contraceptive sex. Rhonheimer concludes that his account is ethically more satisfying because "it integrates nature and its requirements into a broader moral perspective, which is the perspective of the virtues, without focusing in such an exclusive way on the behavioral pattern of the male's contribution to the marital act."[58] Moreover, he challenges his critics to provide a compelling argument in favor of the moral relevance of *never* deliberately impeding insemination during the marital act. He asks them: "Provided there is no proposal to impede conception and therefore no intentional or deliberate connection between impeding insemination and impeding procreation, why is the prevention of insemination still morally relevant or even determinative?"[59]

In response, a man unable to inseminate his wife is unable to procreate. This reveals that the conjugal act is ordered toward a procreative end that is intimately linked to insemination. Thus, a sexual act that impedes insemination necessarily impedes the procreative nature of the conjugal act, and as such is contraceptive. Recall from chapter 1 that the physical structure of a human act limits the moral objects that can be legitimately chosen to specify it from the perspective of the acting person in the same way that matter limits form. Therefore, by its nature, a condomistic sexual act limits the moral objects that can be legitimately chosen by a married couple. Using a condom necessarily impedes the procreative nature of the conjugal act, and as such, the impediment of procreation needs to be included in the moral object chosen by the couple as they describe their action. Thus, despite their further intention to prevent the transmission of the AIDS virus, a couple using a condom for prophylactic purposes cannot claim that they are not engaged in a contraceptive act.

57. For Rhonheimer's response to his critics, see his essay, "The Contraceptive Choice, Condom Use, and Moral Arguments Based on Nature: A Reply to Christopher Oleson," *Natl Cathol Bioeth Q* 7 (2007): 273–292.
58. Ibid., 278.
59. Ibid., 281.

One additional comment needs to be made about this controversy. I think that we have sidelined the most important question in this debate: What does *love* demand of a husband and a wife when one of them is infected with HIV/AIDS? In other words, would a husband who truly loved his wife ever take the chance of exposing her to a lethal virus? Can love ever risk the life of a beloved? I think not. Condom use is not 100 percent effective at preventing the spread of HIV/AIDS.[60] Thus, I do not think that a husband who truly loved his wife would ever put her life at risk by having marital relations with her, even with a condom. In the end, therefore, the only truly authentic Christian response to the disputed question over the moral liceity of prophylactic condom use in marriage must be this: Never condoms. Always abstinence.

Finally, we close with a brief discussion of condom use among unmarried HIV-infected individuals. Critics of the Catholic Church's teaching on contraception often argue that it has hindered efforts to halt the spread of HIV/AIDS, especially in Africa. In response, it is clear that condom promotion is effective in halting HIV/AIDS spread mainly through prostitution, as in Thailand, and also, to some extent, among other high-risk groups, including men who have sex with men.[61] However, there is no evidence that condom use has had a primary role in contributing to HIV decline in more generalized, primarily heterosexual populations like those in Africa, probably because it is difficult to maintain consistent condom use within more regular and, typically, concurrent partnerships.[62] In fact, there are data that suggest that one of the most successful strategies for reducing the spread of HIV/AIDS in this context involves programs that encourage monogamy and fidelity.[63] Moreover, there are data that point

60. One systematic review concludes that consistent use of a condom results in only 80 percent reduction in HIV incidence. See Susan C. Weller and Karen Davis-Beaty, "Condom Effectiveness in Reducing Heterosexual HIV Transmission (Cochrane Review)," in *Cochrane Library*, issue 4 (Chichester, UK: John Wiley and Sons, 2003).

61. Norman Hearst and Sanny Chen, "Condom Promotion for AIDS Prevention in the Developing World: Is it Working?" *Stud Fam Plann* 35 (2004): 39–47.

62. James D. Shelton, "Ten Myths and One Truth about Generalized HIV Epidemics," *Lancet* 370 (2007): 1809–1811. Also see the essay, James D. Shelton, "Confessions of a Condom Lover," *Lancet* 368 (2006): 1947–1949.

63. James D. Shelton, Daniel T. Halperin, Malcolm Potts, Helene D. Gayle, and King K. Holmes, "Partner Reduction Is Crucial for Balanced 'ABC' Approach to HIV Prevention," *BMJ* 328 (2004): 891–893. Also see R. L. Stoneburner and D. Low-Beer, "Population-Level HIV Declines and Behavioral Risk Avoidance in Uganda," *Science* 304 (2004): 714–718.

to a link between a greater availability and use of condoms and high-er—and not lower—HIV infection rates.[64] This may be due in part to a phenomenon known as risk compensation, meaning that when one uses a risk-reduction "technology" such as condoms, one often loses the ben-efit (reduction in risk) by "compensating" or taking greater chances than one would take without the risk-reduction technology. Thus in the long run, it appears that the most effective answer to the HIV/AIDS epidemic involves not promoting condom use, but encouraging male circumcision and challenging individuals to live virtuous and chaste lives that reduce multiple sexual partnerships.[65]

The Use of Contraceptives during and after Sexual Assault

Rape is a great moral evil. It is "the forcible violation of the sexual in-timacy of another person. . . . [It] deeply wounds the respect, freedom, and physical and moral integrity to which every person has a right. . . . It is always an intrinsically evil act."[66] If a woman is in serious danger of be-ing raped, many Catholic moralists have convincingly argued that she can choose to protect herself from her rapist's sperm and the further violation it could cause if it fertilized her egg.[67]

To understand the argument that moral theologians make to justify the use of a contraceptive in the context of a sexual assault, we need to re-call that a couple choosing to contracept is intentionally choosing to en-gage in the sexual act in a manner that would prevent the possible con-ception of their child. To put it another way, the spouses are attempting to choose the unitive dimension of sex while simultaneously rejecting its procreative dimension. Notice, however, that this moral analysis presup-poses that the couple has freely chosen to engage in the sexual act. Oth-

64. Phoebe Kajubi, Moses R. Kamya, Sarah Kamya, Sanny Chen, Willi McFarland, and Norman Hearst, "Increasing Condom Use without Reducing HIV Risk: Results of a Controlled Community Trial in Uganda," *J Acquir Immune Defic Syndr.* 40 (2005): 77–82.

65. For extensive discussion, see Malcolm Potts et al., "Reassessing HIV Preven-tion," *Science* 320 (2008): 749–750; and the monograph by Matthew Hanley and Jokin de Irala, *Affirming Love, Avoiding AIDS: What Africa Can Teach the West* (Philadelphia: The Na-tional Catholic Bioethics Center, 2010).

66. *Catechism of the Catholic Church*, no. 2356.

67. For insightful analysis that includes a historical overview of the theological dis-cussion surrounding the question of contraception and rape, see Martin Rhonheimer, "The Use of Contraceptives under Threat of Rape: An Exception?" *Josephinum Journal of Theology* 14 (2007): 168–181.

erwise, how could they choose one of the dimensions of human sexuality while rejecting the other? Properly understood, therefore, a contraceptive act is every action that, whether in anticipation of a *freely* chosen sexual act or in its accomplishment, proposes, whether as an end or as a means, to render procreation impossible.

By definition, however, an act of rape is not a freely chosen sexual act. Rather, it is an act of violence. For this reason, if a rape victim chooses to use a condom, a diaphragm, or a spermicidal jelly, she would not be contracepting because here she is not choosing to sterilize a freely chosen sexual act. She is not choosing the unitive dimension of sex while simultaneously rejecting its procreative dimension. Indeed, properly speaking, she is not choosing sex at all. Rather, she is choosing to defend herself from a further violation from her rapist and the further perpetuation of an unjust act of sexual violence. This is morally justifiable.

Finally, we should stress the following: though a woman who has been raped may choose either methods that destroy sperm or those that prevent the ovulation of her egg to prevent a pregnancy, she may not attempt to remove, destroy, or interfere with the implantation of an embryo who may have already been conceived. This would constitute a direct abortion and would therefore be immoral. The *Ethical and Religious Directives* of the United States Conference of Catholic Bishops reads as follows: "A female who has been raped should be able to defend herself against a potential conception from the sexual assault. If, after appropriate testing, there is no evidence that conception has occurred already, she may be treated with medications that would prevent ovulation, sperm capacitation, or fertilization. It is not permissible, however, to initiate or to recommend treatment that have as their purpose or direct effect the removal, destruction, or interference with the implantation of a fertilized ovum."[68] As we discussed in chapter 2, it would be gravely unjust to punish a child for the sin of her father.

A Disputed Question: The Morality of Rape Protocols

In recent years, there has been a debate among Catholic moral theologians regarding the use of rape protocols to care for women who have been sexually assaulted.[69] The issue is whether or not potentially aborti

68. *Ethical and Religious Directives for Catholic Health Care Services*, 5th ed., no. 36.
69. For details, see the following essays and the references they cite: Ronald P. Hamel

facient medications should be given to a woman who presents herself in an emergency room after a sexual assault. As I already cited above, the ERDs support the use of contraceptives after sexual assault because this is not a contraceptive act properly so called. However, the ERDs do not provide details as to what constitutes "appropriate testing" or "evidence that conception has occurred."

In response to this lacuna, Catholic moralists have proposed two frameworks for rape protocols to care for victims of sexual assault. The first approach, often called the ovulation approach, tests both for pregnancy and for ovulation and offers contraceptive medication to rape victims only if they are neither pregnant nor ovulating nor recently ovulated.[70] This approach seeks not only to prevent conception resulting from a sexual assault, but also to prevent the destruction of human life if conception has already occurred. Some Catholic moralists have criticized the ovulation approach because they are concerned that it is unnecessarily restrictive.[71] Instead, they propose a second approach, called the pregnancy approach, which tests only for pregnancy and then offers contraceptive medication to rape victims if they are not pregnant.

To resolve this dispute, it is important to point out that emergency contraceptives are not all the same. It is likely that there are emergency contraceptives—for instance, the Yuzpe regimen that is able to prevent pregnancies up to 120 hours after sexual intercourse—that are abortifacients as well.[72] Before prescribing these emergency contraceptives, it would be prudent for a physician to minimize the risk of an abortion with a rape protocol that embraces the ovulation approach. As the Congregation for the Doctrine of the Faith warns: "[A]nyone who seeks to prevent the implantation of an embryo which may possibly have been

and Michael R. Panicola, "Low Risks of Moral Certitude: A Response to Msgr. Mulligan," *Ethics Medics* 28.12 (2003): 2–4; and Peter J. Cataldo, "The USCCB and Rape Protocols," *Ethics Medics* 29.4 (2004): 2–4.

70. The most common version of the ovulation approach is the Peoria Protocol first developed at Saint Francis Medical Center in Peoria, IL, in 1995: *Interim Protocol, Sexual Assault: Contraceptive Treatment Component* (Peoria, Ill.: St. Francis Medical Center, 1995).

71. For discussion, see Ronald P. Hamel and Michael R. Panicola, "Emergency Contraception and Sexual Assault. Assessing the Moral Approaches in Catholic Teaching," *Health Prog* 83 (2002): 12–19.

72. Isabel Rodrigues, Fabienne Grou, and Jacques Joly, "Effectiveness of Emergency Contraceptive Pills between 72 and 120 Hours after Unprotected Sexual Intercourse," *Am J Obstet Gynecol* 184 (2001): 531–537.

conceived and who therefore either requests or prescribes such a pharmaceutical [that has the effect of inhibiting implantation] generally intends abortion."[73] In contrast, as I have argued elsewhere, it is unlikely that the contraceptive Plan B, or levonorgestrel, has post-fertilization effects that would risk the life of an embryo.[74] Therefore, there could be reasons to prudently forsake the ovulation approach for the pregnancy approach when prescribing Plan B for sexual assault. For instance, I think that a Catholic doctor with a practice in a rural setting in Idaho who does not have easy access to the laboratory equipment that is required for the ovulation approach could, with moral assurance, prescribe Plan B to a rape victim who is not pregnant without testing to see if she had ovulated.

The Cross of Infertility and the Use of ART

Infertility is an increasingly common problem in the developed world. According to the widely accepted definition of the American Society for Reproductive Medicine, a couple is infertile when they are unable to achieve a pregnancy after one year of regular, non-contraceptive intercourse.[75] The *Merck Manual of Diagnosis and Therapy*, 18th edition, reports that one in five couples in the United States experiences infertility.[76] Infertility has many causes, including sperm disorders (35% of couples), ovulatory dysfunction (20% of couples), tubal dysfunction (30% of couples), abnormal cervical mucus (5% of couples), and unidentified factors (10% of couples).[77] Given the central role of children in the life of a family, it is not surprising that infertility can cause profound suffering within a marriage. In the Old Testament, Rachel cries to her husband Jacob, "Give me children, or I shall die!" (Gn 30:1). Thus, the Catholic Church is clear that research aimed at reducing human sterility is to be encouraged.[78]

73. Congregation for the Doctrine of the Faith, *Dignitas personae*, no. 23.

74. See "Is Plan B an Abortifacient? A Critical Look at the Scientific Evidence," *Natl Cathol Bioeth Q* 7 (2007): 703–707; and my responses to letters in *National Catholic Bioethics Quarterly* 8.3 (Autumn 2008): 421–425; 11.2 (Summer 2011): 212–213.

75. See the website of American Society for Reproductive Medicine, at http://www .asrm.org/Patients/faqs.html#Q1.

76. Mark H. Beers, Robert S. Porter, and Thomas V. Jones, eds., *Merck Manual of Diagnosis and Therapy*, 18th ed. (Whitehouse Station, N.J.: Merck Research Laboratories, 2006), 1991–1995.

77. Ibid.

78. *Catechism of the Catholic Church*, no. 2375.

In the past several decades, many technological advances that treat infertility have been made. However, what is technically possible is not for that very reason necessarily morally permissible. Rather, as the Congregation for the Doctrine of the Faith has made clear, both the dignity of the human person and the profound meaning associated with human sexuality and procreation determine the moral limits of technological interventions at the beginning of life.[79]

To morally evaluate the different techniques for medically assisted procreation, we have to recall two important principles. First, as we discussed in chapter 2, human persons can never be treated as objects because of their intrinsic dignity. This applies to children, regardless of their stage of development. Second, as I noted earlier in this chapter, the marital act between two spouses is meaningful because human sexuality involves the self-giving of persons. Therefore, if conjugal love is to be authentic, it has to be a complete, mutual, and total self-giving of persons. Otherwise, it attacks the dignity of the spouses and undermines their union. In light of this anthropology, the basic principle that governs the moral evaluation of assisted reproductive technologies (ART) is the following: a medical intervention respects the dignity of persons when it seeks "either to facilitate the natural act [of conjugal love], or to enable the natural act, normally carried out, to attain its proper end."[80] The *Ethical and Religious Directives* of the United States Conference of Catholic Bishops formulates this principle this way: "When the marital act of sexual intercourse is not able to attain its procreative purpose, assistance that does not separate the unitive and procreative ends of the act, and does not substitute for the marital act itself, may be used to help married couples conceive."[81]

Treating Infertility

Judging the Morality of ART

Basically, those procedures that help a couple to conceive without bypassing the need for the conjugal act are good. These include, among oth-

---

79. Cf. Congregation for the Doctrine of the Faith, *Donum vitae*, Introduction; *Dignitas personae*, nos. 4–10.

80. Pope Pius XII, "Allocution to Delegates at the Fourth International Congress of Catholic Doctors, November 26, 1951," in *The Human Body: Papal Teaching*, selected and arranged by the Monks of Solesmes, 114–119 (Boston: St. Paul Editions, 1960), 119.

81. *Ethical and Religious Directives for Catholic Health Care Services*, 5th ed., no. 38.

ers, both hormonal treatments to regularize a woman's reproductive cycle or to boost a man's sperm production and surgical interventions to correct defective fallopian tubes and to reverse other structural defects. These treatments restore the couple to health by treating the underlying disease process that causes the infertility. The infertile couple becomes fertile. In and through their marital acts, they are now able to conceive a child who remains a fruit of their love. The child is begotten and not made.

In contrast, procedures that bypass sexual intercourse are not good. These include, among others, in vitro fertilization (IVF), intracytoplasmic sperm injection (ICSI), and zygote intrafallopian tube transfer (ZIFT). These procedures involve fertilizing a woman's (or a donor's) eggs with her husband's (or a donor's) sperm in a Petri dish in a laboratory and transferring the embryos into her womb. They do not respect the dignity either of the human person or of human procreation because they inherently reduce the child to an object and dissociate the procreative from the unitive dimension of marital love. In other words, regardless of the intentions of the parents involved, these technologies treat the child like an object of market exchange, something manufactured, sold, and bought. Rather than being the fruit of his parents' love expressed in the marital act, the child is now a manmade product, the end result of a technological process that takes place on a laboratory bench. Here, the child is *not* begotten but made. Significantly, these treatments do not treat the underlying disease processes that cause the infertility, and thus they do not restore the couple to health. In truth, the infertile couple remains infertile, because these technologies substitute for, rather than assist, the conjugal act.

Finally, two additional comments: First, one controversial procedure to treat infertility involves the use of drugs that hyperstimulate a woman's ovaries. These drugs—Clomid and Pergonal are commonly used—increase the chances of a couple conceiving a child through sexual intercourse.[82] This therapeutic approach is morally permissible as long as the ovarian stimulation is controlled to reduce the risk of a multi-fetal pregnancy. Abortion can *never* be an option to "reduce" a pregnancy. As *Dignitas personae* makes very clear, *"embryo reduction is an intentional selective abortion."*[83]

82. Treatments used to induce ovulation also appear to increase the overall risk of cancer. See R. Calderon-Margalit et al., "Cancer Risk after Exposure to Treatments for Ovulation Induction," *Am J Epidemiol* 169 (2009): 365–375.

83. Congregation for the Doctrine of the Faith, *Dignitas personae*, no. 21. (original emphasis).

It is a sad commentary on our society that drugs that help infertile couples conceive children are often used in conjunction with abortions that kill the unborn children of those same childless couples. The *Ethical and Religious Directives* of the United States Conference of Catholic Bishops mandate that "only those techniques of assisted conception that respect the unitive and procreative meanings of sexual intercourse and do not involve the destruction of human embryos, or their deliberate generation in such numbers that it is clearly envisaged that all cannot implant . . . may be used as therapies for infertility."[84]

Second, some Catholic moral theologians faithful to the Magisterium have argued that under certain specified conditions, gamete intrafallopian transfer (GIFT) and artificial insemination by husband (AIH) can be performed within marriage without violating the dignity of the human person and of human procreation.[85] Other theologians have disagreed. Given this situation, however, and until the Church teaches otherwise, individual Catholics may choose to use these procedures according to the dictates of a rightly formed conscience and the virtue of prudence.

Judging the Morality of Preimplantation Genetic Diagnosis

Preimplantation genetic diagnosis (PGD or PIGD), and more recently, preimplantation genetic haplotyping (PGH), are technological practices associated with IVF that are used to determine if embryos created in vitro contain particular genetic traits.[86] Such diagnosis is done in order to screen either for desirable embryos that do not carry a genetic defect

84. *Ethical and Religious Directives for Catholic Health Care Services*, 5th ed., no. 39.

85. For details, compare the following essays: John Haas, "Gift? No!," *Ethics Medics* 18.9 (1993): 1–3; and Donald G. McCarthy, "Gift? Yes!," *Ethics Medics* 18.9 (1993): 3–4. Also see the discussion and the references cited in Peter J. Cataldo, "Reproductive Technologies," in *Catholic Health Care Ethics: A Manual for Practitioners*, 2nd ed., ed. Edward J. Furton, Peter J. Cataldo, and Albert S. Morachzewski, O.P., 103–118 (Philadelphia: National Catholic Bioethics Center, 2009).

86. For a scientific review, see Anver Kuliev and Yury Verlinsky, "Preimplantation Genetic Diagnosis: Technological Advances to Improve Accuracy and Range of Applications," *Reprod BioMed Online* 16 (2008): 532–538. Also, see Pamela J. Renwick et al., "Proof of Principle and First Cases Using Preimplantation Genetic Haplotyping: A Paradigm Shift for Embryo Diagnosis," *Reprod BioMed Online* 13 (2006): 110–119. For one of the earliest examples of PGD used to select for a desirable child, see A. H. Handyside, J. G. Lesko, J. J. Tarin, R. M. Winston, and M. R. Hughes, "Birth of a Normal Girl after In Vitro Fertilization and Preimplantation Diagnostic Testing for Cystic Fibrosis," *N Engl J Med* 327 (1992): 905–909.

or for those that do possess a particular genetic trait. For instance, couples have already used PGD to identify both embryos who are genetically matched to already-born siblings in the hope that these embryos could become tissue or organ donors to save the lives of their sick brothers or sisters (the savior sibling scenario),[87] and embryos who are deaf for a deaf couple who wanted a deaf child.[88] These desirable embryos would then be implanted into their mother's womb and allowed to grow to term. Undesirable embryos, on the other hand, would be discarded and destroyed.

The Catholic Church has categorically condemned the practice of preimplantation genetic diagnosis. The Congregation for the Doctrine of the Faith has reasoned as follows:

Preimplantation diagnosis—connected as it is with artificial fertilization, which is itself always intrinsically illicit—is directed toward the *qualitative selection and consequent destruction of embryos*, which constitutes an act of abortion. Preimplantation diagnosis is therefore the expression of a *eugenic mentality* that "accepts selective abortion in order to prevent the birth of children affected by various types of anomalies. Such an attitude is shameful and utterly reprehensible."[89]

Preimplantation genetic diagnosis to identify and to cull undesirable human embryos can never be reconciled with the pursuit of beatitude and human excellence.

Judging the Morality of Donors and Surrogates

With the advent of assisted reproductive technologies, infertile couples are increasingly choosing to obtain or to purchase sperm and eggs from third-party donors. Moreover, women unable to carry a pregnancy to term are using surrogate mothers to carry the child in their womb. Given this, it is not surprising that websites advertizing the sale of sperm and eggs are proliferating on the Internet alongside websites that advertize the services of women willing to be surrogate mothers for a fee. Today, a child can be born who has five "parents": the man who contributed his sperm, the woman who contributed her egg, the woman who carried

87. For one example of this practice, see Yury Verlinsky, Svetlana Rechitsky, William Schoolcraft, Charles Strom, and Anver Kuliev, "Preimplantation Diagnosis for Fanconi Anemia Combined with HLA Matching," *JAMA* 285 (2001): 3130–3133.

88. For commentary, see Neil Levy, "Deafness, Culture, and Choice," *J Med Ethics* 28 (2002): 284–285.

89. Congregation for the Doctrine of the Faith, *Dignitas personae*, no. 22, citing *Evangelium vitae*, no. 63.

the child in her womb, and the infertile couple seeking to have the child. Is this good?

Simply, no. Though donors and surrogates often have very noble intentions—they are seeking to help an infertile couple alleviate their suffering and experience the happiness of having a child—their use in human procreation remains immoral. When a couple marries, they promise each other that their love will be exclusive. Thus, the marriage covenant affords the couple the exclusive right to become father and mother solely through each other. Putting it another way, having babies is something that a husband and a wife do with each other and only with each other. The use of gametes from a third-party donor, however, introduces a third person—often a stranger—into the intimacy of marital life. This is immoral because it violates the unity and integrity of the marriage covenant.

Furthermore, the use of donors and surrogates is also an injustice for the child. It unnecessarily deprives him of the relationships he could have had with his biological parents and introduces potentially confusing relational ambiguities into his life. It is significant that numerous studies have shown that an overwhelming majority (about 80%) of parents who have used gametes from third-party donors do not wish to disclose this to their children.[90] Nondisclosure largely stemmed from a desire to protect the child, suggesting that even these parents intuitively recognized that their use of third-party donors is in some way detrimental to the child's well-being. Therefore, the *Ethical and Religious Directives* of the United States Conference of Catholic Bishops mandate the following: "Because of the dignity of the child and of marriage, and because of the uniqueness of the mother-child relationship, participation in contracts or arrangements for surrogate motherhood is not permitted. Moreover, the commercialization of such surrogacy denigrates the dignity of women, especially the poor."[91]

For the Catholic Church, a child has the right to be conceived, to be

90. For details, see the following papers: A. Brewaeys, "Donor Insemination: The Impact on Family and Child Development," *J Psychosom Obstet Gynaecol* 17 (1996): 1–13; Claes Gottlieb, Othon Lalos, and Frank Lindblad, "Disclosure of Donor Insemination to the Child: The Impact of Swedish Legislation on Couple's Attitudes," *Hum Reprod* 15 (2000): 2052–2056; S. Klock and D. Maier, "Psychological Factors Related to Donor Insemination," *Fertil Steril* 56 (1991): 489–495; and S. Klock, M. Jacob, and D. Maier, "A Prospective Study of Donor Insemination of Recipients: Secrecy, Privacy, and Disclosure," *Fertil. Steril* 62 (1994): 477–484.

91. *Ethical and Religious Directives for Catholic Health Care Services*, 5th ed., no. 42.

carried in the womb, to be brought into the world, and to be brought up by his own biological parents.[92] This is good for the child. All unnecessary attacks of this good, no matter how noble the motivation, threaten the unity and stability of the family. Not surprisingly, such damage would also have repercussions on civil society as a whole.

Judging the Morality of Reproductive Cloning Technology

On February 27, 1997, scientists from Scotland shocked the world when they reported the creation of the first mammalian clone, the famous sheep named Dolly.[93] Using a procedure called somatic cell nuclear transfer (SCNT), these researchers were able to create a practically identical, but younger, copy of an adult sheep by introducing the genetic program of that adult into an ennucleated egg, by activating it so that it becomes an embryo that begins development, and then by implanting it into the uterus of another animal. This was the first time asexual reproduction had been demonstrated in mammals. Since then, many other animals, including goats, cows, mice, pigs, cats, rabbits, dogs, and deer, have been cloned.[94]

There are those who argue that human cloning is a beneficial technical advance to help infertile couples, even same-sex couples, who desire to have a child of their own. For example, a man who does not produce any sperm could still have a child who inherits his genome if he transferred one of his nuclei into an enucleated egg taken from his wife. The resulting cloned embryo would then be implanted into his wife, who would carry the child to term.

At the present time, there appears to be a widespread moral and political consensus against reproductive cloning or cloning for birth. The Pontifical Academy for Life outlined three basic reasons for the immorality of human cloning in a document, *Reflections on Cloning*, published in 1997.[95] First, cloning leads to the radical exploitation of women, who are reduced either to egg-making factories or to wombs to gestate a clone. Next, it also leads to the perversion of basic human relationships, where "a wom-

92. Cf. Congregation for the Doctrine of the Faith, *Donum vitae*, II.A.3.

93. I. Wilmut, A. E. Schnieke, J. McWhir, A. J. Kind, and K. H. S. Campbell, "Viable Offspring Derived from Fetal and Adult Mammalian Cells," *Nature* 385 (1997): 810–813.

94. For a review of the history of somatic cell nuclear transfer technology, see Gabor Vajta, "Somatic Cell Nuclear Transfer in Its First and Second Decades: Successes, Setbacks, Paradoxes, and Perspectives," *Reprod Biomed Online* 15 (2007): 582–590.

95. The Pontifical Academy for Life, "Reflections on Cloning," *Origins* 28 (1998): 14–16.

an could be the twin sister of her mother, lack a biological father, and be the daughter of her grandfather,"[96] and to the acceptance of relationships of domination where some individuals can have such dominion over others that they are able to determine the genetic makeup of other human beings. Finally, human cloning attacks and undermines the dignity of the cloned individual. As the Congregation for the Doctrine of the Faith has taught: "Human cloning is intrinsically illicit in that, by taking the ethical negativity of techniques of artificial fertilization to their extreme, it seeks to *give rise to a new human being without a connection to the act of reciprocal self-giving between spouses* and, more radically, *without any link to sexuality.* This leads to manipulation and abuses gravely injurious to human dignity."[97] Cloning is a process that treats a child as a product who is manufactured in the lab rather than as a person who is procreated in the loving embrace of his father and his mother.

In addition to these reasons, other moralists have emphasized that the low success rate and the high numbers of birth defects often associated with cloned animals created using current cloning protocols heightens the risk that human cloning would produce a sick or dying infant. They have also argued that cloning deprives the cloned individual of an open future.[98] He does not have the freedom to choose his future. Note that each of us was given the challenge and the privilege of discovering our future. We were free to discover the divinely ordained vocations that would give meaning to our lives. We were free to dream about our futures, whether it was the life of a pianist, an athlete, a lawyer, or a priest, and, with God's help, to try to achieve those dreams. However, a cloned child would not have this freedom. He would be born with expectations determined by the life of the individual from whom he was cloned and would be expected to follow in the footsteps of that person. For example, if Michael Jordan was cloned, would anyone expect Michael Jordan Jr. to be anything other than a basketball player? As the Congregation of the Doctrine of the Faith emphatically explained: "If cloning were to be done for *reproduction,* this would impose on the resulting individual a predetermined genetic identity, subjecting him—as has been stated—to a form of

96. Ibid., no. 3.

97. Congregation for the Doctrine of the Faith, *Dignitas personae,* no. 28.

98. For an eloquent defense of a child's right to an open future, see Joel Feinberg, "A Child's Right to an Open Future," in his *Freedom and Fulfillment, Philosophical Essays* (Princeton, N.J.: Princeton University Press, 1992), 76–97.

biological slavery, from which it would be difficult to free himself."[99] This is clearly unjust.

Finally, despite the intrinsic immorality of human cloning, I should point out that the use of cloning technology with plants and animals is not necessarily wrong, especially if it leads to advances that benefit human society and the environment. For instance, cloning technology could be used to propagate lines of drought-resistant rice or stress-resistant wheat. These crops could help combat world hunger. Cloning technology could also be used to repopulate endangered animals, including the giant panda (*Ailuropoda melanoleuca*) and the Sumatran tiger (*Panthera tigris sumatrae*).[100] As I will discuss in chapter 7, plant and animal research is justifiable, in principle, as long as this research respects some basic moral principles.

Common Objections to the Church's Teaching

In our culture, there are those who oppose the Catholic Church's teaching on the use of assisted reproductive technologies. They argue that a couple has the right to use whatever means are available to become parents.[101] According to this argument, every couple—some would even add, every individual, married or not—has a right to a child.

In response, the *Catechism of the Catholic Church* is clear: "A child is not something *owed* to one, but is a *gift*. The 'supreme gift of marriage' is a human person. A child may not be considered a piece of property, an idea to which an alleged 'right to a child' would lead."[102] Putting it another way, a couple does not and cannot have a right to a child because a child is a human person. Can one person ever have the right to another person? Can a man claim a right to a wife, or a woman a right to a husband? No one is en-

---

99. Congregation for the Doctrine of the Faith, *Dignitas personae*, no. 29.

100. For example, see the following papers that describe the cloning of the endangered gaur and the endangered wolf: Robert P. Lanza et al., "Cloning of an Endangered Species *(Bos gaurus)* Using Interspecies Nuclear Transfer," *Cloning* 2 (2000): 79–90; M. K. Kim et al., "Endangered Wolves Cloned from Adult Somatic Cells," *Cloning Stem Cells* 9 (2007): 130–137. For discussion, see the review, Pasqualino Loi, Cesare Galli, and Grazyna Ptak, "Cloning of Endangered Mammalian Species: Any Progress?" *Trends Biotechnol* 25 (2007): 195–200.

101. For one representative example of this position, see John A. Robertson, *Children of Choice* (Princeton, N.J.: Princeton University Press, 1996). Robertson, a legal bioethicist at the University of Texas at Austin, argues for procreative freedom defined as the freedom to decide whether or not to have offspring and to control the use of one's reproductive capacity.

102. *Catechism of the Catholic Church*, no. 2378.

titled to a spouse for the same reason that no couple is entitled to a child—no person is ever entitled to another person. Indeed, as the *Catechism* points out, "in this area, only the child possesses genuine rights: the right 'to be the fruit of the specific act of the conjugal love of his parents,' and 'the right to be respected as a person from the moment of his conception.'"[103]

Therefore, an infertile couple seeking to respect genuine human rights should seek medical advice from physicians who respect the dignity both of the human person and of human procreation, instead of resorting to assisted reproductive technologies. One resource is the Pope Paul VI Institute for the Study of Human Reproduction in Omaha, Nebraska,[104] which has pioneered Natural Procreative (NaPro) Technology, a medical and surgical approach that treats the underlying disease process of which infertility is only a symptom. Their comprehensive method has been successful at curing infertility and, notably, is also less expensive than the assisted reproductive technologies.

Next, there are others who argue that the Church's ban on the use of IVF in the simple case between a husband and a wife is erroneous because of its claim that a child conceived as the product of an intervention of medical or biological techniques cannot be the fruit of his parents' love. As Richard A. McCormick, S.J., puts it, this conclusion "is a *non sequitur*, and both prospective parents and medical technologists would recognize it as such. Sexual intercourse is not the only loving act in marriage."[105] He continues: "When Cardinal Joseph Ratzinger added in a March 14 press conference that the use of IVF and ET is not a loving act but an 'egoistic' one, he was uttering sheer nonsense."[106]

In response, it is important to emphasize that loving someone involves desiring his good. When parents choose to conceive their child with IVF, they inevitably allow others to treat their child as an object who is created in a laboratory. This is true regardless of the reasons they give for allowing this to happen, reasons that could include fulfilling their deepest yearning for a child of their own and enhancing their marital bond. Thus, regardless of their best intentions, parents who use IVF necessarily treat their child as a means—a means to fulfill their reproductive

103. Ibid.
104. For more information, see the Institute's website at www.Popepaulvi.com.
105. Richard A. McCormick, S.J., "The Vatican Document on Bioethics: Two Responses," *America* 156 (1987): 246–248; 248.
106. Ibid.

needs—rather than as end in himself. This objectively undermines the child's dignity and attacks his good. This is not authentic love.

Finally, there are those who have argued that the Church's teaching is erroneous because parents who allow doctors to treat their children in hospitals are no different from parents who allow technicians to create their children in the laboratory. Both involve treating children as objects of technological manipulation. Since the former intervention is clearly good, the argument concludes that the latter one must be good as well.

In response, we should affirm that there is a difference between the two types of interventions. In hospitals, the technological interventions are being accomplished *for* the sake of the child who is sick. As such, the child is still being treated not as a means but as an end. He is being treated as a person in need of healing. In the case of the child conceived in vitro, however, technology is being used *on* him and not *for* him. Thus, the child is being treated not as an end but as a means, in this case, a means to fulfill his parents' desires for a larger family.

To conclude this discussion, we need to acknowledge the struggle of those couples who discover that they are still unable to conceive despite their best efforts to use legitimate approaches to cure their infertility. Aware of their suffering, the Church reminds them of the power of the Cross:

Couples who find themselves in this sad situation are called to find in it an opportunity for sharing in a particular way in the Lord's Cross, the source of spiritual fruitfulness. Sterile couples must not forget that "even when procreation is not possible, conjugal life does not for this reason lose its value. Physical sterility in fact can be for spouses the occasion for other important service to the life of the human person, for example, adoption, various forms of educational work, and assistance to other families and to poor or handicapped children."[107]

In faith, we know that carrying the Cross of the Lord, despite the great suffering involved, can be a great privilege of redemptive value.

A Disputed Question: The Adoption of Abandoned Human Embryos

According to one study performed by the Society for Assisted Reproductive Technology (SART), there are nearly four hundred thousand

---

107. Congregation for the Doctrine of the Faith, *Donum vitae*, II.B.8, quoting *Familiaris consortio*, no. 14.

(396,526) frozen human embryos in over four hundred assisted reproductive technology (ART) facilities in the United States.[108] Sadly, some of these embryos have been abandoned by their parents, who conclude that they have no more need for them. In response to this tragedy, several pro-life groups have suggested that these abandoned embryos should be rescued and implanted into the wombs of wives who are willing to "adopt" them, to bring them to term, and to raise them as one of their own children. Recently, an Evangelical Christian organization founded an embryo adoption agency called the Snowflakes Program.[109] Not surprisingly, this proposal to rescue frozen embryos has raised many ethical questions. It has also sparked a heated debate among Catholic moralists: are there any circumstances in which it would be morally admirable for a woman to seek to have an orphaned embryo implanted in her womb?

Proponents claim that embryo rescue is morally acceptable because both the end—saving the baby—and the means—transferring an embryo from a freezer to a womb—are good. For example, William E. May argues that a married couple may adopt a frozen embryo, which then commits them to further actions, of which the basic one is to give their adopted child a home.[110] This they do, first, when the wife chooses to have the frozen embryo transferred into her womb. They would then continue to do this by giving their adopted child, once born, the home provided by both husband and wife. May concludes that embryo rescue is simply a more sophisticated kind of adoption. Thus, embryo rescue is good.

In contrast, opponents—and I am one of them—claim that embryo rescue is morally unacceptable because it violates the marital covenant.[111]

---

108. David I. Hoffman et al., "Cryopreserved Embryos in the United States and their Availability for Research," *Fertil Steril* 79 (2003): 1063–1069.

109. www.snowflakes.org. For a case study of embryo adoption using the Snowflakes program, see JoAnn L. Davidson, "A Successful Embryo Adoption," *Natl Cathol Bioeth Q* 1 (2001): 229–233. For commentary, see John Berkman, "Adopting Embryos in America: A Case Study and an Ethical Analysis," *Scottish Journal of Theology* 55 (2002): 438–460.

110. William E. May, "The Object of the Acting Woman in Embryo Rescue," in *Human Embryo Adoption*, ed. Thomas V. Berg, L.C., and Edward J. Furton, 135–163 (Philadelphia: National Catholic Bioethics Center, 2006). For further discussion of the pro–embryo adoption position, see the essays by Berkman, Brugger and Ryan in this volume. Also see the essays by Tollefsen, Brown and Eberl, and Brakman, in Sarah Vaughan Brakman and Darlene Fozard Weaver, eds., *The Ethics of Embryo Adoption and the Catholic Tradition* (New York: Springer, 2007).

111. For details, see my essay, "On the Catholic Vision of Conjugal Love and the Mo-

In other words, because of their marriage vows, a husband is given the exclusive right to make his wife pregnant through their marital acts. Becoming pregnant is something a couple does with each other and only with each other. Embryo rescue, however, would rob the husband of the unique and privileged role he should play in establishing a pregnancy in his wife. Instead, his wife would become pregnant through the actions of a third individual, usually the physician, who inserts the embryo into her womb. This undermines the exclusivity of marriage and is therefore unjust. Thus, embryo rescue is not good.

Given the ongoing debate among faithful Catholic moral theologians and until the Church teaches otherwise,[112] individual Catholics may choose to rescue abandoned embryos according to the dictates of a rightly formed conscience that has examined the arguments for and against the morality of such an act.

What then should we do about these frozen human embryos, especially those embryos who have been abandoned by their parents? As I have explained in more detail elsewhere, adoptive parents, instead of implanting their adopted embryo into his adopted mother's womb, could pay to maintain the cryopreservation necessary for the survival of their child until incubators capable of bringing him to term are invented.[113]

---

rality of Embryo Transfer," in *Human Embryo Adoption*, ed. Thomas V. Berg, L.C., and Edward J. Furton (Philadelphia: National Catholic Bioethics Center, 2006), 115–134. For further discussion of the anti–embryo adoption position, see the essays by Pacholczyk, Watt, Tonti-Filippini, and Geach in this volume. Also see the essays by Stempsey, Althaus, and Pacholczyk in Sarah-Vaughan Brakman and Darlene Fozard Weaver, eds., *The Ethics of Embryo Adoption and the Catholic Tradition* (New York: Springer, 2007).

112. The Congregation for the Doctrine of the Faith has raised concerns regarding the practice of embryo adoption but has refrained from making a definitive moral judgment: "This proposal [of embryo adoption], praiseworthy with regard to the intention of respecting and defending human life, presents however various problems not dissimilar to those mentioned above." *Dignitas personae*, no. 19. For commentary on *Dignitas personae* and the adoption of frozen embryos, see the following essays: John S. Grabowski and Christopher Gross, "*Dignitas personae* and the Adoption of Frozen Embryos: A New Chill Factor?" *Natl Cathol Bioeth Q* 10 (2010): 307-328; and Edward J. Furton, "Embryo Adoption Reconsidered," *Natl Cathol Bioeth Q* 10 (2010): 329-347.

113. Austriaco, "On the Catholic Vision of Conjugal Love and the Morality of Embryo Transfer," 131–133. As *Dignitas personae* makes clear, the cryopreservation of human embryos is an attack on their inherent dignity: "Cryopreservation is *incompatible with the respect owed to human embryos;* it presupposes their production *in vitro;* it exposes them to the serious risk of death or physical harm, since a high percentage does not survive the process of freezing and thawing; it deprives them at least temporarily of maternal reception

This would preserve the life of the child without undermining his parents' marital covenant.

Highlighting the Role of Virtue in Bioethics

It should not be surprising that many persons living in our sex-saturated culture, including many Catholics, find it difficult, if not impossible, to understand and to accept the Church's teaching on human sexuality and procreation. As St. Thomas Aquinas eloquently explained in his *Summa theologiae,* unchastity or lust—a vice that is rampant in our overly eroticized society—not only corrupts the virtue of prudence but also begets a blindness of spirit that clouds the intellect and weakens the will.[114] Thus, unchaste individuals who routinely engage in premarital or contraceptive marital sex are often incapable of seeing the truth and the goodness of chaste love.

In light of this, couples struggling with the Church's teachings on human procreation should be invited to grow in the virtue of chastity that orders their sexual desires, by introducing chaste practices into their marriage. Unfortunately, in contemporary culture, chastity is often confused with continence, the virtue that allows one to curb all sexual activity.[115] Chastity is more than simply abstaining from sex. Rather, it is a spiritual discipline that leads the acting person to a self-mastery of his erotic desires so that all sexual activity is ordered according to reason. Chaste practices, including NFP, not only free couples to develop an intimate friendship that respects their dignity as persons, but also allow them to appreciate the truth and the beauty of chaste love.[116] As noted above, it is not surprising that couples who use chaste methods of birth regulation have a lower divorce rate than the average couple. Chastity facilitates the growth of all the virtues, including the virtues of charity, faith, hope, and truth, virtues that can only strengthen a marriage. It also challenges the

and gestation; it places them in a situation in which they are susceptible to further offense and manipulation" (no. 18). Thus, let me emphasize here that I am recommending that adoptive parents pay for the *ongoing* cryopreservation of their embryos, a necessary evil that has to be tolerated until their embryonic children can be brought to term in an advanced incubator.

114. St. Thomas Aquinas, *ST,* IIa-IIae, 53.6; IIa-IIae, 153.5; IIa-IIae, 15.3.

115. Ibid., IIa-IIae, 155.1.

116. For an insightful reflection on the need for chastity in marriage, see Elizabeth Anscombe, *Contraception and Chastity* (London: Catholic Truth Society, 2003).

spouses to a selflessness that is properly ordered to the common good of the family. In the end, it will help them to understand and to live out the Church's vision of human sexuality. The truth and beauty of this moral vision needs to be lived out if it is to be fully appreciated.

Finally, we should acknowledge that initial efforts to grow in the virtue of chastity are often difficult because they involve undoing years of unchaste practices. Therefore, couples striving to become chaste should also be invited to fast. As many of the Church's saints recognized, the discipline of fasting orders the inner life of the individual and keeps the turbulence of sensuality in check. It is not surprising that St. Thomas Aquinas declared that fasting is a guardian of chastity.[117] Fasting is an act of the virtue of abstinence that frees the intellect and liberates the spirit so that the acting person may more easily contemplate heavenly things.[118] In doing so, fasting will help a couple not only to discern, but also to discover for themselves, the physical and spiritual goods that come with temperance and its allied virtues, one of which is the virtue of chastity. Couples should fast to learn how to love well.

117. *ST*, IIa-IIae, 147.1.
118. Ibid.

CHAPTER FOUR

Bioethics and the Clinical Encounter

In the United States, the conviction that the patient is ultimately responsible for making the health-care decisions that involve him—a conviction already articulated in the Nuremberg Code written after World War II to protect the basic rights of patients and research subjects—was codified into law with the passage of the Patient Self-Determination Act (PSDA) of 1990.[1] It requires most hospitals and other health-care institutions to inform their patients at the time of admission, of their health-care decision-making rights, including the following: (1) the right to participate in all health-care decision making regarding their care, including the right to accept or refuse treatment; (2) the right under state law to complete an advance directive for health care; and (3) the health-care institution's policies that allow it to honor these rights. The PSDA also prohibits institutions from discriminating against a patient who does not have an advance directive for health care.

In this chapter, I deal with several issues surrounding the decision-making process of the patient and his physician, as they are understood within the tradition of Catholic bioethics. I begin with a discussion of the identities of the patient and of the health-care professional in the clinical encounter. How are we to understand their particular roles in the struggle with illness? I then move both to the professional-patient relationship that forms the context for many of the health-care decisions entrusted to the patient, and to the question of confidentiality, an essential ingredient that protects the integrity of this relationship. Next, I discuss informed consent, the process that allows a patient (or if he is incapacitated, his surro-

1. For a discussion of the impact of the Patient Self-Determination Act of 1990 on health care services in the United States, see John La Puma, David Orentlicher, and Robert J. Moss, "Advance Directives on Admission: Clinical Implications and Analysis of the Patient Self-Determination Act of 1990," *JAMA* 266 (1991): 402–405. Also see Lawrence P. Ulrich, *The Patient Self-Determination Act: Meeting the Challenges in Patient Care* (Washington, D.C.: Georgetown University Press, 2001).

gate decision maker) to become a prudent participant in all decision making regarding his health care, including a short discussion of the role of
the priest in the pastoral care of an individual who is making decisions in
bioethics. Finally, I conclude by describing three clinical situations when a
medical intervention without informed consent is morally justifiable.

The Clinical Encounter

The Role of the Patient

When contemporary bioethics deals with the clinical encounter between the patient and his health-care professional, it usually emphasizes
the perspective of the physician or the nurse or the health-care provider.
However, it is more important to begin with the patient because it is the
patient who is ultimately responsible for making the health-care decisions
that involve him. He is ultimately responsible because he is the steward
of the gifts of life and health that he has received from God. It is also the
patient who usually initiates his encounter with his health-care provider
when he becomes sick, and who ends it when he is either healed or beyond
healing. In light of this, how are we to understand the patient's role in the
clinical encounter? Who is he called to be, and what is he called to do?

Recall that each one of us is invited by God to attain a happy life,
what the classical authors called beatitude, by following in the footsteps
of the Lord Jesus Christ along the path to perfection. In the mystery of
God's providence, every moment of our lives is part of this divine invitation to grow in holiness. We respond to this call by performing good acts
and by developing the virtues that these good acts engender. Illness too
is an invitation to human excellence. When we are sick, we are being invited to cooperate with God's grace to grow in virtue and to become holy.
From this divine perspective, it is clear that the role of the patient understood from within the Catholic tradition is to become a virtuous patient.
In the face of the suffering that comes with illness, the patient is being
called to become a saint.

Who is the virtuous patient?[2] In responding to this question, we need

2. For insightful discussions regarding the virtuous patient, see Karen Lebacqz,
"The Virtuous Patient," in *Virtue and Medicine*, ed. Earl E. Shelp, 275–288 (Dordrecht:
Kluwer Academic Publishers, 1985); and Stanley Hauerwas, "Practicing Patience: How
Christians Should be Sick," in *Christians among the Virtues*, ed. S. Hauerwas and C. Pinch-
es, 166–178 (Notre Dame, Ind.: University of Notre Dame Press, 1997).

to be careful that we do not answer it solely from the perspective of the health-care professional, who may see his ideal, and thus virtuous, patient as someone who is compliant, uncomplaining, and cheerful. Rather, we should seek an account of the virtuous patient that arises from the particular struggles of the patient as he lives the vulnerability of illness. With this in mind, one empirical study has proposed a model of illness and virtue that is helpful. It identifies four moral challenges for the patient, especially the chronic patient.[3] They are the following: (1) maintaining good relationships with others and participating in the community; (2) maintaining self-respect; (3) being realistic; and (4) being courageous. These are the four primary moral burdens that often loom large in a patient's life.

In response to this study, we can name the virtues of charity, faith, hope, and fortitude as those specific virtues that would allow the patient to act well in light of the moral challenges that he faces during his illness. Charity would dispose the patient to properly order his relationships with his health-care providers, with the other patients, and with his family and friends. It would challenge him to cooperate with them as they seek his healing together. Faith would allow the patient to maintain his identity when his self-understanding and his self-respect are challenged by the apparent indignities of suffering. It would challenge him to remember that first and foremost, he is a human person made in the image and likeness of God. As such, he has an intrinsic dignity that cannot be taken from him. Hope would enable the patient to be realistic even when he is faced with the possibility that he may not be cured. It would challenge him to take his medication responsibly, to care for himself, and to live a steadfast life with his eventual resurrection in mind. Finally, fortitude would enable the patient to be serene in the face of suffering, and to endure the tests, the treatments, and the medical interventions that often come with the struggle against illness. Transformed by these virtues, the patient can become an icon of the suffering Christ who can call those around him, including his physicians, his nurses, and his other health-care providers, to virtue and human excellence. We should also not forget that these virtues, like all the virtues, can clear the intellect, strengthen the will, and discipline the passions, so that the patient can make those prudent deci-

3. Alastair V. Campbell and Teresa Swift, "What Does It Mean to Be a Virtuous Patient? Virtue from the Patient's Perspective," *Scottish Journal of Healthcare Chaplaincy* 5 (2002): 29–35.

sions regarding his health care, both medical and moral, that are integral to human flourishing.

The Vocation of the Health-Care Professional

From within the tradition of Catholic bioethics, the identity of the health-care professional can only be properly understood as a vocation, a God-given mission in this life, whose fulfillment brings both glory to God and happiness to that individual. Every person has a vocation. For their part, physicians, nurses, and other health-care providers are called to imitate the Lord Jesus Christ, who was known as someone who went about doing good and healing those who were ill. They strive to the best of their abilities, with God's help, to cure the sick. However, Jesus' healing mission went further than just caring for those with physical afflictions. He also sought their physical, mental, and spiritual healing so that "they may have life and have it more abundantly" (Jn 10:10). Thus, the work of health-care providers involves more than just curing disease. It has to embrace the physical, psychological, social, and spiritual dimensions of the human being. It is holistic care because it is care for human *persons.*

For the Christian, caring for the sick is an act of love, both for neighbor and for God. In a very real way, Catholic physicians, nurses, and other health-care professionals are called to grow in charity as good Samaritans who stop beside the wounded person, becoming his "neighbor in charity." In doing so, they fulfill a divine and salvific mission acting as ministerial instruments for God's love poured out for the suffering person. As Blessed John Paul II put it in a homily to a conference of Italian doctors: "You are aware of the close relationship, the analogy, the interaction, between the mission of the priest on the one hand and that of the health-care worker on the other: All are devoted, in different ways, to the salvation of the person, and care for his health, to free him from illness, suffering and death, to promote in him life, well-being and happiness."[4] The doctor is to the body as the priest is to the soul.

Next, for the Christian, caring for the sick is also an act of love for God. As the Lord Jesus Himself said: "I was ill and you cared for me" (Mt 25:36). Thus, every Catholic doctor, nurse, or health-care provider should always seek to grow in faith so that he may recognize the presence

4. John Paul II, "Discourse for the 120th Anniversary of the Foundation of the 'Bambin Gesu' Hospital," March 18, 1989, cited in Pontifical Council for Pastoral Assistance, *Charter for Health Care Workers* (Vatican City: Libreria Editrice Vaticana, 1995), no. 5.

of the Lord in his suffering brothers and sisters, and approach them as he would approach the sacramental Lord in the tabernacle. This perspective would challenge the health-care provider to always focus on the person rather than on the tumor or the illness or the infection. It also challenges him to see the patient as a person who has a life filled with dreams, with hopes, and with fears.

Third, health-care workers are called to be guardians and servants of human life, who should constantly and courageously seek to promote and defend human dignity. *Evangelium vitae*, Blessed John Paul II's encyclical on the Gospel of Life, puts it this way:

A unique responsibility belongs to health-care personnel: doctors, pharmacists, nurses, chaplains, men and women religious, administrators and volunteers. Their profession calls for them to be guardians and servants of human life. In today's cultural and social context, in which science and the practice of medicine risk losing sight of their inherent ethical dimension, health-care professionals can be strongly tempted at times to become manipulators of life, or even agents of death. In the face of this temptation their responsibility today is greatly increased. Its deepest inspiration and strongest support lie in the intrinsic and undeniable ethical dimension of the health-care profession, something already recognized by the ancient and still relevant *Hippocratic Oath*, which requires every doctor to commit himself to absolute respect for human life and its sacredness.[5]

Thus, Catholic physicians, nurses, and other health-care providers have the obligation to grow in the virtue of justice so that they may embrace the responsibility to stand up for life in the public square. They do this primarily through the witness of how they live out their professions in accordance with the Gospel of Life.[6] As the Pontifical Council for Pastoral Assistance put it in its *Charter for Health Care Workers*: "In fidelity to the moral law, the health-care worker actuates his fidelity to the human person whose worth is guaranteed by the law, and to God, whose wisdom is expressed by the law."[7] In the end, especially in the presence of tragic human experiences, the Christian is called to bear witness to the consoling truth of the Risen Lord, who takes upon Himself the wounds and ills of humanity, including death itself, and transforms them into occasions of grace and of life.

5. John Paul II, *Evangelium vitae*, no. 89.
6. For an insightful discussion on the vocation of the Catholic physician in an age of secularized medicine, see Don Forsythe, "The Physician's Vocation," *Ethics Medics* 29.2 (2004): 3–4.
7. Pontifical Council for Pastoral Assistance, *Charter for Health Care Workers*, no. 6.

Finally, in the Catholic tradition, much theology can be learned from the prayers of the Church. As an ancient Latin saying went, *lex orandi, lex credendi,* the law of prayer is the law of faith. Not surprisingly, there are numerous prayers that have been written specifically for the intentions of physicians, nurses, and other health-care professionals. Here is one that is based upon a prayer composed by Blessed John Paul II during the Great Jubilee Year.[8] It reveals the vocation of the health-care professional from a liturgical perspective within the Catholic tradition.

Lord Jesus,

Divine Physician, who in your earthly life showed special concern for those who suffer and entrusted to your disciples the ministry of healing, make us ever ready to alleviate the trials of our brethren. Make each one of us, aware of the great mission that is entrusted to him, strive always to be, in the performance of daily service, an instrument of your merciful love. Enlighten our minds, guide our hands, make our hearts diligent and compassionate. Ensure that in every patient we know how to discern the features of your divine Face.

You who are the Way, provide us with the gift of knowing how to imitate you every day as medical doctors not only of the body but of the whole person, helping those who are sick to tread with trust their own earthly path until the moment of their encounter with You.

You who are the Truth, provide us with the gift of wisdom and science in order to penetrate the mystery of the human person and their transcendent destiny as we draw near to them in order to discover the causes of their maladies and find suitable remedies.

You who are the Life, provide us with the gift of preaching and bearing witness to the 'Gospel of Life' in our profession, committing ourselves to defending it always, from conception to its natural end, and to respect the dignity of every human being, and especially the dignity of the weakest and the most in need. Make us O Lord, *Good Samaritans,* ready to welcome, treat, and console those we encounter in our work. Following the example of the holy medical doctors who have preceded us, help us to offer our generous contribution to the constant renewal of health care structures.

You who are Lord, bless our studies and our profession, enlighten our research and our teaching. Lastly, grant to us, having constantly loved and served you

8. XXth International Congress of the Catholic Doctors, June 29, 2000. Available at the website of the Catholic Medical Association: http://www.cathmed.org/about/background/promise_prayer/.

in our suffering brethren, that at the end of our earthly pilgrimage we may contemplate your glorious countenance and experience the joy of the encounter with you in your Kingdom of joy and everlasting peace.

Amen.

Clearly, the physician is called to a commendable and holy vocation in the service of his brothers and sisters for the glorification of his Creator.

The Professional-Patient Relationship

First and foremost, we have to remember that the relationship between the health-care professional and his patient is a relationship between two *persons*, each of whom has immeasurable worth. Thus, the professional-patient relationship has to be grounded in mutual respect, the respect due to persons. This means two things. First, the patient should never be just a case or a disease, an anonymous individual who is used by the health-care professional to exercise his medical knowledge. Second, the professional should never be just an expert who is used by the patient to get information and medical care. Neither the patient nor the physician, as persons, should be used purely as a means to an end.

The distinguished Catholic physician and scholar Edmund Pellegrino has proposed that the healing relationship is grounded in three realities of the clinical encounter.[9] First, there is the fact of illness. Persons become patients when they acknowledge that they need help to alleviate a particular symptom. Because of this ailment, they are no longer free to pursue the things they want out of life without difficulty. Second, there is the act of profession. Here, the physician, nurse, or health-care worker asks, "How may I help you?" Implicit in this question is the promise that the health-care professional possesses the knowledge to heal. This self-imposed trust covenant imposes obligations on the professional from the moment it is made. Finally, there is the act of healing. The promise made to the patient directs the knowledge, techniques, and personal commitment of the health professional who attempts to heal the sick person.

In a similar vein, Blessed John Paul II has called the professional-

9. For more information, see Edmund D. Pellegrino and David C. Thomasma, *A Philosophical Basis of Medical Practice: Toward a Philosophy and Ethic of the Healing Professions* (Oxford: Oxford University Press, 1994). Also see their more recent book, *Helping and Healing: Religious Commitment in Health Care* (Washington, D.C.: Georgetown University Press, 1997). For discussion and responses to Pellegrino's proposal from a secular perspective, see the open peer commentaries in *American Journal of Bioethics* 6 (2006): 72–91.

patient relationship "a meeting between trust and conscience."[10] It is the trust of one person who is sick and suffering and hence in need, who entrusts himself to the conscience of another who can help him in his need and who comes to care for him and to cure him. To put it another way, the professional-patient relationship is a fiduciary relationship— "fiduciary" derives from the Latin word *fiducia*, meaning "confidence" or "trust"—a covenantal relationship based upon trust. The bond of trust between the patient and the physician is vital to the diagnostic and therapeutic process. In order for the health professional to make accurate diagnoses and provide proper treatment recommendations, the patient must be able to communicate all relevant information about an illness. He must be truthful and forthcoming with his medical condition and history. Thus, the professional-patient relationship requires that both persons strive to grow in virtue especially in the virtues of charity, patience, benevolence, truth, understanding, and prudence. It also requires an appropriate level of confidentiality.

Confidentiality and the Professional-Patient Relationship

During the clinical encounter, it is not uncommon for the patient to disclose personal and private information to his health-care providers. In confidence, he entrusts this information to them in the hope that they will use it to heal him. Thus, confidentiality is important in the professional-patient relationship.[11] It arises both from our respect for the dignity of each person who has the right to determine those who are privy to certain confidences about him, and those who are not, and from our need to preserve the professional relationships that are important for the common good.

Two kinds of confidential information are often exchanged in the clinical setting. First, there are natural secrets, information someone happens

10. John Paul II, "To the Participants at Two Congresses of Medicine and Surgery," October 27, 1980, cited in *Charter for Health Care Workers*, no. 2.

11. For an in-depth discussion of confidentiality from the Catholic perspective, see Kevin J. Murrell, "Confidentiality," in *Catholic Health Care Ethics: A Manual for Practitioners*, 2nd ed., ed. Edward J. Furton, Peter J. Cataldo, and Albert S. Moraczewski, O.P., 19–23 (Philadelphia: National Catholic Bioethics Center, 2009). Also see the essay relating medical confidentiality more specifically to professional confidentiality more generally: John M. Haas, "Can You Keep a Secret?" *Ethics Medics* 17.12 (1992): 1–2. For a different perspective taken from the secular bioethics tradition, see the target essay by Kenneth Kipnis, "A Defense of Unqualified Medical Confidentiality," *Am J Bioeth* 6 (2006): 7–18, and the open peer commentaries that follow.

to find out in the course of ordinary conversation that the other person does not want disclosed. One is obligated both in charity and in justice to keep these secrets. If inappropriate disclosure of the secret causes personal distress on the part of the person whom the information is about, then it is a violation of charity. In addition, if the inappropriate disclosure leads to material loss or damage of the reputation of the person whom the secret is about, then it is also a violation of justice.

Second, there are professional secrets, information entrusted to another because he holds a professional capacity. Within the clinical setting, these secrets include, among others, personal histories, symptoms, clinical diagnoses, and prognoses. The physician or nurse has the responsibility to ensure that this privileged information is used only to achieve the purpose for which the patient disclosed this knowledge, that is, the healing of the sick individual. Inappropriate disclosures of these secrets would be a violation of justice. It could also undermine the trust and confidence that grounds the fiduciary relationship between health-care professional and patient, with detrimental effects on both the care the patient may need and the common good that presupposes that patients trust their health-care providers. Not surprisingly, therefore, the medical profession has consistently urged physicians to maintain confidentiality. The Hippocratic Oath, which dates to about 400 BC, enjoins doctors: "What I may see or hear in the course of the treatment or even outside of the treatment in regard to the life of men, which on no account one must spread abroad, I will keep to myself, holding such things shameful to be spoken about."[12] Echoing the oath, Pope Pius XII taught the following in an address to the Italian Medical-Biological Union of St. Luke: "Another of the duties which derive from the eighth commandment is the observance of the professional secret, which must serve and serves the good of the individual and even more of society."[13] The art of medicine presupposes that both patients and physicians respect and honor the integrity of each other's secrets.

Despite the importance of confidentiality in the clinical encounter, however, there are two general categories of circumstances where a physician or

12. Ludwig Edelstein, *Hippocratic Oath: Text, Translation and Interpretation* (Baltimore: Johns Hopkins University Press, 1943), 3.

13. Pope Pius XII, "Allocution to the Italian Medical-Biological Union of St. Luke, November 12, 1944," in *The Human Body: Papal Teaching*, selected and arranged by the Monks of Solesmes, 51–65 (Boston: St. Paul Editions, 1960), 63.

other health-care provider may disclose confidential information without the patient's consent. In each case, the breach of confidentiality is justified because it preserves the common good. Recall that one reason for confidentiality in professional relationships is that these relationships are necessary for the preservation of the common good and the right ordering of society. Thus, if the observance of professional secrecy in a given circumstance would be more harmful than helpful for the common good, then the obligation of secrecy is replaced by an obligation to reveal the secret. To put it another way, a private secret can and should become public knowledge in times of common necessity. As Pope Pius XII taught:

> In [the observance of the professional secret], there can arise conflicts between the public and private interests, or between different elements and aspects pertaining to the common good. In these conflicts, it will often be very difficult indeed to measure and weigh justly the pros and cons for speaking out or keeping silent. In such a dilemma, the conscientious doctor seeks his norm in the basic tenets of Christian ethics, which will help him to pick the right course. These norms, in fact, while they clearly affirm the obligation on the physician to preserve the professional secret, above all in the interest of the common good, do not concede to this an absolute value. For that very common good would suffer were the professional secret placed at the service of crime or injustice.[14]

In a parallel fashion, the Christian tradition has always understood that private goods become public goods in circumstances of common need.[15]

In the first category of circumstances, confidential information may be disclosed without the patient's consent in order to protect society as a whole. Thus, in many states, physicians are morally obligated to report gunshot or stab wounds, because this information is used to preserve the order and well-being of the community. In a similar fashion, hospitals are often legally required to report any cases of certain communicable or infectious diseases to public health authorities, because these pathogens are threats to the welfare of the public at large.

14. Ibid., 63.

15. "The seventh commandment forbids *theft*, that is, usurping another's property against the reasonable will of the owner. There is no theft if consent can be presumed or if refusal is contrary to reason and the universal destination of goods. This is the case in obvious and urgent necessity when the only way to provide for immediate, essential needs (food, shelter, clothing . . .) is to put at one's disposal and use the property of others." *Catechism of the Catholic Church*, no. 2408.

Second, confidentiality may be broken in order to protect an individual whose life may be at risk. In the 1976 *Tarasoff* case, for example, the state Supreme Court of California ruled that a health-care professional has a legal obligation to warn a person whose life has specifically been threatened by a patient.[16] Similar reasoning has been used to justify the actions of those physicians who break confidentiality in order to warn the partners of their HIV-positive patients. As the American College of Physicians and the Infectious Diseases put it: "The confidentiality of patients infected with HIV should be protected to the greatest extent possible, consistent with the duty to protect others and to protect public health."[17] Note, however, that the breaking of confidentiality should be an action of last resort undertaken only after the physician has tried to obtain permission from the patient to involve the third party.[18]

Finally, we should mention a moral dilemma involving confidentiality that often arises in the clinical encounter. Here, a patient tells his health-care providers that they are not to inform his family and loved ones about his medical condition. What should the physician or nurse do if the patient's spouse approaches him for information? Simply, since the common good is not endangered by the health-care provider's silence, he is not morally justified in breaking the confidentiality of his patient. Instead, he should encourage conversation between the patient and his spouse, and their family, so that he can tell them about his medical condition himself.

Health-Care Decisions

Medical Guidance and the Process of Informed Consent

Though the individual patient is ultimately responsible for his health-care decisions, he cannot make his health-care decisions alone. Most significantly, the patient needs expert medical guidance. Therefore, his health-care decisions have to be made in the context of his relationships

16. Supreme Court of California, *Tarasoff v. Regents of the University of California*, 131 Cal. Rptr. 14 (July 1, 1976).

17. American College of Physicians and the Infectious Diseases Society of America. Health and Public Policy Committee, "The Acquired Immunodeficiency Syndrome (AIDS) and Infection with the Human Immunodeficiency Virus (HIV)," *Ann Intern Med* 108 (1988): 460–469, 466.

18. For a Catholic perspective on the question of confidentiality and the HIV/AIDS patient, see Germain Kopaczynski, O.F.M. Conv., "Handling the Truth about HIV/AIDS," *Ethics Medics* 21.7 (1996): 3–4.

with his health-care providers, especially his physicians and his nurses. They are responsible for providing him with their medical expertise so that he can prudently choose the best therapeutic option available to him. They do this by employing the process of informed consent, which involves a personal exchange between the health-care professional and the patient where the physician or the nurse provides information so that the patient becomes properly "informed" of his health-care options.

In contemporary bioethics, informed consent is the name given to the process that allows a patient (or if he is incapacitated, his surrogate decision maker or proxy) to become an informed participant in all decision making regarding his health care.[19] It is grounded in both the moral and the legal right of the patient to direct what happens to him and in the moral and legal duty of the physician to involve the patient in his health care. As we noted above, each patient is ultimately responsible for making the health-care decisions that involve him, because he is the steward of the gifts of life and health that he has received from God. Thus, the patient has to prudently ask questions of his health-care providers so that he understands the health decisions that he has to make, and his health-care providers in turn need to obtain the patient's consent before performing any therapeutic procedures on him. Pope Pius XII affirmed this in a speech that explored the interests of the patient, when he declared: "The doctor has only that power over the patient which the latter gives to him, be it explicitly, or implicitly and tacitly."[20] This teaching was reiterated in the *Charter for Health Care Workers* promulgated by the Pontifical Council for Pastoral Assistance to Health Care Workers, when it explained: "So that the choice may be made with full awareness and freedom, the patient should be given a precise idea of his illness and the therapeutic possibilities, with the risks, the problems and the consequences that they entail. This means that the patient should be asked for an *informed consent.*"[21] The requirement for informed consent is grounded in

19. For an extensive discussion of informed consent, see Jessica W. Berg, Paul S. Appelbaum, Lisa S. Parker, and Charles W. Lidz, eds., *Informed Consent: Legal Theory and Clinical Practice,* 2nd ed. (New York: Oxford University Press, 2001). Also see the comprehensive and magisterial reference text by Fay A. Rozovsky, *Consent to Treatment: A Practical Guide,* 4th ed. (Frederick, Md.: Aspen Publishers, 2007).

20. Pope Pius XII, "Allocution to the First International Congress of Histopathology, September 13, 1952," in *The Human Body: Papal Teaching,* selected and arranged by the Monks of Solesmes, 194–208 (Boston: St. Paul Editions, 1960), 198.

21. Pontifical Council for Pastoral Assistance, *Charter for Health Care Workers* (Vatican City: Libreria Editrice Vaticana, 1995), no. 72 (original emphasis).

the moral duty to respect the human dignity of each patient. The *Ethical and Religious Directives* of the United States Conference of Catholic Bishops include the following: "The free and informed consent of the person or the person's surrogate is required for medical treatments and procedures, except in an emergency situation when consent cannot be obtained and there is no indication that the patient would refuse consent to the treatment."[22]

There are three basic moral and legal requirements for informed consent. First, all the relevant information has to be provided to the patient. This includes the purpose of the procedure, anticipated risks and benefits, reasonable alternatives to the proposed intervention, uncertainties, and hoped-for results. The *Ethical and Religious Directives* state the following: "Free and informed consent requires that the person or the person's surrogate receive all reasonable information about the essential nature of the proposed treatment and its benefits; its risks, side-effects, consequences and cost; and any reasonable and morally legitimate alternatives, including no treatment at all."[23] Information should never be withheld for the purpose of eliciting consent, and truthful answers have to be given in response to direct questions.

Some debate exists over the amount of information that has to be given to the patient for informed consent.[24] Some embrace the *reasonable physician standard:* what would a typical physician say about this intervention? This standard allows the physician to determine the appropriate amount of information that must be disclosed to the patient. However, most studies have shown that the typical physician tells the patient very little. There are others who insist upon the *reasonable patient standard:* what would the average patient need to know in order to be an informed participant in the decision? This standard focuses on the patient. In the United States, the landmark ruling by the U.S. Court of Appeals for the D.C. Circuit, *Canterbury v. Spence,* rejected the physician-based approach to informed con-

22. *Ethical and Religious Directives for Catholic Health Care Services,* 5th ed., no. 26.

23. Ibid., no. 27.

24. For discussion, see Timothy J. Paterick, Geoff V. Carson, Marjorie C. Allen, and Timothy E. Paterick, "Medical Informed Consent: General Considerations for Physicians," *Mayo Clin Proc* 83 (2008): 313–319; and Theodore R. LeBlang, Arnold J. Rosoff, and Christopher White, "Informed Consent to Medical and Surgical Treatment," in *Legal Medicine,* ed. S. Sandy Sanbar, Marvin H. Firestone, Fillmore Buckner, Allan Gibofsky, Theodore R. LeBlang, Jack W. Snyder, Cyril H. Wecht, and Miles J. Zaremski, 6th ed., 343–351 (Philadelphia: Mosby, 2004).

sent, ruling that the physician must disclose all that he should reasonably expect to be relevant to the patient's decision-making process.[25] Finally, there is the *subjective standard:* what would this patient need to know and understand in order to make an informed decision? This standard is the most challenging to incorporate into practice, since it requires tailoring information to each patient. In the end, the health-care professional should prudentially seek to provide as much information as needed on a case-by-case basis so that the patient can properly share in the health-care decision making.

Second, informed consent requires that comprehension of the information exist on the part of the patient. It is the responsibility of both the health-care professional, who has to make sure that the patient understands what has been told to him, and the patient, who has to make the best effort possible to understand his health-care providers. To this end, the *Ethical and Religious Directives* of the United States Conference of Catholic Bishops mandate that professional counseling should be made available to the patient to help him understand what is being explained: "Each person or the person's surrogate should have access to medical and moral information and counseling so as to be able to form his or her conscience. The free and informed health-care decision of the person or the person's surrogate is to be followed so long as it does not contradict Catholic principles."[26]

Third, freedom has to be present in order for informed consent to be legitimate. No coercion or undue influence should be exercised by the health-care professional. However, the health-care provider should still be able to speak with conviction regarding his medical opinion. Nonetheless, he should also explain clearly the reason for this opinion. The patient should also be free to seek a second or even a third opinion. Finally, to encourage voluntariness, the physician should make clear to the patient that he is participating in a decision-making process and is not merely signing a form. Only in this way will the dignity of both the physician and the patient be respected.

Moral Guidance and the Process of Informed Consent

In making decisions in bioethics, the patient needs guidance in two ways. As we discussed above, he needs guidance for his medical decisions,

25. *Canterbury v Spence,* 464 F. 2d at 786.
26. *Ethical and Religious Directives for Catholic Health Care Services,* 5th ed., no. 28.

and here he is guided by his health-care professional in the process of informed consent. However, the patient also needs moral guidance in order to form his conscience so that his decisions will be good ones. This responsibility falls on the patient himself, who needs to seek out pastoral assistance from informed and prudent individuals. For the Catholic patient, and also for a non-Catholic who seeks him out, a well-informed priest can play a unique role in the bioethical decision-making process, given his training as a moral and spiritual counselor.[27] Together, they can seek to choose a health-care option that promotes the overall well-being, both physical and spiritual, of the patient.

What is the role of the priest in bioethics? At the conclusion of his moral encyclical, *Veritatis splendor*, Blessed John Paul II exhorts his fellow bishops, as the pastors of the Church, to accomplish three tasks with regard to the moral life of the people entrusted into their care.[28] First, the Holy Father encourages his brother bishops to preach the moral truth of the Gospel. It is the bishops' common duty and their common grace "to teach the faithful the things that lead them to God, just as the Lord Jesus did with the young man in the Gospel" (cf. Mt 19:16ff). Next, the pope tells the pastors of the Church to be faithful to their sacramental duties. Through the proper administration of the sacraments, the bishops dispense to the Christian people the gifts of grace and sanctification that allow them to act well and to choose the authentic good. Finally, the Holy Father tells the bishops to pray for their people in order to "support believers in their efforts to be faithful to the demands of the faith and to live in accordance with the Gospel." More generally, in his role as a moral guide, and more specifically in his role as a bioethics counselor, these exhortations also apply to the priest who is ordained as a co-worker of the bishops.

First, it is not uncommon for a patient to approach a priest for counsel, simply because the patient lacks a moral framework to help him make the moral judgments that need to be made with regard to his health care. Often, the patient does not even know how to begin the moral reasoning process. The priest is called to assist the patient and help him to form his conscience so that he is able to do what is right and good. However, it is important to emphasize that when a patient comes to the priest, he ap-

27. For insightful discussion, see the essay by Mark J. Seitz, "The Role of the Priest in Bioethical Decision Making," *Natl Cathol Bioeth Q* 4 (2004): 681–689.
28. John Paul II, *Veritatis splendor*, no. 114.

proaches the priest precisely because the priest is a representative of the Church. Thus, the priest has the responsibility to help the patient to hear and to understand the truth of what the Church has to say about the bioethical issues of our day. He is a minister of the Word "in the name of Christ and in the name of the Church."[29] When the Church has not spoken on a particular question—and there are still many pressing bioethics questions that the Magisterium has not yet definitively decided—the priest has to explain this to the patient, presenting the arguments of Catholic moral theologians who are faithful to the Church's teachings. In doing so, the priest acts as a pastor, helping the patient form his conscience, so that he in turn can make the informed decision that he needs to make.

Next, it is not uncommon for patients struggling with the life and death questions common in clinical settings to face fear about their future and guilt about their past. These strong emotions can impair human action, both by clouding the intellect so that the patient cannot see the truth and by weakening his will so that he cannot desire the authentic good. In these situations, the priest is called to act as an instrument of God's grace and mercy as a minister of the sacraments. Through the administration of the sacraments, especially the three sacraments of penance, of anointing, and especially of the Eucharist, the priest can give the patient the graces of hope, to offset fear, of forgiveness, to alleviate guilt, and of charity, to alleviate self-centeredness, so that he can desire and act well.[30] Moreover, the sacraments can assist the patient to move away from those destructive patterns of behavior—those disordered habits—that prevent him from choosing the true, the good, and the beautiful. They can also help the patient strengthen the virtues of charity, faith, hope, and fortitude, among others, which he needs to confront the moral struggles that often accompany illness.

Finally, it is not uncommon for patients to come to the priest for prayer. They come to him because, by virtue of his vocation, the priest is

29. Congregation for the Clergy, *The Priest and the Third Christian Millennium: Teacher of the Word, Minister of the Sacraments, and Leader of the Community* (Vatican City: Libreria Editrice Vaticana, 1999), 14ff.

30. For an insightful commentary on the sacrament of anointing as a healing practice of the Christian community for the care of those who are vulnerable, see M. Therese Lysaught, "Vulnerability within the Body of Christ: Anointing of the Sick and Theological Anthropology," in *Health and Human Flourishing*, ed. Carol R. Taylor and Roberto Dell'Oro, 159–182 (Washington, D.C.: Georgetown University Press, 2007).

an intercessor. As the Letter to the Hebrews reveals: "Every high priest is selected among men and is appointed to represent them in matters related to God" (Heb 5:1). Thus, the priest has to pray for his people, especially those who are struggling with moral dilemmas. He has to intercede for them, asking God to give them the grace to choose and to act well.

Informed Consent and the Incompetent Patient

Informed consent presupposes that the patient is capable of interacting with his health-care provider. Often, however, the patient is incapable of making health-care decisions for himself. In these cases, health-care decisions for the incapacitated patient could rely upon an advance health-care directive, if one is available. Advance health-care directives (AHCDs) are a patient's instructions for health care that become effective if he ever loses his decision-making capacity. Otherwise, if no advance directive is available, health-care decisions could be made by a surrogate decision maker, also called a health-care proxy or a durable power of attorney for health care, who speaks on behalf of the patient. It is important to stress that every individual should think about his health-care decisions while he is still healthy and competent. He should then execute an AHCD and select a trustworthy health-care proxy in the eventuality that both will be needed for his future care.

Informed Consent and the Advance Health-Care Directive

There are three basic types of advance directives. First, there are oral directives. These are the patient's instructions for treatment expressed in conversation with his physician, his family, or his friends. Second, there are written directives that specify the patient's wishes regarding treatment in the event that he is afflicted with any of several medical conditions. Finally, there are proxy directives that designate a specific individual who would report the patient's wishes to his health-care providers, or, if no prior instructions were available, would make decisions for the patient.

Oral directives are the patient's wishes regarding future health-care treatment communicated to his physician, his family, or his friends. In certain states, oral directives to a patient's physician are valid only if they were given in the presence of witnesses.

Written advance directives come in two forms. First there is the *living will*. A living will is a legal document that usually designates specific treatments that the patient does or does not want to receive in case of terminal illness. It is called a "living will" because it takes effect while the patient is still living. Second, there is the *medical care directive*. This type of advance directive is broader than a living will because anyone capable of informed consent can make one. In contrast, many states often require that a patient be terminally or seriously ill in order to write a living will. Often, medical care directives are also more concrete and more complete than living wills, because they contain instructions about specific clinical scenarios that a patient may encounter. These include, among others, the patient's wishes in case he is either in a coma or in the persistent vegetative state (PVS) or suffers permanent brain damage that leaves him totally or permanently incoherent and confused all the time.

Most Catholic bioethicists agree that there are several problems with living wills and medical care directives.[31] First, they may force the patient to make a decision in the present moment about the details of a future medical condition that cannot be known in advance. Therefore, the patient is not capable of making a truly informed moral judgment. Next, advance directives cannot anticipate all the conditions that a patient may have to face. As such, there may be times when an advance directive simply would not apply, leaving the patient's health-care providers in the dark about his health-care wishes. Third, an advance directive may inappropriately constrain the actions of a health-care provider if it is ambiguously written. Consequently, many Catholic bioethicists suggest that a patient who writes an advance directive should simultaneously, as we will discuss below, designate a health-care proxy who will make health-care decisions in his place.

Finally, we should note that an individual physician may refuse to honor a patient's advance directive if the request is contrary to the physician's moral or religious beliefs. The physician should then assist the patient in obtaining a replacement for him. In addition, as the *Ethical and Religious Directives* of the United States Conference of Catholic Bishops make clear,

31. For discussion of some of the problems associated with living wills and advance directives, written from a Catholic perspective, see the pastoral letter of the Bishops of Maryland, "Care of the Sick and Dying," October 14, 1993, at http://mdcatholic .org/Care.htm; and the following essays: Robert Barry, O.P., "Writing a Pro-life Living Will," *Homiletic and Pastoral Review* 92 (1991): 8–17; John A. Leies, "Advance Directives," *Ethics Medics* 21.8 (1996): 1–2, and John S. Grimm, "Living Wills and Health Care Proxies," *Ethics Medics* 26.3 (2001): 3–4. Also, see the essay written from the secular perspective by S. M. Wolf et al., "Sources of Concern about the Patient Self-Determination Act," *N Engl J Med* 325 (1991): 1666–1671.

a Catholic hospital cannot follow a directive that conflicts with Church teaching: "In compliance with federal law, a Catholic health-care institution will make available to patients information about their rights, under the laws of their state, to make an advance directive for their medical treatment. The institution, however, will not honor an advance directive that is contrary to Catholic teaching. If the advance directive conflicts with Catholic teaching, an explanation should be provided as to why the directive cannot be honored."[32] A Catholic hospital should always seek to be faithful to its identity and its mission as an institution that promotes the Gospel of Life.

Informed Consent and the Health-Care Proxy

A health-care proxy, who is also called a durable power of attorney for health care or a surrogate decision maker, is an individual who speaks on behalf of the patient if the patient is incapacitated. This individual could be either a person designated by the person as his health-care proxy or one designated by law. Individual states recognize a hierarchy of family relationships in determining which family member should speak for the patient, though generally all close family members and significant others are involved in a discussion that tries to seek a consensus. This hierarchy is typically the following: the patient's spouse, the adult children of the patient, the parents of the patient, the adult siblings of the patient, a close friend, and then the patient's physician.

The role of the surrogate decision maker is to make decisions on behalf of the incompetent patient.[33] He can do this in two ways. First, he could make choices about treatment decisions based on what he believes the incapacitated person would choose, given his values and preferences. This is the *substituted judgment* standard.[34] If this is not possible, then the surrogate decision maker should determine what is best for the patient's overall good by asking what most reasonable persons would want. This is the *best-interests* standard.[35]

32. *Ethical and Religious Directives for Catholic Health Care Services*, 5th ed., no. 24.

33. For a discussion of surrogate decision making written from the Catholic perspective, see William E. May, "Making Health Care Decisions for Others," *Ethics Medics* 22.6 (1997): 1–3.

34. For further discussion, see Mark R. Tonelli, "Substituted Judgment in Medical Practice: Evidentiary Standards on a Sliding Scale," *J Law Med Ethics* 25 (1997): 22–29.

35. For further discussion, see Norman L. Cantor, "The Bane of Surrogate Decision-Making: Defining the Best Interests of Never-Competent Persons," *J Leg Med* 26 (2005): 155–205.

Ideally, as we noted above, a patient should have both a written directive and a proxy directive or durable power of attorney that designates a particular individual who will act as a health-care proxy. Both complement each other. The written directive would be a guide to assist the proxy in making decisions, and the proxy would be available to clarify any ambiguities in the written directive based upon his familiarity with the moral convictions and wishes of the patient.

Finally, we should note that an individual physician may refuse to honor a patient's or his surrogate's request if the request is contrary to the physician's moral or religious beliefs. As we will discuss in chapter 8, however, health-care providers have an obligation to inform potential patients about their moral objections to certain medical procedures so that these individuals can make a free and informed choice before they enter into the physician-patient relationship.

Exceptions to Informed Consent

There are three major situations when medical intervention without informed consent from a competent patient is morally justifiable. A possible fourth situation involving therapeutic privilege is controversial.

First, there are times when legal or military directives require health-care interventions. Examples include mandatory immunizations for a nation's citizens during a public health crisis, or a military order requiring the use of drugs to protect the health of the armed forces. Here the medical interventions are necessary to protect the common good.

Second, informed consent is not required during medical emergencies. In these situations, typically found in hospital emergency rooms and at scenes of accidents or sudden illness, there is often no time to discuss therapeutic options with the patient or his family in order to obtain consent. The *Ethical and Religious Directives* of the United States Conference of Catholic Bishops state the following: "The free and informed consent of the person or the person's surrogate is required for medical treatments and procedures, except in an emergency situation when consent cannot be obtained and there is no indication that the patient would refuse consent to the treatment."[36] Here the health-care providers can presume consent in order to promote the good of the patient.

Third, there are situations when patients with decision-making capacity waive their prerogative to give informed consent. For a variety of rea-

36. *Ethical and Religious Directives for Catholic Health Care Services,* 5th ed., no. 26.

sons, they may choose not to be informed of their diagnosis, the prognosis, or the risks involved in their health care. They might not even want to make any decisions, choosing to leave all decision making in the hands of either a loved one or a physician. Though this is morally permissible, we should point out that the physician is not required to accept the entire burden that accompanies a patient's waiver of informed consent. He may choose to designate a proxy to share in the health-care decision making.

Finally, there are situations when physicians and family members wish to withhold information, especially an unfavorable medical diagnosis, from the patient, because they fear that it would devastate the individual. Here, medical care is provided without the patient's informed consent. This appeal to therapeutic privilege is problematic, for at least three reasons. First, it often does not work. Patients soon realize that they are not getting better and that all is not well. They also begin to sense that they do not have the whole truth about their medical conditions. Second, it forces the patient's health-care providers to live out a lie. They continuously have to conceal the truth from the sick individual. This undermines the fiduciary relationship between the patient and his doctors and nurses. Finally, it denies the patient the opportunity to prepare for death. The time leading up to death is an especially important and often grace-filled moment in the life of the human being. It is a final opportunity for him to resolve any difficulties he may have with his loved ones, and, more significantly, with his Creator. For these reasons, the appeal to therapeutic privilege is rarely justifiable. Instead, it is preferable to tell the patient the truth about his medical condition and then to help him in charity to carry the cross of this burden. As the *Charter for Health Care Workers* puts it:

"There is a need to establish a relationship of trust, receptivity and dialogue with the patient. . . . In this relationship, the prospect of death is not presented as inescapable, and it loses its anguishing power: the patient does not feel isolated and condemned to death. When the truth is presented to him in this way he is not left without hope, because it makes him feel alive in relationship of sharing and communion. He is not alone with his illness: he feels truly understood, and he is at peace with himself and with others. He is himself as a person. His life, despite everything, has meaning, and dying unfolds with optimistic and transcendent meaning."[37]

37. Pontifical Council for Pastoral Assistance, *Charter for Health Care Workers*, nos. 126–127.

For the Christian, as it is with all human beings, death remains a tragedy. However, the Christian is called to face it with hope, knowing that it is a horror that has been redeemed by the passion, death, and resurrection of Jesus Christ our Lord.

Highlighting the Role of Virtue in Bioethics

The moral virtue of truth, a secondary virtue of the cardinal virtue of justice according to St. Thomas Aquinas,[38] which disposes the acting person to tell the truth when he ought and as he ought, is a virtue that should hold pride of place during the clinical encounter.[39] Truth telling undergirds the fiduciary relationship between a patient and his health-care provider. Without reciprocal honesty, physicians would be unable to make an accurate diagnosis, and patients would be unable to make an informed decision regarding their health care. Thus, physicians should be willing to speak truthfully to their patients even if they are concerned that the truth, especially the truth of a poor prognosis, would be hard for their patients to accept. Interestingly, two empirical studies, separated by twenty years, have revealed that a complete reversal of professional attitudes toward truth telling, in the context of a cancer diagnosis, has happened. In 1961, 90 percent of a sample of 219 U.S. physicians reported that they would *not* disclose a diagnosis of cancer to the patient,[40] while in 1979, 97 percent of a sample of 264 doctors reported that they would.[41] It is praiseworthy that physicians are more willing to speak the truth to their patients.

Like all other human acts, however, an act of truth telling needs to be governed by the virtue of prudence. In other words, the physician should also be cautious with the truth. When surveyed, a considerable number

38. St. Thomas Aquinas, *ST,* IIa-IIae, 109.3.

39. For a theological commentary on the role of the virtue of truth in the clinical encounter, see Fausto B. Gomez, O.P., "Truth Telling: Bioethical Perspective," *Philippiniana Sacra* 33 (1998): 217–238.

40. Donald Oken, "What to Tell Cancer Patients: A Study of Medical Attitudes," *JAMA* 175 (1961): 1120–1128.

41. Dennis H. Novack, Robin Plumer, Raymond L. Smith, Herbert Ochitill, Gary R. Morrow, and John M. Bennett, "Changes in Physicians' Attitudes toward Telling the Cancer Patient," *JAMA* 241 (1979): 897–900. For commentary, see the special issue of the journal of the New York Academy of Sciences: A. Surbone and M. Zwitter, eds., *Communication with the Cancer Patient: Information and Truth, Ann N Y Acad Sci* 809 (1997): 1–540.

of patients express significant reservations about their doctors being completely frank with them regarding their illness.[42] One study revealed that
15 percent of 80 cancer patients queried desired to have minimal detail
about their illness.[43] They simply do not want to know everything about
their condition, particularly if that information is pessimistic or highly threatening. Thus, physicians should prudentially discern the proper
time, the proper place, and the proper manner for their difficult conversations with their patients. They should even be willing to refrain from
speaking if their patients indicate that they do not want to know the
truth. There are also books that provide suggestions on how one should
convey bad news to another.[44] Nonetheless, the virtuous physician cannot lie. He would need to learn how to prudentially live both the virtue
of truth and the virtue of mercy, the heartfelt sympathy for another's distress, impelling us to succor him if we can.[45] Indeed, a virtuous physician
would not be able to be authentically truthful if he was not simultaneously merciful, since he would not be able to speak the truth as he ought.
In the end, as we discussed in chapter 1, the virtues are interconnected
through the virtue of prudence, because there is an essential dependence
of one virtue upon another, such that one cannot exist without the others
in the prudent individual.

42. Ami Shattner, "What Do Patients Really Want To Know?" *QJM* 95 (2002): 135–136.
43. Phyllis N. Butow et al., "The Dynamics Of Change: Cancer Patients' Preferences
For Information, Involvement, And Support," *Ann Oncol* 8 (1997): 857–863.
44. Robert Buckman, *How to Break Bad News: A Guide for Health Care Professionals* (Baltimore: Johns Hopkins University Press, 1992).
45. St. Thomas Aquinas, *ST*, IIa-IIae, 30.1.

CHAPTER FIVE

Bioethics at the End of Life

Since its publication in two medical journals in the United States in 2005, the Groningen Protocol developed in the Netherlands for the killing of a newborn infant who, in the judgment of his physicians, is experiencing unbearable suffering, has generated much controversy.[1] The protocol has five criteria: First, the suffering of the child must be so hopeless and severe that the newborn has no prospects of a future. Second, the suffering of the child must be beyond the remedy of medicine. Third, the parents of the child must give their consent to the deliberate ending of life. Fourth, an independent doctor not involved in the child's medical care must confirm the original diagnosis and prognosis of unbearable suffering. Finally, euthanasia must be performed in accordance with accepted medical practice. The criteria were developed after the Groningen Committee considered twenty-two instances of life-ending interventions, all involving newborn infants with very severe forms of spina bifida, a developmental defect of the spine, that were reported to the Dutch authorities between 1997 and 2004. In these cases and others like them, the authors of the Groningen Protocol concluded that parents and physicians "may concur that death would be more humane than continued life."[2] How are we to evaluate the moral issues raised by Groningen and similar protocols that advocate the so-called mercy killing of patients, even the youngest of patients?

---

1. Eduard Verhagen and Pieter J. J. Sauer, "The Groningen Protocol: Euthanasia in Severely Ill Newborn," *N Engl J Med.* 352 (2005): 959–962; and Eduard Verhagen and Pieter J. J. Sauer, "End-of-Life Decisions in Newborns: An Approach from the Netherlands," *Pediatrics* 116 (2005): 736–739. For commentary, see the essay by Hilde Lindemann and Marian Verkerk, "Ending the Life of a Newborn: The Groningen Protocol," *Hastings Cent Rep* 38 (2008): 42–51; and the insightful exchange of letters to the editor generated by this essay: "Are Their Babies Different from Ours? Dutch Culture and the Groningen Protocol," *Hastings Cent Rep* 38 (2008): 4–8.

2. Verhagen and Sauer, "The Groningen Protocol," 961.

In this chapter, which deals with the moral issues that surround death and the dying process, I begin with a theological account of death. How should a Christian understand death? How should he respond to death? How should he prepare for death? Next, I turn to the two most common scenarios in the clinical setting that raise troubling moral questions at the end of life. The first deals with the management of intense pain that risks hastening the patient's death, while the second deals with the refusal or the discontinuation of medical treatment. I then consider the moral debate surrounding euthanasia and physician-assisted suicide: may a clinician choose to end the life or aid in the ending of a life of a dying or suffering patient? Next, I deal with the treatment of those patients who are incapacitated by severe disorders of consciousness. As Christians, how are we to care for these individuals in either the persistent vegetative state (PVS) or the minimally conscious state (MCS)? May we deny them food and water? Finally, I end with a brief discussion of the clinician's role in end-of-life decisions.

The Christian Meaning of Death

My experience as a hospital chaplain who has also served on ethics consultations in different health-care contexts has taught me that many Catholics, patients and their family members alike, unnecessarily struggle with many of the moral issues raised at life's end because they fear that death is the mere extinction of life, the annihilation of the human person. They have forgotten, or they have never learned, of the hope that is given to us in Jesus Christ. Therefore, it is important that we begin our discussion of the bioethics at the end of life with a brief summary of a Christian theology of death.[3]

As the Gospel reveals, the Christian God is a god not of death but of the living (cf. Lk 29:38). Thus, the Christian faith affirms life even when life is overshadowed by suffering and by death. It can do this because in truth, death is not the end of life. Though death is a natural event—every human being by nature is mortal (cf. Heb 9:27)—sacred Scripture reveals that we were not destined to die (cf. Rom 6:23; 1 Cor 15:21). God's origi-

---

3. For a magisterial and comprehensive theology of death, see Joseph Ratzinger, *Eschatology: Death and Eternal Life*, trans. Michael Waldstein and Aidan Nichols, O.P. (Washington, D.C.: The Catholic University of America Press, 1988), 69–103; Also, see *Catechism of the Catholic Church*, nos. 1005–1020.

nal intention was to give us the grace of immortality so that we could live forever. Death therefore is, and always will be, a tragedy. It is contrary to the plans of the Creator and entered the world as a consequence of sin: "Therefore, just as through one person sin entered the world, and through sin, death, and thus death came to all, inasmuch as all sinned" (Rom 5:12). Thus, we should not be surprised when patients facing their mortality are struck by the injustice of death. It was not supposed to be so.

Death, however, is not the end of the story, because the obedience of Jesus has transformed the curse of death into a blessing (cf. Rom 5:19–21). The Lord's death destroyed not only the one who holds the power of death (cf. Heb 2:14) but also death itself (cf. 2 Tm 1:10). Since death could not hold Him (cf. Acts 2:24), Christ is now the Lord both of the dead and of the living (cf. Rom 14:9). Hence, in light of the Christ's victory over death, death can now be understood as gain (cf. Phil 1:21), as being at home with the Lord (cf. 2 Cor 5:8), as sleep (cf. Jn 11:11), and as a new birth into eternal life (cf. Jn 3:3–8). Death is not the extinction of life: "For those who die in Christ's grace it is a participation in the death of the Lord, so that they can also share his Resurrection."[4]

To sum up, from the perspective of the Gospel, death is much more than the mere separation of the soul from the body. As the *Catechism of the Catholic Church* teaches, in death, God calls man to Himself.[5] This truth is evident in the Church's prayer of commendation at the moment of death:

Go forth, Christian soul, from this world in the name of God the almighty Father, who created you, in the name of Jesus Christ, Son of the living God, who suffered for you, in the name of the Holy Spirit, who was poured out upon you, go forth, faithful Christian. May you live in peace this day, may your home be with God in Zion, with Mary, the virgin Mother of God, with Joseph, and all the angels and saints.[6]

Accordingly, Christians should approach death as a long-awaited encounter with the Lord: in life, we hear His voice, and now at death, we have a chance to see His face. Not surprisingly, the Church urges us to prepare for the hour of our death. Spiritual writers throughout the ages have unanimously taught that the only adequate preparation for death is a vir-

4. *Catechism of the Catholic Church*, no. 1006.

5. Cf. ibid., no. 1011.

6. Pastoral Care of the Sick: Rites of Anointing and Viaticum, no. 220, in *The Rites of the Catholic Church*, vol. 1 (Collegeville, Minn.: Liturgical Press, 1990), 866.

tuous life. This is the work of a lifetime. However, the dying process can often be a graced moment at life's end that allows an individual to more properly face his mortality. Often, it can be a time of healing and reconciliation, a gift from God.[7] Catholic bioethicists working at the end of life need to remember that as moral theologians who are called to help others seek beatitude, they have an important role to play as patients prepare for their death, not only by addressing their moral concerns at life's end, but also by strengthening their hope for immortality.

Preparing for Death

Managing Pain at the End of Life

To prepare for their death, patients need to confront the fears that accompany the dying process. These are legion. However, my pastoral experience has taught me that patients often experience two fundamental fears at life's end that raise bioethical questions. First, they fear the unbearable pain that may plague their dying. Next, they fear a prolonged dying process unnecessarily extended by technological and medical intervention. Catholic bioethicists need to reassure patients that there are virtuous approaches that will help them face and overcome these fears so that they may properly prepare for their death. The *Ethical and Religious Directives* of the United States Conference of Catholic Bishops state: "Catholic health care institutions offering care to persons in danger of death from illness, accident, advanced age, or similar condition should provide them with appropriate opportunities to prepare for death. . . . They should be provided the spiritual support as well as the opportunity to receive the sacraments in order to prepare well for death."[8]

---

7. Ira Byock cites anecdotal evidence suggesting that patients can emerge from the suffering at life's end with a sense of peace and wellness, describing the end of their lives as a time of opportunity for personal growth. See his paper, "The Nature of Suffering and the Nature of Opportunity at the End of Life," *Clin Geriatr Med* 12 (1996): 237–252; and the book by Jana Staton, Roger W. Shuy, and Ira Byock: *A Few Months to Live: Different Paths to Life's End* (Washington, D.C.: Georgetown University Press, 2001). For a now classic study of the dying process that proposes that terminally ill individuals go though five stages of grief, see Elisabeth Kubler-Ross, *On Death and Dying* (New York: Scribner, 1969), and the accompanying volume, *Questions & Answers on Death and Dying* (New York: Touchstone, 1974). Working at the Grief Recovery Institute, Russell Friedman and John W. James have contested the Kubler-Ross Model. See their essay, "The Myth of the Stages of Dying, Death and Grief," *Skeptic* 14 (2008): 37–41.

8. *Ethical and Religious Directives for Catholic Health Care Services*, 5th ed., no. 55.

When cure is not possible, which often happens at life's end, the relief of suffering and the management of pain is the cardinal goal of medicine. Professionally, this is the primary concern of physicians who specialize in palliative medicine, which is the study and management of patients with active, progressive, far-advanced disease, for whom the prognosis is limited and the focus of care is the quality of life.[9] One important—maybe even the most important—challenge for physicians with patients at life's end is to properly manage their pain and to alleviate their fear that their death will be torturous. Here, treatment with analgesic drugs, which are drugs that relieve pain, remains the treatment of choice. These powerful drugs, many of which are opioids that act like the narcotic morphine, can effectively manage pain. However, their use raises moral questions because the administration of these drugs could also hasten death. Can a doctor or a nurse prescribe these medications even if he knows that they could shorten the life of his patients? (Incidentally, there is now data that suggests that the use of opioids and sedatives for various medical indications during a patient's last days of life is not associated with shortened survival.)[10]

Appealing to the principle of double effect, the Catholic moral tradition has proposed that the use of analgesic drugs is morally justifiable even if it could hasten the death of the patient, as long as the patient and his doctor intend only the relief of pain. The hastening of the death of the patient, if it occurs, is only an indirect outcome, a foreseen but unintended side effect, of their act. Recall that a person's intentions are important for judging the morality of his actions because our intentions re-

9. Geoffrey Hanks, Nathan I. Cherny, Nicholas A. Christakis, Marie Fallon, Stein Kaasa, and Russell K. Portenoy, eds., *Oxford Textbook of Palliative Medicine* 4th ed. (Oxford: Oxford University Press, 2009). Significantly, the World Health Organization defines palliative care to also include the spiritual care of patients who are struggling with psychological, social, and religious burdens: World Health Organization: Cancer Pain Relief and Palliative Care: Report of the WHO Expert Committee, Technical Report Series 804 (Geneva: World Health Organization, 1990).

10. For details, see Nigel Sykes and Andrew Thorns, "Sedative Use in the Last Week of Life and the Implications for End-of-Life Decision Making," *Arch Intern Med* 163 (2003): 341–344; and the review by the same authors, "The Use of Opioids and Sedatives at the End of Life," *Lancet Oncol* 4 (2003): 312–318. Also see the discussion by Robert G. Twycross, "Where There Is Hope, There Is Life: A View from the Hospice," in *Euthanasia Examined: Ethical, Clinical, and Legal Perspectives,* ed. John Keown, 141–168 (Cambridge: Cambridge University Press, 1995). For the teaching of the Catholic Church, see *Catechism of the Catholic Church,* no. 2279.

flect our choices, and it is our choices as acts of our wills that make us either good or evil individuals. Thus, in its *Declaration on Euthanasia*, the Congregation for the Doctrine of the Faith, in making the distinction between aggressive palliative care and euthanasia, which is the mercy killing of a patient, concludes that in the former case, "death is no way intended or sought even if the risk of it is reasonably taken; the intention is simply to relieve pain effectively, using for this purpose painkillers available for medicine."[11] Significantly, the importance of using the moral distinction between intending death and intending the relief of pain to distinguish physician-assisted suicide from palliative care was also affirmed by the United States Supreme Court in its landmark case *Washington v. Glucksberg*.[12] Hence, no patient should have to endure unwanted pain, and no doctors and nurses seeking only to relieve the severe pain of their patients should fear moral or legal censure when they administer analgesics, even if this leads to terminal sedation, a state of deep sleep that precedes death.[13] This is not killing. Nevertheless, the Catholic tradition does affirm that it is good for the patient if he is fully conscious at life's end, because he can then properly prepare for and meet death. Thus, a patient should not be deprived of consciousness unless there is a compelling reason to do so. The *Ethical and Religious Directives* of the United States Conference of Catholic Bishops mandate the following: "Patients should be kept as free of pain as possible so that they may die comfortably and with dignity, and in the place where they wish to die. Since a person has a right to prepare for his or her death while fully conscious, he or she should not be deprived of consciousness without a compelling reason."[14]

Finally, the following question often arises: how can one distinguish an intention to relieve the severe pain of a patient from an intention to bring about the death of that patient? Intentions are manifested in intel-

11. Congregation for the Doctrine of the Faith, *Declaration on Euthanasia*, no. III.

12. U.S. 702 (1997). Also see *Vacco v. Quill*, 521 U.S. 793 (1997).

13. For a review of the recent medical literature concerning palliative sedation and suffering, see Patricia Claessens, Johna Menten, Paul Schotsmans, and Bert Broeckaert, "Palliative Sedation: A Review of the Research Literature," *J Pain Symptom Manage* 36 (2008): 310–333; and Jorge H. Eisenchlas, "Palliative Sedation," *Curr Opin Support Palliat Care* 1 (2007): 207–212. For a discussion of the ethics of palliative sedation from within the tradition of secular bioethics, see National Ethics Committee, Veterans Health Administration, "The Ethics of Palliative Sedation as a Therapy of Last Resort," *Am J Hosp Palliat Care* 23 (2006): 483–491.

14. *Ethical and Religious Directives for Catholic Health Care Services*, 5th ed., no. 61.

ligible actions. Did the nurse administer the minimum dose of narcotic to alleviate pain? Did he use the opioid as a treatment of last resort? All of these actions would indicate that the nurse does not intend the death of the patient. On the other hand, we could—and should—question the actions of a physician who prescribes ten times the recommended dose of an opioid to a dying patient even if he claims that he is simply seeking to alleviate the pain of his patient. He is clearly doing more than this.[15]

Refusing Medical Treatment at the End of Life

At life's end, another moral question that is frequently raised involves the refusal and discontinuation of medical treatment. Often, patients think that they need to accept any and all medical treatments that may become available to them, since life is a great good, a gift from God. Thus, they fear that their deaths will become a protracted and agonizing process dictated by physicians and their machines. This does not have to be the case.

As we discussed above, life and health are precious gifts entrusted to each one of us by God. Thus, we each have an obligation to care for them, taking into account the needs of others and the common good.[16] Consequently, we are morally obligated to use all ordinary means to preserve our lives and our health, including food, drink, housing, and health care. Thus, the *Ethical and Religious Directives* of the United States Conference of Catholic Bishops state: "A person has a moral obligation to use ordinary or proportionate means of preserving his or her life."[17] However, life is not an absolute good.[18] We will all die. A time will inevitably come when we should simply accept our inability to impede death. In recognition of this truth, the Catholic tradition teaches that we are not morally obligated to use extraordinary means to maintain our lives.[19] This is the principle of elective extraordinary means. Pope Pius XII gave magisterial expression to this principle when he taught:

15. For a comprehensive discussion of the intelligibility of human actions, see Charles R. Pinches, *Theology and Action: After Theory in Christian Ethics* (Grand Rapids, Mich.: William B. Eerdmans, 2002), 111–166.

16. Cf. *Catechism of the Catholic Church*, no. 2288.

17. *Ethical and Religious Directives for Catholic Health Care Services*, 5th ed., no. 56.

18. *Catechism of the Catholic Church*, no. 2289.

19. For commentary on the Catholic Church's teaching on the prolongation of human life, see Kevin O'Rourke, O.P., "Prolonging Life: A Traditional Interpretation," *Linacre Q* 58 (1991): 12–26; and Michael Panicola, "Catholic Teaching on Prolonging Life: Setting the Record Straight," *Hastings Cent Rep* 31 (2001): 14–25.

Normally, one is held to use only ordinary means—according to the circumstances of persons, places, times and cultures—that is to say, means that do not involve any grave burden for oneself or another. A more strict obligation would be too burdensome for most people and would render the attainment of the higher, more important good too difficult. Life, health, all temporal activities are in fact subordinated to spiritual ends. On the other hand, one is not forbidden to take more than the strictly necessary steps to preserve life and health, as long as one does not fail in some more serious duty.[20]

Note that the distinction between ordinary and extraordinary means is a *moral* and not a medical one. In other words, to say that a procedure constitutes extraordinary means is not to say that it is an experimental procedure that is not commonly used in medical practice. Rather, to say that a procedure constitutes extraordinary means is to say that it constitutes an excessive burden to the patient.[21] This is a moral judgment made by the patient or his designated proxy. It is the patient who determines if a particular medical procedure is beneficial and not unreasonably burdensome to him. He does this by considering its hope for benefit as well as the physical, psychological, and financial costs it will place on him and/or his family. For instance, a patient could decide that a particular surgical procedure is unreasonably burdensome because it is too invasive, without any proportionate hope of cure. He could also decide that the same procedure is burdensome because it would place his family in serious long-term financial debt, again without any proportionate hope of a cure. For any of these and similar reasons, he could judge that the procedure constitutes extraordinary means, and thus, would be morally nonobligatory. Thus, distinguishing extraordinary from ordinary means has to be done on a case-by-case basis. One procedure could be ordinary means for one

20. Pius XII, "The Prolongation of Life, November 24, 1957," *The Pope Speaks* 4 (1958): 393–398; 395–396.

21. In an insightful essay that summarizes the history of the extraordinary-ordinary distinction in the Catholic moral tradition, Kevin Wildes, S.J., discusses five criteria of extraordinary means that have been used by Catholic moralists to define the burden of a medical intervention: impossibility, excessive effort, pain, expense, and fear and repugnance (*vehemens horror*). See his paper, "Ordinary and Extraordinary Means and the Quality of Life," *Theological Studies* 57 (1996): 500–512. Also see the essay by Donald E. Henke, "A History of Ordinary and Extraordinary Means," *Natl Cathol Bioeth Q* 5 (2005): 555–574. For a thoughtful response to Wildes, see Gilbert Meilaender, "*Question Disputata:* Ordinary and Extraordinary Treatments: When Does Quality of Life Count?" *Theological Studies* 58 (1997): 527–531. Meilaender argues that quality-of-life judgments are inappropriate when surrogates are making decisions for incapacitated patients.

individual but extraordinary for another because of different personal circumstances. The *Ethical and Religious Directives* of the United States Conference of Catholic Bishops state: "A person may forgo extraordinary or disproportionate means of preserving life. Disproportionate means are those that in the patient's judgment do not offer a reasonable hope of benefit or entail an excessive burden, or impose excessive expense on the family or the community."[22] Finally, we should point out that for the Catholic moral tradition, all means are considered ordinary means if the patient has not been properly reconciled with God. Everything should be done to ensure that no patient dies with mortal sin on his soul.

In light of our discussion, therefore, it follows that a patient may refuse any or all treatment, or discontinue any treatment, once he judges that the medical intervention constitutes extraordinary care, and thus is morally optional. Recall that it is the responsibility of the patient or his proxy to make this and all other moral judgments at life's end. As such, concluding that a particular medical treatment constitutes extraordinary care is a subjective decision made on objective grounds. For instance, a terminally ill patient whose daughter is getting married could choose to go on a ventilator until sometime after her child's wedding day. Given her desire to see her daughter exchange marriage vows, the patient judges that the ventilator is not burdensome because it sustains the hope that she will be able to see her daughter's wedding. Sometime after the wedding, however, she could then decide that the ventilator is now burdensome because it is very uncomfortable and prevents her from speaking to her family members. Thus, she could reasonably conclude that the ventilator now constitutes extraordinary means. It can now be discontinued without moral condemnation to allow her to say a few important things to her loved ones before she dies.

What is important is that a patient or his proxy must make a moral judgment regarding the quality of the treatment and *not* the quality of the patient's life. For example, consider the following clinical scenario: An elderly patient with advanced Alzheimer's disease develops pneumonia. Should an antibiotic regimen be administered that can effectively clear the infection? There are some who would argue that the antibiotic treatment constitutes extraordinary means because it will not reverse the dementia. It gives the patient no reasonable hope of cure, and thus, should be morally optional. They would probably go on to argue that the patient should be allowed to die from the pneumonia.

22. *Ethical and Religious Directives for Catholic Health Care Services*, 5th ed., no. 57.

This argument, however, is flawed. It is a medical fact that antibiotics are not used to cure Alzheimer's. They are used to fight opportunistic infections. Thus, those who would judge that the antibiotic constitutes extraordinary means would have to provide reasonable reasons for the burden of the treatment itself: Would the antibiotic lead to medical complications? Would it be too expensive for the patient or his family? Without a reason of this type, the antibiotic treatment would remain ordinary means, because it has a reasonable chance of saving the patient's life by clearing the infection. Thus, it would be morally obligatory to provide the antibiotic. In fact, without a reason for judging the treatment burdensome, withholding the antibiotic could constitute an act of omission that directly leads to the death of the patient. In other words, in this scenario, the act of withholding the antibiotic would necessarily include the intention of killing the patient by an act of omission. This type of act would be morally reprehensible. At this point, however, I should note that when a patient is in the active process of dying, he and his caregivers may decide that the potential benefit of the antibiotic treatment—a few infectious-free days of life—may not justify the burden of medical care involved. They may then reasonably conclude that the medical intervention is extraordinary and thus morally optional. This scenario often presents itself during hospice care.

Finally, we should acknowledge that a patient's judgment of extraordinary means has to be reasonable and intelligible to reasonable persons. For example, a diabetic could conclude that his daily injections of insulin are burdensome because they are inconvenient. He could, therefore, argue that he should be allowed to discontinue them. However, this is not reasonable. Daily injections of insulin have become commonplace in the lives of millions of diabetics, and the inconvenience and pain is trivial given the need for these injections to preserve the patient's life. This would be different if the patient had a pathological fear—a vehement repugnance, in Latin, *vehemens horror*—of needles or injections. Here he could reasonably argue that given his particular situation, daily injections of insulin constitute extraordinary means. He could then refuse the injections, though given what is at stake, there would be a moral obligation on the patient's part to honestly seek alternative therapeutic interventions, or to find counseling to overcome his fear. Again, prudent moral choices depend on the unique circumstances of each patient.

Requesting a Do-Not-Resuscitate (DNR) Order

Before 1960, there was little that a physician could do for a patient who suffered a sudden cardiac arrest. In that year, however, a medical team at Johns Hopkins University described the first of now many cardiopulmonary resuscitation (CPR) techniques that can be used to restore circulation and respiration in patients who have suffered a heart attack.[23] Today, CPR is routinely used as the standard of care in emergency scenarios, both in the hospital and elsewhere.

As with any other medical procedure, however, a patient or his proxy may determine that CPR would constitute extraordinary means that is burdensome to the patient. For instance, in several clinical circumstances, including septic shock, acute stroke, metastatic cancer, and severe pneumonia, CPR has been shown to have zero probability of success.[24] In these situations—and there are many other possible scenarios where studies have shown that survival from CPR is extremely limited—the patient could request that his physician sign a do-not-resuscitate (DNR) order to withhold any efforts to resuscitate him in the event of a respiratory or cardiac arrest. In effect, the patient is asking that nothing heroic be done to unduly prolong his life. Here, the patient does not directly will his death. Rather, he declines any future attempt to resuscitate him—attempts at treatment that he judges to be extraordinary means—so that he may be allowed to die in peace. Understood in this way, a DNR order is really a specific type of advance health-care directive, which, as we discussed in chapter 4, is a patient's instructions for health care that will become effective if he ever loses his decision-making capacity.

Finally, all reasonable efforts should be made to provide palliative care to patients who have requested a DNR order.[25] Patients should also be encouraged to properly prepare for death. Patients who are Catholics

23. W. B. Kouwenhoven, James R. Jude, and G. Guy Knickerbocker, "Closed-Chest Cardiac Massage," *JAMA* 173 (1960): 1064–1067.

24. For details and discussion, see Susanna E. Bedell, Thomas L. Delbanco, E. Francis Cook, and Franklin H. Epstein, "Survival after Cardiopulmonary Resuscitation in the Hospital," in *Bioethics: An Introduction to the History, Methods, and Practice* 1st ed., ed. Nancy S. Jecker, Albert R. Jonsen, and Robert A. Pearlman, 202–217 (New York: Jones & Bartlett Publishers, 1997).

25. Often, the completion of a DNR order is the first end-of-life decision made in the clinical setting. As studies of end-of-life practice patterns have shown, the writing of a DNR order is a significant milestone at life's end that helps clinicians realize that their patient is dying. It signals the transition from aggressive curative care to palliative

should be given every opportunity to receive the sacraments and the last rites and be reconciled to God and to their neighbor.

Euthanasia and Physician-Assisted Suicide: The Teaching of the Catholic Church

Euthanasia, which literally means "good death," and is also called mercy killing, is defined by the Congregation for the Doctrine of the Faith as follows: "An action or an omission which of itself or by intention causes death, in order that all suffering may in this way be eliminated."[26] A clinician could intentionally kill a patient by an act of commission such as injecting a poison, or by an act of omission such as withholding essential medication. In either case, what is important is that in both scenarios, the doctor or the nurse intentionally seeks to end the life of the patient. This distinguishes acts of euthanasia from those acts of removing or withholding extraordinary means that were discussed above. Euthanasia may be voluntary, nonvoluntary, or involuntary. It is voluntary when a competent patient requests it; it is nonvoluntary when it is performed on a patient who cannot request it, including infants and incompetent patients; and it is involuntary when it is carried out on a competent patient who does not want it. Physician-assisted suicide is one form of voluntary euthanasia, in which a physician intentionally seeks to help another person, usually a patient suffering from a terminal or a chronically debilitating disease, to take his own life, usually by providing him with a lethal dose of a drug that he can use to kill himself. In this scenario, the physician is cooperating with the patient who seeks his own death.

At the time of this writing, some form of euthanasia or physician-

care. However, other work has also revealed that clinicians often prioritized the needs of other patients over those who are dying, especially if the latter have a DNR order in place. Bioethicists need to remind health-care professionals that a DNR is not an abbreviation for "do not respond." For details and discussion, see Joseph J. Fins, *A Palliative Ethic of Care* (Sudbury, Mass.: Jones and Bartlett Publishers, 2006), 73–77; 121–125.

26. Congregation for the Doctrine of the Faith, *Declaration on Euthanasia*, no. II. Proponents of legalized euthanasia and physician-assisted suicide would like to reframe the language of the euthanasia debate. For example, they propose that the designation "physician-assisted suicide" should be replaced by the "value-neutral" term "physician-assisted dying." In response, changing words does not change the reality of the acts of physician-assisted dying would still involve a suicide with the patient's ending of his own life. For discussion, see Kathryn L. Tucker and Fred B. Steele, "Patient Choice at the End of Life: Getting the Language Right," *J Leg Med* 28 (2007): 305–325.

assisted suicide is legal in the Netherlands, Belgium, Switzerland, and Luxembourg.[27] The Netherlands—considered the test case for legalized euthanasia—has legally permitted euthanasia and physician-assisted suicide since a Dutch Supreme Court decision in 1984, though its parliament formally approved a bill permitting these practices only in 2001.[28] In the United States, physician-assisted suicide was legalized in Oregon in 1994 with the passage of the Death with Dignity Act in a voter referendum.[29] Washington State became only the second state in the United States to sanction physician-assisted suicide with the passage of Proposition 1000 on November 4, 2008.

Bluntly, acts of euthanasia and physician-assisted suicide—including the acts of infanticide advocated by the Groningen Protocol—are gravely evil. As the *Ethical and Religious Directives* of the United States Conference of Catholic Bishops make clear: "Catholic health-care institutions may never condone or participate in euthanasia or assisted suicide in any way. Dying patients who request euthanasia should receive loving care, psychological and spiritual support, and appropriate remedies for pain and other symptoms so that they can live with dignity until the time of natural death."[30] Acts of euthanasia or physician-assisted suicide are acts of murder.

There are at least five moral arguments against the practices of euthanasia and physician-assisted suicide.[31] First, there is the argument that appeals to the intrinsic inviolability of innocent human life. As many people of different religions and none acknowledge, human beings are of great and equal worth, and as such, should be respected by others and

27. For a history of the euthanasia movement, see Ian Dowbiggin, *A Concise History of Euthanasia: Life, Death, God, and Medicine* (Lanham: Rowman and Littlefield Publishers, 2005).

28. For a comprehensive overview of the practice of euthanasia in the Netherlands, see Raphael Cohen-Almagor, *Euthanasia in the Netherlands: The Policy and Practice of Mercy Killing* (Dordrecht: Kluwer Academic Publisher, 2004).

29. For a penetrating analysis of the social and philosophical context of the physician-assisted suicide debate in Oregon, see Robert P. Jones, *Liberalism's Troubled Search for Equality: Religion and Cultural Bias in the Oregon Physician-Assisted Suicide Debates* (Notre Dame, Ind.: University of Notre Dame Press, 2007).

30. *Ethical and Religious Directives for Catholic Health Care Services,* 5th ed., no. 60; cf. *Catechism of the Catholic Church,* nos. 2280–2283.

31. For an insightful discussion of the contemporary debate over the legalization of euthanasia, see Wesley J. Smith, *Forced Exit: Euthanasia, Assisted Suicide, and the New Duty of Die* (New York: Encounter Books, 2006); and Neil M. Gorsuch, *The Future of Assisted Suicide and Euthanasia* (Princeton, N.J.: Princeton University Press, 2006).

protected by society. The Catholic Church teaches that every human life, no matter how impaired this life may be, whether it is beleaguered with suffering, disability, ignorance, or even sin, remains, in itself, something of great value, because "it remains forever in a special relationship with the Creator. . . . God alone is the Lord of life from its beginning until its end: no one can under any circumstance claim for himself the right directly to destroy an innocent human being."[32] As the Gospel reveals, human life is a trust that has been put into our stewardship by God, and thus it is not ours to dispose of. Therefore, as practices that intentionally end the lives of innocent human beings, euthanasia and physician-assisted suicide are gravely evil. The Congregation for the Doctrine of Faith teaches: "No one is permitted to ask for this act of killing, either for himself or herself or for another person entrusted to his or her care, nor can he or she consent to it, either explicitly or implicitly. Nor can any authority legitimately recommend or permit such an action. For it is a question of the violation of the divine law, an offense against the dignity of the human person, a crime against life, and an attack on humanity."[33]

Second, there is the argument that appeals to the integrity of the medical profession. Both euthanasia and physician-assisted suicide would undermine the medical profession by eroding the trust of patients in their physicians as caregivers. If doctors were permitted to engage in practices that harm their patients, then patients would never know if their doctors were truly acting in their best interests. As the American Geriatric Society (AGS) acknowledges: "Historically, the fundamental goal of the doctor/patient relationship has been to comfort and to cure. To change the physician's role to one in which comfort includes the intentional termination of life is to alter this alliance and could undermine the trust between physician and patient."[34] Given the legalization and acceptance of euthanasia in their society, it should not be surprising that many Dutch patients, before they will check themselves into hospitals, insist on writing contracts assuring that they will not be killed without their explicit consent.[35] Accounts like this reveal that legalized euthanasia has weakened the fiduciary relationship between the health-care professional and

32. Congregation for the Doctrine of the Faith, *Donum vitae*, Introduction, no. 5.

33. Congregation for the Doctrine of the Faith, *Declaration on Euthanasia*, no. II.

34. At http://www.americangeriatrics.org/Products/Positionpapers/vae94.shtml.

35. *House of Lords Report* HL Paper, 21-I of 1993–1994 Session at 66; cited in Gorsuch, *The Future of Assisted Suicide and Euthanasia*, 126.

his patient to the detriment of sound medical practice and of the common good.

Third, there is the argument that appeals to society's commitment to support palliative medicine. In an era driven by cost containment, both euthanasia and physician-assisted suicide would undermine our society's commitment to care for the dying. Promoting euthanasia in all its forms would be cheaper than developing often more expensive and more effective strategies for palliative care. As Neil Gorsuch has chronicled, there is already some evidence that economic considerations play a role in the decision-making process that governs euthanasia and physician-assisted suicide in the Netherlands.[36]

Fourth, there is the argument that appeals to the protection of the sick and the aged. As the American Geriatric Society (AGS) argues, legalization of euthanasia and physician-assisted suicide would "open the door to abuse of the frail, disabled, and economically disadvantaged of society, by encouraging them to accept death prematurely rather than to burden society and family."[37] Over twenty years ago, it was reported that Governor Richard D. Lamm of Colorado had suggested that elderly people who are terminally ill have a "duty to die and get out of the way."[38] Though his statement generated a firestorm of criticism at the time, there are scholars who have endorsed his view, suggesting that the old and the infirm have a duty to die when they become a burden to their loved ones and to society at large.[39] With rising health-care costs, it is not unreasonable to think that the elderly face increasing pressure to avoid having their families foot the bill for extended palliative care.

36. Gorusch, *The Future of Assisted Suicide and Euthanasia*, 128–129. Zbigniew Zylicz has also documented at least one case in the Netherlands where the acceptance of euthanasia motivated one clinician to forgo basic palliative care. See the essay, "Palliative Care and Euthanasia in the Netherlands," in Kathleen Foley and Herbert Hendin, eds., 122–143 *The Case against Assisted Suicide: For the Right to End-of-Life Care* (Baltimore: Johns Hopkins University Press, 2002), 141.

37. At http://www.americangeriatrics.org/Products/Positionpapers/vae94.shtml.

38. "Gov. Lamm Asserts Elderly, if Very Ill, Have 'Duty to Die,'" *New York Times*, published March 29, 1984, at http://query.nytimes.com/gst/fullpage.html?res= 9E01 E5D91E39F93AA15750C0A962948260&sec=health&spon=&pagewanted=1. An editor's note on the website reports that Gov. Lamm later denied that he had ever said that the elderly or the terminally ill have a duty to die. Rather, Gov. Lamm commented: "I was essentially raising a general statement about the human condition, not beating up on the elderly."

39. John Hardwig, "Is There a Duty to Die?" *Hastings Cent Rep* 27 (1997): 34–42.

Finally, there is the slippery slope argument: legalizing euthanasia and physician-assisted suicide could eventually lead to the acceptance of euthanasia for incompetent persons—the killing of the comatose, the demented, and the severely handicapped—and the euthanasia of competent persons without their consent. The Dutch experience with legalized euthanasia provides much support for this slippery slope argument. A survey taken in 1990, eleven years *before* the Dutch Parliament formally approved a bill permitting assisted suicide and euthanasia, revealed that doctors intentionally sought to shorten more lives without a patient's consent than lives with that consent.[40] It was their primary aim to kill 10,558 patients, 5,450 (52%) of whom had not explicitly asked to have their lives shortened.[41] This trend has continued: as Dr. Herbert Hendin and his colleagues have shown, in 1995, 948 patients were put to death without their consent, while over 80 percent of 1,896 patients were killed with opiates that were administered with the explicit intent of causing death, without the request or the consent of these patients.[42] The data suggest that the legalization of euthanasia has led to the exploitation and the killing of Dutch patients without their consent. It appears that they are being killed because their physicians have assumed the power to determine that their lives are not worth living. The legalization of euthanasia has undermined the integrity of the medical profession in the Netherlands and has led to the killing of innocent persons. For this, and the other reasons discussed above, both euthanasia and physician-assisted suicide are morally reprehensible. They attack the good not only of the human person, but also of his community as a whole.

Not surprisingly, Blessed John Paul II has emphatically denounced all forms of euthanasia, including physician-assisted suicide, with a confirmation of the ordinary Magisterium of the Church: "[I]n harmony with the Magisterium of my Predecessors and in communion with the Bishops of the Catholic Church, *I confirm that euthanasia is a grave violation of the law of God,*

40. John Keown, "Euthanasia in the Netherlands: Sliding Down the Slippery Slope?" in *Euthansia Examined: Ethical, Clinical and Legal Perspectives,* ed. John Keown, 261–296 (Cambridge: Cambridge University Press, 1995), 278.

41. Ibid.

42. Herbert Hendin, Chris Rutenfrans, and Zbigniew Zylicz, "Physician-Assisted Suicide and Euthanasia in the Netherlands. Lessons from the Dutch," *JAMA* 277 (1997): 1720–1722. For more extensive discussion, see Herbert Hendin, *Seduced by Death: Doctors, Patients, and the Dutch Cure* (New York: Norton, 1996); and Herbert Hendin, "The Dutch Experience," *Issues Law Med* 17 (2002): 223–246.

since it is the deliberate and morally unacceptable killing of a human person. This doctrine is based upon the natural law and upon the written word of God, is transmitted by the Church's Tradition and taught by the ordinary and universal Magisterium."[43] According to the pope, euthanasia is a false mercy, even when it is not motivated by a selfish refusal to be burdened with the life of someone who is suffering. Rather, true compassion leads not to the killing of the person whose suffering we cannot bear, but to the sharing of another's pain as he approaches death. The alternative to performing euthanasia and physician-assisted suicide, therefore, is to enter into solidarity with the suffering patient and to accompany him as he approaches death.

Common Objections

The Appeal to Autonomy and Self-Determination

Respect for autonomy—respect for individual freedom and choice—remains one of the most widely accepted moral principles in our liberal societies of the West.[44] In his book *Life's Dominion*, the legal scholar Ronald Dworkin presents an argument for a strong right for personal autonomy at the end of life.[45] He begins by explaining how one's dying is a critical part of one's life. It is important because how we die can impact and shape the overall meaning and narrative structure of our lives. Dworkin writes: "There is no doubt that most people treat the manner of their deaths as of special, symbolic importance: they want their deaths, if possible, to express and in that way to vividly confirm the values that they believe most important to their lives."[46] Therefore, Dworkin argues that each individual person should be given the freedom to choose a death that completes the integrity and coherence of his life as he understands it. For those who believe that human life is sacred and intrinsically inviolable because of the human contribution that shapes it, euthanasia or physician-assisted suicide, according to Dworkin, may sometimes support, rather than undermine, that value.

43. John Paul II, *Evangelium vitae*, no. 65.

44. For a discussion of the importance of autonomy in contemporary ethical reflection, see the essays in James S. Taylor, ed., *Personal Autonomy* (New York: Cambridge University Press, 2005).

45. Ronald Dworkin, *Life's Dominion* (New York: Alfred A. Knopf, 1993).

46. Ibid., 211.

To respond, God created human beings as rational and free creatures. As such, we are called to perfect ourselves and establish our identities as moral beings through our free choices and the acts that arise from them. Therefore, the capacity to choose freely is indeed a great good deserving of respect. However, autonomy and the freedom to determine oneself are not absolute goods that can, in themselves, morally justify human action. Murderers or adulterers or thieves who freely choose to kill, or to betray, or to steal, by virtue of their free choices, are still not morally justified in their actions. Rather, actions are good because they realize some human or communal perfection. As we already discussed above, the prohibition against euthanasia and physician-assisted suicide reflects the conviction that these actions undermine and attack not only the fundamental human good of life, but also the important communal good of the fiduciary relationship between the health-care professional and his patient. These goods are worthwhile even if the patient does not affirm or appreciate them. Thus, euthanasia and physician-assisted suicide, regardless of personal choice, are intrinsically evil in the same way that murder, adultery, and lying, regardless of personal choice, are morally reprehensible. By their very nature, these practices distort and sully both the meaning and the narrative structure of an individual's life.

Finally, and somewhat ironically, we should consider the following: if autonomy were in fact such a great good that should be respected absolutely, why then would it be morally acceptable for someone to choose to destroy it, by putting an end to his life, and thus, his capacity to be autonomous?[47] This question is especially pressing since studies have shown that depression is strongly associated with the desire to die, including the wish for euthanasia and physician-assisted suicide, suggesting that many patients seeking euthanasia at life's end may not be as autonomous as some may think they are.[48]

47. For an insightful and powerful response to the objection that appeals to autonomy and self-determination, see Daniel Callahan, "Reason, Self-Determination, and Physician-Assisted Suicide," in *The Case against Assisted Suicide: For the Right to End-of-Life Care*, ed. Kathleen Foley and Herbert Hendin, 52–68 (Baltimore: Johns Hopkins University Press, 2002).

48. According to one study, people experiencing depression or other emotional or psychological distress are four times more likely to seek euthanasia or assisted suicide than patients with similar symptoms without the distress: Marije L van der Lee, Johanna G. van der Bom, Nikkie B. Swarte, A. Peter M. Heintz, Alexander de Graeff, and Jan van den Bout, "Euthanasia and Depression: A Prospective Cohort Study among Termi-

The Appeal to Compassion

As we noted at the beginning of this chapter, the Groningen Protocol justifies the killing of severely handicapped infants by appealing to mercy: death would put an end to these children's "unbearable" suffering. Proponents of euthanasia and physician-assisted suicide argue that no one should endure pointless suffering and that physicians and other health-care professionals have a mandate to alleviate the suffering of their patients. Therefore, they insist that these practices should be made available to terminally ill patients as a merciful and compassionate way to deliver them from their pain. This would allow them "to die with dignity."[49]

To respond, as Blessed John Paul II taught in his allocution to the 19th International Conference of the Pontifical Council for Health Pastoral Care, euthanasia, even if it is motivated by sentiments either of a misconstrued compassion or of a misunderstood preservation of dignity, "actually eliminates the person instead of relieving the individual of suffering."[50] The Holy Father continues: "True compassion, on the contrary, encourages every reasonable effort for the patient's recovery. At the same time, it helps draw the line when it is clear that no further treatment will serve this purpose."[51] Thus, according to the pope, dying patients should be accompanied lovingly to the end of their lives with acts that lessen their suffering to "dispose them to prepare their souls for the encoun-

---

nally Ill Cancer Patients," *J Clin Oncol* 23 (2005): 6607–6612. Importantly, another study has revealed that patients with depression were more likely to change their minds about desiring euthanasia or assisted suicide: Ezekiel J. Emanuel, Diane L. Fairclough, and Linda L. Emanuel, "Attitudes and Desires Related to Euthanasia and Physician-Assisted Suicide among Terminally Ill Patients and Their Caregivers," *JAMA* 284 (2000): 2460–2468.

49. Dr. Timothy Quill, a physician who made headlines in 1991 when his essay describing how he assisted a terminally ill woman named Diane to commit suicide was published in the *New England Journal of Medicine*, has argued that the legalization of physician-assisted suicide would give the severely ill the freedom to avoid a lingering and painful death. For his and other arguments supporting the acceptance of physician-assisted suicide that appeal to compassion, see Timothy E. Quill and Margaret P. Battin, eds., *Physician-Assisted Dying: The Case for Palliative Care and Patient Choice* (Baltimore: Johns Hopkins University Press, 2004).

50. John Paul II, "To the Participants in the 19th International Conference of the Pontifical Council for Pastoral Health Care, November 12, 2004," *Natl Cathol Bioeth Q* 5 (2005): 153–155; 154.

51. Ibid.

ter with the heavenly Father."[52] Palliative care, and not euthanasia, is the compassionate response to suffering at life's end.[53] As we already noted above, with recent advances in palliative medicine, there is no medical or moral reason why any dying patient should have to endure unwanted pain today.

Finally, a few words about the death-with-dignity movement. According to physician and assisted-suicide advocate, Dr. Timothy Quill, "suicide could be appropriate for patients if they did not want to linger comatose, demented or incontinent."[54] For Quill and other proponents of euthanasia, patients have to be delivered not only from pain, but also from "undignified" conditions such as those just mentioned. They should be allowed to die "with dignity." Implicit in their argument, however, is the suggestion that the old, the ill, the infirm, and the disabled have less human dignity than the young, the healthy, the robust, and the abled. This assertion needs to be challenged. Felicia Ackerman formulates the objection to what she calls this "bigoted and superficial view of human dignity" with a question: "Does Dr. Quill really want to endorse the view that human dignity resides in the bladder and the rectum?"[55] Clearly, this cannot be true.

In response, to understand the death-with-dignity movement, one must recognize that Quill and his associates endorse an account of human dignity that posits that this dignity is extrinsic. In other words, according to this account, to affirm that someone has dignity is to affirm that he is in some *subjective* way worthy of the esteem of others. In this sense, sipping soup with a spoon is dignified while slurping it directly from the bowl is not. Here, dignity is a quality that depends upon how others perceive us. It is a dignity that can be gained or lost as the circumstances of our lives

52. Ibid.

53. Significantly, several research studies of patients at the end of life have shown that psychological, existential, and social reasons are more often associated with a desire to die than medical reasons, including pain, suggesting that the spiritual care of dying patients has to be an essential component of a culture of life that opposes euthanasia. See the review of the research by Peter L. Hudson et al., "Desire for Hastened Death in Patients with Advanced Disease and the Evidence Base of Clinical Guidelines: A Systematic Review," *Palliat Med* 20 (2006): 693–701.

54. Jane Gross, "Quiet Doctor Finds a Mission in Assisted Suicide Case," *New York Times*, January 2, 1997, B1.

55. Felicia Ackerman, "Assisted Suicide, Terminal Illness, Severe Disability, and the Double Standard," in *Physician Assisted Suicide: Expanding the Debate*, ed. Margaret P. Battin, Rosamond Rhodes, and Anita Silvers, 149–162 (New York: Routledge, 1998), 151.

change. Quill and his colleagues embrace this account of attributed human dignity, because they, like many liberal philosophers, posit that an individual's dignity is rooted in his autonomy, which can be gained or lost. Thus, it is not surprising that they conclude that coma, dementia, and incontinence are "undignified" conditions. These are conditions where patients have suffered the loss of their ability to function independently. They have lost their autonomy.

This account of attributed human dignity stands in stark contrast with the account described in chapter 2, which posits that human dignity properly understood is intrinsic.[56] According to this rival account put forward by the Catholic tradition, to affirm that someone is dignified is to affirm that he is in some *objective* way worthy of the respect of others. Here, dignity is an intrinsic quality that does not depend only on how others perceive us. It is an *inherent* dignity that can be possessed only in the absolute sense—one either has it completely or does not have it at all—since one is either a human being or not one at all. Therefore, it can neither be diminished nor lost simply because one is comatose or demented or incontinent. To put it another way, according to this account of human dignity, a human being can die in an undignified manner—a situation that should be prevented by a patient's health-care providers using all moral means available—but he cannot die "without dignity." Until he ceases to be human, the patient retains his intrinsic dignity regardless of his illness, his disability, or his age.

Which one of these two accounts of human dignity is the true one? As I explained in chapter 2, human dignity is inherent, essential, and proper to the human being because he is made in the image and likeness of God. This justification, however, would not convince Quill and his secular associates. However, as we will describe in chapter 8, an intrinsic account of human dignity is also the only account that can coherently sustain a liberal society. Therefore, by the standards of liberalism itself—the same liberalism that motivates Quill and his colleagues to value autonomy—patients who are comatose, demented, or incontinent retain their dignity, and as such, do not need to be "delivered" from these conditions.

56. Note that to claim that human dignity is intrinsic, as the Catholic moral tradition does, is not to deny that human beings also have an attributed dignity that is extrinsic in nature. Clearly, a guest who slurps his French onion soup directly from the serving bowl is undignified. However, the account of human dignity described here affirms that this attributed dignity does not and cannot constitute the foundation for the human dignity that grounds the moral discourse in a liberal society.

The Difference between Killing and Letting Die

In a famous essay published in the *New England Journal of Medicine,* James Rachels argued that there is no moral difference between killing a patient—active euthanasia—and allowing him to die—withdrawing or withholding the use of extraordinary means that may prolong the life of that patient.[57] Thus, he concludes that those who accept the validity of the principle of elective extraordinary means should also accept the legitimacy of euthanasia and physician-assisted suicide.

To make his case, Rachels asks his readers to compare the following two scenarios. In the first scenario, Smith stands to gain a large inheritance if anything should happen to his six-year-old cousin. One evening while the child is taking his bath, Smith sneaks into the bathroom and drowns the child, and then arranges things so that it will look like an accident. In the second scenario, Jones also stands to gain if anything should happen to his six-year-old cousin. Like Smith, Jones sneaks in planning to drown the child in his bath. However, just as he enters the bathroom, Jones sees the child slip and hit his head, and fall face down in the water. Jones is delighted; he stands by, ready to push the child's head back under if it is necessary, but it is not necessary. With only a little thrashing about, the child drowns all by himself, "accidentally," as Jones watches and does nothing. Rachels asks: Smith killed his cousin while Jones allowed his to die. Is there really a moral difference between the two acts? Rachels argues that there is none. He, therefore, concludes that there is no moral difference between intentionally killing someone and withholding or withdrawing some means in order to allow him to die.

To respond, Rachels is right in arguing that there is no moral difference between Smith who kills his cousin and Jones who allows his to die. However, what he fails to realize is that there is a moral difference between allowing someone to die by withholding morally *obligatory* means and allowing someone to die by withholding morally *optional* means. Jones was morally obligated to help his drowning cousin because everyone is morally obligated to do whatever is reasonable to help someone who is drowning. Thus, his inaction made him culpable for his cousin's death. His act of omission was an act of intentional killing. Contrast this with

57. James Rachels, "Active and Passive Euthanasia," *N Engl J Med* 292 (1975): 78–80. For a more comprehensive account of Rachels's advocacy of euthanasia, see his book, *The End of Life: Euthanasia and Morality* (New York: Oxford University Press, 1986).

an altered scenario. Here, Jones is paralyzed and in a wheelchair. He sees his cousin fall into the bath. Helplessly, Jones watches, does nothing, allowing his cousin to die. Here, Jones is not culpable for his cousin's death because paralyzed individuals are not morally obligated to help someone who is drowning if there is nothing reasonable they could have done. Thus, paralyzed Jones's act of omission is not an act of murder.

Withdrawing extraordinary means is not identical to killing a patient because here, the doctor is withdrawing morally optional means that are prolonging the patient's life. This is morally permissible because the death of the individual is only a foreseen but an unintended consequence of a morally upright act, the withdrawal of elective extraordinary means. This is not the same as withdrawing ordinary means. Withdrawing ordinary means to cause the patient to die—also called passive euthanasia—is identical to killing the person, because, by definition, the doctor is morally obligated to use all ordinary means to try and keep his patients alive. Again, the key distinction that is presupposed in the moral distinction between "killing" and "allowing to die" is the distinction between ordinary and extraordinary means.

Caring for Patients with Disorders of Consciousness

Diagnosis and Classification

On March 31, 2005, just after nine o'clock in the morning, Terri Schiavo died at Woodside Hospice in Pinellas Park, Florida, thirteen days after her feeding tube was withdrawn. Terri had been in the persistent vegetative state (PVS) for fifteen years, and her dying generated much public debate over the morality and legality of withdrawing hydration and nutrition from patients suffering from profound disorders of consciousness:[58] may we deny food and water to PVS patients and other patients with similar conditions?[59]

58. For a comprehensive review of disorders of consciousness, see Adrian M. Owen, "Disorders of Consciousness," *Ann N Y Acad Sci* 1124 (2008): 225–238.

59. For detailed accounts of the Terri Schiavo case and a discussion of the ethical questions that it raised, see David Gibbs III, *Fighting for Dear Life* (Bloomington, Minn.: Bethany House Publishers, 2006); Diana Lynne, *Terri's Story: The Court-Ordered Death of an American Woman* (Nashville, Tenn.: Cumberland House Publishing, 2005); Rita L. Marker, "Terri Schiavo and the Catholic Connection," *Natl Cathol Bioeth Q* 4 (2004): 555–569; and Daniel P. Sulmasy, O.F.M., "Terri Schiavo and the Roman Catholic Tradition of Forgoing Extraordinary Means of Care," *J Law Med Ethics* 33 (2005): 359–362. For perspec-

The persistent vegetative state is a severe disorder of consciousness that can result after traumatic brain injury.[60] Patients in the PVS are awake but appear not to be aware. They are able to fall asleep and to wake up but are externally characterized by the complete absence of awareness, either of themselves or of their environment. PVS patients are not brain dead. They are able to breathe on their own, to digest food, and to respond to pain. They may even exhibit reflexive crying or smiling behaviors. Significantly, some recent studies have suggested that some PVS patients may still retain cognitive function and awareness despite the absence of external behavior indicators.[61] Patients in the PVS are able to live for extended periods of time as long as they are provided with water, food, and shelter. There are also well-documented cases of recovery from PVS, even after many years, though medical science is still unable to distinguish with any certainty those patients who will recover from those who will not.[62]

PVS should not be confused with other disorders of consciousness. For instance, patients in coma have complete failure of the arousal system.[63]

tives from the tradition of secular bioethics, see Arthur L. Caplan, James J. McCarthy, and Dominic A. Sisti, eds., *The Case of Terri Schiavo: Ethics at the End of Life* (New York: Prometheus Books, 2006).

60. Multi-Society Task Force on PVS, "Medical Aspects of the Persistent Vegetative State—First of Two Parts" and "Medical Aspects of the Persistent Vegetative State—Second of Two Parts," *N Engl J Med* 330 (1994): 1499–1508 and 1572–1579; and Bryan Jennett, *The Vegetative State: Medical Facts, Ethical and Legal Dilemmas* (Cambridge: Cambridge University Press, 2002).

61. For details, see the review by Adrian M. Owen and Martin R. Coleman, "Detecting Awareness in the Vegetative State," *Ann N Y Acad Sci* 1129 (2008): 130–138; and the groundbreaking paper, Martin M. Monti et al., "Willful Modulation of Brain Activity in Disorders of Consciousness," *N Engl J Med* 362 (2010): 579–589.

62. For one example, see Marco Sara et al., "An Unexpected Recovery from Permanent Vegetative State," *Brain Inj* 21 (2007): 101–103. Also see A. Estraneo et al., "Late Recovery after Traumatic, Anoxic, or Hemorrhagic Long-lasting Vegetative State," *Neurology* 75 (2010): 239–245 and Keith Andrews, "Recovery of Patients after Four Months or More in the Persistent Vegetative State," *BMJ* 306 (1993): 1597–1600. Interestingly, there is a report that the administration of zolpidem, a sleeping pill sold as Ambien, can transiently arouse patients in the vegetative state. See Ralf Clauss and Wally Nel, "Drug Induced Arousal from the Permanent Vegetative State," *NeuroRehabilitation* 21 (2006): 23–28. A study published in 1991 that followed eighty-four patients with a firm diagnosis of PVS discovered that 41 percent became conscious by six months, 52 percent regained consciousness by one year, and 58 percent recovered consciousness within three years. See Harvey Levin et al., "Vegetative State after Closed-Head Injury: A Traumatic Coma Data Bank Report," *Arch Neurol* 48 (1991): 580–585.

63. For a description of the Glasgow Coma Scale and the new Full Outline of UnResponsiveness (FOUR) Score, both of which are used to assess the level of consciousness

They are unable to wake up from a deep state of unconsciousness. They manifest minimal reflexive behaviors. In contrast, patients in the minimally conscious state (MCS) are distinguished from patients in the PVS or in a coma by the partial preservation of conscious awareness that manifests itself in external behaviors.[64] They may be able to follow simple commands, to reach for objects, or to engage in purposeful behavior. One physician has suggested that the MCS is an intermediate state between a persistent vegetative state and a permanent vegetative state where a *persistent* vegetative state becomes a permanent vegetative state either three months after an anoxic injury from oxygen deprivation or a year after traumatic injury.[65] Recovery from MCS to higher states of consciousness has been documented.[66] Clearly, states of consciousness fall along a continuum where the upper boundary of a particular type of disorder of consciousness is necessarily arbitrary.

Finally, PVS should not be confused with the locked-in syndrome. Patients in the locked-in syndrome are fully conscious and aware of themselves and their environment.[67] However, they are unable to communicate because their body is completely paralyzed. Vertical eye movement and blinking are usually the only voluntary movements that are left intact. These gravely disabled patients too, should be provided with water, food, and shelter.[68]

---

in patients with significant brain injury and to diagnose coma, see Eelco F. Wijdicks, "Clinical Scales for Comatose Patients: The Glasgow Coma Scale in Historical Context and the New FOUR Score," *Rev Neurol Dis* 3 (2006): 109–117.

64. Steven Laureys and Melanie Boly, "What Is It Like to be Vegetative or Minimally Conscious?" *Curr Opin Neurol* 20 (2007): 609–613.

65. Joseph J. Fins, "Rethinking Disorders of Consciousness: New Research and Its Implications," *Hastings Cent Rep* 35 (2005): 22–24.

66. For example, see Christine M. Taylor, Vanessa H. Aird, Robyn L. Tate, and Michele H. Lammi, "Sequence of Recovery during the Course of Emergence from the Minimally Conscious State," *Arch Phys Med Rehabil* 88 (2007): 521–525. There is also a report that the administration of zolpidem, a sleeping pill sold as Ambien, can transiently arouse patients in the minimally conscious state. See James L. Shames and Haim Ring, "Transient Reversal of Anoxic Brain Injury-Related Minimally Conscious State after Zolpidem Administration: A Case Report," *Arch Phys Med Rehabil* 89 (2008): 386–388.

67. Steven Laureys et al., "The Locked-In Syndrome: What Is It Like to Be Conscious But Paralyzed and Voiceless?" *Prog Brain Res* 150 (2005): 495–511.

68. For a tragic case study that describes the euthanasia of a patient in the locked-in syndrome in the Netherlands, see Erwin J. Kompanje, Inez D. de Beaufort, and Jan Bakker, "Euthanasia in Intensive Care: A 56-year-old Man with a Pontine Hemorrhage Resulting in a Locked-In Syndrome," *Crit Care Med* 35 (2007): 2428–2430.

Providing Food and Water

How are we to care for patients who are not able to eat or to drink
without assistance, because they have a disorder of consciousness? On
March 20, 2004, in an address to the participants of the International Congress on Life-Sustaining Treatments and the Vegetative State,
Blessed John Paul II taught that the administration of food and water,
even when provided by artificial means, represents a natural means of preserving life:

> I should like particularly to underline how the administration of water and
> food, even when provided by artificial means, always represents a *natural means*
> of preserving life, not a *medical act*. Its use, furthermore, should be considered,
> in principle, *ordinary* and *proportionate*, and as such morally obligatory, insofar
> as and until it is seen to have attained its proper finality, which in the pres-
> ent case consists in providing nourishment to the patient and alleviation of his
> suffering.[69]

According to the pope, providing food and water to a patient in the vegetative state always constitutes ordinary care as long as it nourishes the individual, and as such, is morally obligatory.

On August 1, 2007, the Congregation for the Doctrine of the Faith
published a document that definitively interpreted the papal allocution
made several years earlier. In response to a question regarding the moral
obligations involved in feeding and hydrating a patient in the vegetative
state, the CDF stated the following: "The administration of food and
water even by artificial means is, in principle, an ordinary and proportionate means of preserving life. It is therefore obligatory to the extent
to which, and for as long as, it is shown to accomplish its proper finality,
which is the hydration and nourishment of the patient. In this way, suffering and death by starvation and dehydration are prevented."[70] Clear-

69. John Paul II, "On Life-Sustaining Treatments and the Vegetative State: Scientific Advances and Ethical Dilemmas," *Natl Cathol Bioeth Q* 4 (2004): 573–576, 575. For a
comprehensive analysis of this allocution that shows that it is in continuity with the
Catholic moral tradition, see Peter J. Cataldo, "Pope John Paul II on Nutrition and Hydration: A Change of Catholic Teaching?" *Natl Cathol Bioeth Q* 4 (2005): 513–536. For an
overview of the immediate reactions to the pope's comments, see Germain Kopaczynski, O.F.M. Conv., "Initial Reactions to the Pope's March 20, 2004, Allocution," *Natl
Cathol Bioeth Q* 4 (2005): 473–482.

70. Congregation for the Doctrine of the Faith, "Responses to Certain Questions
Concerning Artificial Nutrition and Hydration, August 1, 2007," *Origins* 37 (2007): 242–

ly, the Church has discerned that providing food and water to patients constitutes ordinary care as long as it is effective, and as such, is morally obligatory. Thus, the *Ethical and Religious Directives* of the United States Conference of Catholic Bishops affirms:

In principle, there is an obligation to provide patients with food and water, including medically assisted nutrition and hydration for those who cannot take food orally. This obligation extends to patients in chronic and presumably irreversible conditions (e.g., the "persistent vegetative state") who can reasonably be expected to live indefinitely if given such care. Medically assisted nutrition and hydration become morally optional when they cannot reasonably be expected to prolong life or when they would be "excessively burdensome for the patient or [would] cause significant physical discomfort, for example resulting from complications in the use of the means employed."[71]

The pope's authoritative comments during his allocution resolved a debate among Catholic moral theologians regarding the moral necessity of providing food and drink to PVS, MCS, or comatose patients, even if this requires the use of a tube directly into the patient's stomach, his intestine, or his vein.[72] The opposing perspectives in the debate over the moral necessity of providing food and water to permanently unconscious patients were highlighted in two, apparently contradictory, statements published by the Texas and the Pennsylvania Bishops Conferences in the early 1990s.[73] According to sixteen Texas bishops—two of Texas's eigh-

---

245. John J. Hardt and Kevin O'Rourke, O.P., have published a commentary challenging the conclusions of the CDF's statement by appealing to canon law: "Nutrition and Hydration: The CDF Response, In Perspective," *Health Prog* 88 (2007): 44–47. Their arguments have been convincingly refuted by Edward Peters, himself a canonist: "Hardt and O'Rourke Err in Minimizing the Scope of CDF Response," *Natl Cathol Bioeth Q* 8 (2008): 14–15. Cardinal Justin Rigali and Bishop William Lori have also responded to Hardt and O'Rourke: "On Basic Care for Patients in the 'Vegetative' State: A Response to Dr. Hardt and Fr. O'Rourke," *Health Prog* 89 (2008): 70–72.

71. *Ethical and Religious Directives for Catholic Health Care Services*, 5th ed., no. 58.

72. Depending upon the medical needs of the patient, artificial hydration and nutrition can be provided by nasogastric feeding tubes inserted through the nose into the stomach, or by percutaneous endoscopic gastrostomy (PEG) feeding tubes inserted directly into the stomach or the small intestine. While nasogastric tubes are often used only on a short-term basis—they can cause ulcers in the nostrils or in the throat—PEG tubes are used on a more long-term basis for the care of disabled patients. For a review of the science and medicine of tube feeding, see Khursheed N. Jeejeebhoy, "Enteral Feeding," *Curr Opin Gastroenterol* 18 (2002): 209–212.

73. For a comprehensive overview of the historical and moral debate within the

teen bishops did not sign the document on hydration and nutrition—
the withdrawal of artificial hydration and nutrition from patients in the
vegetative state can be morally justified if the patient or his proxy deems
them burdensome and thus morally optional.[74] The bishops base their argument on the principle of elective extraordinary means discussed above,
suggesting that there are times when feeding and hydrating the patient in
the vegetative state can be deemed futile and thus burdensome.

In contrast to the bishops of Texas, the bishops of Pennsylvania concluded: "[T]he feeding [of permanently unconscious patients] regardless of whether it be considered as treatment or as care is serving a life-
sustaining purpose. Therefore, it remains an ordinary means of sustaining life and should be continued."[75] The bishops argued that supplying
nourishment sustains life, and as such, is beneficial as long as it is able
to preserve life. Moreover, they note that so far as it can be determined
by observation, the unconscious patient is not experiencing the anguish
that would be borne by a conscious person who is receiving artificial hydration and nutrition. Finally, they point out that resources are available
in society to help families of PVS patients who may find that caring for
their incapacitated loved one constitutes a financial difficulty or a personal burden. In light of these observations, the bishops of Pennsylvania
conclude that feeding and hydrating either the PVS, the MCS, or the comatose patient cannot be considered burdensome as long as the food and
water nourishes the individual.[76]

Catholic tradition surrounding the provision of artificial nutrition and hydration to the
permanently unconscious patient, see the essays in Ronald P. Hamel and James J. Walter, eds., *Artificial Nutrition and Hydration and the Permanently Unconscious Patient: The Catholic Debate* (Washington, D.C.: Georgetown University Press, 2007).

74. Joint Statement by 16 of the 18 Texas Catholic Bishops and the Texas Conference
of Catholic Health Facilities, "On Withdrawing Artificial Nutrition and Hydration,"
Origins 20 (1990): 53–55.

75. Catholic Bishops of Pennsylvania, "Nutrition and Hydration: Moral Considerations," *Origins* 21 (1992): 541–553. For a similar argument, see the document by the National Conference of Catholic Bishops Committee for Pro-Life Activities, "Nutrition
and Hydration: Moral and Pastoral Reflections," *Origins* 21 (1992): 705–712.

76. Some moral theologians have suggested that artificial hydration and nutrition
is clearly a burden, not necessarily because it is a burden for the patient himself, but
because caring for the patient, especially for months or for years, can easily become a
burden for his family and/or his professional caregivers. See Thomas A. Shannon and
James J. Walter, "The PVS Patient and the Forgoing/Withdrawing of Medical Nutrition and Hydration," in *Bioethics*, 4th ed., ed. Thomas A. Shannon (Mahway, N.J.: Paulist Press, 1993), 173–198; 188. Kevin O'Rourke, O.P., has also voiced concerns about the

Significantly, the statement from the bishops of Texas ends with the following: "All care and treatment should be directed toward the total well-being of the person in need. Because of the high value of temporal health and life, the presumption is made that the necessary steps will be taken to restore health or at least avert death. However, the temporal concerns must always be subordinated to the patient's spiritual needs and obligations."[77] The last sentence suggests that their moral position arises from an interpretation of the papal allocution by Pope Pius XII on elective extraordinary means already discussed above that has been championed by Kevin O'Rourke, O.P. As we cited above, Pope Pius XII had said the following: "A more strict obligation [than the use of ordinary means to prolong life] would be too burdensome for most men and would render the attainment of the higher, more important good too difficult. Life, health, all temporal activities, are in fact subordinated to spiritual ends."[78] O'Rourke suggests that according to Pope Pius XII, "anything that would make the attainment of the spiritual goal of life less secure or seriously difficult would be a grave burden and would be considered

---

financial burden that is incurred by a family caring for a PVS patient: Kevin O'Rourke, O.P., "Open Letter to Bishop McHugh: Father Kevin O'Rourke on Hydration and Nutrition," *Origins* 19 (1989): 351–352. In response, we must distinguish between the burden specifically associated with nourishing a patient in the vegetative state using a feeding tube, and those burdens more generally associated with the care of a severely disabled loved one. Only the former should be used to evaluate the burden of tube feeding. For the most part, the latter burdens—though often very difficult and inconvenient—cannot be used to justify withdrawing artificial hydration and nutrition from a patient in the vegetative state, especially when health-care costs are borne in the most part by insurance coverage. Otherwise, a similar argument could be made for a family's decision to stop feeding and hydrating a wheelchair-bound quadriplegic who is completely dependent upon others for his care. Caring for a disabled family member is part of the responsibilities and obligations that comes with being family, and it is clear from published narratives that family members are able to learn the basic medical skills required to provide adequate food and water using a feeding tube to a husband or a wife or a child in the vegetative state. It is also important to invite the local church parish and the community at large to contribute to the care of our disabled neighbors. So often, contemporary bioethics fails to recognize the communitarian dimension of human life. For a true account of a 34-year-old Buffalo firefighter who was cared for by his family while he was unconscious and in a vegetative state, see Rich Blake, *The Day Donny Herbert Woke Up: A True Story* (Nevada City, Calif.: Harmony Books, 2007). Donny Herbert woke up after ten years.

77. Texas Bishops, "On Withdrawing Artificial Nutrition and Hydration," 55.
78. See his "The Prolongation of Life, November 24, 1957," *The Pope Speaks* 4 (1958): 393–398; 396.

an optional or extraordinary means to prolong life."[79] Thus, apparently echoing the bishops of Texas, O'Rourke concludes that artificial hydration and nutrition can be withdrawn as extraordinary means because it is a burdensome and futile medical intervention that cannot help the PVS patient pursue the spiritual goal of life.[80]

In response, O'Rourke's interpretation of the papal allocution is erroneous because it would justify too much. Clearly, there are individuals who are born with severe mental handicaps that might prevent them from pursuing the spiritual goal of life. And yet, all reasonable people would concede that they have a right to ordinary or basic care. As William May has pointed out, for example, if O'Rourke's interpretation of Pius XII is correct, it would justify a decision not to stop the reparable arterial bleeding of an infant suffering from Trisomy 21, who has no cognitive abilities.[81] May argues: "Such a baby is not and never will be able to pursue the spiritual goal of life, nor will prolonging its life by stopping the bleeding from the artery *enable* it to pursue this goal, but surely this is ordinary and nonburdensome treatment."[82] He concludes his comments on John Paul II's teaching on the caring of PVS patients this way: "Obviously, John Paul II does not agree with [O'Rourke's] interpretation of the teaching of Pius XII, and rightly so."[83]

Finally, we should acknowledge that the teaching of Blessed John Paul II articulated in his remarks on March 20, 2004, does not preclude the withdrawal of a feeding tube when food and water is no longer needed, and or when food and water fail to nourish the patient. The former applies to clinical scenarios where artificial hydration and nutrition are temporarily provided to a patient who, for a brief period, cannot eat or drink. The latter applies to those cases where a dying patient's body is unable to assimilate any and all nutrients. At this point, artificial hydration and nutrition fails to attain its proper finality of nourishing the patient,

79. Kevin O'Rourke, O.P., "Evolution of Church Teaching on Prolonging Life," *Health Prog* 69 (1988): 28–35; 32.

80. For a defense of this moral argument, see Jason T. Eberl, "Extraordinary Care and the Spiritual Goal of Life: A Defense of the View of Kevin O'Rourke, O.P.," *Natl Cathol Bioeth Q* 5 (2005): 491–501. For a critique of and response to Eberl's paper, see Mark S. Latkovic, "The Morality of Tube Feeding PVS Patients: A Critique of the View of Kevin O'Rourke, O.P.," *Natl Cathol Bioeth Q* 5 (2005): 503–513.

81. William E. May, "An End to the Debate?" *Natl Cathol Bioeth Q* 4 (2004): 451–452.

82. Ibid., 452.

83. Ibid.

and as such, becomes burdensome and morally optional. In fact, continuing to feed and to hydrate these individuals can lead to breathing difficulties and excessive fluid accumulation, which can make the dying process unnecessarily more difficult for the patient and his loved ones.

A Common Objection Again: The Appeal to Autonomy and Self-Determination

In a commentary that appeared several weeks after Blessed John Paul II's allocution to the international conference considering the care of vegetative state patients, Arthur Caplan, the de facto dean of the corps of secular bioethicists, criticized the papal directive because, in his view, it undermines a powerful social consensus in the United States that affirms a patient's right to refuse medical treatment.[84] He continues: "Not only does the Pope's order undermine these rights [to refuse medical treatment], but his claims that withdrawing feeding tubes is cruel and a form of euthanasia are mistaken."[85] For Caplan, bioethics at the end of life is driven by the mandate to protect a patient's autonomy: "The Pope's aim in reminding us that all people, even those in permanent comas or vegetative states, are human beings deserving of compassion and care is important. But he is wrong about what confers dignity on the sick and the dying. It is not about artificially feeding them against their will, but about finding ways to let their will be respected."[86] Self-determination, according to Caplan, always trumps the obligation to feed and hydrate a patient.

In response, the pope's directive does not undermine a patient's right and responsibility for his health-care decisions. The right remains intact. However, this right is not absolute. As we discussed above, a patient may refuse only medical treatment that has been deemed burdensome, and as such, is morally optional. He should not refuse ordinary means of care. For instance, most reasonable persons would agree that a patient may not simply refuse to eat or to drink while he is in the hospital. In his allocution, Blessed John Paul II makes a determination that essentially agrees with the bishops of Pennsylvania: a reasoned reflection upon the medical

---

84. Arthur Caplan, "Must We All Die with a Feeding Tube? Pope's Directive Undermines Patients' Medical Rights," April 6, 2004, Breaking Bioethics at MSNBC.com, at http://www.msnbc.msn.com/id/4669899/.

85. Ibid.

86. Ibid.

and societal circumstances surrounding artificial hydration and nutrition suggests that in most cases, providing food and water to a permanently unconscious patient—like providing food and water to a paralyzed, conscious, and alert patient with quadriplegia—is not burdensome, and as such, is not morally optional. Consequently, neither the patient nor his proxy, nor his health-care professional, may withdraw food and water until artificial hydration and nutrition fails to attain its proper finality of nourishing and hydrating the patient.

The Clinician's Role in End-of-Life Decisions

In two different kinds of clinical scenarios at life's end, a physician may want to refuse a treatment requested by a patient. First, a patient (or his proxy) may request a medical intervention that offers no medical benefit. In these situations, numerous physicians and secular bioethicists have argued that a doctor should be allowed to withhold or to withdraw such treatments, even over the objections of the competent patient or his family. However, this movement to give physicians a right to refuse futile treatment has not met with much success.[87] One possible reason for this is the absence of a consensus within the medical community, either on a specific definition of futility or on an empirical basis, for deciding what further treatment would be futile. Instead, recent commentators have emphasized the need for physicians to talk to their patients and their families when they believe that further treatment will have no benefit. The doctor has to help his patient see that treatments that offer no medical benefit are simply hopeless efforts to delay the inevitable. In other words, the clinician needs to help the patient and his family understand that further medical interventions would constitute extraordinary care. These conversations can take place only within a relationship of trust where the doctor makes clear that he is not abandoning or giving up on his patient but actually has his best interests in mind.

Second, a patient may request a medical intervention that is immoral. Examples include a request either for euthanasia, for physician-assisted suicide, or for the withdrawal of food and water, to cause death. In these cases, the physician is morally obligated not to comply with his patient's request, even if the request comes from a competent patient. Thus, the *Eth-*

87. For details and discussion, see Paul R. Helft, Mark Siegler, and John Lantos, "The Rise and Fall of the Futility Movement," *N Engl J Med* 343 (2000): 293–296.

ical and Religious Directives of the United States Conference of Catholic Bishops makes clear that "the free and informed judgment made by a competent adult patient concerning the use or withdrawal of life-sustaining procedures should always be respected and normally complied with, unless it is contrary to Catholic moral teaching."[88] The physician may not even refer the patient to another physician willing to do these procedures because such a referral could, as we will discuss in chapter 8, constitute an act of material cooperation with the patient's immoral act that would make the physician morally culpable. Thus, it is recommended that physicians preempt such requests by publicizing their opposition to immoral medical procedures, so that prospective patients are aware that these services would not be available to them while they are under the care of the clinician. At the present time, as we will discuss further in chapter 8, clinicians are legally protected by conscience clauses that prevent them from being coerced to perform medical treatments that they consider morally reprehensible.

Highlighting the Role of Virtue in Bioethics

Catholic bioethicists working at the end of life need to remember that they have an important role to play as patients prepare for their death, not only by addressing their moral concerns at life's end but also by boosting the virtue of hope. The moral virtue of hope specifically strengthens the human agent to withstand threats to his well-being in the world by grounding him in an expectation that he will successfully attain his goal. Josef Pieper describes the act of hoping as a reaching out toward happiness: "Hope, like love, is one of the very simple, primordial dispositions of the living person. In hope, man reaches 'with restless heart,' with confidence and patient expectation toward . . . the arduous 'not yet' of fulfillment, whether natural or supernatural. As a characteristically human endeavor, then, hoping incarnates a reaching out for anything that is perceived as good, and for the anticipated fulfillment that the possession of something good brings."[89] Moral hope begets courage. It enables the person to endure life's difficulties in expectation of attaining a good.

At the end of one's life, however, the moral virtue of hope—human

---

88. *Ethical and Religious Directives for Catholic Health Care Services,* 5th ed., no. 59.

89. Josef Pieper, *On Hope,* trans. Mary Frances McCarthy S.N.D. (San Francisco: Ignatius Press, 1986), 27.

hope—is not enough. In the face of death, the believer needs the *theological* virtue of hope—Christian hope—that is grounded in the merciful power of God, who has promised us salvation.[90] As we saw in chapter 1, theological hope is a gift that unites the Christian with God as his supreme and ultimate good. It orders human longing and expectation by placing the human desire for happiness within the context of both God's invitation to share the intimacy of His inner life and His power to effect the same. As the Holy Father, Pope Benedict XVI, explained in his encyclical on hope, entitled *Spe salvi* (Saved in Hope), from the Latin *spe salvi facti sumus* (in hope we were saved) (cf. Rom 8:24): "It is, however, hope—not yet fulfillment; hope that gives us the courage to place ourselves on the side of good even in seemingly hopeless situations, aware that, as far as the external course of history is concerned, the power of sin will continue to be a terrible presence."[91] Sacred Scripture portrays Christian hope as a journey in absolute confidence, based on the divine promise, toward the kingdom of God. It is centered on a specific event, namely, the Second Coming of Christ, with its glorious consequences, including our resurrection and our possession of the perfected Kingdom (cf. Mt 25:34). The Act of Hope in the *Baltimore Catechism* beautifully expresses the essence of this theological virtue: "O my God! Relying on Thy infinite goodness and promises, I hope to obtain pardon of my sins, the help of Thy grace, and life everlasting, through the merits of Jesus Christ, my Lord and Redeemer."[92] The Christian who hopes develops a connatural clinging to God in the sure expectation that his Creator will provide whatever is needed for him to attain true happiness.

How does one strengthen the virtue of hope in a person facing his mortality so that he may intend, decide, and execute good acts at the end of his life? There are at least three pastoral practices that could help here. First, the dying patient should be reminded of God's providence in his life. He should be invited to reflect upon his life to identify those specific times when God sustained him through the difficult and painful moments of his past. These memories are important because they are the fingerprints of God on our lives. They can ground the theological virtue

90. For a comprehensive discussion on Christian hope, see Bernard Olivier, O.P., *Christian Hope*, trans. Paul Barrett, O.F.M. Cap. (Westminster: Newman Press, 1963).

91. Benedict XVI, *Spe Salvi*, no. 36.

92. *A Catechism of Christian Doctrine*, rev. ed. of the Baltimore Catechism, No. 3 (Paterson, N.J.: St. Anthony Guild Press, 1949), ix.

of hope, especially when we realize that the God who has saved us in the past is an unchanging and eternal God who will continue to save us in the future: "Let us hold fast to the confession of our hope without wavering, for he who has promised is faithful" (Heb 10:23). Next, the Christian should be encouraged to meditate on the reality of heaven. He should be reminded that heaven is "the ultimate end and fulfillment of the deepest human longings, the state of supreme, definitive happiness."[93] By his death and resurrection, our Lord Jesus Christ has opened heaven to us, making us partners in His heavenly glorification to enjoy forever the perfect life with the Most Holy Trinity and with the Virgin Mary, the angels, and all the saints.[94] This is the truth that lies beyond the valley of the shadow of death. It is the truth that can sustain our hope as we face all the difficult moments of life, including and especially our death. Finally, the Catholic should be invited to prepare for his encounter with his Creator with prayer and the sacraments, especially the sacraments of penance, of the anointing of the sick, and of the Eucharist. As the *Catechism of the Catholic Church* teaches, "the prayer of the Church and personal prayer nourish hope in us."[95] In the end, the Christian is called to make the prayer of St. Paul his own: "May the God of hope fill you with all joy and peace in believing, so that by the power of the Holy Spirit you abound in hope" (Rom 15:13). Ultimately, of course, it is God the Holy Spirit, source of hope, who accompanies us as we walk the final journey home.

93. *Catechism of the Catholic Church*, no. 1024.
94. Cf. ibid., no. 1026.
95. Ibid., no. 2657.

CHAPTER SIX

Bioethics, Organ Donation, and Transplantation

On May 23, 2004, the *New York Times* published a story that described the sale of a kidney in an international organ trafficking ring that operated in Israel, South Africa, and Brazil.[1] Mr. Alberty Jose da Silva, a thirty-eight-year-old slum resident living in Recife, Brazil, was flown to South Africa, where he sold his kidney for six thousand dollars to an Israeli broker, who transplanted it into a forty-eight-year-old woman from Brooklyn, who paid just over sixty thousand dollars for the organ. The kidney transfer was one of more than one hundred suspect transplants performed in less than two years at St. Augustine's, a hospital in Durban, South Africa. Though the sale and the purchase of human organs is illegal in most countries, the Brooklyn woman's husband was confident that there was nothing wrong with what he and his wife had done: "I felt helpless, because she was going to die," he said. "Helping her get that kidney was the best thing that I have ever done for anyone in my entire life."

In this chapter, which deals with the bioethics of organ transplantation, I begin with a brief history of organ transplantation to set the stage for our moral analysis. I then move to the ethical framework that is used to justify the practice of organ donation and exchange: organ donation is an act of self-giving that should be motivated by charity. Next, I discuss the moral issues raised by proposals to procure organs from aborted and disabled donors. May organs be procured from aborted fetuses, anencephalic infants, and unconscious patients in the vegetative state? I then move to the issue raised by our opening vignette of this chapter. Given the lack of available organs from these and more noncontroversial sourc-

---

1. Larry Rohter, "The Organ Trade: A Global Black Market: Tracking the Sale of a Kidney on a Path of Poverty and Hope," *New York Times*, May 23, 2004, at http://query .nytimes.com/gst/fullpage.html?res=9C0CE0DD163EF930A15756C0A9629C8B63&fta= y&scp=1&sq=organ%20trade%20global%20black%20market&st=cse.

es, several bioethicists have raised the issue of financial compensation for organ donation to encourage higher "donation" rates. How should we evaluate this proposal and other suggestions that legitimate the sale and purchase of human organs? After this, I move to questions of allocation: Who should receive the limited numbers of organs that are donated every year? What criteria should be used to triage potential organ recipients? Finally, I end with a critical survey of the debate surrounding the definition of death and the neurological criteria that equate brain death with death, concluding that the available evidence indicates that brain-dead patients are not dead.

Organ Transplantation

A Historical Framework

The first successful kidney transplant from one living human being to another, at the Peter Brent Brigham Hospital in Boston on December 23, 1954, was the breakthrough that established the field of human organ transplantation on firm scientific foundations.[2] The medical team led by Dr. Joseph E. Murray removed a kidney from Ronald Herrick and implanted it into his identical twin brother Richard, the victim of a fatal kidney disease. Richard recovered quickly and went on to live nine more years until he died of a heart attack. Transplants of a lung, a liver, and a heart followed within the next decade, though these were not successful in the long term because surgeons were not able to overcome the immune barrier: the donated organs were eventually rejected and destroyed by the recipient's immune system.

The next major breakthrough in transplant medicine involved the discovery of drugs that could suppress the immune system, thus preventing the rejection of a donated organ. The first such immunosuppressant was 6-mercaptopurine, discovered by Robert Schwarts and Walter Dameshek at Tufts University in 1959.[3] However, it was the discovery, in 1978, of the drug cyclosporine A that catalyzed the rapid growth of transplantation in the 1980s.[4] More recent discoveries, including the development of the

2. J. P. Merrill, J. E. Murray, J. H. Harrison, and W. Guild, "Successful Homotransplantation of Human Kidney between Identical Twins," *JAMA* 160 (1956): 277–282.

3. R. Schwartz, A. Eisner, and W. Dameshek, "The Effect of 6-Mercaptopurine on Primary and Secondary Immune Responses," *J Clin Invest* 38 (1959): 1394–1403.

4. R. Y. Calne et al., "Cyclosporine A Initially as the Only Immunosuppressant in 34

drug FK-506, have allowed organ donation and transplantation to become routine. According to the tally of the Organ Procurement and Transplantation Network (OPTN), nearly 450,000 organ transplantations have been performed in the United States in the past twenty years.[5]

Finally, the history of organ transplantation in the United States has been punctuated by four important pieces of legislation. First, in 1968, the National Conference of Commissioners on the Uniform State Laws and the American Bar Association approved the Uniform Anatomical Gift Act (UAGA) to encourage organ donation in the country and to address some of the legal and ethical issues associated with transplantation.[6] The UAGA established the legal foundation for cadaveric organ donation as well as the individual's right to sign a document agreeing to have his organs donated. By 1973, every state in the United States had adopted the recommendations of the UAGA, facilitating the growth of organ transplantation. Next, in 1980, the Uniform Determination of Death Act (UDDA) was approved by the National Conference of Commissioners on the Uniform State Laws and endorsed by the President's Commission for the Study of Ethical Problems in Medicine and Biomedical and Behavioral Research. It embraced the neurological, or brain-dead, criteria for death that will be discussed in greater detail later in this chapter. Third, in 1984, the U.S. Congress passed the National Organ Transplant Act (NOTA) that established the Organ Procurement and Transplantation Network (OPTN), to maintain a national registry for organ matching. The act not only made recommendations for uniform standards for organ procurement but also made the buying and selling of human organs illegal. Finally, the Organ Donation and Recovery Improvement Act, which was signed into law in 2004, established a federal grant program to provide assistance to living donors for travel and subsistence expenses. It also funded public awareness programs to increase organ dona-

Recipients of Cadaveric Organs: 32 Kidneys, 2 Pancreases, and 2 Livers," *Lancet* 2 (1979): 1033–1036.

5. Updated information can be found at the website of the Organ Procurement and Transplantation Network, at http://optn.transplant.hrsa.gov.

6. For details, see Alfred M. Sadler, Jr., Blair L. Sadler, and E. Blythe Stason, "The Uniform Anatomical Gift Act: A Model for Reform," *JAMA* 206 (1968): 2501–2506. The UAGA has undergone several revisions, most recently in 2006. For commentary, see Joseph L. Verheidjde, Mohamed Y. Rady, and Joan L. McGregor, "The United States Revised Uniform Anatomical Gift Act (2006): New Challenges to Balancing Patient Rights and Physician Responsibilities," *Philos Ethics Humanit Med* 2 (2007): 19.

tion. Collectively, these laws have helped to increase the number of organ transplants in the United States. However, a disparity still exists between the supply and the demand for human organs, and it is a sad reality that according to the OPTN, in 2007, nearly six thousand patients in the United States died while waiting for an organ transplant.

A Moral Framework

How can we justify the procurement and transplantation of human organs? Since the pontificate of the Servant of God, Pope Pius XII (1939–1958), the Catholic Church has explicitly supported the donation and transplantation of organs from both the dead and the living. With regard to donation after death, the *Catechism of the Catholic Church* teaches the following: "Organ donation after death is a noble and meritorious act and is to be encouraged as an expression of generous solidarity."[7] Here the *Catechism* echoes Pope Pius XII, who taught: "A person may will to dispose of his body and to destine it to ends that are useful, morally irreproachable and even noble, (among them the desire to aid the sick and suffering). One may make a decision of this nature with respect to his own body with full realization of the reverence which is due it. . . . This decision should not be condemned but positively justified."[8] Pope Pius XII also reminded his audience, however, that the cadaver of a human person, though it is not intrinsically valuable, should still be respected, because the respect for the dignity of the human person, made in the image and likeness of God, requires that we also honor his mortal remains. As the pope taught in the same speech:

The human body deserves to be regarded entirely differently [from the dead body of an animal]. The body was the abode of a spiritual and immortal soul, an essential constituent of a human person whose dignity it shared. Something of this dignity still remains in the corpse. We can say also that, since it is a component of man, it has been formed 'to the image and likeness' of God. . . . Finally, the dead body is destined for the resurrection and eternal life. This is not true of the body of an animal.[9]

Therefore, the human cadaver can never be regarded simply as a collection of body parts. Moreover, as the Holy Father noted in another ad-

---

7. *Catechism of the Catholic Church*, no. 2296.

8. Pope Pius XII, "Allocution to a Group of Eye Specialists, May 14, 1956," in *The Human Body: Papal Teaching*, selected and arranged by the Monks of Solesmes, 378–384 (Boston: St. Paul Editions, 1960), 381.

9. Ibid., 380–381.

dress to a congress of surgeons, the human person is not the master, but only the steward, of his own life and of his body: "God alone is the lord of man's life and bodily integrity, his organs and members and faculties, those in particular which are instruments associated in the work of creation. Neither parents, nor husband or wife, nor even the very person concerned, can do with these as he pleases."[10] Accordingly, no one can treat either his or another's body or organs as property because no one owns them.

With regard to donation from a living donor to another person, the *Catechism* approves of the practice, as long as it respects the moral law: "Organ transplants are in conformity with the moral law if the physical and psychological dangers and risks to the donor are proportionate to the good that is sought for the recipient."[11] The specific moral requirements of this teaching have been clarified over the past fifty years. Initially, Catholic moralists were unwilling to endorse organ donation and transplantation between two living persons because they could not justify a medical procedure that mutilated the healthy donor.[12] Their theological opinion stemmed from the basic principle that God is the ultimate Lord of human life. Therefore, they reasoned that mutilation, any kind of act that injures or impairs bodily integrity, is an immoral act that violates the dominion of God, unless—and this is the principle of totality—the removal of the bodily part leads to the well-being and integrity of the whole. Pope Pius XII taught that three conditions govern the moral licitness of surgical operations:

First, that the continued presence or functioning of a particular organ within the whole organism is causing serious damage or constitutes a menace to it; next, this damage must be remediable or at least can be measurably lessened by the mutilation in question, and the operation's efficacy in this regard should be well assured; finally, one must be reasonable certain that the negative effect, that is, the mutilation and its consequences, will be compensated for by the

10. Pope Pius XII, "Allocution to the Fourth International Congress of Surgeons, May 20, 1948," in *The Human Body: Papal Teaching*, selected and arranged by the Monks of Solesmes, 95–100 (Boston: St. Paul Editions, 1960), 97.

11. *Catechism of the Catholic Church*, no. 2296.

12. For an overview of the early moral debates surrounding the donation and transplantation of human organs between living persons, see the essay by Gerald Kelly, "The Morality of Mutilations: Towards a Revision of the Treatise," *Theological Studies* 17 (1956): 322–344.

positive effect: elimination of danger to the whole organism, easing of pain, and so forth.[13]

In light of this analysis, Catholic moralists were initally unwilling to endorse organ donation between the living because, in their judgment, the mutilating surgery associated with procuring an organ could not be condoned, inasmuch as the mutilation is not ordered to the welfare of the donor's body. Pope Pius XII agreed with their moral analysis, declaring that the principle of totality could not be used to justify organ transplants among the living.[14]

In time, however, the majority of Catholic moral theologians soon accepted an alternative theological proposal, first articulated by Bert Cunningham, C.M., which recommended that the self-giving of one's own organs could be justified by the principle of charity.[15] This theological opinion has since become part of the moral teaching of the Catholic Church. According to this reasoning, the healthy person who donates a kidney to a patient is making a genuine act of sacrifice modeled after the Lord's sacrifice of Himself on the Cross. In doing so, the donor fulfills the Lord's great commandment to His disciples: "This is my commandment, that you love one another as I have loved you. Greater love has no man than this, that a man lay down his life for his friends" (Jn 15:12–13). Organ donation is an act of self-gift of the human person.[16]

---

13. See his "Allocution to Delegates at the 26th Congress of Urology, October 8, 1958," in *The Human Body: Papal Teaching,* selected and arranged by the Monks of Solesmes, 277–281 (Boston: St. Paul Editions, 1960), 277–278. For discussion, see Gerald Kelly, S.J., "Pope Pius XII and the Principle of Totality," *Theological Studies* 16 (1955): 373–396. Also see the essay by John Haas, "The Totality and Integrity of the Body," *Ethics Medics* 20.1 (1995): 1–3.

14. See his "Allocution to a Group of Eye Specialists, May 14, 1956."

15. Bert Cunningham, C.M., *The Morality of Organic Transplantation* (Washington, D.C.: The Catholic University of America Press, 1944).

16. Germain Grisez has argued that the procurement of organs from the living can also be justified by the principle of double effect. He proposes that the object of the surgery on the donor is not the harm done to the person, but rather, is the removal of the donated organ, with, as its resulting effects, the mutilation of the donor's body (the evil effect) and the restoration to health of the recipient (the good effect). According to Grisez, the principle of double effect would justify this surgery, as long as the surgeon and the donor did not intend the mutilation of the donor's body. See Grisez, *The Way of the Lord Jesus,* vol. 2, *Living a Christian Life,* 542–543. This argument is troubling. Why could a surgeon not justify removing the beating heart from a patient imminently dying, by arguing that the object of the surgery is not the death of the donor, but rather, is the removal of the donated organs, with, as its resulting effects, the death of the donor (the evil effect) and the saving of the life of the recipient (the good effect)? In both scenarios,

To reconcile this reasoning with the moral conviction that no one can unjustifiably mutilate himself or allow another to violate his bodily integrity, Catholic moralists made the distinction between the anatomical and the functional integrity of the donor, and then argued that only the latter is necessary for the bodily integrity that must be maintained and respected by surgeon and patient. Thus, the donation of organs that maintains the functional integrity of the donor, including, for example, the transfusion of blood, the removal of a kidney, or the resection of part of a liver, is morally permissible, because the loss of these organs does not lead to the loss of blood, kidney, or liver function. In contrast, the donation of any organs that destroys a patient's functional integrity, including the donation either of one eye or of an entire lung, is immoral since the donor needs both eyes and both lungs in order to see and to breathe normally.[17] In the same way, the donation of organs that leads to the direct sterilization of the donor, since it would lead to the loss of his functional integrity, would be illicit.[18] Thus, the *Ethical and Religious Directives* of the United

the mutilation of, and the death of, the patient, result from the removal of the organs, and in both cases, the surgeon and the patient could say that they do not intend the evil effect. And yet, we agree that a surgeon cannot remove an unpaired vital organ from a patient even if it could help another patient. We agree because we acknowledge that one cannot remove a beating heart from a living donor, without necessarily intending his death. Recall from chapter 1 that the physical structure of a human act constrains the legitimate moral objects that could be used to specify it. For this reason, I argue that one cannot remove a nonvital organ from a living donor without necessarily intending his mutilating injury, because the acting person must include this moral object into the specification of his action if he is to remain intelligible and morally coherent.

17. For a discussion of the moral issues raised by suggestions that the elective amputations of healthy limbs of patients suffering from body integrity identity disorder, also known as apotemnophilia, could be a potential course of limbs for transplantation, see my essay "Requests for Elective Amputation: A Moral Perspective," *Ethics Medics* 36, no. 2 (2011): 1–2.

18. Recently, surgeons have successfully transplanted an ovary from one woman into her identical twin. The recipient of the ovary went on to conceive and give birth to a healthy baby girl. See Sherman J. Silber, Gedis Grudzinskas, and Roger G. Gosden, "Successful Pregnancy after Microsurgical Transplantation of an Intact Ovary," *N Engl J Med* 359 (2008): 2617–2618. Though the donation of one gonad, either a single ovary or a single testicle, would not destroy the donor's functional integrity, I propose that its transplantation into the recipient would profoundly affect the recipient's personal identity, since it alters his ability to give himself away to another in the conjugal act, and as such, is morally prohibited. As I will discuss in more detail later in this chapter, personal identity is defined by the Pontifical Academy for Life, in its document on xenotransplantation, as "the relation of an individual's *unrepeatability* and *essential core* to his *being a*

States Conference of Catholic Bishops state: "Catholic health care institutions should encourage and provide means whereby those who wish to do so may arrange for the donation of their organs and bodily tissue, for ethically legitimate purposes, so that they may be used for donation and research after death."[19]

In sum, in the tradition of Catholic bioethics, organ transplantation from both the dead and the living can be morally justified by appealing to charity, with the added caveat that organ donation between living persons must maintain the functional integrity of the donor. As Blessed John Paul II emphasized in an address to an International Congress on Transplants: "Every organ transplant has its source in a decision of great ethical value: 'the decision to offer without reward a part of one's own body for the health and well-being of another person.' Here precisely lies the nobility of the gesture, a gesture which is a genuine act of love."[20] In an earlier speech to the First International Congress of the Society for Organ Sharing, the pope had explained the moral limits for this charitable gift: "A person can only donate that of which he can deprive himself

---

person (ontological level) and *feeling* that he is a person (psychological level)." The Academy goes on to conclude, "in general, the implantation of a foreign organ into a human body finds an ethical limit in the degree of change that it may entail in the identity of the person who receives it." Regarding animal-to-human organ transplants, it concludes that organs "such as the encephalon and the gonads, are indissolubly linked with the personal identity of the subject because of their specific function, independently of their symbolic implications. Therefore one must conclude that, whereas the transplantation of these last can never be morally legitimate, because of the inevitable objective consequences that they would produce in the recipient or in his descendants." Though the Catholic Church has not yet made a definitive pronouncement regarding human-to-human gonadal transplants, I propose that this moral argument, for the same reasons articulated by the Pontifical Academy for Life, also prohibits the transplantation of human gonads from one person to another. See the Pontifical Academy's document "Prospects for Xenotransplantation: Scientific Aspects and Ethical Considerations," at http://www.vatican.va/roman_curia/pontifical_academies/acdlife/documents/rc_pa_acdlife_doc_20010926_xenotrapianti_en.html. For commentary on this document, see Basil Cole, O.P., "'Prospects for Xenotransplantation': A Brief Overview," *Natl Cathol Bioeth Q* 2 (2002): 391–397. Finally, for a comprehensive moral analysis of uterine transplantation, see Renee Mirkes, O.S.F., "The Ethics of Uterus Transplantation," *Linacre Q* 75 (2008): 112–131. Mirkes concludes that a uterine transplantation from either a menopausal woman or a woman required to undergo a hysterectomy for therapeutic reasons to a recipient who would be able to conceive naturally, in principle, is morally permissible.

19. *Ethical and Religious Directives for Catholic Health Care Services*, 5th ed., no. 63.

20. John Paul II, "Address to the International Congress on Transplants, August 29, 2000," *Natl Cathol Bioeth Q* 1 (2001): 89–92; 90.

without serious danger or harm to his own life or personal identity, and for a just and proportionate reason."²¹ As we have seen before, the moral standard for organ transplantation, as it is for other medical interventions, is that it respects the integrity and the dignity of the human person.

Significantly, we need to emphasize that all donors and recipients have to give their informed consent prior to the surgical removal and transplantation of organs. As the *Catechism of the Catholic Church* makes clear, the donor must give his free and informed consent prior to his death, or his next of kin must do so at the time of his death: organ transplantation "is not morally acceptable if the donor or his proxy has not given explicit consent."²² Informed consent is a necessary component of the Church's teaching on the morality of organ donation and transplantation for at least two reasons. First, informed consent affirms and protects the intrinsic dignity and inviolability of the human person, who is free. As Pope Pius XII made clear: "Unless circumstances impose an obligation, we must respect the liberty and spontaneity of the parties involved. Ordinarily, the deed [of organ donation] cannot be presented as a duty or as an obligatory act of charity. In proposing it, an intelligent reserve must certainly be maintained in order to avoid serious internal and external conflicts."²³ Next, informed consent respects the essential formality of the donated organ as a gift that one person gives to another. Thus, as the Holy Father, Pope Benedict XVI, taught in an address to the participants of the international congress A Gift for Life: Considerations on Organ Donation, held in Rome from November 6–8, 2008: "With frequency, organ transplantation takes place as a completely gratuitous gesture on the part of the family member who has been certifiably pronounced dead. In these cases, informed consent is a precondition of freedom so that the transplant can be characterized as being a gift and not interpreted as a coercive or abusive act."²⁴ Informed consent guarantees that the gift of a donated organ remains precisely that, a gift.

21. John Paul II, "Address to the First International Congress of the Society for Organ Sharing, June 20, 1991," *L'Osservatore Romano*, English ed., June 24, 1991, 1–2; 2.

22. *Catechism of the Catholic Church*, no. 2296. Pope Pius XII had taught the following: "Generally speaking, doctors should not be permitted to undertake excisions or other operations on a corpse without the permission of those charged with its care, and perhaps even in the face of objections previously expressed by the person in question." See his "Allocution to a Group of Eye Specialists, May 14, 1956," 382.

23. Pius II, "Allocution, May 14, 1956," 381.

24. Benedict XVI, "Address of His Holiness Benedict XVI to Participants at an

Finally, I should point out that this requirement for informed consent rules out a system of organ procurement that favors replacing informed with presumed consent. Such a system of presumed consent, which has already been adopted as social policy in numerous Catholic nations in Europe, would automatically register all adults as organ donors unless they opt out. It would make organ donation the default position, permitting surgeons to retrieve organs from every dead patient who has not explicitly objected to such a surgical intervention.[25] Since it rejects informed consent, such a system would undermine the dignity of the organ donor as a charitable gift-giver and the formality of the donated organ as a gift. Therefore, I propose that individual Catholics and Catholic institutions, especially Catholic hospitals, must reject presumed consent and not cooperate with this unjust system of organ procurement.

Procuring Organs from Aborted and Disabled Donors

The shortage of available organs for transplantation has prompted different individuals and organizations to propose that aborted, anencephalic, and unconscious individuals in the vegetative state should be considered as potential sources for human organs. Not surprisingly, these proposals have raised numerous moral issues and concerns.

In recent years, the transplantation of fetal cells and tissues into the brain and/or spinal cord has been pursued as a potential cure for numerous diseases of the central nervous system, including Parkinson's disease and Huntington's disease, just to name two.[26] Since the United States

---

International Congress Organized by the Pontifical Academy of Life," at http://www.vatican.va/holy_father/benedict_xvi/speeches/2008/november/documents/hf_ben-xvi_spe_20081107_acdlife_en.html.

25. For one example of such a proposed system of presumed consent, see Danielle Hamm and Juliet Tizzard, "Presumed Consent for Organ Donation," *BMJ* 336 (2008): 230. Also see the debate between Veronica English, "Is Presumed Consent the Answer to Organ Shortages? Yes" *BMJ* 334 (2007): 1088; and Linda Wright, "Is Presumed Consent the Answer to Organ Shortages? No." *BMJ* 334 (2007): 1089. For further discussion, see my essay, "Presumed Consent for Organ Procurement: A Violation of the Rule of Informed Consent?" *Natl Cathol Bioeth Q* 9 (2009): 55–62.

26. For scientific reviews of cell-based therapies for Parkinson's disease and for Huntington's disease, see R. Laguna Goya, P. Tyers, and R. A. Barker, "The Search for a Curative Cell Therapy in Parkinson's Disease," *J Neurol Sci* 265 (2008): 32–42; and Anne E. Rosser and Stephen B. Dunnett, "Neural Transplantation in Patients with Huntington's Disease," *CNS Drugs* 17 (2003): 853–867, respectively.

Congress passed the National Institutes of Health (NIH) Revitalization Act in 1993, allowing for unrestricted use of fetal tissue for experimentation, these transplanted cells have often been derived from aborted fetuses. Is this practice morally licit?

In response, Pope Blessed John Paul II taught the following in his encyclical, *Evangelium vitae:*

This moral consideration [of abortion] also regards procedures that exploit living human embryos and foetuses—sometimes specifically "produced" for this purpose by *in vitro* fertilization—either to be used as "biological material" or as *providers of organs or tissue for transplants* in the treatment of certain of certain diseases. The killing of innocent human creatures, even if carried out to help others, constitutes an absolutely unacceptable act.[27]

The Congregation for the Doctrine of the Faith, in its instruction *Dignitas personae,* has confirmed this moral prohibition:

It needs to be stated that there is a duty to refuse to use such "biological material [of illicit origin]" even when there is no close connection between the researcher and the actions of those who performed the artificial fertilization or the abortion, or when there was no prior agreement with the centers in which the artificial fertilization took place. This duty springs from the necessity to *remove oneself,* within the area of one's own research, *from a gravely unjust legal situation and to affirm with clarity the value of human life.*[28]

There are at least three reasons for this moral prohibition. First, the use of fetal tissues and cells for transplantation and research tends to legitimize abortion and to lead to future abortions. There is evidence that women who are about to have an abortion overwhelmingly approve of fetal research, possibly because they need an option that would alleviate the anxiety and guilt associated with their choice to end their pregnancy.[29] Another survey revealed that 12 percent of the women queried reported that they would more likely elect to have an abortion if they could donate tissue for fetal tissue transplantation.[30] It is clear that the possibility

27. John Paul II, *Evangelium vitae,* no. 63.

28. Congregation for the Doctrine of the Faith, *Dignitas personae,* no. 35 (original emphasis).

29. Fionn Anderson, Anna Glasier, Jonathan Ross, and David T. Baird, "Attitudes of Women to Fetal Tissue Research," *J Med Ethics* 20 (1994): 36–40. Also see the essay by Douglas K. Martin, "Abortion and Fetal Tissue Transplantation," *IRB* 15 (1993): 1–4.

30. Douglas K. Martin et al., "Fetal Tissue Transplantation and Abortion Decisions: A Survey of Urban Women," *CMAJ* 153 (1995): 545–552.

of using fetal tissue for therapeutic purposes would encourage women to choose abortion when they may not have done so. Next, the use of fetal tissues for transplantation and research would require collaboration with the abortion industry, which should be strenuously discouraged. As I will discuss in chapter 8, cooperation with evil has to be avoided when at all possible, lest our actions lead not only to scandal, but also to complicity with the evil acts of others. Finally, some ethicists have raised concerns about the informed consent obtained from women who have chosen to donate fetal tissue for transplantation after they have aborted their child, suggesting that the decision to abort disqualifies the mother from playing any role in the disposition of her fetal child's remains.[31] Would we allow a woman who has killed her two-year-old daughter to donate her child's organs for transplantation at a pediatric hospital?

Next, the use of anencephalic infants as organ donors has also been proposed as a means to decrease the shortage of transplantable organs.[32] As we described in chapter 2, anencephalics are born without a forebrain, a complete skull, and a scalp, though they have a functioning brainstem. Consequently, they are often able to breathe, to suck, and to engage in spontaneous movements of their eyes, their arms and legs, and their faces, on their own. The lifespan of an anencephalic neonate is generally very short. Many die within a few hours, less than half survive more than a day, and fewer than 10 percent survive more than a week.[33] However, because these neonates often do not receive aggressive treatment to keep them alive, their potential lifespan is probably longer than their current actual lifespan.

Initially, the Council on Ethical and Judicial Affairs of the American Medical Association (AMA) proposed that organs may be taken from living anencephalic infants without a pronouncement of death, provided that the parents initiate the discussion and that other transplantation standards of care are retained.[34] The council justified its proposal by ar-

31. James Burtchaell, "University Policy on Experimental Use of Aborted Fetal Tissue: Case Study," *IRB* 10 (1988); 7–11; Mary B. Mahowald, "Placing Wedges along a Slippery Slope: Use of Fetal Neural Tissue for Transplantation," *Clin Res* 36 (1988): 220–222; and K. Nolan, "The Use of Embryo or Fetus in Transplantation: What There Is to Lose," *Transplant Proc* 22 (1990): 1028–1029.

32. Robert D. Truog and John C. Fletcher, "Anencephalic Newborns: Can Organs Be Transplanted before Brain Death?" *N Engl J Med* 321 (1989): 388–391.

33. M. Jaquier, A. Klein, and E. Boltshauser, "Spontaneous Pregnancy Outcome after Prenatal Diagnosis of Anencephaly," *BJOG* 113 (2006): 951–953.

34. Council on Ethical and Judicial Affairs, American Medical Association, "The

guing the following: "The use of the anencephalic neonate as a live donor
is a limited exception to the general standard [that donors of vital organs
be first declared dead] because of the fact that the infant has never experienced, and will never experience, consciousness."[35]

In response, the Committee on Doctrine of the United States Conference of Catholic Bishops concluded the following: "It is most commendable for parents to wish to donate the organs of an anencephalic child for
transplants that may assist other children, but this may never be permitted before the donor child is certainly dead."[36] In other words, procuring
vital organs from an anencephalic child is meritorious as long as this does
not kill the child. No one may take the life of an innocent human being,
even if the taking of that life would benefit others. Finally, to respond
specifically to the argument advanced by the AMA Ethics Council to justify anencephalic donation, a human being retains his inviolability even
if he is unconscious or is unable to experience consciousness, because, as
we discussed in chapter 2, human dignity is intrinsic and depends solely
on the humanity of the human being. Incidentally, a study of twelve anencephalic infants at Loma Linda University Medical Center in California, who were supported with intensive care measures for one week to facilitate a declaration of brain death, revealed that anencephalic infants do
not make good organ donors.[37] Successful organ donation did not occur
from any of the infants because the hypoventilation—the breathing difficulty—that eventually kills the anencephalic child renders vital organs
unsuitable for transplantation. The authors concluded that with the restrictions of the law in place at that time, more specifically the dead-

Use of Anencephalic Neonates as Organ Donors," *JAMA* 273 (1995): 1614–1618. The
AMA reversed its position at its Interim Meeting, held December 3–6, 1995, in Washington, D.C.: Council on Ethical and Judicial Affairs, "Anencephalic Infants as Organ Donors," Council on Ethical and Judicial Affairs Report C-I-88, available on www
.ama-assn.org/ama1/pub/upload/mm/369/ceja_ci88.pdf. For a critique of the initial
position of the AMA from a team of physicians, see D. Alan Shewmon, Alexander M.
Capron, Warwick J. Peacock, and Barbara L. Schulman, "The Use of Anencephalic Infants as Organ Sources: A Critique," *JAMA* 261 (1989): 1773–1781.

35. Council on Ethical and Judicial Affairs, "The Use of Anencephalic Neonates as
Organ Donors," 1617–1618.

36. Committee on Doctrine, National Conference of Catholic Bishops, "Moral Principles Concerning Infants with Anencephaly," *Origins* 26 (1996): 276. For commentary,
see Benedict Ashley, O.P., "Moral Principles Concerning Infants with Anencephaly:
Observations on the Document," *L'Osservatore Romano*, September 23, 1998, 8.

37. Joyce L. Peabody, Janet R. Emery, and Stephen Ashwal, "Experience with Anencephalic Infants as Prospective Organ Donors," *N Engl J Med* 321 (1989): 344–350.

donor rule, it would not be feasible to procure solid organs for transplantation from anencephalic infants. The *Ethical and Religious Directives* of the United States Conference of Catholic Bishops makes clear: "The use of tissue or organs from an infant may be permitted after death has been determined and with the informed consent of the parents or guardians."[38]

Finally, several commentators have proposed that organs should be procured from patients in the vegetative state for whom a decision has already been taken to withdraw treatment to allow them to die.[39] They justify their proposal by claiming that "there is no clear moral distinction between allowing to die by omission of treatment and more actively ending life, for instance, by injection of a fatal substance. The outcome is the same."[40]

In response, as discussed in chapter 5, there is a moral difference between killing a patient and allowing him to die. The key distinction presupposed in the moral distinction between "killing" and "allowing to die" is the distinction between withdrawing ordinary and withdrawing extraordinary means. One may not procure the vital organs of a patient in the vegetative state—thus killing him—even if the taking of that patient's life would benefit others, because no one may take the life of an innocent human being, even if the taking of that life would benefit other individuals. As the *Catechism of the Catholic Church* teaches: "It is not morally admissible directly to bring about the disabling mutilation or death of a human being, even in order to delay the death of other persons."[41]

In conclusion, in light of all the proposals to obtain organs from severely disabled persons, we should heed the warning of Blessed John Paul II, who condemned all abuses that could occur in the name of transplant medicine: "Nor can we remain silent in the face of other more furtive, but no less serious and real, forms of euthanasia. These could occur for example when, in order to increase the availability of organs for transplants, organs are removed without respecting objective and adequate criteria which verify the death of the donor."[42] Organ transplantation is a laudable practice only if it respects the dignity of the human person.

38. *Ethical and Religious Directives for Catholic Health Care Services,* 5th ed., no. 65.

39. R. Hoffenberg et al., "Should Organs from Patients in Permanent Vegetative State Be Used for Transplantation?" *Lancet* 350 (1997): 1320–1321.

40. Ibid., 1321.

41. *Catechism of the Catholic Church,* no. 2296.

42. John Paul II, *Evangelium vitae,* no. 15.

Procuring Organs from Animal and Bioengineered Donors

As numerous commentators have observed, the transplantation of organs from one animal species into another, a proposal called xenotransplantation, could potentially relieve the chronic shortage of human organs available for transplantation. To date, chimpanzee, baboon, and pig organs have been transplanted into human recipients with limited success.[43] However, recent technological innovations have enhanced the feasibility of xenotransplantation. First, pigs have been genetically engineered that lack many of the molecular signals that would elicit an immune response in a human donor.[44] The availability of these animals should mitigate rejection from the human recipient's immune system. Second, careful selection and/or genetic engineering of pig herds should minimize the risk of porcine cross-species virus infection into human recipients.[45] Third and finally, a recent report has described a technique that could be used to suppress pig viruses in pig organs prior to human transplantation.[46] With these developments, xenotransplant experts believe that we are now on the threshold of the first clinical trials involving animal-to-human organ transplantation, suggesting that the first clinical application may involve pig heart xenografting as a bridging method to sustain the life of a patient awaiting a human heart.[47]

To examine the ethical issues raised by these technological advances, the Pontifical Academy for Life published a study entitled "Propects for Xenotransplantation: Scientific Aspects and Ethical Considerations," on September 26, 2001.[48] In the study, the Pontifical Academy concluded that xenotransplantation is morally acceptable in principle, as long as three conditions are met. First, physicians have to ensure the safety of all hu-

43. For a scientific review of the field of xenotransplantation, see B. Sprangers, M. Waer, and A. D. Billiau, "Xenotransplantation: Where Are We in 2008?" *Kidney Int* 74 (2008): 14–21.

44. Hao-Chih Tai et al., "Progress in Xenotransplantation Following the Introduction of Gene-Knockout Technology," *Transpl Int* 20 (2007): 107–117.

45. Roumiana Boneva and Thomas M. Folks, "Xenotransplantation and Risks of Zoonotic Infections," *Ann Med* 36 (2004): 504–517.

46. Jagdeece Ramsoondar et al., "Production of Transgenic Pigs That Express Porcine Endogenous Retrovirus Small Interfering RNAs," *Xenotransplantation* 16 (2009): 164–180.

47. Burcin Ekser and David K. Cooper, "Update: Cardiac Xenotransplantation," *Curr Opin Organ Transplant* 13 (2008): 531–535.

48. Pontifical Academy for Life, "Prospects for Xenotransplantation: Scientific Aspects and Ethical Considerations," at http://www.vatican.va/roman_curia/pontifical_academies/acdlife/documents/rc_pa_acdlife_doc_20010926_xenotrapianti_en.html.

man recipients. Second, surgeons need to preserve the personal identity of the person receiving the animal organ, concluding, "in general, the implantation of a foreign organ into a human body finds an ethical limit in the degree of change that it may entail in the identity of the person who receives it."[49] In making these recommendations, the Pontifical Academy for Life was simply reiterating the teaching of Popes Pius XII and Blessed John Paul II, who had upheld the moral legitimacy of xenotransplantation, in principle, on the condition that "the transplanted organ must not impair the integrity of the psychological or genetic identity of the person receiving it; and there must also be a proven biological possibility that the transplant will be successful and will not expose the recipient to inordinate risk."[50] Third, the Pontifical Academy also insisted that scientists prevent all unnecessary animal suffering and that they respect the biodiversity and balance of species in the animal world.

Finally, a word about bioengineered organs: several years ago, a mother of two became the first transplant patient to receive an organ that was grown to order in a laboratory.[51] Claudia Castillo underwent an operation in Barcelona to replace her windpipe after tuberculosis had left her unable to breathe. The bioengineered organ was created in the laboratory using Mrs. Castillo's own stem cells, using a donor trachea to provide the mechanical framework. The medical advance came two years after surgeons in the United States had transplanted seven patients with bladder tissue grown in the laboratory.[52] Bioengineering organs using stem cells obtained using morally licit techniques could potentially revolutionize organ transplantation without raising any ethical problems, other than those associated with a typical surgical procedure.

Organ Trafficking: A Moral Analysis

As we described in the opening vignette of this chapter, there is a global market for the sale and purchase of human organs.[53] It is estimated that

49. Ibid., no. 10.

50. John Paul II, "Address to the International Congress on Transplants," 91, citing Pope Pius XII, "Allocution to a Group of Eye Specialists, May 14, 1956."

51. A. Tonks, "Patient Makes Good Recovery after Transplant of a Bioengineered Airway," *BMJ* 337 (2008): a2676.

52. Anthony Atala et al., "Tissue-Engineered Autologous Bladders for Patients Needing Cystoplasty," *Lancet* 367 (2006): 1241–1246.

53. Nancy Scheper-Hughes, "The Global Traffic in Organs," *Curr Anthropol* 41 (2000): 191–224.

5–10 percent of the kidney transplants performed annually throughout the world can be attributed to organ trafficking and transplant tourism.[54] Despite attempts by some Catholic moralists to justify organ sales using the thought of St. Thomas Aquinas, Pope Pius XII, or Blessed John Paul II,[55] the Catholic Church has consistently opposed the commercialization of human organs, though it has acknowledged that a reasonable stipend can be given to the donor to compensate him for lost wages and other costs that he may have accrued because of the transplantation procedure. The *Ethical and Religious Directives* of the United States Conference of Catholic Bishops is clear in this regard when it directs that during the procurement and transplantation of organs, "economic advantages should not accrue to the donor."[56] Both state and federal laws in the United States also prohibit the buying and selling of human organs. The National Organ Transplant Act (NOTA) makes it illegal to "acquire, receive, or transfer any human organ for valuable consideration for use in organ transplantation."[57] Similarly, the Uniform Anatomical Gift Act (UAGA), as it was revised in 1987, makes it a felony to "knowingly for valuable consideration purchase or sell" cadaveric organs for transplantation.[58] Finally, the medical and transplant community has also condemned both organ trafficking and organ tourism.[59]

The primary reason for the Church's prohibition against the commercialization of human organs is that the ban protects the dignity of the gift-giver and the character of the donated organ as a free gift that is given by the donor in charity. Blessed John Paul II explained it as follows:

Love, communion, solidarity and absolute respect for the dignity of the human person constitute the only legitimate context of organ transplantation. It is essential not to ignore the moral and spiritual values which come into play when

---

54. Debra A. Budiani-Saberi and Francis L. Delmonico, "Organ Trafficking and Transplant Tourism: A Commentary on the Global Realities," *Am J Transplant* 8 (2008): 925–929.

55. For two examples, see Nicholas Capaldi, "A Catholic Perspective on Organ Sales," *Christ Bioeth* 6 (2000): 139–151; and Mark J. Cherry, "Body Parts and the Market Place: Insights from Thomistic Philosophy," *Christ Bioeth* 6 (2000): 171–193. For a critical response to these two essays, see William E. Stempsey, S.J., "Organ Markets and Human Dignity: On Selling Your Body and Soul," *Christ Bioeth* 6 (2000): 195–204.

56. *Ethical and Religious Directives for Catholic Health Care Services*, 5th ed., no. 30.

57. National Organ Transplant Act, 1984 Pub L No. 98-507, 3 USC §301.

58. Uniform Anatomical Gift Act, §4,8A ULA 15 (1987).

59. "The Declaration of Istanbul on Organ Trafficking and Transplant Tourism," *Transplantation* 86 (2008): 1013–1018.

individuals, while observing the ethical norms which guarantee the dignity of the human person and bring it to perfection, freely and consciously decide to give a part of themselves, a part of their own body, in order to save the life of another human being. In effect, the human body is always a personal body, the body of a person. The body cannot be treated as a merely physical or biological entity, nor can its organs and tissues ever be used as items for sale or exchange. Such a reductive materialist conception would lead to a merely instrumental use of the body, and therefore of the person. In such a perspective, organ transplantation and the grafting of tissue would no longer correspond to an act of donation but would amount to the dispossession or plundering of the body.[60]

This theme recurred in the address of the Holy Father, Pope Benedict XVI, to the participants of an international congress on organ transplants organized by the Pontifical Academy for Life:

The possibility of organ sales, as well as the adoption of discriminatory and utilitarian criteria, would greatly clash with the underlying meaning of the gift that would place it out of consideration, qualifying it as a morally illicit act. Transplant abuses and their trafficking, which often involve innocent people like babies, must find the scientific and medical community ready to unite in rejecting such unacceptable practices. Therefore they are to be decisively condemned as abominable.[61]

The buying and selling of human organs is incompatible with the moral framework that is used to justify the procurement and transplantation of human organs. It would transform organ donors from givers to vendors, and donated organs from gifts to merchandise. As such, it has to be rejected as a morally illicit practice.

A Common Objection: The Regulated Sale of Organs

In recent years, voices favoring the regulated sale of organs, particularly of kidneys obtained from living persons, have become more audible. As

60. Pope Blessed John Paul II, "Address of His Holiness John Paul II to Participants of the First International Congress of the Society for Organ Sharing, June 20, 1991," no. 3, at http://www.vatican.va/holy_father/john_paul_ii/speeches/1991/june/documents/hf_jp-ii_spe_19910620_trapianti_en.html.

61. Pope Benedict XVI, "Address of His Holiness Benedict XVI to Participants at an International Congress Organized by the Pontifical Academy for Life, November 7, 2008," at http://www.vatican.va/holy_father/benedict_xvi/speeches/2008/november/documents/hf_ben-xvi_spe_20081107_acdlife_en.html.

one representative of this view, Arthur J. Amatas, a past president of the American Society of Transplant Surgeons, has proposed that the regulated commercialization of living kidney donation would greatly increase the supply of kidneys, not only saving lives but also lowering the number of patients who have to suffer dialysis.[62] In this system of "compensated donation," organ donors would receive payment from the government or a government-approved agency. In brief, Amatas defends his proposal by arguing that a system of compensated donation would both save lives and protect individual liberty. In particular, he suggests that compensated donation would respect the freedom of individual donors: "I am advocating not that people be treated by others as property, but only that they have the autonomy to treat their own parts as property."[63] Finally, to respond to critics who argue that the commercialization of human organs would exploit the poor, Amatas counters by suggesting that compensated donation, among other benefits, would actually give the financially disenfranchised the possibility of bettering their lives.

In response, as we discussed above, a system of compensated donation would undermine the moral framework used to justify organ donation, the framework grounded upon the conviction that the donated organ is a free and charitable gift of self. Instead, the organ becomes a commodity that drives a commercial transaction. Not surprisingly, financial considerations, rather than the health and welfare of recipients and donors, tend to become a priority for the involved parties. One report from Pakistan, comparing the health of commercialized donors to a control population of nonpaid donors, revealed a high incidence of both hepatitis C and B in the donors, who had sold their kidneys, suggesting that the financial incentives had resulted in a lower standard of care for the organ vendors.[64] Next, compensated donation *does* lead to the exploitation of the poor. Amatas's appeal to the autonomy of the indigent Filipino or the

62. Arthur J. Amatas, "A Gift of Life Deserves Compensation: How to Increase Living Kidney Donation with Realistic Incentives," Cato Institute Policy Analysis No. 604: November 7, 2007. Also see Michael B. Gill and Robert M. Sade, "Paying for Kidneys: The Case against Prohibition," *Kennedy Inst Ethics J* 12 (2002): 17–45. For a response to these proposals, see Gabriel M. Danovitch and Francis L. Delmonico, "The Prohibition of Kidney Sales and Organ Markets Should Remain," *Curr Opin Organ Transplant* 13 (2008): 386–394.

63. Amatas, "A Gift of Life," 16.

64. S. A. Naqvi et al., "Health Status and Renal Function Evaluation of Kidney Vendors: A Report from Pakistan," *Am J Transplant* 8 (2008): 1444–1450.

underprivileged Pakistani who sells his kidney to the American tourist is misleading. It fails to recognize that neither organ vendor is free nor autonomous when both are confronted with the choice either of selling their organs or of letting their children starve.[65] Therefore, a system of compensated donation, especially one that is targeted primarily at those who have no other alternative to provide resources for themselves or their families, is inherently coercive. Moreover, as we discussed earlier, individual autonomy is not an absolute good. It is governed by the truth. In this case, the truth that the sale of human organs undermines the dignity of the human donor places legitimate limits on the autonomy of the donor, even one who may be wealthy enough not to experience the coercive nature of organ sales. Finally, there is empirical evidence from Hong Kong and Israel that suggests that the commercialization of organ donation would decrease the rate of noncommercial living and deceased donation.[66] This is not unexpected. Why should someone choose to freely give away his organ in Boston when the potential recipient could simply purchase a kidney in Manila?

Allocating Organs: A Moral Framework

The need for donated organs far exceeds the number of available organs. How should we distribute and allocate these scarce organs to the many sick and dying patients on the transplant waiting list? The method of distribution and allocation of donations will literally mean that some people will live while others will die.

In justice, common goods have to be given not equally, but proportionately according to each citizen's contributions and needs. This is reasonable. The family without any food should receive more from the common purse than the family with plenty. In transplant medicine, therefore, the organ transplant network should allocate human organs to recipients based on their particular need. Determining this need involves a complex algorithm that takes into account both the efficiency of organ use and

65. For a case report that illustrates the danger of allowing vulnerable persons to engage in the commercial sale of their organs, see Miram Epstein, "The Ethics of Poverty and the Poverty of Ethics: The Case of Palestinian Prisoners in Israel Seeking to Sell Their Kidneys in Order to Feed Their Children," *J Med Ethics* 33 (2007): 473–474.

66. Gabriel M. Danovitch and Alan B. Leichtman, "Kidney Vending: The 'Trojan Horse' of Organ Transplantation," *Clin J Am Soc Nephrol* 1 (2006): 1133–1135.

the urgency of patient need.[67] At the present time, this algorithm assigns a donor organ to a particular recipient based upon the following criteria: the closeness of the immunological match between the organ and the recipient, the urgency of the medical need of the recipient, the time spent by the recipient on the waiting list, and the distance separating the donor organ and the recipient.[68]

Finally, the allocation of scarce organs has raised specific disputed questions regarding particular patient populations. For instance, bioethicists are asking if alcoholics who have damaged their own livers should compete equally with patients who need a liver through no fault of their own.[69] Some suggest that alcoholics should receive a lower priority for liver transplantations because they are morally responsible for their medical conditions. In contrast, I propose that moral responsibility should not be used as a criterion for the allocation of moral resources, not only because it is difficult to quantify moral culpability—is an individual who is genetically predisposed toward alcoholism less culpable than another who is not?—but also because including moral criteria in allocating medical resources would undermine the practice of medicine—should a physician treat a stab victim before he treats the victim's assailant who is in greater need of medical attention? Medicine should be motivated, first and foremost, by the desire to treat the sickest among us who would benefit most from that treatment.

Defining Death

A Philosophical Framework

As Pope Benedict XVI reminded the Church and the world in his speech to the international congress on organ transplants mentioned earlier in this chapter, vital organs can be taken only from a person who has been declared dead: "It is helpful to remember, however, that the indi-

---

67. For a discussion of the algorithm that governs the allocation of kidneys in the United States, see Gabriel M. Danovitch and J. Michael Cecka, "Allocation of Deceased Donor Kidneys: Past, Present, And Future," *Am J Kidney Dis* 42 (2003): 882–890.

68. For discussion from the perspective of the Catholic moral tradition, see John Haas, "Ethics of Organ Allocation," in *Proceedings of the International Congress: A Gift for Life. Considerations on Organ Donation, November 6–8, 2008*, in press.

69. For comment and discussion, see Daniel Brudney, "Are Alcoholics Less Deserving of Liver Transplants?" *Hastings Cent Rep* 37 (2007): 41–47.

vidual vital organs cannot be extracted except *ex cadavere*."[70] As the *Ethical and Religious Directives* of the United States Conference of Catholic Bishops makes clear, "such [donated] organs should not be removed until it has been medically determined that the patient has died."[71] It is not surprising, therefore, that Catholic and other bioethicists continue to try to answer the following question accurately and truthfully: how do we know that someone is dead?

The debate over the validity of different criteria for death is a complex one.[72] As different scholars grappling with this issue have pointed out, however, the dispute can be clarified by distinguishing the three levels of discourse that are present in the arguments put forward by every side in the debate.[73]

First, every interlocutor in the debate has a *definition* of death. This involves the conceptual basis underlying that individual's understanding of death. Three dominant categories of definitions for death exist in the brain-death literature:[74]

1. *Biological definitions:* Basically, death involves the loss of the physiological integrative unity of the body. This definition is species-*non*specific and corresponds to the ordinary understanding of "death." This is also the mainstream rationale for brain death in both secular[75] and Catholic circles, including both Working Groups of the Pontifical Academy of

70. Benedict XVI, "Address of His Holiness Benedict XVI to Participants at an International Congress Organized by the Pontifical Academy of Life," at http://www.vatican.va/holy_father/benedict_xvi/speeches/2008/november/documents/hf_ben-xvi_spe_20081107_acdlife_en.html.

71. *Ethical and Religious Directives for Catholic Health Care Services,* 5th ed., no. 64.

72. For a more extensive discussion of the debate surrounding brain death, see my essay, "Is the Brain-Dead Patient *Really* Dead?" *Studia Moralia* 41 (2003): 277–308. Also see the insightful commentary by James DuBois, "Avoiding Common Pitfalls in the Determination of Death," *Natl Cathol Bioeth Q* 7 (2007): 545–550.

73. James L. Bernat, Charles M. Culver, and Bernard Gert, "On the Definition and Criterion of Death," *Ann Intern Med* 94 (1981): 389–394. Also see Karen Gervais, *Redefining Death* (New Haven, Conn.: Yale University Press, 1986).

74. For discussion, see D. Alan Shewmon, "The Brain and Somatic Integration: Insights into the Standard Biological Rationale for Equating 'Brain Death' with Death," *J Med Philos* 26 (2001): 457–478.

75. James L. Bernat, "A Defense of the Whole-Brain Concept of Death," *Hastings Cent Rep* 28 (1998): 14–23; and President's Commission for the Study of Ethical Problems in Medicine and Biomedical and Behavioral Research, *Defining Death* (Washington, D.C.: Government Printing Office, 1981).

Sciences.[76] These individuals propose that loss of the entire brain leads immediately and necessarily to the loss of bodily integrity. This is the so-called whole-brain or total-brain formulation of the brain-death criteria.

2. *Psychological definitions:* Basically, death involves the permanent loss of consciousness or other essential human properties associated with personhood. This definition is species-specific. This is the rationale advocated by those who propose that death occurs when an individual loses only those parts of his brain associated with the "higher" functions of human being, including the abilities to think, feel, and reason.[77] This is the so-called higher-brain or neocortical formulation of the brain-death criteria. Psychological definitions are problematic because they inherently assert that human beings and other nonhuman animals die in radically different ways. This is contrary to reason and to everyday experience.

3. *Sociological definitions:* Basically, death involves the loss of socially conferred membership in the human community. This definition is *culture-specific*, and it is the rationale advocated by those who believe that death is an arbitrary, culturally relative, social construct, which presently in developed countries happens to be brain-based.[78] Sociological definitions are problematic because they inherently assume that a human being could be alive in a particular culture while dead in another, if the two cultures had different definitions of death. Again, this is contrary to reason and to everyday experience. A truly dead person should be considered dead in every time, in every place, and in every culture.

Note that disagreements at this first level of discourse would involve philosophical arguments. There is no need for medical expertise here, since

76. C. Chagas, "Conclusions," in *Working Group on the Artificial Prolongation of Life and the Determination of the Exact Moment of Death, October 19–21, 1985,* Scripta Varia 60 (Vatican City: Pontifical Academy of Sciences, 1986), 113–114; and R. J. White, H. Angstwurm, and I. Carrasco de Paula, "Final Considerations Formulated by the Scientific Participants," in *Working Group on the Determination of Brain Death and its Relationship to Human Death, December 10–14, 1989,* Scripta Varia 83 (Vatican City: Pontifical Academy of Sciences, 1992), 81–82.

77. As a representative example of this position, see Robert M. Veatch, "The Impending Collapse of the Whole-Brain Definition of Death," *Hastings Cent Rep* 23 (1993): 18–24.

78. As representative examples of this position, see J. Lachs, "The Element of Choice in Criteria of Death," in *Death: Beyond Whole-Brain Criteria,* ed. R. M. Zaner, 233–251 (Dordrecht: Kluwer Academic Publishers, 1988); and M. S. Pernick, "Back from the Grave: Recurring Controversies over Defining and Diagnosing Death in History," in *Death: Beyond Whole-Brain Criteria,* ed. R. M. Zaner, 17–74 (Dordrecht: Kluwer Academic Publishers, 1988).

definitions of death arise primarily from one's anthropological vision of the human person.

Second, every interlocutor has a set of *criteria* for death that he uses to determine when his particular definition of death has been fulfilled. For instance, if an individual held that death involved the permanent loss of consciousness (a psychological definition for death), it is likely that he would also embrace a set of criteria for death that included the destruction of those parts of the brain necessary for consciousness. At this level of discourse, disagreements would involve both philosophical and medical arguments. Philosophers would need to understand human biology before they would be able to identify and distinguish the criteria that would be needed to meet their definition of death.

Finally, every interlocutor in the brain-death debate has a list of clinical *tests* for death that is used to evaluate whether his criteria for death have been satisfied. To return to our individual who held that death involved the permanent loss of consciousness, his list of tests could include either an MRI or a CT scan or EEG measurements, medical procedures that could determine whether the critical parts of the brain necessary for consciousness are still intact or not. At this level of discourse, disagreements would involve predominantly medical arguments over how clinical tests best ascertain criteria for death.

The Neurological Criterion for Death

With these philosophical distinctions in mind, we now turn to the debate over brain death. For hundreds, if not thousands, of years, the absence both of respiration and of pulsation of the arteries—what is now called the pulmonary-respiratory criterion for death—was acknowledged as the definitive sign for death. This social consensus began to change in 1968, when the Ad Hoc Committee of the Harvard Medical School first proposed the concept of brain death as a more accurate definition for death.[79] In the early 1980s, this definition was codified into law in the United States when the President's Commission proposed a model statute for brain death, the Uniform Determination of Death Act, in which the commission specified two criteria for determining death: (1) irreversible cessation of circulatory and respiratory functions, or (2) irreversible ces-

79. "A Definition of Irreversible Coma: Report of the Ad Hoc Committee of the Harvard Medical School to Examine the Definition of Brain Death," *JAMA* 205 (1968): 337–340.

sation of all functions of the entire brain, including the brainstem. Since then, this second criterion, called the whole brain or total brain neurological criterion for death, has been endorsed by all the states in the United States and by many other nations. The commission justified its recommendations by arguing that the brain is the integrating organ of the human body and that loss of the brain inevitably leads to loss of bodily integrity, and thus to death.[80] Today, patients who fulfill the total brain dead neurological criterion are routinely declared dead.

On August 29, 2000, Blessed John Paul II addressed the 18th International Congress of the Transplantation Society that was being held in Rome.[81] His brief discourse to that meeting of physicians was significant because it was the first explicit statement by a pope regarding the diagnosis of death by neurological criteria. It was hailed by many as the long-awaited magisterial pronouncement on the brain-death controversy that had divided moralists, physicians, and lawyers, both within the Catholic Church and within society at large, vindicating the prevailing opinion that death of the whole brain is an adequate definition for the death of the human being.

The pope's argument presented at the international conference in Rome in support of the neurological criterion for death is relatively straightforward. First, John Paul II adopts a biological definition for death. He says that the "death of the person is a single event, consisting in the total disintegration of that unitary and integrated whole that is the personal self."[82] According to the pope, this disintegration results from "the separation of the life-principle (or soul) from the corporal reality of the person."[83] Presupposed in this definition of death is a Christian anthropology that acknowledges two truths. First, the human being is an embodied spirit, a substantial unity of body and soul. Second, the soul is the formal principle of the body, that principle that integrates and unifies the body, making it what it is. Note that this definition of the soul is extremely important because it lies at the heart of the pope's argument: if death is the separation of the soul from the body, and the soul is the integrating principle of the body, then the *only* empirical data for the absence of the

80. See the analysis by James L. Bernat, "The Definition, Criterion, and Statute of Death," *Semin Neurol* 4 (1984): 45–51.

81. Pope Blessed John Paul II, "Address to the 18th International Congress on Transplants," *Natl Cathol Bioeth Q* 1 (2001): 89–92.

82. Ibid., 90.

83. Ibid.

soul will be the loss of bodily integration. Next, the pope presumes that the scientific and medical communities have shown that total brain death leads to the loss of bodily integration: "Specifically, [death] consists in establishing, according to clearly determined parameters commonly held by the international scientific community, the complete and irreversible cessation of all brain activity (in the cerebrum, cerebellum and brain stem). This is then considered the sign that the individual organism has lost its integrative capacity."[84] Thus, the Holy Father concludes that "the fact of death, namely the complete and irreversible cessation of all brain activity, if rigorously applied, does not seem to conflict with the essential elements of a sound anthropology."[85]

A Disputed Question: The Validity of the Whole Brain Death Criterion

In the past decade, D. Alan Shewmon, a neurologist at the University of California, Los Angeles, has challenged the medical evidence that has been used to argue that the brain-dead patient has lost his bodily integrity. Most significantly, Shewmon has published a study of approximately 175 cases of diagnosed brain-dead patients with survival exceeding one week.[86] One patient, named T.K., was brain-dead for over twenty years. He spent over half that time at home under the care of his family, who fed him and maintained the ventilator that was needed to keep him breathing. While brain-dead, T.K. had grown, had overcome infections, and had healed wounds. T.K.'s case—and his is only one of many documented in Shewmon's paper—is a clear demonstration that total brain death patients are able to maintain a physiological stability and integrity superior to that found in many ICU patients still considered alive. Shewmon concluded that brain death patients are not dead because they still manifest the physiological integration that would be missing in truly dead individuals. To put it another way, total brain dead patients are not dead because they do not meet the biological definition of death. In sum, T.K. and the other whole brain dead patients, who survive for many years, challenge the consensus that the neurological criterion satisfies the bio-

84. Ibid., 91.
85. Ibid.
86. D. Alan Shewmon, "Chronic 'Brain Death': Meta-analysis and Conceptual Consequences," *Neurology* 51 (1998): 1538–1545.

logical definition of death. Clearly, if whole brain death patients have not lost the integrative capacity endorsed by the pope as the definitive sign of life, then they *really* are not dead.

The publication of Shewmon's critique of the whole brain criterion for death has generated much debate within secular and Catholic circles. Significantly, many physicians and secular philosophers concede that the whole brain dead patient retains some integrative capacity. James Bernat, the preeminent defender of the total brain death criterion, admits: "Of course Alan Shewmon is correct that not all bodily system integration and functions of the organism as a whole are conducted by the brain (though most are) and that the spinal cord and other structures serve relevant roles."[87] Jeff McMahan, a philosopher who specializes in the questions surrounding death and dying, writes: "If the familiar claims about the necessary role of the brain in integrating the functions of an organism are empirical claims, I think that Shewmon's cases and arguments force the defender of brain death to admit defeat."[88] Next, in an essay published in the influential *New England Journal of Medicine*, Robert Truog and Franklin G. Miller acknowledge, "The uncomfortable conclusion to be drawn from this literature [the scientific and medical literature including Shewmon's research] is that although it may be perfectly ethical to remove vital organs for transplantation from patients who satisfy the diagnostic criteria of brain death, the reason it is ethical cannot be that we are convinced they are really dead."[89] Finally, in its recent white paper on the determination of death, the President's Council of Bioethics has concluded: "Patients diagnosed with total brain failure ... certainly retain enough somatic integrity to challenge claims that the body immediately becomes 'a disorganized collection of organs' once the brainstem is disabled. In addition, advances in intensive care techniques, displayed in cases of prolonged somatic 'survival' after 'whole brain death' challenge claims that the body cannot continue in its artificially supported state beyond a short window of time."[90]

87. James L. Bernat, "The Whole-Brain Concept of Death Remains Optimum Public Policy," *J Law Med Ethics* 34 (2006): 35–43; 41.

88. Jeff McMahan, "An Alternative to Brain Death," *J Law Med Ethics* 34 (2006): 44–48; 46.

89. Robert D. Truog and Franklin G. Miller, "The Dead Donor Rule and Organ Transplantation," *N Engl J Med* 359 (2008): 674–675.

90. President's Council on Bioethics, *Controversies in the Determination of Death: A White*

Though these commentators—and there are others—concede that the brain-dead patient is not dead by the standards of the biological definition of death, they disagree on the consequences of this admission. Bernat acknowledges the conceptual difficulties with the whole brain death criterion for death, but continues to support it because "on the public policy level its shortcomings are relatively inconsequential."[91] McMahan, on the other hand, would like to replace the whole-brain criterion with a "higher-brain" criterion that equates death not with the loss of biological integrity, but with loss of consciousness and personhood. To put it another way, McMahan would like to replace a biological definition with a psychological definition for death. He is not alone in making this proposal.[92] However, as Robert Truog points out, the higher-brain criterion would not only declare PVS patients and anencephalic infants dead, but would also be counterintuitive: "The notion that a spontaneously breathing patient who is surviving with only minimal nursing care is actually dead is extremely counterintuitive, and it is hard to imagine how this view could ever be acceptable to the public at large. Declaring these patients as dead 'by definition' would seem to contradict all of our common sense notions of what it is to be alive."[93] Thus, notwithstanding the problems with the whole brain dead criterion, Truog does not think that any change in public policy is likely. Finally, the President's Council on Bioethics has defended the validity of the whole brain dead criterion by proposing that the presence of the organism should be verified not by the presence of its bodily integration, but by the presence of its "fundamental work." According to the council, organisms "*must*—and *can* and *do*—engage in commerce with the surrounding world."[94] This is the definitive work of the organism as an organism. Moreover, this "openness to the world," according to the council, is manifested in the organism's ability to act on its own behalf, especially in its ability to take in food and water, and even more basically, in its ability to

---

Paper by the President's Council on Bioethics (Washington, D.C.: President's Council on Bioethics, 2008), 44–45.

91. Bernat, "The Whole-Brain Concept," 41.

92. Also see Veatch, "The Impending Collapse of the Whole-Brain Definition of Death"; and Stuart J. Youngner and Edward T. Bartlett, "Human Death and High Technology: The Failure of the Whole-Brain Formulations," *Ann Inter Med* 99 (1983): 252–258.

93. Robert D. Truog, "Brain Death—Too Flawed to Endure, Too Ingrained to Abandon," *J Law Med Ethics* 35 (2007): 273–281, 276.

94. President's Council on Bioethics, *Controversies*, 60.

breathe. Therefore, according to the white paper, "if there are no signs of consciousness *and* if spontaneous breathing is absent *and* if the best clinical judgment is that these neurophysiological facts cannot be reversed, [it] would lead us to conclude that a once-living patient has now died."[95] Despite this disagreement among the commentators, however, their agreement is clear: the whole brain dead patient has not lost his integrative capacity, and as such he is not dead by the standards of the biological definition of death that is presupposed by Blessed John Paul II and an authentic anthropology.

Shewmon's work has also generated a lot of controversy among Catholic moralists. In a statement published by the Pontifical Academy of Sciences entitled, "Why the Concept of Brain Death Is Valid as a Definition of Death," a working group of neurologists and others, including several Catholic prelates, endorsed the whole brain death criterion, declaring: "An important clarification is that brain death is not a synonym for death, does not imply death, or is not equal to death, but 'is' death."[96] The working group reaffirmed the orthodox line by claiming that the brain is the central integrator of the body, and as such, is absolutely essential for the integration of the human being. It also challenged Shewmon's argument that the brain-dead patient is integrated, by asserting that with respect to keeping somatic organs functioning after the brain has died, "it is extremely difficult and, with rare exceptions (not, as Dr. Shewmon suggests, 'common' exceptions), fails after a few days."[97] Moreover, the working group also argued that the brain-dead patient has in fact lost his bodily integrity: "The rare subjects who are brain dead, but whose organs survive for weeks or months, indicate that some organs such as the kidney and the digestive system can function independently of the brain, but whether they can integrate with each other is less clear."[98] In other words, according to the working group from the Pontifical Academy of Sciences, the whole brain dead patient has indeed lost his integrative capacity, and as such, he is dead by the standards of the biological definition of death.

95. Ibid., 64.

96. Antonio Battro et al., "Why the Concept of Brain Death Is Valid as a Definition of Death," in *The Signs of Death: The Proceedings of the Working Group, 11–12 September 2006,* ed. Marcelo Sanchez Sorondo, *Scripta Varia 110,* 5–13 (Vatican City: Pontifical Academy of Sciences, 2007), 5.

97. A. M. Battro et al., "Response to the Statement and Comments of Prof. Spaemann and Dr. Shewmon," in *The Signs of Death,* 14–20, at 15.

98. Ibid., 16.

Notably, a dissenting group of scholars, some of whom are also members of the Pontifical Academy for Life, has independently published a collection of essays that is critical of the whole brain dead criterion.[99] Like Shewmon, these Catholic scholars do not think that the brain-dead patient has lost his bodily integrity. He is still alive.

Finally, in the second edition of his textbook, *Catholic Bioethics and the Gift of Human Life*, William E. May refers to a novel Thomistic argument—I will call it the radical capacity for sentience (RCS) argument—that suggested that the presence or the absence of the radical capacity for sentience, defined here as the ability to have sensations or experiences, can be used to discern the presence or absence of human life.[100] The RCS argument has been used to argue for the validity of the whole brain death definition for death: since the human brain is required for sentience, loss of the brain inevitably leads to loss of the radical capacity for sentience and thus to human death. Integral to this argument is the premise that animals are defined by their radical capacity for sentience: an animal is a sentient creature. Thus, according to this argument, loss of the whole brain, and therefore, the loss of the radical capacity for sentience, necessarily involves a substantial change that transforms a human being into something that is not even an animal. Convinced by the veracity of the RCS argument, Professor May concludes that "bodies" that really are brain-dead "are *not* human or even mammalian."[101]

In response, the RCS argument is flawed.[102] It presupposes an ambiguous criterion for the material foundation for a radical capacity that links the radical capacity for sentience to a part of the human body that is *necessary* for that radical capacity to be actualized. However, this criterion is inadequate, because in many cases, a radical capacity cannot be linked to a single organ. Therefore, I propose that it is more accurate to link the material foundation for a radical capacity to the part that is both necessary *and sufficient* for that capacity. To illustrate the robustness of my proposal, consider the following query: what is the material foundation for

99. Roberto de Mattei, ed., *Finis Vitae: Is Brain Death Still Life?* (Rome: Consiglio Nazionale delle Rescherche, 2006).

100. William E. May, *Catholic Bioethics and the Gift of Human Life*, 2nd ed. (Huntington, Ind.: Our Sunday Visitor Press, 2008), 352–353.

101. Ibid., 353.

102. For a more detailed discussion of this argument, see my essay, "In Defense of the Loss of Bodily Integrity as a Criterion for Death: A Response to the Radical Capacity Argument," *Thomist* 73 (2009): 647–659.

the radical capacity to reproduce? With the RCS criterion—that a material foundation is a part that is necessary for the radical capacity to be actualized—there are multiple material foundations for reproduction. For the woman, her ovaries, her uterus, and her vagina would all fulfill this criterion. Instead, in light of my proposal, I would suggest that since all of these organs together are necessary *and sufficient* for reproduction, then it is more fitting, at a minimum, to identify the entire reproductive system as the material foundation for the radical capacity for reproduction.

With this in mind, the material foundation for the radical capacity for sentience, at a minimum, is the entire nervous system, because the entire nervous system is both necessary and sufficient for sentience. In theory, therefore, in order to determine if a human being has died, that is, undergone a substantial change such that he is neither a rational nor a sentient creature, we would have to determine if he has completely and irreversibly lost the functioning of his entire nervous system. In reality, however, this is not possible, because the nervous system innervates every tissue of the whole human being. To put it another way, we could never lose the entire the nervous system without losing the organism. Thus, the only real sign for the death of the human being must be the loss of the human organism, which as we discussed above, necessarily involves the loss of the patient's bodily integrity. Since the whole brain-dead patient retains this integrity, he is alive.

In sum, as Blessed John Paul II reemphasized in his discourse to the International Congress of the Transplantation Society, the only reliable indicator for the separation of the soul from its body is the loss of bodily integration. This follows directly from the definition that the soul is the formal principle of the body that unifies and integrates the body, making it what it is. Alan Shewmon has made a scientifically supported argument—a convincing one, in my opinion—that the whole brain dead patient retains his bodily integrity. In response, the working group from the Pontifical Academy of Sciences has suggested that this is not the case. However, their riposte is a weak one. How can they explain the growth and the homeostatic stability of T.K., who grew and fought off infections for nearly two decades, while totally brain-dead? He certainly had as much bodily integrity as those imminently dying patients in intensive care units (ICUs) throughout the world, whose bodily systems are kept functioning by chemical and mechanical assistance. Rather, T.K.'s physiological integrity suggests that he and other brain-dead patients are still alive. Moreover, the President's Council on Bioethics' proposal is also flawed.[103] Its suggestion that the life of the organism is best identified not with its bodily integrity but with its "fundamental work," in this case, with its ability to breathe spontaneously, cannot be reconciled with an authentic anthropology that acknowledges that the soul is the sole principle of unity and integrity of the organism. If the brain-dead patient is truly dead because he is unable to breathe spontaneously, then how, if not for the presence of a soul, do we explain the somatic integrity of the brain-dead patient?

Death from a Systems Perspective

As I have described in detail elsewhere, from the systems perspective, the body is a dynamic, complex, and seamlessly integrated network, not of organs nor of cells, but of *molecules,* including DNA, RNA, lipids, and proteins, connected by reaction pathways that generate shape, mass, energy, and information transfer over the course of a human lifetime.[104] In contrast to the prevailing reductionist and mechanistic view, the organism is seen here as a single, unified whole, a complex and dynamic network of interacting molecules that appear and then disappear in time. It is an embodied process that has both spatial and temporal manifestations. From the systems perspective, this particular pattern, this organization of the molecules of the human being, would be a manifestation of his immaterial soul.

Within this framework, death would coincide with the disintegration of the molecular network that makes up the body as a whole. This view rejects the idea that one organ in the body is essential for integration. Rather, the whole system is integrated and united by the soul. Undoubtedly, Alan Shewmon, would agree with this perspective. In one essay, he has argued that his data also show that there is an inherent non-localizability for integration. In other words, "each part of the body, especially the brain, contributes to the stability, robustness, and richness of the body's vitality and unity, but no one part or even combination of parts constitutes that vitality or unity."[105] Note that this is not a return to the traditional

103. For Alan Shewmon's critical response to the President Council of Bioethics' novel proposal to justify the brain death criterion, see his "Brain Death: Can It Be Resuscitated?" *Hastings Cent Rep* 39 (2009): 18–24.

104. Austriaco, "On Static Eggs and Dynamic Embryos: A Systems Perspective." The systems perspective was first discussed in relationship to death in Austriaco, Cole, and May, "Reply to Fr. Ashley," *Natl Cathol Bioeth Q* 1 (2001): 9–11.

105. Shewmon, "The Brain and Somatic Integration," 472.

cardio-pulmonary criteria, since the absence of respiration and circulation does not immediately lead to the disintegration of the body (otherwise, we could never use CPR to restore bodily function). Instead, death would occur when enough time has passed after the cessation of respiration and circulation, such that individual cells scattered randomly throughout the body would die from lack of oxygen. This sporadic but system-wide loss of cells would quickly and necessarily lead to the irreversible loss of molecular integrity of the whole system, and thus, to death.

A Disputed Question: Organ Procurement from a Non-Heart-Beating Donor with a DNR

Finally, one argument that is often leveled against critics of the whole brain criteria for death is that abandoning the neurological standard would exacerbate the already limited supply of transplantable organs, thus leading to more deaths of patients on the organ waiting list.[106] This is a utilitarian argument that does not hold privileged status within the Catholic moral tradition. The loss of transplantable organs would be an acceptable price to pay if abandoning the whole brain criterion would protect the lives of innocent and vulnerable human beings. However, it is still important to ascertain the effects of replacing the brain-death criteria with a systems-based standard for death on organ transplantation procedures.

At the outset, we should acknowledge that a systems-based understanding of death does not necessarily have to lead to the end of organ transplantation. The Catholic Church's moral prohibition against the donation of unpaired vital organs from a living individual is based upon the Church's moral prohibitions against murder and suicide—harvesting a beating heart from a living human being would necessarily lead to his death because it would stop his circulation, killing him—and no one, including the individual himself, is morally permitted to do this. However, this no longer applies to the person whose heart and lungs have stopped functioning: Removing a living heart or another "vital" organ from a living human being, whose body lacks respiration and circulation, does not lead to the patient's death.[107] The patient's death, the disintegration of

106. For a representative example of this argument, see Bernat, "The Whole-Brain Concept of Death Remains Optimum Public Policy."

107. For a similar perspective from Alan Shewmon, see his "'Brainstem Death,' 'Brain Death' and 'Death': A Critical Re-evaluation of the Purported Equivalence," *Issues Law Med* 14 (1998): 128–129.

his body, occurs from the lack of oxygen experienced by individual cells scattered throughout his body and not from the removal of his heart. In other words, after asystole, the moment when the heart stops beating, the heart ceases to be a vital organ for the life of the individual. In fact, from the systems perspective, after the cessation of respiration and circulation, none of a human being's organs is vital. Thus, after asystole, it should now be morally permissible for the still-living individual to donate his once, but no longer vital, organs as a last act of charity before his death.[108]

Critics could object by asserting that the removal of a non-beating heart is in fact an act that kills the patient, because it would preclude any possibility of autoresuscitation, the spontaneous recovery of the heart. In response, I distinguish that preventing resuscitation can be equivalent to killing a person. For instance, someone who intentionally prevents a nurse from performing CPR on an injured man, so that the man dies, would be guilty of murder. However, this act is an act of murder only because in this context, it is morally justifiable, in fact morally obligatory, to come to this injured man's aid. Contrast this scenario with the following: a physician prevents a nurse from performing CPR on his patient with a DNR order so that his patient would be allowed to die. In this alternative case, the physician is not guilty of murder. In fact, he is preventing the nurse from performing an immoral act—the resuscitation of a patient who, for a morally justified reason, has asked not to be resuscitated—that does not respect the dignity of the person, who should be allowed to refuse an extraordinary means of medical intervention. The DNR order is morally determining in this clinical case. In the same way, I propose that it should be morally licit for a surgeon to remove a non-beating heart as long as the patient has requested a morally justifiable DNR. Moreover, to avoid the possibility of scandal, the prudent surgeon could choose to wait ten minutes after the heart has stopped beating before procuring the donor's organs. After this time period, there is evidence to suggest that human autoresuscitation is unlikely.[109]

---

108. Note the difference between this argument and the argument made by some bioethicists who would like to have the non-beating heart donor declared dead. For a representative example of the latter argument, see James M. Dubois, "Non-Heart-Beating Organ Donation: A Defense of the Required Determination of Death," *J Law Med Ethics* 27 (1999): 126–136. Here, I am proposing that the non-beating heart donor is still alive. However, after asystole, he is now morally permitted to donate his once, but no longer, vital organs before he dies.

109. The true incidence and predictors of autoresuscitation in humans remain un-

Highlighting the Role of Virtue in Bioethics

Two different clusters of virtues should play a role in the practice of organ transplantation. As we discussed above, the donation of organs should be motivated by the virtue of charity, which disposes the agent to act to promote the good of another. We will consider charity in greater detail in chapter 8. However, two other moral virtues can support and encourage organ donation. The first is the virtue of liberality, in Latin *liberalitas*, which predisposes the acting person to use his possessions well.[110] This virtue makes a person generous according to right reason such that he is willing to give freely of his wealth without need of or expectation of praise. Liberality consists in giving, for the love of God, generous help to those in need. It is a more excellent justice. The second is the virtue of magnificence, which, as St. Thomas Aquinas explained, adds to the virtue of liberality.[111] It belongs to this moral virtue to make use of our wealth to do something great. "Great" here takes the work of magnificence from what pertains to the individual and extends it to what concerns God or the community. Both of these virtues would predispose the human agent—in an analogous manner, of course, since his organs do not belong to him as his possessions do—to the charitable act of organ donation. A liberal and magnificent individual would be more likely to donate his kidney in charity—a supreme act of generosity—if the opportunity presented itself to him. Thus, efforts to increase organ donation should target individuals who are already inclined to be generous: blood banks, volunteer associations, and civic charities should be preferred sites for recruiting new organ donors. Members of the clergy and consecrated men and women should be encouraged to consider organ donation.

---

known, though two reviews have described autoresuscitation (also called the Lazarus phenomenon) five minutes or longer after cardiorespiratory arrest in approximately half of the published case studies. For details, see Wolfgang H. Maleck et al., "Unexpected Return of Spontaneous Circulation after Cessation of Resuscitation (Lazarus Phenomenon)," *Resuscitation* 39 (1998): 125–128; and V. Adhiyaman and R. Sundaram, "The Lazarus Phenomenon," *J R Coll Physicians Edinb* 32 (2002): 9–13. The Maastrich protocol developed at the University of Zurich requires at least ten minutes to elapse after cardiorespiratory arrest before starting organ procurement. This waiting time did not compromise the quality of organs procured. For details, see Markus Weber et al., "Kidney Transplantation from Donors without a Heartbeat," *N Engl J Med* 347 (2002): 248–255.

110. St. Thomas Aquinas, *ST,* IIa-IIae, 117.

111. Ibid., 134.

In contrast, the allocation of organs needs to be governed by the virtue of justice, the moral virtue that consists of the constant and firm will in the human agent to give what is due to God and to neighbor.[112] Notice that justice is understood here as a virtue of the individual, as St. Thomas Aquinas explained, rather than as a characteristic trait of society and its institutions, as John Rawls and other modern philosophers would have it.[113] Classically, there are two kinds of justice. Commutative justice is the virtue that is concerned with the mutual dealings between two persons, while distributive justice is the virtue that is concerned with the dealings between society as a whole and its citizens as its parts.[114] In transplant medicine, the former governs the relationship between the transplant surgeon and his patient, who is in need of an organ, by ensuring that the surgeon practices medicine with the best interests of his patient in mind, while the latter governs the relationship between the organ distribution network and the individual organ recipients, by ensuring that the distribution network distributes organs fairly and equitably. As we discussed above, the organ transplant network should allocate human organs to recipients based on their particular need. Though determining this need involves a complex algorithm that takes into account both the efficiency of organ use and the urgency of patient need, in the end, the process should be shaped not only by the numbers generated by this algorithm, but also by just administrators motivated by compassion and mercy.

Finally, the culture of organ donation and transplantation should be permeated by the virtue of gratitude. St. Thomas Aquinas describes gratitude as a virtue connected to justice that predisposes the individual to be thankful for a benefit received.[115] He goes on to explain that thankfulness is due first to God, then to our parents, to our country, and finally, to our benefactors. In light of this hierarchy of thanksgiving, an organ donor should appreciate that his organs are gifts from his Creator, which he has shared with another, while an organ recipient should also realize that his new organ is a gift given to him from the Lord through the generosity of the donor. Practically speaking, therefore, the virtue of grati-

112. *Catechism of the Catholic Church*, no. 1807.

113. John Rawls has posited that justice is the first virtue of social institutions. See his landmark monograph, *A Theory of Justice* (Cambridge, Mass.: Harvard University Press, 1971), 3.

114. St. Thomas Aquinas, *ST*, IIa-IIae, 61.1.

115. Ibid., IIa-IIae, 106.

tude should motivate both, the organ donor and the recipient, to prayer. Both should pray for the welfare and salvation of the other. The recipient too should resolve to live as excellent a life as possible to honor the generosity and the gift of the donor. He would accomplish this by incorporating practices in his life that would preserve and promote his own health and the health of the organ he has received. In doing so, he acknowledges the magnificence of the act of self-giving that has preserved his life. Gratitude should change and shape his life.

CHAPTER SEVEN

Research Bioethics from the Bench to the Bedside

On May 16, 1997, President Bill Clinton apologized to the eight remaining survivors of a government-funded syphilis study, conducted between 1932 and 1972, in Tuskegee, Alabama, by the U.S. Public Health Service.[1] The nearly four hundred participants who had been enrolled in the Tuskegee Syphilis Study, most of whom were poor, illiterate, African American sharecroppers, had not given, and were not asked for, their informed consent, and were not informed of their diagnosis. Furthermore, rather than end the study, the Tuskegee scientists chose to withhold penicillin from the study participants even though they were aware that the drug could have cured them of their illness. The study continued until a leak to the press generated a public scandal that ended the research program. By then, nearly a quarter of the participants had been allowed to die from syphilis or from medical complications related to the disease. Not surprisingly, the Tuskegee study has been described as "arguably the most infamous biomedical research study in U.S. history."[2] In response to the press report and the public firestorm that it created, the federal government commissioned the Belmont Report (1979) that led to the establishment of institutional review boards nationwide to monitor all experimentation with human subjects.[3]

1. "Remarks by the President in Apology for Study Done in Tuskegee," May 16, 1997, at http://clinton4.nara.gov/textonly/New/Remarks/Fri/19970516–898.html.

2. Ralph V. Katz et al., "The Tuskegee Legacy Project: Willingness of Minorities to Participate in Biomedical Research," *J Health Care Poor Underserved* 17 (2006): 698–715; 698. For details and further discussion on the Tuskegee Study, see James H. Jones, *Bad Blood: The Syphilis Experiment*, rev. ed. (New York: Free Press, 1993); and Fred D. Gray, *The Tuskegee Syphilis Study: The Real Story and Beyond* (Montgomery, Ala.: NewSouth Books, 2002).

3. For discussion of *The Belmont Report*, see James F. Childress, Eric M. Meslin, and Harold T. Shapiro, eds., *Belmont Revisited: Ethical Principles for Research with Human Subjects* (Washington, D.C.: Georgetown University Press, 2005).

In this chapter, which deals with the moral questions raised by bio-medical research, I will begin with a discussion of the vocation of the sci-entist, by focusing on recent papal addresses to the Pontifical Academy of Sciences. According to the popes, the scientist is a professional who is called to serve the human person by discovering the truth about cre-ation and by improving society through technological advances. I then deal with experiments with human subjects: what are the moral limits for protocols that involve human participants, especially experiments that target developmentally immature human beings, such as embryos and fe-tuses? Next, I address two specialized areas of biomedical research in-volving human subjects, genetic engineering and neuroscience, which have been the focus of much recent ethical debate. I continue with a parallel discussion of the morality of animal testing: how can one justify the rou-tine, and sometimes lethal, experiments that are done with monkeys, rab-bits, and mice, in laboratories throughout the world? Finally, I close with a discussion of the moral controversy surrounding stem cell research and the emerging field of regenerative medicine.

The Vocation of the Scientist

Like the health care professional considered in chapter 4, the research scientist has a specific vocation prepared by the Lord. As Blessed John Paul II explained to the members of the Pontifical Academy of Sciences, a scientist is a way of being someone, rather than just a way of doing some-thing: "Every scientist, through personal study and research, completes himself and his own humanity. You [scientists] are authoritative witness-es to this. Each one of you, indeed, thinking of his own life and his own experience, could say that research has constructed and in a certain way has marked his personality."[4] Like everyone else who has a vocation, a sci-entist is called to pursue his research endeavors for his own salvation and for the salvation of others.

In his many addresses to the Pontifical Academy of Sciences, Blessed John Paul II highlighted three important dimensions of the scientist's vo-cation. First, the scientist is a person who is called to seek truth: "The search for truth is the task of basic science. The researcher who moves

---

4. John Paul II, "Address to the Plenary Session on the Subject 'Science and the Fu-ture of Mankind,' November 13, 2000," in Pontifical Academy of Sciences, *Papal Addresses to the Pontifical Academy of Sciences*, 385–388, 387.

on this first versant of science, feels all the fascination of St. Augustine's words: '*Intellectum valde ama,*' 'he loves intelligence' and the function that is characteristic of it, to know truth."[5] More specifically, the scientist uses both his capacity to reason and his faculty for wonder, "to understand in an ever better way the particular reality of man in relation to the biological-physical processes of nature, to discover always new aspects of the cosmos, to know more about the location and the distribution of resources, the social and environmental dynamics, and the logic of progress and development."[6] In this way, the scientist ascertains the laws that govern the created order we call the universe, and in doing so, manifests our dominion over and stewardship of creation. Ultimately, and this is significant, according to Blessed John Paul II, science leads us to a better understanding of the human person: "Scientific truth, which is itself a participation in divine Truth, can help philosophy and theology to understand ever more fully the human person and God's Revelation about man, a Revelation that is completed and perfected in Jesus Christ."[7]

Next, according to the Holy Father, in seeking the truth, the scientist is also a person who is called to seek God. He is a person who is in a unique position to perceive the transcendence of a reality that points to its Creator: "The scientist's condition as a sentinel in the modern world, as one who is the first to glimpse the enormous complexity together with the marvelous harmony of reality, makes him a privileged witness of the plausibility of religion, a man capable of showing how the admission of transcendence, far from harming the autonomy and the ends of research, rather stimulates it to continually surpass itself in an experience of self-transcendence which reveals the human mystery."[8] The scientist, by virtue of his vocation, is called to an encounter with God, the Creator of heaven and earth. Indeed, undertaking scientific research can be a form of wor-

---

5. John Paul II, "Address to the Plenary Session (Commemoration of Albert Einstein), November 10, 1979," in Pontifical Academy of Sciences, *Papal Addresses to the Pontifical Academy of Sciences,* 239–244, 239.

6. John Paul II, "Address to the Plenary Session on the Subject 'Science and the Future of Mankind, November 13, 2000," 387.

7. John Paul II, "Address of John Paul II to the Members of the Pontifical Academy of Sciences, November 10, 2003," at http://www.vatican.va/holy_father/john_paul_ii/speeches/2003/november/documents/hf_jp-ii_spe_20031110_academy-sciences_en.html.

8. John Paul II, "Scientists and God: General Audience, Wednesday, 17 July 1985," *L'Osservatore Romano,* July 22, 1985; 1.

ship, because "by exploring the greatest and the smallest, [it] contributes to the glory of God which is reflected in every part of the universe."[9]

Finally, the pope explains that in seeking truth, the scientist is called to a life of service to his brothers and sisters: "Scientists, therefore, precisely because they 'know more,' are called to 'serve more.' Since the freedom they enjoy in research gives them access to specialized knowledge, they have the responsibility of using it wisely for the benefit of the entire human family."[10] This call to service bears fruit in the benefits that science can bring to society through basic research and technological innovation. Thus, the Holy Father insisted that scientific knowledge is ordered not to the private good of the individual scientist or even to the limited good of a particular group of individuals, but to the common good of society as a whole: "You are asked to work in a way that serves the good of individuals and of all humanity, while always being attentive to the dignity of every human being and to respect for creation."[11] This moral charge is an integral dimension of the scientist's vocation and his professional calling in life. As the Congregation for the Doctrine of the Faith, quoting the Second Vatican Council, put it: "Science and technology require, for their own intrinsic meaning, an unconditional respect for the fundamental criteria of the moral law: That is to say, they must be at the service of the human person, of his inalienable rights and his true and integral good according to the design and will of God."[12] In sum, in pursuing their experimental protocols and clinical trials, scientists must always strive to grow in virtue and in human excellence if they are to remain faithful to their vocation to serve both God and the human person.

Experimentation with Adult Human Subjects: Biomedical Research and Clinical Trials

According to the registry maintained by the U.S. National Institutes of Health, there were approximately 93,900 clinical trials taking place in

9. John Paul II, "Address to Scientists, Jubilee of Scientists, May 25, 2000," at http://www.vatican.va/holy_father/john_paul_ii/speeches/documents/hf_jp-ii_spe_20000525_jubilee-science_en.html.

10. John Paul II, "Address to the Plenary Session on the Subject 'The Cultural Values of Science,'" in Pontifical Academy of Sciences, Papal Addresses to the Pontifical Academy of Sciences, 389–391, 390.

11. John Paul II, "Address to Scientists, Jubilee of Scientists, May 25, 2000."

12. Congregation for the Doctrine of the Faith, Donum vitae, I-6.

173 countries in the middle of 2010.[13] Most of these clinical trials include both interventional and observational studies that involve human subjects. Interventional studies admit research subjects who are assigned by the investigator to a protocol or other medical intervention so that treatment outcomes can be measured, while observational studies admit subjects who are simply observed by the research investigators.

What are the moral guidelines for clinical research and experimental trials? The ethical parameters that should govern experimentation with human subjects were first articulated in the Nuremberg Code, which was written in 1947 in response to the atrocities carried out by Nazi scientists on vulnerable subjects, and were later developed in the Declaration of Helsinki, first adopted in 1964, by the World Medical Association.[14] Both documents protect and promote the dignity of the research subject. They mandate that all research subjects must be kept safe, because no research is more valuable than the well-being and life of the human participants in the clinical trial or experimental study. Moreover, they insist that all participants must give their informed consent to research, and be allowed to discontinue participation in the clinical trial at any time. Therefore, physician-investigators and other scientists must be qualified to supervise the experimental trials involving human subjects, they must avoid causing harm, injury, or death, and they must discontinue their experiments if they discover that their research might cause the same. Next, the code and the declaration require that a research program involving human subjects, to be morally justified, must be based on prior animal studies, and must not only be valuable to society, but also provide a reasonable benefit proportionate to the burden requested of the research participant. Finally, Helsinki prescribed that in designing their clinical trial or experiment, researchers must try neither to exclude nor to unfairly burden a particular population of potential human subjects unless there is an overwhelming reason to do so.

The Catholic Church has endorsed the ethical principles summarized in the Nuremberg Code and the Declaration of Helsinki. First, as the

13. ClinicalTrials.gov (http://www.clinicaltrials.gov) is a registry of federally and privately supported clinical trials conducted in the United States and around the world.

14. For commentary, see George J. Annas and Michael A. Grodin, eds., *The Nazi Doctors and the Nuremberg Code: Human Rights in Human Experimentation* (Oxford: Oxford University Press, 1995); and Ulf Schmidt and Andreas Frewer, eds., *History and Theory of Human Experimentation: The Declaration of Helsinki and Modern Medical Ethics* (New York: Franz Steiner Publishers, 2007).

Catechism of the Catholic Church makes clear, science and technology are precious resources when they are placed at the service of the human person and promote his integral development for the benefit of all.[15] More specifically, scientific experiments on human individuals or groups that can contribute to healing the sick and the advancement of public health are also praiseworthy.[16] However, these experiments must be governed by moral principles that respect the dignity of the human person:

> Research or experimentation on the human being cannot legitimate acts that are in themselves contrary to the dignity of persons and to the moral law. The subjects' potential consent does not justify such acts. Experimentation on human beings is not morally legitimate if it exposes the subject's life or physical and psychological integrity to disproportionate or avoidable risks. Experimentation on human beings does not conform to the dignity of the person if it takes place without the informed consent of the subject or those who legitimately speak for him.[17]

To be justified, human experimentation has to respect the moral law.[18]

Of these moral guidelines for clinical trials and experiments with human subjects, one of the most important is the requirement for informed consent. As we discussed in chapter 4, there are several necessary elements for informed consent in the clinical encounter. The patients must understand the therapeutic protocol involved, they must be made aware of any reasonable alternatives to the proposed intervention if one is available, and they must appreciate the risks and the benefits associated with the medical intervention. They must then give their free consent to the medical intervention. These requirements for informed consent also apply to human experimentation where the therapeutic protocol is replaced by the experimental protocol of the clinical trial.

Finally, it is important to acknowledge that there is an important and morally significant difference between medical care and experimental regimens. The former is ordered primarily toward the good of the patient. It is patient-centered, and as such, is governed by professional standards of

---

15. Cf. *Catechism of the Catholic Church*, no. 2293.

16. Ibid., no. 2292.

17. Ibid., no. 2295.

18. For a succinct summary of Catholic principles and guidelines for clinical research, see Catholic Medical Association and the National Catholic Bioethics Center, "Catholic Principles and Guidelines for Clinical Research," *Natl Cathol Bioeth Q* 7 (2007): 153–165.

care. In contrast, the latter is ordered primarily toward the common good by generating knowledge that could improve the health care of a particular patient population. This difference justifies the use of mock drugs, commonly called placebos, which have no therapeutic effect, in clinical trials as long as reasonable safeguards are taken to minimize the risk to the participants in the study.[19] Thus, it is clearly immoral if patients assigned a placebo would be substantially more likely to suffer serious and permanent harm or even death. On the other hand, placebo-controlled trials for a new treatment for the common cold or for male pattern baldness would be moral, since the discomfort associated with these conditions does not impair health or cause severe discomfort. Therefore, participants of an experimental study must be told that their involvement in the clinical trial includes the risk that they may not receive any treat-

19. Critics have proposed that the use of placebos is immoral when an alternative effective treatment is available. They argue that randomizing patients to give a subpopulation of them sham medication violates the therapeutic obligation of physicians when an alternative treatment exists that could treat their illness. Thus, these commentators argue for the validity of the principle of clinical equipoise, a principle that is thought to be an ethical foundation for the design and conduct of clinical trials with human subjects. Clinical equipoise requires that there must be a state of uncertainty in the expert medical community between the treatment under investigation and the existing standard of care. In other words, clinical equipoise would prevent physician-investigators from incorporating placebo controls in their clinical trials when an effective treatment for the illness in question is available. For representative views from those critical of placebo trials, see Kenneth J. Rothman and Karin B. Michels, "The Continuing Unethical Use of Placebo Controls," *N Engl J Med* 331 (1994): 394–398; and Benjamin Freedman, Kathleen C. Glass, and Charles Weijer, "Placebo Orthodoxy in Clinical Research. II: Ethical, Legal, and Regulatory Myths," *J Law Med Ethics* 24 (1996): 252–259. In response, others have pointed out that the objection fails to recognize and acknowledge the difference between medical care and clinical trials. The former is ordered toward the good of the patient, while the latter is ordered toward the common good. When effective treatments exist, there must be a compelling methodological reason to conduct a placebo-controlled trial. However, if that reason exists, then placebos may be included in a clinical trial as long as their use does not lead to serious harm. For more extensive discussion of this response to the objection, see Franklin G. Miller and Howard Brody, "A Critique of Clinical Equipoise: Therapeutic Misconception in the Ethics of Clinical Trials," *Hastings Cent Rep* 33.3 (2003): 19–28. Also see Alex John London, "Clinical Equipoise: Foundational Requirement or Fundamental Error," in *The Oxford Handbook of Bioethics*, ed. Bonnie Steinbock, 571–596 (Oxford: Oxford University Press, 2007). Finally, and significantly, there are data that suggest that placebos can have a therapeutic effect even if patients know that they have received a sham treatment. For details, see Ted J. Kaptchuk et al., "Placebos without Deception: A Randomized Controlled Trial in Irritable Bowel Syndrome," *PLoS ONE* 5 (2010): e15591.

ment whatsoever for their ailment, as long as this does not lead to serious harm. This is an important dimension of the process of informed consent in the context of experimental trials with human subjects.

Experimentation with Immature Human Subjects: Embryo, Fetal, and Child Research

Many experimental research programs require the participation of persons who are unable to give their free and informed consent. These vulnerable individuals include, among others, psychiatric patients, incarcerated prisoners, young children, and unborn fetuses and early human embryos. As we discussed in chapter 4, informed consent in therapeutic situations can be given by a proxy who acts on behalf of the incompetent patient to protect and further the patient's good. A parallel scenario also applies for a nontherapeutic study or clinical trial. A moral consensus exists among Catholic moral theologians that proxy consent for incompetent individuals, including children, can be justified for nontherapeutic studies as long the patient or the prisoner or the child is not exposed to significant risk or harm.[20] Germain Grisez has identified a significant risk as a risk that is "beyond the level of life's common risks."[21] This ordinary-risk standard is a reasonable one. In these cases, the proxy serves the common good while exercising responsible stewardship over his charges.

With regard to unborn human persons, however, the Magisterium of the Catholic Church is clear: proxy consent can never be given for the participation of fetuses or embryos in nontherapeutic experimental research. The Congregation for the Doctrine of the Faith explained this moral prohibition as follows:

As regards experimentation, and presupposing the general distinction between experimentation for purposes which are not directly therapeutic and experimentation which is clearly therapeutic for the subject himself, in the case in point one must also distinguish between experimentation carried out on embryos which are still alive and experimentation carried out on embryos which are dead. If the embryos are living, whether viable or not, they must be respected just like any other human person; experimentation on embryos which is not

20. For discussion and a summary of the theological debate surrounding proxy-consent for incompetent individuals, see William E. May, "Proxy Consent for Nontherapeutic Experimentation," *Natl Cathol Bioeth Q* 7 (2007): 239–248.

21. Grisez, *Living a Christian Life, The Way of the Lord Jesus,* vol. 2, 534.

directly therapeutic is illicit. No objective, even though noble in itself, such as a foreseeable advantage to science, to other human beings or to society, can in any way justify experimentation on living human embryos or foetuses, whether viable or not, either inside or outside the mother's womb. The informed consent ordinarily required for clinical experimentation on adults cannot be granted by the parents, who may not freely dispose of the physical integrity or life of the unborn child. Moreover, experimentation on embryos and foetuses always involves risk, and indeed in most cases it involves the certain expectation of harm to their physical integrity or even their death. To use human embryos or foetuses as the object or instrument of experimentation constitutes a crime against their dignity as human beings having a right to the same respect that is due to the child already born and to every human person.[22]

Unborn human persons are particularly vulnerable individuals because of their developmental immaturity, and as such, nontherapeutic experiments with them necessarily involve risks that exceed the ordinary, common risk standard. They can never be morally justified.

Experimentation with Human Subjects: Genetic Engineering and Genethics

Though the human genome published at the dawn of the twenty-first century—three billion DNA bases, twenty or so thousand genes, and thirteen years of labor—remains a landmark achievement in the history of science,[23] it is only one of many genomes that have been or are being deciphered. The publication of these genomes, each of which is a complete catalog of all the genes of an organism, raises numerous moral questions. In particular, the post-genomic age will have to struggle with the ethics of genetic manipulation. When, if ever, is it morally permissible to modify genes in plants, in animals, and especially, in human beings? This will be the fundamental question for a post-genomic ethics that deals with the moral issues raised by genetics—a field some have called "genethics"[24]—because it grapples with the possibility of altering the very nature of nature, especially of human nature, itself.

22. Congregation for the Doctrine of the Faith, *Donum vitae*, I-4.
23. International Human Genome Sequencing Consortium, "Initial Sequencing and Analysis of the Human Genome," *Nature* 409 (2001): 860–921; and J. Craig Venter et al., "The Sequence of the Human Genome," *Science* 291 (2001): 1304–1351.
24. David Suzuki and Peter Knudtson, *Genethics: The Clash between the New Genetics and*

With regard to genetic engineering involving human subjects, a distinction must be made between genetic manipulations that are ordered toward the cure or the alleviation of human disease—gene therapy—and those genetic manipulations that are ordered toward the alteration of the human genome for nontherapeutic purposes—gene enhancement. Moreover, gene therapies can be further divided into two categories. Somatic cell gene therapy seeks to eliminate or reduce the effects of genetic defects in a patient's somatic cells, which include all his cells other than his reproductive cells. Examples of this genetic approach include clinical trials to correct primary immunodeficiencies, a group of inherited genetic diseases that compromise a patient's immune response.[25] Here, physicians and genetic engineers use different viruses and other means to introduce normal genes into a patient's diseased immune cells in the hope of reversing the symptoms of the illness. Gene therapy could also be used to treat cancer by introducing genes into the cancer cells, making them more susceptible to chemotherapy or radiation, and to cure AIDS by genetically altering the patient's white blood cells so they are resistant to HIV infection. The effects of these genetic manipulations would be limited to the patient himself. In contrast, germ cell gene therapy seeks to correct a genetic defect in a patient's germ cells, that is, his sperm cells or her egg cells, so that his or her children will be free of the genetic disease. It has not yet been performed on human beings, though experimental protocols have already been developed to correct genetic defects in mice and in their progeny. In theory, the effects of this kind of genetic manipulation would extend to all the patient's descendents and would permanently change the human gene pool.

To evaluate the morality of these technologies, Blessed John Paul II has articulated the basic moral norm regarding the genetic manipulation of human subjects: "All interference in the [human] genome should be done in a way that absolutely respects the specific nature of the human species, the transcendental vocation of every being and his incomparable dignity."[26] In an address to the Pontifical Academy of Sciences, he also

---

Human Values (Cambridge, Mass.: Harvard University Press, 1990). Also see the excellent anthology: Justine Burley and John Harris, eds., *A Companion to Genethics* (Malden, Mass.: Blackwell Publishers, 2002).

25. Adrian J. Thrasher, "Gene Therapy for Primary Immunodeficiencies," *Immunol Allergy Clin North Am* 28 (2008): 457–471.

26. John Paul II, "Address to the Plenary Session on the Subject 'Human Genome; Alternative Energy Sources for Developing Countries; the Fundamental Principles of

acknowledged the promise of genetic interventions that lead to the healing of patients: "A strictly therapeutic intervention whose explicit objective is the healing of various maladies such as those stemming from deficiencies of chromosomes will, in principle, be considered desirable, provided it is directed to the true promotion of the personal well-being of man and does not infringe on his integrity or worsen his conditions of life. Such an intervention, indeed, would fall within the logic of the Christian moral tradition."[27] Pope Benedict XVI has reiterated this teaching: "The Church appreciates and encourages the progress of the biomedical sciences which open up unprecedented therapeutic prospects until now unknown, for example, through the use of somatic stem cells, or treatment that aims to restore fertility or cure genetic diseases."[28] In other words, according to both these popes, gene therapy, in principle, is good.

More recently, the Congregation for the Doctrine of the Faith (CDF) has further specified a prudential distinction in its moral evaluation of both somatic and germ cell therapy. First, the CDF approved of somatic cell gene therapy: "Procedures used on somatic cells for strictly therapeutic purposes are in principle morally licit."[29] This kind of gene therapy is laudable because it seeks "to restore the normal genetic configuration of the patient or to counter damage caused by genetic anomalies or those related to other pathologies."[30] In contrast, the CDF is cautious about germ line gene therapy. In the same document, it concluded that "in the present state of research, it is not morally permissible to act in a way that may cause possible harm to the resulting progeny," in part because the risks connected to any genetic manipulation are considerable.[31] Therefore, until technological innovation improves the safety of these genetic modifications, germ cell gene therapy should be out of bounds for human

Mathematics and Artificial Intelligence', October 28, 1994," in Pontifical Academy of Sciences, *Papal Addresses to the Pontifical Academy of Sciences*, 358–363, 360.

27. John Paul II, "Dangers of Genetic Manipulation: Address to Members of the World Medical Association, October 29, 1983," *L'Osservatore Romano*, December 5, 1983, 10–11.

28. Benedict XVI, "Address of His Holiness Benedict XVI to the Participants in the Plenary Session of the Congregation for the Doctrine of the Faith, January 31, 2008," at http://www.vatican.va/holy_father/benedict_xvi/speeches/2008/january/documents/hf_ben-xvi_spe_20080131_dottrina-fede_en.html.

29. Congregation for the Doctrine of the Faith, *Dignitas personae*, no. 26.

30. Ibid.

31. Ibid.

subjects.[32] Finally, in its discussion of the morality of genetic modifications, the CDF adds that somatic gene therapy, to be morally licit, must
not only seek to minimize the risk to the patient but also require his informed consent.

With regard to the genetic alterations of human subjects that are not
directly curative, especially alterations that seek to "improve" or "enhance" human nature, Blessed John Paul II has reasoned that this kind of
biological manipulation is morally problematic: "No social or scientific
usefulness and no ideological purpose could ever justify an intervention
on the human genome unless it be therapeutic, that is its finality must be
the natural development of the human being."[33] The CDF has justified
this prohibition by noting that genetic manipulation for the enhancement
of human nature is inherently eugenic and, as such, would lead to the
marginalization of individuals:

> Some have imagined the possibility of using techniques of genetic engineering
> to introduce alterations with the presumed aim of improving and strengthen-
> ing the gene pool. Some of these proposals exhibit a certain dissatisfaction
> or even rejection of the value of the human being as a finite creature and per-
> son. Apart from technical difficulties and the real and potential risks involved,
> such manipulation would promote a eugenic mentality and would lead to in-
> direct social stigma with regard to people who lack certain qualities, while
> privileging qualities that happen to be appreciated by a certain culture or so-
> ciety; such qualities do not constitute what is specifically human. This would
> be in contrast with the fundamental truth of the equality of all human beings
> which is expressed in the principle of justice, the violation of which, in the
> long run, would harm peaceful coexistence among individuals.[34]

In other words, genetic enhancement would be unjust because it would
widen the gap between the haves and the have-nots. It could potentially
lead to the creation of a genetically enhanced "superior" class of individu-

---

32. For a concise summary of the arguments made for and against germ line gene
therapy in contemporary bioethics, see Eric T. Juengst, "Germ-Line Therapy: Back to
Basics," *J Med Philos* 16 (1991): 587–592. For a response to Juengst from the Catholic moral tradition, see James J. Walter, "Human Germline Therapy: Proper Human Responsibility or Playing God?" in *Design and Destiny*, ed. Ronald Cole-Turner, 119–143 (Cambridge, Mass.: MIT Press, 2008).

33. John Paul II, "To the Union of Italian Jurists," December 5, 1987, cited in Pontifical Council for Pastoral Assistance, *Charter for Health Care Workers*, no. 13.

34. Congregation for the Doctrine of the Faith, *Dignitas personae*, no. 27.

als with advantages over their genetically non-augmented peers that far exceed any benefits that parents are now able to give their children through education or training. Moreover, according to the CDF, germ cell gene therapy would inevitably undermine the common good by contributing to a culture of domination, where one class of individuals would eventually be able to regulate, and therefore to limit, the genetic future of another group of persons:

Furthermore, one wonders who would be able to establish which modifications were to be held as positive and which not, or what limits should be placed on individual requests for improvement since it would be materially impossible to fulfill the wishes of every single person. Any conceivable response to these questions would, however, derive from arbitrary and questionable criteria. All of this leads to the conclusion that the prospect of such an intervention would end sooner or later by harming the common good, by favouring the will of some over the freedom of others.[35]

Social justice requires that the commonweal seek to use its limited resources to improve the wellbeing of those at its margins, rather than to further marginalize them by enhancing an elite few far above the norm.

Genetic Testing of Human Subjects

With developments in genetics, it is now possible to identify individuals who are likely, or more likely than the typical person, to develop a particular disease. Genetic testing in adults can be undertaken for several reasons. A diagnostic genetic test can be used to verify the cause of a patient's symptoms; a pre-symptomatic test can be used to determine if a patient carries the mutated gene for a particular disease, for example, Huntington's disease, before symptoms manifest themselves; and a predispositional test may identify a higher-than-average probability for developing a disease. All of these uses can be incorporated into medical care that is consistent with a virtuous life. Therefore, as the bishops of the United States point out, the Catholic Church "welcomes [genetic] testing when it functions as an extension of sound medical practice."[36] However, in the same document, the bishops condemn any prenatal testing to

---

35. Ibid.

36. United States Conference of Catholic Bishops, *Critical Decisions: Genetic Testing and its Implications* (Washington, D.C.: USCCB, 1996).

detect genetic defects so that an abortion can be performed. As we discussed in chapter 2, however, prenatal testing to detect genetic defects to give families advance warning of a disease or disabling condition, so that they can make adequate preparations for the care of their child, is laudable. Finally, the bishops raise several cautions about the proper use and abuse of genetic information: "If someone tests positive [for a genetic mutation that predisposes the individual to a disease], should this information be available to insurance companies, whose financial success depends on minimizing risk? Potential employers? Potential marriage partners? What if the existence of a gene disposing to homosexuality is confirmed? Who should have access to test results? These simple examples illustrate the enormous potential for abuse."[37] These questions raise complex moral questions that will require not only prudence, but also the other virtues to discern well, likely on a case-by-case basis.

Finally, the prospects of genetic testing raise the issue of the prophylactic or preventive removal of body parts or organs. For instance, women who carry mutations in either the *BRCA1* or the *BRCA2* genes routinely undergo surgeries to remove their breasts and their ovaries before these organs develop tumors.[38] Can these medical interventions be justified for individuals whose family history and/or genetic testing indicate a highly elevated cancer risk? As we discussed in chapter 6, the Catholic moral tradition recognizes that the removal of a bodily part can be justified if the surgical intervention leads to the well-being and integrity of the whole. Recall that Pope Pius XII taught that three conditions govern the morality of a surgical procedure that removes a human organ:

First, that the continued presence or functioning of a particular organ within the whole organism is causing serious damage or constitutes a menace to it; next, this damage must be remediable or at least can be measurably lessened by the mutilation in question, and the operation's efficacy in this regard should be well assured; finally, one must be reasonably certain that the negative effect, that is, the mutilation and its consequences, will be compensated for by the positive effect: elimination of danger to the whole organism, easing of pain, and so forth.[39]

37. Ibid.

38. For a review, see S. Marquez-Calderon and A. Llamos-Mendez, "Effectiveness of Preventive Interventions in BRCA 1/2 Mutation Carriers: A Systematic Review," *Int J Cancer* 121 (2007): 225–231.

39. Pius XII, "Allocution to Delegates at the 26th Congress of Urology, October 8, 1958," 277–278.

Prophylactic surgery to remove genetically mutated breasts and ovaries appears to fulfill these criteria, and, therefore, is morally justifiable. Some may suggest that the excision of organs cannot be condoned because these body parts are not a present threat to the woman since they are not yet cancerous. However, there is scientific evidence that the development of cancer is a gradual and progressive process that can precede the appearance of a malignant tumor by months and even by years.[40] Thus, it is not unreasonable to argue that breasts and ovaries with *BRCA1* or *BRCA2* mutations are already diseased even if they have not yet developed tumors at the time of the prophylactic surgery.

Experimentation with Human Subjects: Neuroscience and Neuroethics

The Decade of the Brain proclaimed by President George H. W. Bush on July 17, 1990, ended at the turn of the millennium. Nonetheless, the rapid progress in neuroscience that was catalyzed by the ten-year effort "to enhance public awareness of the benefits to be derived from brain research"[41] has continued. Significant scientific and technological advances include the invention of functional magnetic resonance imaging (fMRI) to map brain activity, and the discovery of drugs that enhance cognition and strengthen memory. Not surprisingly, these milestones have also heralded the birth of a specialized focus in bioethics now called "neuroethics," which grapples with the moral questions raised by possible technological and pharmacological interventions that affect the human brain.[42]

One insightful commentator has identified three emerging issues in contemporary neuroethics that exemplify the wide range of moral issues that are being raised by developments in neuroscience, including the enhancement of normal brain function, the court-ordered exploitation of psychopharmacopia to rehabilitate socially undesirable behaviors, and the

40. For a discussion of how *BRCA1* mutations contribute to the gradual development of breast tumors in mice models, see Steven G. Brodie and Chu-Xia Deng, "BRCA1-Associated Tumorigenesis: What Have We Learned from Knockout Mice?" *Trends Genet* 17 (2001): S18–S22.

41. Project on the Decade of the Brain, "Presidential Proclamation 6158," at http://www.loc.gov/loc/brain/proclaim.html.

42. For an overview of the emerging field of neuroethics, see the essays in Walter Glannon, *Defining Right and Wrong in Brain Science: Essential Readings in Neuroethics* (Washington, D.C.: Dana Press, 2007); and the comprehensive text by Neil Levy, *Neuroethics: Challenges for the 21st Century* (Cambridge: Cambridge University Press, 2007).

application of neurotechnology to "read minds."[43] To illustrate the ethical complexity of these technological advances, I will consider here the moral questions raised by the discovery of psychotropic drugs that have been used to improve the mood, cognition, or behavior of patients struggling with mental illness.

Psychotropic or psychoactive drugs that act primarily upon the central nervous system to alter brain function are routinely used to help those struggling with a wide range of mental troubles. Three categories of drugs will be considered here with the following moral question in mind: should they also be used to enhance normal human function?[44] First, selective seratonin reuptake inhibitors (SSRIs) are a class of antidepressants used in the treatment of depression and anxiety disorder. However, they can also be used to enhance the mood of healthy individuals. A handful of studies with healthy subjects has already demonstrated that taking SSRIs— fluoxetine (Prozac) would be one example of this class of drugs—reduces self-reported negative passions, including fear and hostility, without affecting positive affects such as happiness and excitement.[45] The drugs also increase one's sociability and enhance cooperativity in laboratory interactions and test scenarios. Next, stimulant medications, such as methylphenidate (Ritalin) and amphetamines (Adderol), are used to treat attention deficit hyperactivity disorder (ADHD) by regulating the amounts of the neurotransmitters dopamine and norepinephrine in the brain. However, like the SSRIs, these drugs can also be taken by healthy individuals, in this case to boost those cognitive functions involved in problem solving and planning.[46] In colleges throughout the country, these drugs are being taken, without prescription, by healthy students who wish to stay alert and focused for studying, for test taking, and even for partying. A sur-

43. Martha J. Farah, "Emerging Ethical Issues in Neuroscience," *Nat Neurosci* 5 (2002): 1123–1129.

44. For a comprehensive discussion of the scientific and ethical issues discussed here, see *Brain Science, Addiction, and Drugs: An Academy of Medical Sciences Working Group Report* (London: Academy of Medical Sciences, 2008), at http://www.acmedsci.ac.uk/download .php?file=/images/project/BrainSci.pdf.

45. For details, see Brian Knutson et al., "Selective Alteration of Personality and Social Behavior by Serotonergic Intervention," *Am J Psychiatry* 155 (1998): 373–379; and Wai S. Tse and Alyson J. Bond, "Serotonergic Intervention Affects Both Social Dominance and Affiliative Behavior," *Psychopharmacology (Berl)* 161 (2002): 324–330.

46. R. Elliot et al., "Effects of Methylphenidate on Spatial Working Memory and Planning in Healthy Young Adults," *Psychopharmacology (Berl)* 131 (1997): 196–206.

vey in the scientific journal, *Nature*, revealed that 62 percent of the 1,400 respondents from sixty countries—most of whom were scientists—had taken the drug Ritalin without prescription, to enhance concentration and to improve focus on a specific task.[47] For some, this practice is the academic equivalent to doping in sports. Finally, the ampakines, a novel class of psychoactive compounds that facilitate learning and memory, are being used to treat Alzheimer's disease and schizophrenia patients. However, like the other cognitive enhancers described above, these drugs can also be used to boost memory in healthy individuals.[48] The United States military has even explored the use of ampakines to increase military effectiveness by allowing soldiers to function in a sleep-deprived state.[49] Again, should these drugs be used to enhance human function in healthy individuals?

The Catholic Church has remained fairly silent on the majority of moral issues raised by neuroscience, recognizing that many of the decisions involving this technology have to be governed by prudence. Clearly, pharmacotherapy to help patients struggling with mental distress is morally justifiable as long as care is taken to ensure the safety of those receiving the drugs. As Blessed John Paul II reminded a conference on illnesses of the human mind: "Whoever suffers from mental illness *always* bears God's image and likeness in themselves, as does every human being. In addition, they *always* have the inalienable right not only to be considered as an image of God and therefore as a person, but also to be treated as such."[50] But what about the use of cognitive enhancers to better normal human function? The Catholic Church has yet to speak definitively on this matter. However, it is noteworthy that the President's Council on Bioethics has discussed the moral implications of technology that is used to enhance human function to produce "superior performance" to determine whether or not such improvements compromise the humanity and

47. For details see Brendan Maher, "Poll Results: Look Who's Doping," *Nature* 452 (2008): 674–675.

48. For details, see the scientific review by Gary Lynch, "AMPA Receptor Modulators as Cognitive Enhancers," *Curr Opin Pharmacol* 4 (2004): 4–11.

49. For details see the report, "DARPA's Preventing Sleep Deprivation Program, October 2007," at http://www.darpa.mil/Docs/PSD_info_paper_Oct07_200807180945043.pdf.

50. John Paul II, "Mentally Ill Are Also Made in God's Image," International Conference for Health Care Workers on Illnesses of the Human Mind, November 30, 1996, *L'Osservatore Romano*, December 11, 1996, 9.

individuality of the human agent.[51] In its report, the council raised concerns that drugs used to enhance human function could lead to unfairness and inequality, to overt and subtle social coercion and constraint, to detrimental side effects that would undermine the individual's health and well-being, and most significantly, to the distortion of the true dignity of excellent human activity. These possibilities would be inimical to the pursuit of human flourishing, and, thus, would support prohibitions against use of these drugs in healthy individuals.

In light of our emphasis on virtue in bioethics, however, I also suggest that we could address the moral concerns raised by cognitive enhancers—and other biotechnological interventions that could enhance human function—by asking the following question: would use of these cognitive enhancers allow the human agent to grow in virtue and human excellence? In some scenarios, the use of these psychoactive drugs could help the human agent to better attain the end of his vocation in the service of the common good without any harmful effects. For instance, taking cognitive enhancers to help an air traffic controller to more accurately and efficiently keep track of airplanes would be laudable. It would make the individual a more excellent professional. In other scenarios, however, the use of these drugs would encourage the acting person to develop vices inimical to human flourishing. For example, taking Ritalin to better one's performance on the Medical College Admissions Test (MCAT) would be reprehensible. It would make the student a cheater, since medical schools presuppose that the test evaluates the native cognitive abilities of their applicants. In sum, a virtue ethic should help us to properly appropriate technological interventions that enhance human function without making us lose sight of the goal of seeking human excellence.

Experimentation with Animals and Plants

Over 20 million animals are used every year in the United States as models for biological and medical research to study human physiology and anatomy, human disease and injury, and human development and psychology.[52] Increasingly, scientists are using genetic techniques to engineer

51. President's Council on Bioethics, *Beyond Therapy: Biotechnology and the Pursuit of Happiness* (Washington, D.C.: President's Council on Bioethics, 2003), 101–157.

52. Bernard E. Rollin, "The Moral Status of Animals and Their Use as Experimental Subjects," in *A Companion to Bioethics*, 2nd ed., ed. Helga Kuhse and Peter Singer, 495–509 (New York: Blackwell Publishers, 2009), 499.

animals so that they more closely mimic the biology of human patients. For example, as we discussed in chapter 6, molecular biologists have genetically altered pigs so that their organs could be transplanted into human patients. Virologists studying HIV have also generated mice whose own immune cells have been replaced by their human counterparts.[53] These mice will help biologists better understand the complex physiological changes that give rise to AIDS.

Researchers also use plants routinely for basic research. They seek not only to understand the physiology of these organisms, but also to apply this knowledge to genetically modify food crops to create variants that are resistant to disease or to drought.[54] As one illustration of this approach, genetic engineers have made "golden rice" by inserting two genes into a rice plant that allow the rice to make beta-carotene, a precursor of pro-vitamin A.[55] This transgenic crop was developed as a fortified food to be used in areas where there is a shortage of dietary vitamin A, potentially preventing malnourishment and blindness in many children. Humanized mice and genetically engineered rice are only two examples of the varied ways in which the biomedical researchers use, test, and modify animals and plants in the laboratory.

In principle, the Catholic Church is supportive of animal research. The Church teaches that God entrusted the animals to the stewardship of those whom He created in His own image and likeness, and that animals do not and cannot have the dignity ascribed to human beings. Hence, it is legitimate to use animals for food, for clothing, and for biomedical research "if it remains within reasonable limits and contributes to caring for or saving human lives."[56] This use would include the genetic engineering of animals.[57] However, all effort must be taken to minimize the suffering of the animal subjects because "it is contrary to human dig-

53. Tatsuji Nomura, Takeshi Watanabe, and Sonoku Habu, eds., *Humanized Mice*, Current Topics in Microbiology and Immunology 324 (Berlin: Springer, 2008).

54. For an introduction to genetically modified crops, see Nigel G. Halford, *Genetically Modified Crops* (London: Imperial College Press, 2003).

55. X. Ye et al., "Engineering the Provitamin A (beta-carotene) Biosynthetic Pathway into (Carotenoid-Free) Rice Endosperm," *Science* 287 (2000): 303–305.

56. *Catechism of the Catholic Church*, no. 2417.

57. In principle, as we discussed in chapter 6, the Pontifical Academy of Life has endorsed the genetic modification of animals that would be altered so that their organs could be transplanted into a human patient. For a contrary position, see Nicholas Tonti-Filippini, John I. Fleming, Gregory K. Pike, and Ray Campbell, "Ethics and Human-Animal Transgenesis," *Natl Cathol Bioethics Q* 6 (2006): 689–704.

nity to cause animals to suffer or die needlessly."[58] The Pontifical Academy of Life has also commented: "Moreover, there is a place for research, including cloning, in the vegetable and animal kingdoms, wherever it answers a need or provides a significant benefit for man or for other living beings, provided that the rules for protecting the animal itself and the obligation to respect the biodiversity of species are observed."[59] Within reason, animals have a legitimate place in biomedical research that seeks to benefit human society.

Likewise, the Catholic Church is generally supportive of plant research. The Church has cautiously endorsed the promise of genetically modified (GM) foods, though it has not passed any definitive judgment on the moral questions raised by agribiotechnology. In an address for the Jubilee of the Agricultural World, Blessed John Paul II said the following:

"Fill the earth and subdue it; and have dominion over the fish of the sea and over the birds of the air" (Gn 1:28). These famous words of Genesis entrust the earth to man's use, not abuse. They do not make man the absolute arbiter of the earth's governance, but the Creator's "co-worker": a stupendous mission, but one which is also marked by precise boundaries that can never be transgressed with impunity. This is a principle to be remembered in agricultural production itself, whenever there is a question of its advance through the application of biotechnologies, which cannot be evaluated solely on the basis of immediate economic interests. They must be submitted beforehand to rigorous scientific and ethical examination, to prevent them from becoming disastrous for human health and the future of the earth.[60]

This precautionary stance has also been adopted by the United States Conference of Catholic Bishops in its reflections on food, farmers, and farmworkers: "[W]e believe that use of genetically altered products should proceed cautiously with serious and urgent attention to their possible human, health, and environmental impacts."[61] The bishops of the United States conclude with prudent advice: "The driving force in this debate [over GM foods] should not be profit or ideology, but how hunger can

58. Catechism of the Catholic Church, no. 2418.

59. Pontifical Academy of Life, "Reflections on Cloning," no. 4.

60. John Paul II, "Jubilee of the Agricultural World, Saturday, November 11, 2000," at http://www.vatican.va/holy_father/john_paul_ii/speeches/documents/hf_jp-ii_spe _20001111_jubilagric_en.html.

61. United States Conference of Catholic Bishops, For I was Hungry and You Gave Me Food: Catholic Reflections on Food, Farmers, and Farmworkers (Washington, D.C.: USCCB, 2003), 28, at http://www.usccb.org/bishops/agricultural.shtml.

be overcome, how poor farmers can be assisted, and how people partici-pate in the debate and decisions."[62] In contrast, the National Conference of Bishops of Brazil has opposed GM crops, arguing that the use of GM foods involves potential risks to human health; that the technology ben-efits a small group of large corporations to the detriment of small family farmers; and that these crops would damage the environment.[63]

The disagreement between the two national conferences of Catholic bishops regarding the use of GM crops highlights the lack of clarity in this moral debate and the numerous, often unverifiable, claims and coun-terclaims that have been put forward by the opposing sides.[64] Critics ar-gue that this technological innovation is morally problematic for sever-al reasons.[65] First, they contend that genetically modifying crops would harm the environment, by leading, for example, to the uncontrolled spread of foreign genes into nontarget plant species, including, and prob-lematically, weeds.[66] These "superweeds" would then become herbicide-resistant, potentially jeopardizing the food supply of the poor. Critics also cite one controversial study that suggested that pollen from geneti-

62. Ibid.

63. Comissão Pastoral da Terra, "Declaração sobre os transgenicos" (Pastoral Com-mission for the Land of the Catholic Bishops Conference of Brazil, "Declaration on Transgenic Organisms"), at http://www.cptnac.com.br/?system=news&action=read&id =1230&eid=88.

64. For two essays that highlight the main fault lines in the debate over GM foods within the Catholic tradition, see Sean McDonaugh, "Genetic Engineering Is Not the Answer," *America* 192 (2005): 8–10; and Gerald D. Coleman, "Is Genetic Engineering the Answer to Hunger?" *America* 192 (2005): 14–17.

65. For a comprehensive discussion of the ethical and social issues raised by GM crops, see Nuffield Council on Bioethics, *Genetically Modified Crops: The Ethical and Social Issues* (London: Nuffield Council on Bioethics, 1999), at http://www.nuffieldbioethics. org/go/ourwork/gmcrops/publication_301.html; and Jane Rissler and Margaret Nel-lon, *Perils amidst the Promise: Ecological Risks of Transgenic Crops in a Global Market* (Washing-ton, D.C.: Union of Concerned Scientists, 1993). Also see the two essays by Sean Mc-Donaugh, S.S.C., "Will Biotech Agriculture Feed the World?" *East Asian Pastoral Review* 43 (2006): 88–95; and Daniel Kroger, O.F.M., "Genetically Modified Crops: An Assess-ment from a Christian Ethical Perspective," *East Asian Pastoral Review* 40 (2003): 243–258.

66. In a controversial paper, Quist and Chapela suggested that genetically engineered genes had inadvertently been transferred from GM crops to wild species of maize in Mexico: David Quist and Ignacio H. Chapela, "Transgenic DNA Introgressed into Traditional Maize Landraces in Oaxaca, Mexico," *Nature* 414 (2001): 541–543. Though initially disputed, the conclusions of this paper have been confirmed for the most part by A. Piñeyro-Nelson et al., "Transgenes in Mexican Maize: Molecular Evidence and Methodological Considerations for GMO Detection in Landrace Populations," *Mol Ecol* 18 (2009): 750–761.

cally modified corn causes high mortality rates in monarch butterfly caterpillars, suggesting that GM crops could poison the birds and insects that would inevitably ingest these plants in the field.[67] Next, opponents of GM foods have identified potential risks for human beings, suggesting that these products could cause an allergic reaction in people.[68] Finally, they argue that the spread of GM agriculture could unjustly undermine the livelihood of small-scale subsistence farmers, who would be unable to compete with powerful agribusiness corporations.[69]

In contrast, proponents of GM foods have pointed to the potential benefits to agricultural productivity that could alleviate global hunger and malnutrition.[70] The creation of golden rice, to be fed to human populations experiencing a vitamin A deficiency, illustrates this possibility. Genetic modification could also be used to create more nutritious and healthier food crops, including plants that contain medically significant drugs and vaccines. Next, pro-GM advocates claim that genetically engineered pest and disease resistance could reduce the need for pesticides, thereby decreasing the environmental threat from these toxic chemicals. Finally, they propose that farmers in developing countries could benefit from transgenic crops, though a fairly high level of national institutional capacity would be required to ensure that farmers have access to suitable innovations on competitive terms.[71]

67. John E. Losey, Linda S. Rayor, and Maureen E. Carter, "Transgenic Pollen Harms Monarch Larvae," *Nature* 399 (1999): 214. The findings of this study have been challenged by, among others, the following papers: Richard L. Hellmich et al., "Monarch Larvae Sensitivity to Bacillus thuringiensis-purified Proteins and Pollen," *Proc Natl Acad Sci USA* 98 (2001): 11925–11930; and Diane E. Stanley-Horn et al., "Assessing the Impact of Cry1Ab-expressing Corn Pollen on Monarch Butterfly Larvae in Field Studies," *Proc Natl Acad Sci USA* 98 (2001): 11931–11936.

68. One study has suggested that genetically modified soybeans that had been changed to include a gene from the Brazil nut are allergenic for human individuals who are allergic to the nut: Julie A. Nordlee et al., "Identification of a Brazil-Nut Allergen in Transgenic Soybeans," *N Engl J Med* 334 (1996): 688–692. For commentary, see Clive Meredith, "Allergenic Potential of Novel Foods," *Proc Nutr Soc* 64 (2005): 487–490. Also see the extensive report that examines the health risks associated with GM soybeans: Andrew Marshall, "GM Soybeans and Health Safety—A Controversy Reexamined," *Nat Biotechnol* 25 (2007): 981–987.

69. Robert Ali Brac De La Perriere and Franck Seuret, *Brave New Seeds: The Threat of GM Crops to Farmers* (London: Zed Books, 2001).

70. For extensive discussion, see Martina McGloughlin, "Ten Reasons Why Biotechnology Will Be Important to the Developing World," *AgBioForum* 2 (1999): 163–174.

71. Terri Raney, "Economic Impact of Transgenic Crops in Developing Countries," *Curr Opin Biotech* 17 (2006): 174–178.

To summarize the parameters of the moral conversation: creating GM crops to alleviate human hunger is commendable as long as care is taken to minimize the risk to consumers. However, at present, morally evaluating this technology cannot be divorced from a moral analysis of the agribiotech industry, a potentially exploitative corporate structure that seeks to maximize profit rather than to seek a profit margin commensurable with the promotion of the common good. As the Pontifical Council for Justice and Peace taught: "Modern biotechnologies have powerful social, economic and political impact locally, nationally and internationally. They need to be evaluated according to the ethical criteria that must always guide human activities and relations in the social, economic and political spheres. Above all, the criteria of justice and solidarity must be taken into account."[72] In sum, the production and sale of genetically engineered crops, to be moral, has to consider the legitimate needs not only of the scientists and investors who contributed to their development, but also of the farmers whose livelihood would be shaped by the technology.

Finally, we end with a brief discussion regarding the patenting of genes and genetically modified living organisms: is this practice morally permissible? A patent is a set of exclusive rights granted by a state to an inventor for a fixed period of time that allows the inventor, through the courts, to stop rivals from making, using, or selling his invention without his permission in exchange for his agreement to share the details of his invention with the public.[73] In 1980, the United States Supreme Court granted a patent to a microbiologist for a genetically engineered microorganism that could clean up oil spills in the ocean.[74] It was the first American patent granted for a living organism. In 1987, the United States Patent and Trademark Office (PTO) ruled that all nonnaturally occurring, nonhuman multicellular living organisms are patentable subject matter.[75] Among the notable patents issued by the PTO subsequent to this ruling was for the Harvard OncoMouse, a transgenic mouse genetically engineered to develop cancer for the purpose of cancer research.[76] To date, patents have been granted for animal and human genes, for animal and human cells, and for

72. Pontifical Council for Justice and Peace, *Compendium of the Social Doctrine of the Church* (Vatican City: Libreria Editrice Vaticana), no. 474.

73. George C. Elliott, "A Brief Guide to Understanding Patentability and the Meaning of Patents," *Acad Med* 77 (2002): 1309–1314.

74. *Diamond v. Chakrabarty*, 447 U.S. 303 (1980).

75. See 1077 PTO Off. Gazette 24 (April 21, 1987).

76. U.S. Pat. No. 4,736,866 (April 12, 1988).

genetically modified plants and animals. Significantly, on March 29, 2010, a United States federal judge in New York invalidated seven patents related to the two genes *BRCA1* and *BRCA2*, which, when mutated, have been associated with breast cancer.[77] The ruling was appealed.

The Magisterium of the Catholic Church has not made any definitive statements regarding gene patents. At this point, it is important to stress the distinction between patenting *human* genes and patenting *animal* or *plant* genes, a distinction that follows from the radically different natures of human beings and of nonhuman organisms. Regarding the former practice, Blessed John Paul II has commented: "We rejoice that numerous researchers have refused to allow discoveries made about the [human] genome to be patented. Since the human body is not an object that can be disposed of at will, the results of research should be made available to the whole scientific community and cannot be the property of a small group."[78] Like human organs, human genes should not be treated as commodities or as property, because the human person is not the master, but only the steward, of his own life, his body, and therefore, his genes. Regarding the practice of patenting animals, plants, and/or their genes, on the other hand, the bishops of the United States have proposed the following:

Both public and private entities have an obligation to use their property, including intellectual and scientific property, to promote the good of all people. To ensure that the benefits of emerging technologies are widely shared, patents should be granted for the minimum time and under the minimum conditions necessary to provide incentives for innovation. Agricultural products and processes developed over time by indigenous people should not be patented by outsiders without consent and fair compensation. To ensure that poor countries can take advantage of new technologies, strategies and programs will be needed to help transfer these technologies affordably. The driving force in this debate should not be profit or ideology, but how hunger can be overcome, how poor farmers can be assisted, and how people participate in the debate and decisions.[79]

77. *Association for Molecular Pathology v. United States Patent and Trademark Office*, No. 09 Civ 4515 (S.D.N.Y. March 29, 2010).

78. John Paul II, "Address to the Plenary Session on the Subject 'Human Genome; Alternative Energy Sources for Developing Countries; the Fundamental Principles of Mathematics and Artificial Intelligence,' October 28, 1994," in Pontifical Academy of Sciences, *Papal Addresses to the Pontifical Academy of Sciences*, 358–363, 360.

79. United States Conference of Catholic Bishops, *For I Was Hungry and You Gave Me Food*, 31.

The bishops conclude that the patenting of life genes is not inherently immoral as long as all reasonable efforts are undertaken to avoid the exploitation of the poor.

Within contemporary society, there is an ongoing debate surrounding the legitimacy of life patents. Opponents cite three common reasons for their position.[80] First, they argue that living organisms, as creatures of God, should not be equated with human technical inventions. They continue by suggesting that the patenting of life forms promotes an irreverent materialistic conception of life. Next, opponents contend that a gene sequence is not a conventional chemical substance, but is more like an information code with different functions. Thus, the holder of a patent that describes one commercial use should not receive a monopoly on all possible functions. Finally, critics claim that patents hinder scientific research and development, not only by creating a climate of secrecy in science that would hinder the normal exchange of information that is essential for scientific discovery, but also by preventing the reasonable use of living organisms in laboratories.

In contrast, proponents of life patents justify the patent system as a way to promote technological progress in a manner akin to the justification given in the United States Constitution.[81] Patents, including patents for bioengineered organisms and their genes, promote this progress by providing financial incentives for innovation and by requiring inventors to disclose their inventions, which would enable others skilled in the field to test and to improve on them. Moreover, advocates propose that the extent to which life patents contribute to the commodification of living beings is not clear, since patents do not provide an affirmative right to use an invention but only provide a right to bar others from using it. Therefore, proponents conclude that patenting living organisms and their de-

80. For a representative moral analysis that is opposed to life patents, see Christoph Then, *The True Cost of Gene Patents: The Economic and Social Consequences of Patenting Genes and Living Organisms, A Greenpeace Document* (Hamburg: Greenpeace, 2004). Also see the essays by Rebecca Dresser, "Ethical and Legal Issues in Patenting New Animal Life," *Jurimetrics Journal* 28 (1988): 399–435; and Robert P. Merges, "Intellectual Property in Higher Life Forms: The Patent System and Controversial Technologies," *Maryland Law Review* 47 (1988): 1051–1075.

81. The Copyright and Patent Clause of the U.S. Constitution empowers Congress "to promote the Progress of Science and useful Arts, by securing for limited Times to Authors and Inventors the exclusive Right to their respective Writings and Discoveries" (article 1, section 8, clause 8).

rivatives is a practice that actually promotes the common good by accelerating technological advance.[82]

In conclusion, in light of the arguments proffered by both sides of this debate, the statement of the bishops of the United States remains a reasonable one. In principle, the practice of patenting nonhuman organisms and their genes should be morally permissible, as long as all precaution is taken in justice to consider and respect the legitimate needs of the stakeholders involved, especially the poorest of the poor.[83] It would be comparable to the morally acceptable practice of treating nonhuman organisms as property, property that we commonly call crops, livestock, and pets. Ownership gives the owner of the plant or the animal certain rights, including the right to breed and to sell the organism, and the right to prevent others from doing the same with his property. In a parallel manner, patenting would be a practice that gives the inventor analogous rights over his intellectual property.

Experimentation with Human Cells: Stem Cell Research and Regenerative Medicine

A typical adult human being is made up of trillions of cells of different types. There are one hundred and twenty or so of these different cell types—bone cells, skin cells, muscle cells, and blood cells are only some of these types—each with its own unique shape and function. These specialized cells are called differentiated cells because they have different functions. In general, these specialized cells have two basic characteristics. First, they have a limited lifespan. In other words, in the laboratory,

82. The Committee on Intellectual Property Rights in Genomic and Protein Research and Innovation of the National Research Council has concluded: "For the time being, it appears that access to patented inventions or information inputs into biomedical research rarely imposes a significant burden for biomedical researchers." See their report, *Reaping the Benefits of Genomic and Proteomic Research: Intellectual Property Rights, Innovation and Public Health* (Washington, D.C.: National Academies of Sciences, 2006). However, there are studies that suggest that gene patents do inhibit biomedical innovation. For instance, see E. Richard Gold, Warren Kaplan, James Orbinski, Sarah Harland-Logan, and Sevil N-Marandi, "Are Patents Impeding Medical Care and Innovation?" *PLoS Med* 7 (2010): e1000208; and James P. Evans, "Putting Patients before Patents," *Genetics in Medicine* 12 (2010): 204–205.

83. For a theological commentary that suggests that gene patenting ought to be more highly regulated and that it ought to be regulated with international participation, see Lisa Sowle Cahill, "Genetics, Commodification, and Social Justice in the Globalization Era," *Kennedy Inst Ethics J* 11 (2001): 221–238.

a population of these cells can divide only about fifty times or so before growing old and dying. Second, when they divide, these specialized cells can produce only daughter cells of their own type. Thus, a skin cell can produce only other skin cells, while a muscle cell can produce only other muscle cells. They are unipotent cells.

Differentiated human cells and tissues are routinely cultured in laboratories throughout the world for experiments of different types. They are essential elements of numerous research programs that seek to uncover the secrets of both normal and diseased cells. Blessed John Paul II has acknowledged the importance of these research efforts to better understand the most intimate mechanisms of life: "It must be emphasized that new techniques, such as the cultivation of cells and tissues, have had a notable development which permits very important progress in biological sciences."[84] Differentiated human cells are also used to identify and to test novel drugs that could be used to treat disease and genetic anomalies. In principle, experimental protocols using human cells and tissues should be morally permissible, as long as the cells are obtained with the informed consent of the volunteers or the patients who gave them to science.

In addition to the numerous kinds of differentiated cells, the human being also has a different category of cells called stem cells. These cells are rare. In contrast to skin, muscle, and other differentiated cells, stem cells are relatively nonspecialized and are therefore called "undifferentiated" cells. Stem cells too have two basic characteristics. First, they are immortal. In the laboratory, stem cells will continue to divide and to grow as long as they are kept in a suitable environment and receive all necessary nutrients. Second, when they divide, stem cells can produce cells of different cell types. Thus, a stem cell could produce a skin cell or a muscle cell or a liver cell, depending on the particular environment it finds itself in. Like the stem of a plant that can produce branches or leaves or flowers, a stem cell can generate a variety of different cell types.

In human beings, as in other animal species, there are two general classes of stem cells. Embryonic stem cells, or ES cells, are stem cells that are harvested from five-day-old human embryos that are destroyed in the process. In theory, they are able to produce all of the one hundred and twenty or so cell types that are found in an adult's body, and are there-

84. John Paul II, "Address to the Study Week on the Subject 'Modern Biological Experimentation,'" in Pontifical Academy of Sciences, *Papal Addresses to the Pontifical Academy of Sciences*, 253–256, 255.

fore called pluripotent stem cells. Adult stem cells, or AS cells, are stem cells that are found in different tissues in human beings at a later stage of development. Adult stem cells include stem cells taken from, among other tissues, bone marrow, fetal cord blood, fat, and liver. They are able to produce many, but not all, of the one hundred and twenty or so cell types in the adult body, and are, therefore, called multipotent stem cells. There are scientific papers that suggest that adult stem cells—especially stem cells from the bone marrow and from the testicle—may be as pluripotent as embryonic stem cells, though these results remain controversial.[85]

Stem cell research has generated much excitement since human embryonic stem cells were discovered more than ten years ago at the University of Wisconsin–Madison.[86] First, many scientists believe that stem cells are exciting because they will soon revolutionize medicine by catalyzing the emergence of the new field of regenerative medicine. Regenerative medicine will allow physicians to replace lost or damaged cells with stem cells or differentiated cells derived from them.[87] Second, scientists also believe that stem cells will be useful laboratory tools, not only to better understand the origin and causes for many chronic and acute diseases, but also to develop drugs to treat these illnesses.[88] Both approaches could lead to cures that would alleviate the suffering of millions.

Many chronic and acute injuries that are common in the developed world involve the loss or death of a particular cell type in the patient. Chronic conditions include Parkinson's disease, a degenerative disease of the central nervous system that results from the loss of specialized nerve cells in the brain that secrete dopamine, and juvenile, or type 1, diabetes, a metabolic disease associated with the loss of specialized cells in the pancreas that secrete insulin into the blood. Acute conditions include spinal

85. For representative papers, see the following: Andreea Ianus et al., "In vivo Derivation of Glucose-Competent Pancreatic Endocrine Cells from Bone Marrow without Evidence of Cell Fusion," *J Clin Invest* 111 (2003): 843–850; and Sabine Conrad et al., "Generation of Pluripotent Stem Cells from Adult Human Testis," *Nature* 456 (2008): 344–349. For a review of the scientific literature, see M. R. Alison and S. Islam, "Attributes of Adult Stem Cells," *J Pathol* 217 (2009): 144–160.

86. James A. Thomson et al., "Embryonic Stem Cell Lines Derived from Human Blastocysts," *Science* 282 (1998): 1145–1147. (Erratum, *Science* 282 (1998): 1827.)

87. For a comprehensive discussion of regenerative medicine, see Richard L. Gardner, "Stem Cells and Regenerative Medicine: Principles, Prospects and Problems," *C R Biol* 330 (2007): 465–473.

88. John D. McNeish, "Stem Cells as Screening Tools in Drug Discovery," *Curr Opin Pharmacol* 7 (2007): 515–520.

cord injury and heart attacks, which are debilitating because they lead to the death of cells in the spinal cord and in the heart respectively.

Proponents of regenerative medicine hope to treat these diseases and others like them by using stem cells to replace the lost or damaged cells. Let us say that an adult—let us call him Jim—gets Parkinson's disease fifty years from now. Regenerative medicine would allow Jim's physician to use stem cells to cure him of this affliction. The physician would simply take stem cells (or cells derived from them) and introduce them into his patient's nervous system. Since these cells have the ability to become cells of different types, the hope is that they would repair the diseased Parkinson's brain by becoming new dopamine-producing nerve cells, thus replacing the specialized nerve cells that had been lost. The same would hold true for treating heart attacks. If Jim suffers a heart attack fifty years from now, regenerative medicine would allow his cardiologist to simply inject stem cells (or cells derived from them) into his blood stream. The hope would be that these cells would migrate to and regenerate Jim's heart by becoming new heart cells—called cardiomyocytes—thus replacing the heart cells that were killed during the heart attack.

Finally, while regenerative medicine promises to lead directly to cures, scientists also believe that stem cells taken from patients with different diseases could themselves be used as research tools in the laboratory to better understand the origins and development of disease. For instance, stem cells obtained from a patient with amyotrophic lateral sclerosis, or Lou Gehrig's disease, could help scientists to comprehend the gradual deterioration of motor neurons that occurs during the course of this debilitating neuromuscular disease. In this way, disease-specific stem cells used as research tools could lead indirectly to cures for many illnesses. Not surprisingly, stem cell research is a promising source of hope for many patients.

Is stem cell research a moral practice? At the outset, it is important to stress that not all stem cell research is controversial. A moral consensus exists applauding and encouraging the development of cell-replacement therapies that arise from human adult stem cell research. However, much moral and political debate surrounds human embryonic stem cell research because it is associated with the destruction of human embryos. As Pope Benedict XVI explained to a conference of stem cell biologists:

Research, in such cases, irrespective of efficacious therapeutic results is not truly at the service of humanity. In fact, this research advances through the suppression of human lives that are equal in dignity to the lives of other human individuals and to the lives of the researchers themselves. History itself has condemned such a science in the past and will condemn it in the future, not only because it lacks the light of God but also because it lacks humanity.[89]

This scientific practice is gravely immoral because it leads to the death of innocent human beings, and, as such, attacks the inviolable dignity of the human person.

Finally, many people think that the Catholic Church is against all human stem cell research. This is inaccurate. As we discussed above, the Catholic Church is opposed to any and all research programs that attack and undermine the dignity of the human person, especially any experiments that lead to the death of innocent human beings. However, the Church would enthusiastically support all morally acceptable research that seeks to alleviate the suffering of the sick. Indeed, though the Church is opposed to destructive human embryo research, several dioceses, including all the dioceses in South Korea[90] and the Archdiocese of Sydney,[91] have funded efforts to develop adult stem cell technology. Finally, on May 19, 2010, the Vatican announced a joint initiative with an international pharmaceutical company named Neostem, Inc., to raise awareness and to expand research for adult stem cell therapy.[92]

Common Objections

The Use of "Surplus" Human Embryos for Stem Cell Research

As we mentioned in chapter 3, approximately four hundred thousand human embryos are being stored in cryogenic freezers in several hundred assisted reproductive technology (ART) facilities in the United States. Of

89. Benedict XVI, "Address of His Holiness Benedict XVI to the Participants in the Symposium on the Theme: 'Stem Cells: What Future for Therapy?' Organized by the Pontifical Academy for Life, September 16, 2006," at http://www.vatican.va/holy_father/benedict_xvi/speeches/2006/september/documents/hf_ben-xvi_spe_20060916_pav_en.html.

90. "S Korea's Catholic Church Funding Stem-Cell Research," *Taipei Times*, October 6, 2005, at http://www.taipeitimes.com/News/world/archives/2005/10/06/2003274635.

91. "New Grant for Research on Adult Stem Cells from Catholic Church," Archdiocese of Sydney Media Release, July 25, 2005, at http://www.sydney.catholic.org.au/News/MR/2005725_1026.shtml.

92. "Catholic Church Announces Adult Stem Cell Venture with Neostem," at http://www.catholicnewsagency.com/news/catholic-church-announces-adult-stem-cell-venture-with-neostem/

these, approximately eleven thousand embryos are available for research.[93] Moreover, a survey of 2,210 fertility patients has revealed that 495 (49%) of the 1,020 respondents who had stored frozen embryos were somewhat or very likely to donate their embryos for research purposes.[94] Therefore, proponents of stem cell research have suggested that these "surplus" embryos should be made available to scientists working to obtain embryonic stem cells, especially since many of these "spare" embryos are already destined for destruction.[95]

In response, would we be morally justified if we proposed that terminally ill children in a pediatric oncology unit should be made available to scientists who would kill them to study their diseased organs, especially since they are already destined for death? Of course not! Until he dies, the human being, whether he is an embryo or a child, has an intrinsic dignity that needs to be respected. Therefore, even if he is about to die, the human being cannot be killed, even if killing him would lead to the cure of a chronic disease. The instruction *Dignitas personae* makes this very clear: "Proposals to use these embryos for research or for the treatment of disease *are obviously unacceptable because they treat the embryos as mere 'biological material' and will result in destruction.*"[96] As we discussed in chapter 3, abandoned human embryos could be adopted by parents who would pay to maintain the cryopreservation necessary for the survival of their child until incubators capable of bringing him to term are invented. This would preserve the life of the child without undermining his parents' marital covenant.

The Benefits of Embryonic Stem Cell Research

Proponents of human embryonic stem cell research often accuse opponents of destructive human embryo research of being anti-patient because

93. David I. Hoffman et al., "Cryopreserved Embryos in the United States and Their Availability for Research," *Fertil Steril* 79 (2003): 1063–1069.

94. Anne D. Lyerly and Ruth R. Faden, "Embryonic Stem Cells: Willingness to Donate Frozen Embryos for Stem Cell Research," *Science* 317 (2007): 46–47. In Spain, nearly 50 percent of couples who were interviewed after undergoing IVF chose to donate their surplus embryos for stem cell research. See Jose Luis Cortes et al., "Spanish Stem Cell Bank Interviews Examine the Interest of Couples in Donating Surplus Human IVF Embryos for Stem Cell Research," *Cell Stem Cell* 1 (2007): 17–20. For an overview of the scientific literature, see Kristina Hug, "Motivation to Donate or Not Donate Surplus Embryos for Stem-Cell Research: Literature Review," *Fertil Steril* 89 (2008): 263–277.

95. Ethics Committee of the American Society for Reproductive Medicine, "Donating Spare Embryos for Stem Cell Research," *Fertil Steril* 91 (2009): 667–670.

96. Congregation for the Doctrine of the Faith, *Dignitas personae*, no. 19.

banning this research would prevent scientists from discovering cures for a multitude of diseases. This objection often presupposes that the moral course of action is the one that alleviates the most human suffering.

In response, adult stem cell research remains one morally acceptable pro-patient alternative to the destructive human embryo research associated with human embryonic stem cell research. In fact, a quick search on clinicaltrials.gov, the website that tracks all clinical trials currently being undertaken in the United States, reveals that adult stem cells are already being used to treat human disease. As one example, at the Texas Heart Institute at St. Luke's Episcopal Hospital in Houston, Texas, patient-specific adult stem cells are already being tested on patients who have suffered heart attacks to see if they will help restore the structure and function of the damaged heart.[97] In contrast, at the time of this writing, there are only two clinical trials for therapies based on human embryonic stem cells.[98] Adult stem cells have also been used to restore sight to those blinded by burns.[99] In light of this, it is reasonable to argue that pro-patient advocates should invest our limited research funds into developing adult stem cell research that is already reaping benefits at the bedside rather than in embryonic stem cell work that has yet to bear fruit. As the Congregation for the Doctrine of the Faith points out, "Therapeutic protocols in force today provide for the use of adult stem cells and many lines of research have been launched, opening new and promising possibilities."[100]

Furthermore, there are several alternatives that may allow scientists to obtain pluripotent stem cells without destroying human embryos. Here, we summarize and consider four proposals for alternative sources of human pluripotent stem cells that were described by the President's Council on Bioethics.[101]

97. "First Clinical Trial in the World to Treat a Heart Attack Patient with a Special Stem Cell Type," Texas Heart Institute Media Release, April 8, 2008, at http://www.texasheart.org/AboutUs/News/StemCellPress_040408.cfm. Also see the newspaper article: Nicholas Wade, "The Uncertain Science of Growing Heart Cells," *New York Times*, March 14, 2005, at http://query.nytimes.com/gst/fullpage.html?res=9C0DE1D71 53CF937A25750C0A9639C8B63&sec=health&spon=&pagewanted=all.

98. Andrew Pollack, "F.D.A. Approves a Stem Cell Trial," *New York Times*, January 23, 2009, at http://www.nytimes.com/2009/01/23/business/23stem.html?_r=1. Jill U. Adams, "Stem Cell Trial Sets Sight on Blindness," *Los Angeles Times*, January 10, 2011.

99. Paolo Rama et al., "Limbal Stem Cell Therapy and Long-Term Corneal Regeneration," *N Engl J Med* 363 (2010): 147–155.

100. Congregation for the Doctrine of the Faith, *Dignitas personae*, no. 31.

101. The President's Council on Bioethics, *White Paper: Alternative Sources of Pluripotent Stem Cells* (Washington, D.C.: President's Council on Bioethics, 2005).

According to the first proposal, human pluripotent stem cells could be harvested from early IVF embryos that have already died, as evidenced by the irreversible cessation of cell division.[102] Some of these dead embryos could, however, contain individual cells that are still alive, cells that could be used to obtain pluripotent stem cells. This approach would be comparable to organ donation from adult individuals who have died. In this case, the dead embryo would donate his cells to science for the benefit of others.

This first proposal has generated much debate among ethicists and moral theologians. It is based on an attractively simple ethical idea: it should be permissible to obtain cells from embryos that have died, as long as their deaths have not been caused or hastened for that purpose. However, several ethicists have argued that it is hard to know when an early human embryo is truly dead. Others are worried that we could not know if our taking of the individual living cell from the dead embryo would allow it to become an embryo on its own right. If so, then we would have returned to our original objections to destructive human embryo research. Finally, and this is of particular concern for the Catholic, this proposal may necessitate cooperating with the immoral practices of infertility clinics that use IVF techniques to create human embryos in the laboratory.

According to the second proposal, human pluripotent stem cells could be obtained from individual cells obtained by biopsy of an early human embryo.[103] For this proposal to work, scientists would have to find a stage in early embryonic development where the removal of one or a few cells by biopsy would neither harm the embryo nor destroy the capacity of these collected cells to be used as a source of pluripotent stem cells. Preliminary studies have shown that pluripotent stem cells can be derived from individual cells taken from human embryos, but in these experiments, all of the cells in the embryos were used for the tests, destroying the embryo.

Like the first proposal, this proposal has generated much debate among ethicists and moral theologians. In accordance with the teaching of the Catholic Church, several ethicists have argued that we could never justify exposing the human embryo to the harm intrinsic to experimen-

102. Donald W. Landry and Howard A. Zucker, "Embryonic Death and the Creation of Human Embryonic Stem Cells," *J Clin Invest* 114 (2004): 1184–1186; and Donald W. Landry et al., "Hypocellularity and Absence of Compaction as Criteria for Embryonic Death," *Regen Med* 1 (2006): 367–371.

103. Irina Klimanskaya et al., "Human Embryonic Stem Cell Lines Derived from Single Blastomeres," *Nature* 444 (2006): 481–485. (Erratum, *Nature* 444 (2006): 512.)

tal manipulation, no matter how small, when the technical intervention would have no direct benefit to the embryo himself. Using human beings for purposes of no benefit to them and without their informed consent would be an act of injustice. Moreover, a similar concern exists as the one described above for the first proposal: we could never know if our taking of the individual cell from the embryo would allow it to become an embryo on its own right. Once again, this would raise the original objections to destructive human embryo research.

According to the third proposal, variants of which include either altered nuclear transfer (ANT) or altered nuclear transfer–oocyte assisted reprogramming (ANT-OAR), pluripotent human stem cells could be obtained from non-embryonic biological artifacts created by using genetic tricks to manipulate eggs and cells.[104] Experiments with mice suggest that this approach does lead to the production of pluripotent mouse stem cells.[105]

This third proposal has generated much heated debate, especially among Catholic ethicists and moral theologians.[106] Critics are concerned that this proposal would lead to the creation of disabled embryos that would be killed by scientists rather than the creation of non-embryos that could be legitimate sources of pluripotent stem cells. They raise a critical question: what criteria should be used to distinguish bona fide embryos from non-embryos? Though advocates of this proposal have proposed such criteria and have argued that they can be used to provide moral guidance for ANT or for ANT-OAR, these proposals remain controversial. Furthermore, there is the added concern that procuring the large numbers of human eggs needed to accomplish this proposal could lead to the commercialization of human reproductive tissue and the exploitation of women, especially poor women, in the developing world.

Finally, according to the fourth proposal, pluripotent human stem

104. William B. Hurlbut, Robert P. George, and Marcus Grompe, "Seeking Consensus: A Clarification and Defense of Altered Nuclear Transfer," *Hastings Cent Rep* 36 (2006): 42–50; Hadley Arkes et al., "Production of Pluripotent Stem Cells by Oocyte-Assisted Reprogramming: Joint Statement with Signatories," *Natl Cathol Bioeth Q* 5 (2005): 579–583.

105. Alexander Meissner and Rudolf Jaenisch, "Generation of Nuclear Transfer-Derived Pluripotent ES Cells from Cloned Cdx2-deficient Blastocysts," *Nature* 439 (2006): 212–215.

106. For a summary and commentary on the ANT debate among Catholic ethicists and moral theologians, see J. Thomas Petri, O.P., "Altered Nuclear Transfer, Gift, and Mystery: An Aristotelian-Thomistic Response to David L. Schindler," *Natl Cathol Bioeth Q.* 7 (2007): 729–747.

cells could be obtained from reprogrammed differentiated cells taken from adult human beings.[107] This proposal is the most exciting of the four proposals described by the President's Council on Bioethics, especially since a consensus exists for its moral acceptability. To date, it is also the proposal that has attained the most scientific success: on November 20, 2007, two research teams, one in Japan and the other in the United States, independently reported that they had successfully reprogrammed adult human cells into pluripotent stem cells called induced pluripotent stem (iPS) cells, which were indistinguishable from pluripotent stem cells taken from human embryos.[108] The scientists took the differentiated human cells and were able to reprogram them into nondifferentiated stem cells simply by introducing four genes into their nucleus. Two weeks later, a team from M.I.T. used the technique to cure sickle-cell anemia in mice, providing proof-of-principle that this nuclear reprogramming, or induced pluripotent stem cell (iPS) technology, could be used for regenerative medicine.[109] Though the iPS technique needs to be developed before it can be used to treat human patients, numerous commentators agree that it should lead to the end of the stem cell wars. It is not surprising that Dr. Ian Wilmut, the creator of Dolly the cloned sheep, has already announced that he and his laboratory have abandoned their plans to pursue cloning technology to obtain patient-specific embryonic stem cells.[110] Instead, his team has decided to focus all their efforts into perfecting the nuclear reprogramming (iPS) approach.

Experimentation with Novel Life: The Creation of Human/Animal Chimeras and Hybrids

According to ancient Greek mythology, a chimera was a creature with a lion's head, a goat's body, and a serpent's tail. In biology, a chimera is an

107. Christopher J. Lengner, "iPS Cell Technology in Regenerative Medicine," *Ann N Y Acad Sci* 1192 (2010): 38–44.

108. Kazutoshi Takahashi et al., "Induction of Pluripotent Stem Cells from Adult Human Fibroblasts by Defined Factors," *Cell* 131 (2007): 861–872; and Junying Yu et al., "Induced Pluripotent Stem Cell Lines Derived from Human Somatic Cells," *Science* 318 (2007): 1917–1920.

109. Jacob Hanna et al., "Treatment of Sickle Cell Anemia Mouse Model with iPS Cells Generated from Autologous Skin," *Science* 318 (2007): 1920–1923.

110. Sally Lehrman, "Dolly's Creator Moves Away from Cloning and Embryonic Stem Cells," *Scientific American*, July 2008, at http://www.sciam.com/article.cfm?id=no-more-cloning-around.

organism whose body is composed of tissues or of cells from distinct species. For example, goat-sheep chimeras, known as geeps, have been generated by combining embryonic cells from sheep and from goats.[111] Each cell of the chimera contains the genetic material from either one of the parental species but not both. Chimeras have to be distinguished from hybrids, which are organisms produced when two different species interbreed, either via normal copulation or by in vitro fertilization. Mules, for instance, are hybrids produced when a female horse mates with a male donkey. Each cell of the hybrid contains a mixture of genetic material inherited from both parental species.[112] In principle, the creation of non-human interspecies chimeras or hybrids is morally permissible for a reasonable purpose. Most persons would not condemn the actions of a man who bred horses and donkeys to generate the mules that regularly travel up and down the Kaibab Trail of the Grand Canyon carrying supplies. Even sacred Scripture refers approvingly to the practice of grafting one plant onto another to create a plant chimera (cf. Rom 11:17–24). Nonetheless, care has to be taken to avoid any unnecessary animal suffering.

In recent years, however, technical advances that would also allow scientists to make human/animal chimeras and hybrids have generated controversy. First, as we discussed in chapter 6, it is now possible for human beings to receive transplanted animal parts. Recall that, in principle, this technology should be morally permissible, as long as surgeons ensure the safety of and preserve the identity of the human recipient while preventing all unnecessary animal suffering. Next, it is now also possible for scientists to create both chimeric animals that contain human tissues or cells, and hybrid animals whose cells contain one or more human genes. An example of the latter is the patented Harvard OncoMouse

111. Carole B. Fehilly, S. M. Willadsen, and Elizabeth M. Tucker, "Interspecific Chimaerism between Sheep and Goat," *Nature* 307 (1984): 634–636; and S. Meinecke-Tillman and B. Meinecke, "Experimental Chimaeras—Removal of Reproductive Barrier between Sheep and Goat," *Nature* 307 (1984): 637–638.

112. For an insightful discussion of chimeras and hybrids, see Tara L. Seyfer, "An Overview of Chimeras and Hybrids," *Natl Cathol Bioeth Q* 6 (2006): 37–49. Also see the ethical analysis by Neville Cobbe, "Cross-Species Chimeras: Exploring a Possible Christian Perspective," *Zygon* 47 (2007): 599–628; and the two responses to Cobbe's essay: Stephen M. Modell, "Approaching Religious Guidelines for Chimera Policymaking," *Zygon* 47 (2007): 629–641; and Bernard E. Rollin, "On Chimeras," *Zygon* 47 (2007): 643–647.

mentioned earlier in this chapter, which is a transgenic mouse whose cells contain a human cancer gene. The OncoMouse and other genetically engineered mice like it are routinely used as animal models for human disease. In principle, the use of this technology should also be morally legitimate, especially if research with the chimeric or hybrid animal promotes human health. Finally, it is now possible to create animal/human hybrids, either by using in vitro technology to fertilize an animal egg with a human sperm, or by using cloning technology to replace the nucleus of an animal egg with a nucleus taken from a human cell. Stem cell advocates have promoted the latter method to create human embryonic stem cells.[113] This last technological advance is morally problematic because it risks creating a disabled human being who is treated and manipulated as an experimental subject, undermining his dignity.[114] As the Congregation for the Doctrine of the Faith explained in *Dignitas personae:* "From the ethical standpoint, such procedures [to create human/animal hybrids] represent an offense against the dignity of human beings on account of *the admixture of human and animal genetic elements capable of disrupting the specific identity of man.*"[115] To be faithful to his vocation, the virtuous scientist has to respect the moral law, especially the moral imperative to respect and to protect the dignity of the human person.

Highlighting the Role of Virtue in Bioethics

As we acknowledged at the beginning of this chapter, the search for truth is the basic task of the scientist as he strives to understand the natural order in creation. For this, he needs the intellectual virtues, especially the three virtues of understanding, *intellectus* in Latin; of sure-knowledge, *scientia* in Latin; and of wisdom, *sapientia* in Latin, that shape the speculative intellect.[116] From my experience, bench scientists and physician-

113. For one prominent example of this proposal from the scientist who cloned the sheep, Dolly, see Ian Wilmut, "The Moral Imperative for Human Cloning," *New Sci* 181 (2004): 16–17. Recent research has shown that this approach to obtain human stem cells may not be scientifically feasible: Young Chung et al., "Reprogramming of Human Somatic Cells Using Human and Animal Oocytes," *Cloning Stem Cells* 11 (2009): 213–223.

114. For the same reason, I have argued that the creation of a human/primate chimera should also be avoided. See my "How to Navigate Species Boundaries: A Reply to *The American Journal of Bioethics*," *Natl Cathol Bioeth Q* 6 (2006): 61–71.

115. Congregation for the Doctrine of the Faith, *Dignitas personae*, no. 33.

116. For a comprehensive discussion of the intellectual virtues as they are understood

scientists acquire the virtues of understanding and of sure-knowledge during their professional training. With the virtue of understanding, they are able to grasp well the self-evident first principles of knowledge, for example, that the whole is greater than its parts. Then with the virtue of sure-knowledge, they are able to reason from these basic truths and the data of their experiments to the conclusions of their particular field of expertise, whether it be biology, chemistry, or physics. However, scientists, often through no fault of their own, are not trained to acquire—or even to desire—the virtue of wisdom. And yet, it is this virtue that would dispose them to grasp the moral dimensions of their work. Where the virtue of science would dispose the researcher working at the Whitehead Institute at M.I.T. to discover the genetic basis for the pluripotency of human embryonic stem cells, the virtue of wisdom would dispose him to properly understand his findings within the moral, historical, philosophical, and theological context not only of human history and civilization, but also, for the scientist of faith, of Divine Providence.

Wisdom is the virtue that perfects the intellect, so that the human agent can consider the particular conclusions he has made with his reason in light of an ultimate explanation for reality.[117] St. Thomas Aquinas distinguished three kinds of wisdom.[118] The first is a purely natural wisdom, an acquired virtue usually associated with metaphysics, the study of being, which allows the human person to comprehend the cause for and the overall structure of reality.[119] The human intellect formed by natural wisdom finds itself at the threshold of the supernatural. With natural wisdom, the philosopher is able to reason from the structure of reality to its ultimate cause, who is God, but is then unable to go further. For this next

within the Thomistic tradition, see M. Rose Emmanuella Brennan, *The Intellectual Virtues according to the Philosophy of St. Thomas* (Palo Alto, Calif.: Pacific Books, 1941).

117. As St. Thomas Aquinas explained, in contrast to *scientia*, which is the virtue that disposes the human agent to acquire causal knowledge within a specific field, *sapientia* is the virtue that allows the human agent to acquire knowledge with respect to highest causes. See his *Summa theologiae*, Ia-IIae, 57.2.

118. For a comprehensive discussion of the virtue of wisdom as it was understood by the Thomistic tradition, see Kieran Conley, O.S.B., *A Theology of Wisdom* (Dubuque, Iowa: Priory Press, 1963).

119. For a magisterial attempt to order the different branches of human knowledge into a sapiential whole, see Benedict Ashley, O.P., *The Way toward Wisdom* (South Bend, Ind.: University of Notre Dame Press, 2006). Significantly, this approach to wisdom begins with the data of the physical sciences that is not only familiar, but also acknowledged by most scientists, as certain and true knowledge.

step, he needs a second kind of wisdom, supernatural wisdom, an infused virtue that is associated with theology, the study not only of God as He has revealed Himself to us, but also of all things as they relate to Him, which allows the human person to comprehend the mystery of God's inner life and His providence in history. Finally, there is the gift of wisdom, an infused wisdom given by the Holy Spirit that produces a connatural knowledge of God and of His creation in the believer. This gift of wisdom disposes the human agent to know God intimately as a lover knows his beloved. It allows him to make judgments about divine and created things all in light of God as the highest cause. To different degrees, natural, supernatural, and infused wisdom would dispose the scientist to make practical and moral judgments about his experiments and his research plan, in light of his overall vocation to serve God and his society.

Of course, the vocation of the scientist spelled out at the beginning of this chapter, and presupposed here in this discussion of the role of wisdom in research bioethics, is at odds with the secular worldview that permeates and saturates most of the laboratories and hospitals in the West. Nonetheless, all scientists, believers and nonbelievers alike, should seek to cultivate some form of wisdom so that they can appreciate the personal, social, and moral implications of their research. As a priest-scientist myself, I have discovered that a significant number of bench researchers and physician scientists are not familiar with even the major fault lines of the bioethical debates that are consuming our society. Busy with their personal and professional responsibilities, many have not considered the moral implications of their work. This is unfortunate, since they are at the front lines of many of the technological research programs that have generated these disagreements. Therefore, scientists, even those who do not profess any religious faith, should be encouraged to grow in the virtue of wisdom. They can do this by contemplating the big questions of life.

The primary act of wisdom, contemplation, challenges the individual to seek an ultimate explanation for all that is. First and foremost, it demands an answer to the question: why is there anything rather than nothing? Though grappling with this question may not lead the nonbelieving scientist to the First Cause who is God—the road to belief is often blocked not by intellectual but by moral obstacles—the very act of contemplation may challenge him to pause in wonder, even for a moment, allowing him to properly consider the moral dimensions of his work. Professor Shinya Yamanaka, the Japanese scientist who discovered the nuclear reprogramming protocol that generates human induced pluripotent (iPS) stem cells without destroying human embryos, has admitted that his groundbreaking research was motivated by a moment of wonder when he realized that the human embryos in his laboratory reminded him of his daughters.[120] His insight—a moment of wisdom—has changed the course of bioethical discourse in our society for the better.

120. Martin Fackler, "Shinya Yamanaka: Risk Taking Is in His Genes," *New York Times,* December 11, 2007, at http://www.nytimes.com/2007/12/11/science/11prof.html.

CHAPTER EIGHT

Catholic Bioethics in a Pluralistic Society

On Friday, February 27, 2009, the new administration of President
Barack Obama announced that it intended to rescind a Bush administration rule granting broad protections to doctors, nurses, and other health-
care workers who refuse to perform or assist in abortions or in sterilization procedures because of their religious beliefs or moral convictions.[1]
More specifically, the Bush Provider Refusal Rule blocks federal funding to healthcare facilities that do not allow their employees to distance
themselves from medical procedures that they find morally objectionable.
Supporters of the regulation, including the United States Conference of
Catholic Bishops and the Catholic Health Association, which represents
all of the Catholic hospitals in the United States, claim that the rule protects the right of health-care workers to care for their patients in accord
with their conscience, especially in light of the growing effort in our society to force doctors to perform or to make referrals for abortions and
sterilizations.

In contrast, opponents, including the American Medical Association,
the National Association of Chain Drug Stores, and Planned Parenthood,
argue that the Bush rule places women in jeopardy by making it harder
for them to get the medical care they need. Moreover, they suggest that
the Bush "Refusal Clause" undermines the basic health-care rights of patients—especially women—who should have access to accurate and complete reproductive health information and to all legal medical procedures.

On February 18, 2011, the U.S. Department of Health and Human Services issued its new federal guidelines that changed and rescinded the conscience clauses that had protected the rights of medical staffers who object to procedures for religious or moral reasons. The publication of these
guidelines was met with declarations of disappointment by the United

1. David Stout, "Obama Set to Undo 'Conscience' Rule for Health Workers," *New York Times*, February 27, 2009, at http://www.nytimes.com/2009/02/28/us/politics/28web-abort.html?hp.

States Conference of Catholic Bishops and the Christian Medical Association. This ongoing dispute raises troubling questions regarding the place, in a liberal democracy, of the citizen of faith who seeks to pursue his professional calling without fear of persecution or coercion. How is the Catholic citizen called to pursue a virtuous life in this plural and divisive context?

In this chapter, which deals with bioethics in a pluralistic society and the moral issue of cooperation in evil, I begin by locating Catholic bioethics in our contemporary cultural landscape. Basically, the Catholic citizen striving for virtue needs to understand that he is living in a society that is at the same time postmodern, secular, and liberal. It is a society that will inherently oppose his efforts to faithfully live out his moral convictions and fulfill the Christ-given mandate to evangelize and transform the world. Therefore, he is being called to speak and to live the truths of the Gospel of Life with courage and joy as a witness to the transforming power of grace.

Next, I consider the following question: how then is the Catholic citizen supposed to speak the truths of the faith within this social context? In response, I suggest that the methodology of tradition-constituted inquiry pioneered by Alasdair MacIntyre, after the example of St. Thomas Aquinas, would provide the citizen of faith with an approach to constructively engage in dialogue with rival moral traditions, without surrendering the absolute and universal claims of the Catholic moral tradition. To illustrate this approach, I will defend the intrinsic dignity of the human person by appealing to the internal standards of the liberal tradition itself, a tradition that is often critical of the moral teachings of the Catholic Church.

Finally, moving from the theoretical to the practical, I confront the issues of cooperation, complicity, and conscience, which inevitably arise in the moral experience of those who live and work in a pluralistic society: how should the Catholic citizen avoid, limit, and distance himself from the evils committed in a pluralistic society so that he may live the truths of the Gospel? Or to put it another way, how should the Catholic citizen live in a liberal democracy composed not only of moral friends, but also of moral strangers?

Locating Catholic Bioethics in a Pluralistic Society

To locate Catholic bioethics within the moral discourse of contemporary society, we need to begin with a discussion of the pluralism that saturates our culture in the West. It is a pluralism that emerges from a social context that is simultaneously postmodern, secular, and liberal. Each of these characteristics contributes to the variegated texture of our moral landscape that sees Catholic bioethics as just one of many equally legitimate rival traditions that are competing for the allegiance of autonomous citizens within a liberal democracy.

Most significantly, our culture is postmodern. Literally speaking, the term describes the period that comes after modernity. More specifically, it refers to a philosophical, artistic, and cultural worldview that is suffused with a deep suspicion of reason and its ability to attain truth.[2] As Jean-François Lyotard, the French philosopher and literary theorist, explained, individuals in postmodern societies no longer have faith in the meta-narratives—the all-encompassing explanations for the human condition proposed by philosophies, political ideologies, and religions—that used to give people an understanding of what makes life meaningful.[3] Instead, in our postmodern world, different, often contradictory, narratives of what constitutes the true and the good compete for our attention and our allegiance. This has led both to a fragmentation of knowledge in society and to a crisis of truth. Blessed John Paul II described this postmodern condition in his encyclical *Fides et Ratio* as follows:

Recent times have seen the rise to prominence of various doctrines which tend to devalue even the truths which had been judged certain. A legitimate plurality of positions has yielded to an undifferentiated pluralism, based upon the assumption that all positions are equally valid, which is one of today's most widespread symptoms of the lack of confidence in truth. Even certain conceptions of life coming from the East betray this lack of confidence, denying truth its exclusive character and assuming that truth reveals itself equally in different doctrines, even if they contradict one another. On this understanding, everything is reduced to opinion; and there is a sense of being adrift.[4]

Within this social context, citizens are asking themselves and each other: Whose beliefs are valid? Whose morality is binding? Whose worldview is true? Sadly, as the pope acknowledged, many individuals have become

2. For insightful introductions to postmodernism and postmodernity, see Stanley J. Grenz, *A Primer on Postmodernism* (Grand Rapids, Mich.: William B. Eerdmans, 1996); and Douglas R. Groothuis, *Truth Decay: Defending Christianity Against the Challenges of Postmodernism* (Downers Grove, Ill.: InterVarsity Press, 2000).

3. Jean-François Lyotard, *The Postmodern Condition: A Report on Knowledge* (Minneapolis: University of Minnesota Press, 1984).

4. John Paul II, *Fides et Ratio*, no. 5.

convinced that they will not be able to answer these questions with certitude. They have decided that their only legitimate option is to settle for a pluralism of plausible worldviews. Thus, as the Holy Father has noted, the postmodern worldview "has given rise to different forms of agnosticism and relativism which have led philosophical research to lose its way in the shifting sands of widespread skepticism."[5] Indeed, some postmodern philosophers—Richard Rorty especially comes to mind—assert that our society must realize that it can attain only provisional truth, reduced in many ways to mere opinion.[6] These individuals have been accused, rightly, in my opinion, of relativism and irrationalism.[7] The inevitable result of these philosophical trends is the exaltation of pluralism and the promotion of tolerance as the supreme social virtue in a postmodern world.

Not surprisingly, contemporary bioethics mirrors the experience of pluralism in postmodernity.[8] Kevin Wildes, S.J., has categorized the diverse methodologies in contemporary bioethics and has put them into two groups.[9] On the one hand, foundational methods presuppose a ra-

5. Ibid.

6. Richard Rorty has claimed that philosophers should acknowledge the radical temporality of knowledge. He argues that knowledge always remains provisional and tied to the historical and cultural context that produced it. See his *Contingency, Irony, and Solidarity* (Cambridge: Cambridge University Press, 1989), 2–69. For a concise discussion of the philosophical position advocated by Rorty and other thinkers of his ilk, see John E. Thiel, *Nonfoundationalism* (Minneapolis, Minn.: Fortress Press, 1994), 1–37.

7. Thomas Oden has suggested that we call this flavor of postmodernity "ultramodernity," to distinguish it from other brands of postmodernity that are not epistemologically relativistic or nihilistic. See his "The Death of Modernity and Postmodern Evangelical Spirituality," in *The Challenge of Postmodernism*, 2nd ed., ed. David Dockery, 19–33 (Grand Rapids, Mich.: Baker Book House, 2001), 26–28.

8. For an extensive discussion of the state of contemporary bioethics in a postmodern society that concludes that a canonical, content-full secular morality cannot be discovered, see H. Tristam Engelhardt, Jr., *The Foundations of Bioethics*, 2nd ed. (Oxford: Oxford University Press, 1996).

9. Kevin Wm. Wildes, S.J., *Moral Acquaintances: Methodology in Bioethics* (Washington, D.C.: Georgetown University Press, 2000). Pluralism also exists within the tradition of Catholic bioethics. There are Catholic moral theologians who are critical not only of the method used in traditional Catholic bioethics—the method described in this book—but also of some of the conclusions reached by that method. For introductory accounts of Catholic bioethics that are critical of the Church's teaching, see James F. Drane, *More Humane Medicine: A Liberal Catholic Bioethics* (Edinboro: Edinboro University of Pennsylvania Press, 2003); and Kelly, *Contemporary Catholic Health Care Ethics*. For a retort to David F. Kelly, see my review of his book in the *Natl Cathol Bioeth Q* 5.2 (Summer 2005): 425–428.

tionalistic formulation in which theory "requires a set of normative principles governing all rational beings and providing a dependable procedure for reaching definitive moral judgments and decisions."[10] The moral
approach described in this book, a Thomistic natural law account that
grounds virtue in an understanding of the perfections of human nature,
would be one specific example of a foundational approach. Others would
include utilitarianism, deontologism, and contractarianism, just to name
a few.[11] These approaches presuppose that morality is objective and universally applicable because it is grounded in moral principles that act as
a foundation for the moral theory. In contrast, nonfoundational methods "construe ethical theory in terms of a process of reflective equilibrium that tests ethical beliefs against other moral and nonmoral beliefs
with the aim of developing a set of beliefs that fit together."[12] The process of reflectively balancing considered judgments is usually set within
a conceptual framework of a liberal society that is held together by a social contract.[13] Nonfoundational methods include principlism, likely the

10. Wildes, *Moral Acquaintances*, 23, citing Stanley G. Clarke and Evan Simpson, *Anti-Theory in Ethics and Moral Conservatism* (Albany: SUNY Press, 1989), 3–5.

11. Utilitarianism—the work of Peter Singer is a good example of this approach—posits that a universal calculation that maximizes the interests of human agents is the basic starting point for moral theory. Among others, the more important human inter-ests, according to Singer, are those in avoiding pain, in developing one's abilities, in sat-isfying basic needs for food and shelter, in enjoying warm personal relationships, and in being free to pursue one's projects without interference. For details, see Peter Singer, *Practical Ethics*, 2nd ed. (Cambridge: Cambridge University Press, 1999). In contrast, deon-tologism—the work of Alan Donagan is cited by Wildes—is a moral theory grounded in a theory of a system of laws or precepts, binding upon rational creatures as such, the content of which is ascertainable by human reason. See Alan Donagan, *A Theory of Mo-rality* (Chicago: University of Chicago Press, 1977). Finally, contractarianism—the the-ory propounded by bioethicist Robert Veatch is paradigmatic of this approach—seeks to address questions of medical ethics by appealing to contracts. Veatch models the physician-patient relationship within a social context constituted by three contracts. The first contract is a basic contract summed up by several principles, including benefi-cence, autonomy, honesty, avoiding killing, justice, and contract keeping. The second contract exists between society and different professional groups, symbolized by the process of licensure. The third contract is the physician-patient relationship. According to Veatch, the basic norms and principles that govern ethical behavior would be those ones articulated by ideal contractors. For more details, see Robert Veatch, *A Theory of Medical Ethics* (New York: Basic Books, 1981).

12. Wildes, *Moral Acquaintances*, 23.

13. Reflective equilibrium, the process of reflectively balancing considered judgments, is a method of doing moral and political philosophy originally developed by John Raw-ls. According to Rawls, one can justify one's ethical beliefs by seeking coherence among

most influential moral perspective in the tradition of secular bioethics, and secular casuistry.[14] These approaches presuppose that there is a common morality held by different persons but that this common morality is open to numerous interpretations.[15] In the end, the multiplicity of approaches to doing bioethics in contemporary society illustrates well the deep moral ambiguities that exist in our postmodern culture. It should not be surprising that this diversity of moral accounts has generated a landscape that is marred by rancorous debate over different aspects of the moral life.

Next, our society is secular. If a postmodern society, by definition, has

---

them. John D. Arras describes this method as one that "involves the attempt to bring our most confident ethical judgments, our ethical principles, and our background social, psychological, and philosophical theories into a state of harmony or equilibrium." See his "The Way We Reason Now: Reflective Equilibrium in Bioethics," in *The Oxford Handbook of Bioethics*, ed. Bonnie Steinbock, 46–71 (Oxford: Oxford University Press, 2007), 47.

14. Principlism—a perspective associated with Tom L. Beauchamp and James F. Childress—has also received semi-official recognition in *The Belmont Report*, created by the United States government in response to the Tuskegee Syphilis Study described in the opening paragraphs of chapter 7. This moral theory posits that ethical decision making and problem solving in bioethics is best undertaken by appealing to four clusters of moral principles: respect for autonomy, nonmaleficence, beneficence, and justice. According to Beauchamp and Childress, these principles articulate a common morality, a set of norms shared by all persons committed to the moral life. Moreover, they propose that these prima facie binding principles can be specified, weighed, and balanced to resolve every moral dilemma. For discussion, see Tom L. Beauchamp and James F. Childress, *Principles of Biomedical Ethics*, 6th ed. (Oxford: Oxford University Press, 2009). For a brilliant critique of principlism by two Catholic moralists, see John Finnis and Anthony Fisher, O.P., "Theology and the Four Principles of Bioethics: A Roman Catholic View," in *Principles of Health Care Ethics*, ed. Raanan Gillon, 31–44 (New York: John Wiley and Sons, 1993). Next, casuistry—currently being promoted by Albert Jonsen and Stephen Toulmin in bioethics—seeks appropriate moral judgments through an intimate acquaintance with particular situations and the historical record of similar cases. Casuists propose that most moral impasses can be resolved by focusing on points shared by similar moral cases rather than on moral principles. For details, see Albert R. Jonsen and Stephen Toulmin, *The Abuse of Casuistry: A History of Moral Reasoning* (Berkeley: University of California Press, 1988).

15. This claim to a common morality that exists for all individuals is contentious. Some philosophers deny its existence, pointing to the persistent disagreements over abortion, population control, embryo research, assisted suicide, as empirical evidence for their view. For discussion, see the essays in Gene Outka and John P. Reeder Jr., eds., *Prospects for a Common Morality* (Princeton, N.J.: Princeton University Press, 1993); and H. Tristam Engelhardt Jr., ed., *Global Bioethics: The Collapse of Consensus* (Salem, Mass.: M&M Scrivener Press, 2006).

lost its confidence in reason, a secular society has lost its confidence in faith. For many, this loss of faith in faith can be traced back to the religious turmoil of the Reformation and the Counter-Reformation.[16] For example, Jeffrey Stout has proposed that the secular worldview emerged as the unanticipated response to the religious crisis of authority in the seventeenth century.[17] Confronted by conflicting epistemological claims by Catholics on the one hand and by Protestants on the other, René Descartes and his philosophical descendants of the Enlightenment attempted to reconstruct knowledge and reground it on secular foundations based on reason alone. In more recent years, this project to create a post-Christian secular society in the West has also been motivated by the search for a practical political philosophy that would provide a basis for reasoned agreement in a constitutional democracy, where sharp disagreements, of both religious and nonreligious origin, threaten to lead to conflict. Most prominently, the influential political philosopher John Rawls has argued that democracies can survive only if they exclude comprehensive doctrines, those religious or moral or philosophical worldviews held by a limited number of citizens, from the public square.[18] In Rawls's view, it would not be reasonable to expect a Muslim to endorse a Christian worldview as the basis for social and political life in a pluralistic society, or vice versa. Therefore, according to Rawls, since no single comprehensive doctrine can be universally accepted by all reasonable citizens in a democracy, no comprehensive doctrine can serve as the basis for the legitimate use of coercive political power. Consequently, drawing on what he calls the "idea of public reason," Rawls argued that citizens of a liberal democracy should limit their political arguments to ones that they can justify to one another using publicly available—and

16. For commentary on the secularization of contemporary society from a Catholic perspective, see the conversation between Joseph Ratzinger (now the Holy Father, Benedict XVI) and Jürgen Habermas, *The Dialectics of Secularization* (San Francisco: Ignatius Press, 2007).

17. Jeffrey Stout, *The Flight from Authority: Religion, Morality, and the Quest for Autonomy* (Notre Dame, Ind.: University of Notre Dame Press, 1981). For another magisterial narrative that traces the story of faith's decline in modernity, see Charles Taylor, *A Secular Age* (Cambridge, Mass.: Harvard University Press, 2007).

18. Rawls claimed that to maintain a truly liberal society, "it is normally desirable that the comprehensive philosophical and moral views we are wont to use in debating fundamental political issues should give way in public life." See his *Political Liberalism* (New York: Columbia University Press, 1993), 10. For an introductory overview to Rawls and his seminal ideas, see Thomas Pogge, *John Rawls: His Life and Theory of Justice* (Oxford: Oxford University Press, 2007).

thus secular—values and standards.[19] Not surprisingly, this proposal and others like it have secularized the public square and created a divisive social context that dismisses any argument that appears to be motivated by religious convictions. Blessed John Paul II lamented this secularization of Christendom in his encyclical *Veritatis splendor:* "Dechristianization, which weighs heavily upon entire peoples and communities once rich in faith and Christian life, involves not only the loss of faith or in any event its becoming irrelevant for everyday life, but also, and of necessity, *a decline or obscuring of the moral sense.*"[20]

Contemporary bioethics too has undergone a process of secularization. Many of the early bioethicists, including Joseph Fletcher, Paul Ramsey, and Richard McCormick, S.J., were theologians motivated by their religious convictions to consider the moral questions raised by science and technology.[21] Nonetheless, as the field matured, philosophers, lawyers, physicians, and health-care providers became involved in the ongoing conversation. This process led to the marginalization of religious voices in bioethics, especially since the theologians working in bioethics were simultaneously adapting their message, by appealing to a neutral nonpartisan language that they could use to dialogue with the world.[22] Today, moral arguments made by Catholic bioethicists, and, a fortiori, by the Magisterium of the Catholic Church, are dismissed simply because they are perceived to be

19. Other contemporary liberal scholars agree with Rawls. According to Robert Audi, for example, "one should not advocate or promote any legal or public policy restrictions on human conduct unless one not only has and is willing to offer, but is also *motivated by,* adequate secular reason." See his essay, "The Separation of Church and State and the Obligations of Citizenship," *Philosophy and Public Affairs* 18 (1989): 259–296, 284. For responses to this view that propose that religious arguments *do* have a proper place in liberal democracies, see Michael W. McConnell, "Secular Reason and the Misguided Attempt to Exclude Religious Argument from Democratic Deliberation," *Journal of Law, Philosophy and Culture* 1 (2007): 159–174; and John Haldane, "Public Reason, Truth, and Human Fellowship: Going beyond Rawls," *Journal of Law, Philosophy and Culture* 1 (2007): 175–190.

20. John Paul II, *Veritatis Splendor,* no. 106. (original emphasis)

21. David W. Smith, "Religion and the Roots of the Bioethics Revival," in *Religion and Medical Ethics: Looking Back, Looking Forward,* ed. Allen Verhey, 9–18 (Grand Rapids, Mich.: William B. Eerdmans, 1996).

22. For descriptions of this secularization process, see Daniel Callahan, "Religion and the Secularization of Bioethics," *Hastings Cent Rep* 20 (1990): S2–S4; Stephen Lammers, "The Marginalization of Religious Voices in Bioethics," in *Religion and Medical Ethics,* 19–43; and S. Joseph Tham, L.C., "The Secularization of Bioethics," *Natl Cathol Bioeth Q* 8 (2008): 443–453.

theological arguments that are judged irrelevant in a secular age.[23] Not un-expectedly, this too has contributed to the polarization of contemporary moral discourse.

Finally, our society is liberal. Liberals highlight individual autonomy as the fundamental value of a liberal society, where autonomy here is con-ceived in terms of the absence of interference with an individual's choice of and pursuit of his personal goals.[24] Thus, they propose that the state should be guided by an ideal that fosters a plurality of reasonable concep-tions of the good life, guarantees the freedom and equality of its citizens, and maintains a just distribution of the goods to its citizens. These so-cial conditions would give individual human agents the freedom not only to discover—or even to invent—their own rationale for the good life, but also to enable them to pursue it without undue interference. Within a liberal society, therefore, liberals posit that the state should be neutral with regard to the different conceptions of a good life—the different ac-counts of morality—chosen by its citizens. Instead, they propose that the state is responsible for formulating and maintaining those rules and procedures that would enable its citizens to live out their own conception of a good life, without undue interference from others. Indeed, for liber-als, moral pluralism is a sign not of social decay, but of social health. It promotes the ideal of a society of moral agents choosing freely for them-selves, and willingly tolerating a pluralism of moralities, because of their commitment to the supreme value of moral autonomy.

Not unexpectedly, contemporary bioethics has been heavily influenced by liberalism and its ideals.[25] As several commentators have acknowl-edged, secular bioethics in the United States has been closely allied with

23. When the Congregation for the Doctrine of the Faith published *Dignitas personae*, its instruction on bioethics on December 12, 2008, Insoo Hyun, chair of the Ethics and Public Policy Committee at the International Society for Stem Cell Research, dismissed its argument by concluding, "The Vatican is entitled to its theological position." See "Vatican Formalizes Rules on Human Stem-cell Research," *Nature* 456 (2008): 852.

24. For a helpful introduction to contemporary liberal political theory and its crit-ics, see Christopher Wolfe and John Hittinger, eds., *Liberalism at the Crossroads* (Lanham, Md.: Rowman and Littlefield, 1994). This notion of autonomy is linked to what Isaiah Berlin famously called "negative liberty." See his essay, "Two Concepts of Liberty," in *Four Essays on Liberty*, 118–172 (Oxford: Oxford University Press, 1969).

25. For an insightful account of how liberalism manifests itself in contemporary scholarship in bioethics, see Mark B. Brown, "Three Ways to Politicize Bioethics," *Am J Bioeth* 9.2 (2009): 43–54; and the peer commentaries responding to this target article in the same issue of the journal.

liberalism since it was established as a profession in the late 1960s and early 1970s.[26] Partly as a reflection of the cultural upheavals of this tumultuous period in American history, and partly in response to the ethical concerns raised by the exploitation of human research subjects during the Tuskegee Syphilis Study, the field became focused on personal liberty and individual rights. Medical sociologist Paul Wolpe has persuasively argued that there is a link between "the triumph of autonomy in American bioethics" and the individualistic culture of the United States more generally.[27] It is not surprising, therefore, that the moral questions surrounding human health, human procreation, or human death were often framed, early within the tradition of secular bioethics, in terms of whether or not a particular medical intervention unduly limits the autonomy of the individuals involved. Moreover, though there are mainstream scholars who have become uncomfortable with the obsession with autonomy in secular bioethics,[28] it is still not uncommon for secular bioethicists to appeal to personal liberty or to patient choice to justify their moral claims. Even a cursory glance through a current textbook in secular bioethics will quickly reveal that the ideals of liberalism and its emphasis on individual freedom continue to dominate contemporary bioethics. Consequently, as we have seen throughout this book, it should not be surprising that secular bioethicists are often critical of the Catholic moral tradition, precisely because it appears to unjustly limit the autonomy of persons as they seek to live, to reproduce, and to die.

In sum, the contemporary moral landscape is fragmented because our postmodern society has abandoned the search for authentic truth and has settled instead for a plurality of incommensurable worldviews. Ironically, however, this secular and liberal culture also seeks to mute religious voices in the public square: citizens of faith are allowed to live out their mor-

26. For details, see the discussion in Renee C. Fox, "The Evolution of American Bioethics: A Sociological Perspective," in *Social Science Perspectives on Medical Ethics*, ed. G. Weisz, 201–220 (Philadelphia: University of Pennsylvania Press, 1990); Daniel Callahan, "Individual Good and the Common Good: A Communitarian Approach to Bioethics," *Perspectives in Biology and Medicine* 46 (2003): 496–507; and H. Tristam Engelhardt Jr., "The Ordination of Bioethicists as Secular Moral Experts," *Social Philosophy and Policy* 19 (2002): 59–82.

27. Paul Root Wolpe, "The Triumph of Autonomy in American Medical Ethics: A Sociological View," in *Bioethics and Society: Constructing the Ethical Enterprise*, ed. Raymond DeVries and Janardan Subedi, 38–59 (New York: Prentice Hall, 1998).

28. For example, see Onora O'Neill, *Autonomy and Trust in Bioethics* (Cambridge: Cambridge University Press, 2002); and the essay by G. M. Stirrat and R. Gill, "Autonomy in Medical Ethics after O'Neill," *J Med Ethics* 31 (2005): 127–130.

al convictions as long as they do not obstruct or inhibit the lives of their fellow citizens who do not share their beliefs. However, this attempt to constrain the Christian cannot be reconciled with the Christ-given mandate to evangelize and to transform the world, so that the Father's will be done on Earth as it is in Heaven. As our risen Lord tells us through His apostles: "Go, therefore, and make disciples of all nations, baptizing them in the name of the Father, and of the Son, and of the holy Spirit, teaching them to observe all that I have commanded you" (Mt 28: 19–20).[29] Thus, the Catholic citizen trying to faithfully live out his moral convictions and his baptismal promises will inevitably find himself opposed by many in a liberal society. He, therefore, is called to speak passionately, to propose respectfully, and to live joyfully the truths of the Gospel in this countercultural context.

Articulating Catholic Bioethics in a Pluralistic Society

How is the Catholic citizen supposed to articulate the truths of his tradition in a culture where moral discourse is marked by strident and apparently interminable disagreement between widely divergent worldviews? One approach is to describe his worldview from the ground up, beginning with its metaphysical foundations. For example, take the affirmation of the intrinsic dignity of the human person described in chapter 2. The Catholic citizen could explain this bedrock claim of the Catholic moral tradition by first defending the existence of God as the First Cause, using the principle of sufficient reason that asserts that every contingent fact—including the universe—must have an explanation.[30] He could then appeal to philosophical arguments to show that the human being is a creature with a stable nature beginning at conception and ending at death, which differs in kind from the other animal species in our world because he is free to think and to will. Finally, he could argue that these characteristics confer a unique moral status upon the human being as long as he exists.

In making this argument, however, the Catholic citizen would be opposed at every turn by moral strangers, interlocutors with whom he does not share a common moral and philosophical vision.[31] These opponents

---

29. Cf. *Catechism of the Catholic Church*, nos. 848–849; 2816–2821.

30. For discussion, see Alexander R. Pruss, *The Principle of Sufficient Reason* (Cambridge: Cambridge University Press, 2007).

31. H. Tristam Engelhardt Jr., has proposed the distinction between moral friends

could, and would probably, dispute, among other things, the legitimacy of the principle of sufficient reason,[32] the truth of the claim that natural kinds exist,[33] and the validity of the affirmation that human beings are free.[34] Moral strangers would even quibble over the rules of evidence and debate—for instance, the admissibility of appeals to nonmaterial entities or the cogency of metaphysical reasoning—that should govern the resolution of their moral contest. As the American philosopher Alasdair MacIntyre has observed, it is not clear how any dispute between moral strangers would or could ever be resolved, given these fundamental disagreements: "Debate between fundamentally opposed standpoints does occur but it is inevitably inconclusive. Each warring position characteristically appears irrefutable to its own adherents; indeed in its own terms and by its own standards of arguments it *is* in practice irrefutable. But each warring position equally seems to its opponents to be insufficiently warranted by rational arguments."[35] Once again, we are confronted by the question: how is the Catholic citizen supposed to articulate the truths of his tradition in a postmodern, secular, and liberal society?

In response, I propose that the methodology of tradition-constituted inquiry pioneered by MacIntyre would provide the Catholic citizen with an approach to constructively engage in dialogue with moral strangers and their rival traditions. According to MacIntyre, rational inquiry should be conceived as a craft that is undertaken by an individual who is part of a community with its own tradition.[36] Each community, like each person

---

and moral strangers. Moral friends are those individuals with whom we share a contentfull morality with its internal rules of evidence and inference. Moral strangers, on the other hand, are those citizens who do not share these moral premises. See his *The Foundation of Bioethics*, 2nd ed. (New York: Oxford University Press, 1996), 6–9.

32. For example, Quentin Smith and William Lane Craig have critiqued the metaphysical foundations of the principle of sufficient reason in their *Theism, Atheism, and Big Bang Cosmology* (Oxford: Clarendon Press, 1993), 178–191.

33. For example, Myles Burnyeat has argued that an Aristotelian/Thomistic ontology is not credible, and moreover "ought to be junked." See his "Is an Aristotelian Philosophy of the Mind Still Credible?" in *Essays on Aristotle's De Anima*, ed. Martha Nussbaum and Amelie Oksenberg Rorty, 15–26 (Oxford: Clarendon Press, 1995).

34. For example, evolutionary biologist William Provine claims that human freedom is an illusion because we are determined by material factors. See his "Evolution and the Foundation of Ethics," in *Science, Technology, and Social Progress*, ed. Steven L. Goldman, 253–267 (Bethlehem, Pa.: Lehigh University Press, 1989).

35. Alasdair MacIntyre, *Three Rival Versions of Moral Enquiry* (Notre Dame, Ind.: University of Notre Dame Press, 1990), 7.

36. For MacIntyre's discussion on communal knowing and the rationality of tradi-

with his or her own unique narrative, has its own unique tradition shaped by the historical contingencies it has faced. As such, for MacIntyre, it is not surprising that different traditions often have different standards of rational justification based upon different sets of background beliefs, different moral authorities, and different accounts of the good life. Consequently, within MacIntyre's account of intellectual inquiry, there is no expectation that there is one set of rational standards that transcends communal differences and is accessible to all persons.

Despite his disregard for tradition-independent standards of rationality, however, MacIntyre does propose that rational debate is still possible, because adherents of one community with its own native tradition can learn the internal standards of justification accepted by an alien tradition. This would allow them to critique the alien tradition and to respond to criticisms from the rival community on its own terms, with its own standards of rationality. Individuals who engage in this task would be translators, who are able not only to speak the language of both communities, but also to mediate the rational discourse needed to resolve conflicts between the two rival traditions.

St. Thomas Aquinas is an example, par excellence, of a multi-tradition translator who could speak the language of multiple historical communities.[37] As MacIntyre tells the story, Aquinas's achievement was to bring together rival Augustinian and Aristotelian traditions in his own synthesis.[38] For the Angelic Doctor, the theologian doing theology first casts his opponent's case in the best possible light, before demonstrating its inadequacies. His own brilliance was acknowledged precisely because he had perfected this art.[39] The added complexity arising from our postmodern

tions, which he formally defines as historically extended, socially embodied arguments, see his *Whose Justice? Which Rationality?* (Notre Dame, Ind.: University of Notre Dame Press, 1988), 349–369. For commentary, see Ian Markham, "Faith and Reason: Reflections on MacIntyre's 'Tradition-Constituted Enquiry,'" *Religious Studies* 27 (1991): 259–262; Jean Porter, "Tradition in the Recent Work of Alasdair MacIntyre," in *Alasdair MacIntyre*, ed. Mark C. Murphy, 38–69 (Cambridge: Cambridge University Press, 2003); and, especially, Christopher Stephen Lutz, *Tradition in the Ethics of Alasdair MacIntyre* (Lanham, Md.: Lexington Books, 2004).

37. For an insightful commentary on St. Thomas Aquinas and his conviction that one can engage in learned thinking only within an intellectual tradition, see Serge-Thomas Bonino, O.P. "To Be a Thomist," *Nova et Vetera* 8 (2010):763–773.

38. MacIntyre, *Three Rival Versions*, 82–148.

39. Josef Pieper writes of St. Thomas: "[Thomas] challenges the opponent not at the weakest spot in his position—too cheap a procedure for Thomas, who was noble in

age is that casting an opponent's case in the best possible light may mean that one has to first presuppose the validity of all of one's opponent's assumptions and his particular standards for rational justification, before showing either that they would still lead to insurmountable inconsistencies and self-contradiction in the rival tradition or that they would be affirmed by the claims of the opponent's own worldview.[40] This is the way of tradition-constituted inquiry.[41]

Finally, to illustrate MacIntyre's approach to rational debate in a postmodern context, we return to the dispute over the nature of human dignity. As we have already discussed, there are those who hold that human dignity is fundamentally intrinsic, because it is constitutive of human identity. On the other hand, there are those who hold that human dig-

---

more than name—but, rather, he meets him precisely in the area of his strongest arguments. Often enough Thomas is the first to bring the actual forces of these arguments to light; frequently, it is through his formulations that the objections of his adversaries gain persuasive power." See his *The Silence of St. Thomas*, trans. J. Murray, S.J., and D. O'Conner (New York: Pantheon Books, 1957), 22.

40. The Catholic Church claims that its moral teachings, because they are grounded in the natural law, are binding on all human beings: "The natural law, present in the heart of each man and established by reason, is universal in its precepts and its authority extends to all men" (*Catechism of the Catholic Church*, no. 1956). In assuming the validity of all his opponent's presuppositions in tradition-constituted inquiry, the Catholic citizen does not have to surrender the absolute and universal claims of his own tradition. Rather, he simply chooses to focus not on the epistemological claims of his own tradition, but on the claims of the rival tradition, in order to articulate the truths of his own tradition in the language of its rival. Indeed, the Angelic Doctor, himself, recognized that "if our opponent believes nothing of divine revelation, i.e., he does not accept the authority of the Christian tradition, there then is no longer any means of proving the articles of faith by reasoning, but only of answering his objections—if he has any—against faith" (*ST*, Ia, 1.8), Note here that St. Thomas does not deny the universal applicability of Christianity's theological claims to truth in spite of his recognition that they are not universally justifiable to all people. Truth remains true for one's opponent even if one cannot justify it to him in the language of his own tradition.

41. As an aside, I think that St. Thomas Aquinas would have agreed with this postmodern approach to rational discourse. At the end of his work *On the Perfection of the Spiritual Life*, he addressed his critics in the following way: "If anyone desires to send me a reply, his words will be very welcome to me. For the surest way to elucidate truth and to confound error is by confuting the arguments brought against the truth. Solomon says, 'Iron sharpens iron, so a man sharpens the countenance of a friend' (Prov 27:17). And may the Lord God, blessed forever, judge between us and them. Amen." See St. Thomas Aquinas, *The Religious State: The Episcopate and the Priestly Office: A Translation of the Minor Work of the Saint, On the Perfection of the Spiritual Life*, ed. John Proctor (Westminster, Md.: Newman Press, 1950), 164.

nity is solely extrinsic, because it is rooted in personal autonomy, which can be gained or lost during life. In our postmodern society, commentators claim that the debate over human dignity is an interminable one that cannot and will never be resolved. It simply has to be acknowledged as a reality of a plural and liberal society. I disagree. Using the methodology of tradition-constituted inquiry, I will argue that only an *intrinsic* account of human dignity can sustain the ideals of a liberal society. Thus, by the standards of liberalism itself, every human being, regardless of his developmental stage, merits the protection accorded to all adult human beings in a liberal society simply because he is a human being.

What role does human dignity play in a liberal society that values human rights and human equality?[42] As Yehoshua Arieli has convincingly argued, one cannot understand the meaning of human dignity and other such concepts used in the Universal Declaration of Human Rights and its subsequent formulations in the other architectonic documents and constitutions of our liberal society if we deal with them without reference to their textual context.[43] These texts reveal that the invocation of the dignity of the human person was the response of the Free World to the ideologies of Germany, Japan, and Italy during World War II, in general, and of National Socialism in Hitler's Germany, in particular. For instance, the preamble of the Universal Declaration of Human Rights declared, in part:

Whereas recognition of the inherent dignity and of the equal and inalienable rights of all members of the human family is the foundation for freedom, justice and peace in the world, Whereas disregard and contempt for human rights have resulted in barbarous acts which have outraged the conscience of mankind . . . Whereas, it is essential, if man is not to be compelled to have recourse, as a last resort, to rebellion against tyranny and oppression, that human rights should be protected by the rule of law . . .[44]

In this wording, the societies of the Free World made three arguments, arguments that Klaus Dicke has called the founding function of human

42. The discussion that follows is based in the most part on my essay, "Debating Embryonic Dignity in a Liberal Society," *Stem Cell Reviews* 1 (2005): 305–308.

43. Yehoshua Arieli, "On the Necessary and Sufficient Conditions for the Emergence of the Doctrine of the Dignity of Man and His Rights," in *The Concept of Human Dignity in Human Rights Discourse*, ed. David Kretzmer and Eckart Klein, 1–17 (The Hague: Kluwer Law International, 2002).

44. Preamble to the Universal Declaration of Human Rights, in Carol Devine, Carol Rae Hansen, and Ralph Wilde, eds., *Human Rights: The Essential Reference* (Phoenix, Ariz.: Oryz Press, 1999), 277.

dignity.[45] First, they affirmed that human dignity is something that is and has to be recognized. As Dicke makes clear, however, it is important to note that the Universal Declaration excludes an interpretation of "recognition" as the act that constitutes dignity. Human dignity is not, and cannot be, conditioned, either by government policy, societal approval, or the fulfillment of some norm. Second, the citizens of the Free World affirmed that this recognition of human dignity is the foundation of freedom, justice, and peace. It is the basis for human rights. Third, they affirmed that this inherent dignity is a quality possessed by "all members of the human family." Thus, it is the reason for the equality and unity of mankind. In the end, liberal societies affirmed human dignity in the twentieth century in order to reaffirm the autonomy, the rights, and the equality of especially those human beings who had been exploited, and in many cases killed, by tyrannical governments.

With this historical context in mind, however, it should be clear that only an intrinsic account of human dignity can sustain the ideals of a liberal society. Again, by intrinsic dignity, I mean a dignity that is inherent to, and not conferred upon, the human being, simply because of the kind of being that he is. First, as we discussed in chapter 5, if human dignity is solely extrinsic, requiring the possession of particular—usually mental—traits, then those who are mentally disabled, are comatose, are senile, or are newborns would not have dignity according to this criterion. Often these are the weakest and most vulnerable human beings, precisely those individuals who are most in need of the protection that a concept of human dignity is intended to provide in a liberal society.

Second, if human dignity is extrinsic, it reduces human beings to what a government, a people in general, or a community in particular, values about them, whether it be consciousness, moral agency, or autonomy. In principle, however, this invalidates the very reason for ascribing human dignity to human beings in a liberal society—to shield them from the arbitrary will of governments, peoples, or communities. Only an intrinsic account of human dignity can protect the rights of human beings against those who would marginalize them, by denying them moral status.

Finally, if human dignity is extrinsic, then not everyone is equal. There

45. Klaus Dicke, "The Founding Function of Human Dignity in the Universal Declaration of Human Rights," in *The Concept of Human Dignity in Human Rights Discourse*, ed. David Kretzmer and Eckart Klein, 111–120 (The Hague: Kluwer Law International, 2002), 114.

will always be individuals who manifest more or less of a particular trait. For example, there will always be individuals who are more intelligent, more conscious, more autonomous, more productive, or more aware of themselves, than others. Only an intrinsic account of human dignity based solely on the common humanity of all human beings can adequately explain the ideal of human equality that grounds a liberal society.

In sum, there are two ways of speaking about Catholic bioethics in a pluralistic society. With moral friends, the Catholic citizen can articulate and defend the claims of his moral tradition with sound arguments that appeal to the content-full morality and the worldview that they share. In line with this approach, the narrative in this book is directed toward moral friends who affirm the premises of the Catholic moral tradition. In contrast, with moral strangers, the citizen of faith could use the approach of tradition-constituted inquiry to dialogue with citizens belonging to other moral traditions. He is called to demonstrate the truth-claims of the Catholic tradition by using the epistemological standards of its rivals. Both of these approaches will take not only much ingenuity and patience, but also great charity. Like St. Thomas Aquinas, the effective multi-tradition translator must seek to be a virtuous individual.

Living Catholic Bioethics in a Pluralistic Society

Cooperating with Evil Acts

Each of us lives as part of an extensive social network of moral agents who are acting to achieve both good and evil purposes, whether by good or evil means. Clearly, there may be times when we choose to involve ourselves as accomplices in the evil acts of others. However, there are also other times, especially in a pluralistic society, when, without our consent, our good acts may assist others to achieve their evil purposes. For example, take the Catholic postal worker whose employment at the post office allows pornographers to distribute their obscene materials to others, or the Catholic receptionist whose services on the first floor of a secular hospital facilitates the performance of IVF procedures eight floors above. Almost anything we do can be an occasion, opportunity, or means, for someone else to do something wicked. In bioethics, questions of cooperation in evil arise when a Catholic health-care provider or pharmacist is asked to participate in morally troubling procedures, which today can include, among others, assisted reproduction for individuals and couples, physician-assisted suicide in Oregon, where it is now legal, or the distribution of RU-486, the abortifacient pill, to college students. How should the Catholic citizen decide if he should go forward with his contemplated good acts, when he can foresee that his acts may, in some way, facilitate the evil acts of others?

Traditionally, the Catholic moral tradition, in reflecting upon the issue of cooperation in evil, has begun with the distinction between formal and material cooperation.[46] If the cooperator shares in the principal agent's evil intent—in other words, if he too desires, chooses, and approves of the evil purpose chosen by the principal agent—then he *formally* cooperates in the evil act and shares in the culpability of the principal agent.[47] Formal cooperation is morally illicit, always and everywhere. The nurse who assists a physician during an illicit procedure such as an abortion with the intention of taking over in case of necessity is guilty of formal cooperation and is as morally culpable for the abortion as the surgeon is.

In contrast, if the cooperator does not share in the principal agent's

46. For comprehensive overviews of the Catholic moral tradition's reflection on cooperation with evil from a diversity of perspectives, see Orville N. Griese, "The Principle of Material Cooperation," in *Catholic Identity in Health Care: Principles and Practice* (Braintree, Mass.: Pope John Center, 1987), 373–416; Russell E. Smith, "The Principles of Cooperation in Catholic Thought," in *The Fetal Tissue Issue: Medical and Ethical Aspects*, ed. Peter Cataldo and Albert Moraczewski, O.P., 81–92 (Braintree, Mass.: Pope John Center, 1994); Germain Grisez, *The Way of the Lord Jesus*, vol. 3: *Difficult Moral Questions* (Quincy, Ill.: Franciscan Press, 1997), 871–898; James Keenan, S.J., "Collaboration and Cooperation in Catholic Health Care," *Australasian Catholic Record* 77 (2000): 163–174; and Anthony Fisher, O.P., "Cooperation in Evil: Understanding the Issues," in *Cooperation, Complicity and Conscience*, ed. Helen Watt, 27–64 (London: Linacre Center, 2005).

47. Though the discussion here focuses on individuals, questions of cooperation in evil also arise for Catholic institutions, especially hospitals and health-care organizations that enter into partnerships with secular institutions. As the *Ethical and Religious Directives* of the United States Conference of Catholic Bishops makes clear, "new partnerships can pose serious challenges to the viability of the identity of Catholic health-care institutions and services, and their ability to implement these Directives in a consistent way, especially when partnerships are formed with those who do not share Catholic moral principles" (*Ethical and Religious Directives for Health Care Services*, 5th ed., part 6, Introduction). The moral analysis described here for individuals facing dilemmas involving cooperation with evil can be easily applied to institutions confronting similar scenarios. For discussion, see Russell E. Smith, "The Principles of Cooperation and Their Application to the Present State of Health Care Evolution," in *The Splendor of Truth and Health Care*, ed. Russell E. Smith, 217–231 (Braintree, Mass.: Pope John Center, 1995); and National Catholic Bioethics Center, "Cooperating with Non-Catholic Partners," *Ethics Medics* 23.11 (1998): 1–5.

evil intent, if he does not approve of the evil act, then he *materially* cooperates in the evil act. The scrub nurse in the operating room who cares for patients before, during, and after all surgeries, who sometimes finds himself involved in an illicit procedure as an occasional bystander, is involved in material cooperation as long as he does not consent to that procedure. There are two categories of material cooperation. *Immediate* material cooperation occurs when the cooperator participates in circumstances that are essential to the commission of an act, such that the principal agent's act could not occur without this participation. Immediate material cooperation in evil acts is not licit. However, when this immediate material cooperation occurs under duress, the culpability of the cooperator is diminished or eliminated altogether. For instance, a prisoner of war who is forced by his captors to engage in sexual intercourse with a woman because he fears for his life, is not culpable of that rape, even though his act remains a grave evil. As the ethicists at the National Catholic Bioethics Center conclude: "Considered in itself, immediate material cooperation in evil is wrong, but its culpability is significantly reduced or eliminated if done through a legitimate fear of losing a great good."[48] In contrast, *mediate* material cooperation occurs when the cooperator participates in circumstances that are not essential to the commission of the act. This kind of cooperation can be morally justifiable in certain circumstances, if there is an adequate and grave reason for lending such assistance. For example, the custodian who cleans the offices of an abortion clinic after hours to financially support his family would be involved in mediate material cooperation with the activities of his employers.

The prudent individual needs to ask himself three questions when he is considering mediate material cooperation with the evil acts of another agent. First, he has to determine the moral gravity of the evil act. A morally more serious reason would be required for someone to cooperate with a physician performing a procedure that sterilizes a patient permanently than for someone to work with a grocery store manager selling condoms that sterilize individual procreative acts. Next, the prudent man would have to access the closeness of his act to the evil act that it would facilitate. A morally more serious reason would be required for the anesthetist who cooperates with the surgeon performing a sterilization than for the scrub nurse who provides nothing more than routine nursing care for the sterilized patient. The former scenario of the anesthesi-

48. National Catholic Bioethics Center, "Cooperating with Non-Catholic Partners," 3.

ologist would be an example of *proximate* mediate cooperation—it is more closely associated with the sterilization itself—while the latter case of the scrub nurse is an example of *remote* mediate cooperation. Finally, the virtuous cooperator would have to examine the reason for his cooperation and be able to provide a proportionate justification for it. A scrub nurse with five children who would be unable to find another job elsewhere in the city to support his family would be able to better justify his material cooperation with occasional illicit procedures in the operating room than a scrub nurse who is able to easily pursue other employment opportunities. The virtuous individual is called to do all that is reasonable to avoid cooperating in evil acts, even if this is inconvenient, because the acts that we choose, as I have emphasized numerous times throughout this book, make us into either virtuous saints or vicious sinners.

Finally, the prudent individual would have to consider the question of scandal. Scandal is an attitude or behavior that in itself is evil or has the appearance of evil and that leads another to think or to do evil.[49] As is apparent from the strong words used by the Lord Jesus Christ with regard to giving scandal to little children (cf. Lk 17:1–2), it is a grave offense, if by one's deed or by omission, another is deliberately led into thinking or doing evil. A virtuous cooperator needs to do what is reasonable to make sure that his act of material cooperation is not a cause of scandal. He would do this by making sure that he has explained his moral convictions to others, so that they will not be misled by his actions. Thus, the scrub nurse who works in the operating room even when occasional illicit procedures are done, in order to support his family's livelihood, would have to be outspoken about his moral convictions in support of the Gospel of Life so that his colleagues, his patients, and his fellow citizens are aware that he is not formally cooperating in, or condoning, these procedures in even a minimal way.

In the end, the virtue of prudence has to play a significant role in a moral agent's decision to cooperate in an evil act. Cooperation in evil can be allowed in certain circumstances if it is material, mediate, and relatively remote, if it would not be a cause for scandal, and if there is a proportionately serious reason for that cooperation. This is a prudential judgment that needs to be made on an act-by-act basis. St. Alphonsus Liguori explained why such cooperation is not contrary to the law of charity, despite the fact that it presents the occasion of an evil act:

49. *Catechism of the Catholic Church*, no. 2284.

The reason is because when you place an indifferent act without an evil intention, if the other person chooses to abuse it so as to accomplish his sin, you
are not bound to prevent that sin except by the law of charity. And since charity does not obligate with a grave inconvenience, you do not sin by providing
your cooperation with a just reason; then the sin of the other person does not
proceed from your cooperation, but by the malice of that person who abused
your act.[50]

In other words, according to St. Alphonsus, when a human agent has done
all that is reasonable to prevent an evil act, he is not guilty of that act even
if it is facilitated by his own good actions, because it is the principal agent
who is guilty of abusing the cooperator's goodness.

Finally, in the same way that individuals are morally forbidden from
cooperating with evil acts, institutions too, especially Catholic institutions forming partnerships with non-Catholic health-care organizations
and providers, are forbidden from cooperating with evil acts. This is especially true with grave moral evils. The *Ethical and Religious Directives* of the
United States Conference of Catholic Bishops explicitly states: "Catholic
health care organizations are not permitted to engage in immediate material cooperation in actions that are intrinsically immoral, such as abortion, euthanasia, assisted suicide, and direct sterilization."[51] Indeed, the
Ethical and Religious Directives reminds the Catholic institution that it has
the responsibility to make sure that all of its activities done with its non-
Catholic partner "must be limited in accord with the moral principles
governing cooperation."[52]

Appropriating Evil Acts

As we discussed above, there are times when our good acts could assist others to achieve their evil purposes. However, there are also times
when a virtuous agent has to consider if he should incorporate the fruits
or byproducts of another agent's past evil act into his own activity. Law
professor M. Cathleen Kaveny has proposed a new analytical category,
called appropriation of evil, in order to deal with this scenario.[53] While

50. St. Alphonsus de Liguori, *Theologia Moralis*, vol. 1, ed. Leonard Gaude (Rome: Ty-
pographia Vaticana, 1905), 357, cited by Orville N. Griese, *Catholic Identity in Health Care:
Principles and Practice* (Braintree, Mass.: Pope John Center, 1987), 389.

51. *Ethical and Religious Directives for Catholic Health Care Services*, 5th ed., no. 70.

52. Ibid., no. 69.

53. M. Cathleen Kaveny, "Appropriation of Evil: Cooperation's Mirror Image," *Theological Studies* 61 (2000): 280–313.

cooperation deals with cases where one agent's good acts facilitate another person's evil action in the future, appropriation deals with cases where one agent's good acts benefit from another person's evil action done in the past. In bioethics, questions of appropriation include, among others, the morality of conducting research using data procured by immoral means, the legitimacy of using cells and cell lines obtained from an aborted fetus, and the possibility of adopting therapies, in one's medical practice, with embryonic stem cell lines derived from the destruction of human embryos.

Kaveny proposes that the prudent individual should ask himself several questions when he is considering appropriating the fruits of another agent's evil acts. These questions parallel those asked by agents considering cooperating with evil. First, the appropriator needs to determine if he is making use of the wrongful act's fruits as if it were his own action, that is, as if it were an action that he would have engaged in himself given the opportunity and/or necessity. In this type of situation, the appropriator "adopts" or "ratifies" the evil act and assumes moral responsibility for it. This kind of appropriation, formal appropriation if you will, is the moral equivalent of "using someone else to do the dirty work."[54] The molecular biologist who obtains an embryonic stem cell line for use in his laboratory so he does not have to spend the funds required to obtain and to destroy human embryos himself would be guilty of formal appropriation, because he cannot but also intend the destruction of the human embryos required for the generation of the purchased cell line.

Next, if the appropriator does not consent to the original evil act, a case of material appropriation if you will, he would have to access the gravity of the wrongdoing to be appropriated, to determine whether he has a just claim to the fruits or byproducts of the principal agent's evil act, and to see if his appropriation would generate unavoidable scandal that appears to condone the evil act done. Finally, he would also need a grave reason—a proportionate good in relation to the evil done—to justify his appropriation of the fruits of the wrongful act. For one, he would have to consider if there are other ways, which do not involve making use of the fruits of another's evil act, for him to achieve his good purposes. If there are other less tainted options, then he would have to forgo the appropriation to avoid any possible complicity in the completed evil act.

In sum, in a manner parallel to the moral analysis of cooperation, a

54. Ibid., 307.

reasoned reflection upon the appropriation of evil suggests that it could be allowed for individual agents in certain circumstances, if it is material appropriation, if it would not be a cause for scandal, and if there is a proportionately serious reason for that appropriation that would bring about a proportionate good. Catholic institutions, however, should not participate in the appropriation of evil, even if it is material appropriation, because of the greater possibility of scandal. The *Ethical and Religious Directives* of the United States Conference of Catholic Bishops state with regard to cooperation and by extension to appropriation: "The possibility of scandal must be considered when applying the principles governing cooperation. Cooperation, which in all other respects is morally licit, may need to be refused because of the scandal that might be caused."[55]

Doing Research with Morally Controversial Biological Materials

In recent years, there has been much moral controversy surrounding two categories of human cell lines and biological materials obtained from and with them: cell lines derived from aborted human fetuses and cell lines derived from cultured human embryos who are killed in the process. May a scientist of good conscience use these materials?

In response, in its most recent *Instruction* on bioethics, the Congregation for the Doctrine of the Faith has explained that scientists of good conscience should not use biological materials of illicit origin, to distance themselves from evil and to avoid scandal: "This duty springs from the necessity to remove oneself, within the area of one's own research, from a gravely unjust legal situation and to affirm with clarity the value of human life."[56] Scientists should also refrain from these morally controversial cell lines because using these biological materials may also lead to further acts of grave evil. For instance, it is not unreasonable to predict that the use of a human embryonic stem cell line could lead to scientific discoveries that would prompt other scientists to desire more cell lines of this type, and thus to destroy more human embryos. In the end, heroic acts are demanded of scientists of good conscience who seek to respect and protect the inviolability and the dignity of human life in a culture that does not hesitate to instrumentalize human beings.

Significantly, in reaching the conclusion discussed above, *Dignitas personae* explicitly rules out the criterion of independence that had been

---

55. *Ethical and Religious Directives for Catholic Health Care Services*, 5th ed., no. 71.
56. Congregation for the Doctrine of the Faith, *Dignitas personae*, no. 35.

proposed by some moralists who had suggested that a scientist of good conscience could avail himself of morally controversial biological materials as long as he is not involved in the actual destruction of the human being that was necessary for the derivation of that material.[57] In our current political and social climate, the Congregation for the Doctrine of the Faith has discerned that prudence dictates that we strenuously avoid any complicity or even any hint of complicity with evil in science.

Finally, it is important to emphasize that *Dignitas personae* makes two additional points, both of which are critically important in this discussion. First, it also acknowledges that a citizen of good conscience may have grave and morally proportionate reasons to justify the use of morally controversial biological materials. For instance, certain vaccines used in the United States and elsewhere were developed using cells obtained from the corpses of aborted fetuses.[58] May families of good conscience vaccinate their children with these morally controversial reagents? In response, the *Instruction* explains that "danger to the health of children could permit parents to use a vaccine which was developed using cell lines of illicit origin."[59] However, according to *Dignitas personae*, these parents retain the duty to make known their disagreement and to ask that their health-care system make other types of vaccines available.

Next, the *Instruction* makes the distinction between those scientists who make the decision to use morally controversial cell lines and those scientists who have no say in the matter: "Moreover, in organizations where cell lines of illicit origin are being utilized, the responsibility of those who make the decision to use them is not the same as that of those who have no voice in such a decision."[60] Those scientists in the former category—usually called the principal investigators of their laboratories—have a greater responsibility to make sure that their research groups witness to the absolute dignity and to the sacredness of human life.[61]

57. For one articulation of an argument that embraces the so-called criterion of independence see Ron Hamel and Michael R. Panicola, "Embryonic Stem Cell Research: Off Limits? Two Ethicists Discuss a Technological Breakthrough in the Context of Catholic Health Care," *Health Progress* 87.5 (September–October 2006): 23–29.

58. For discussion, see Angel Rodríguez Luño, "Ethical Reflections on Vaccines Using Cells from Aborted Fetuses," *Natl Cathol Bioeth Q* 6 (2006): 453–459; and Alexander R. Pruss, "Complicity, Fetal Tissue, and Vaccines," *Natl Cathol Bioeth Q* 6 (2006): 461–470.

59. Congregation for the Doctrine of the Faith, *Dignitas personae*, n. 35.

60. Ibid.

61. For further discussion, see my essay, "Using Morally Controversial Human Cell Lines after *Dignitas personae*," *Natl Cathol Bioeth Q* 10 (2010): 265–272.

Respecting Conscientious Objection

As we discussed in chapter 1, an individual's conscience is his interior guide to morality. It is the human intellect, inasmuch as it discerns right and wrong conduct. Once the human agent has made a judgment of conscience—once he has decided if an act, either his own or another's, is either good or evil—he has the right, all things considered, to act in conscience, and in freedom, to make moral decisions. As the Second Vatican Council taught: "[The human person] must not be forced to act contrary to his conscience. Nor must he be prevented from acting according to his conscience."[62] This right to act according to one's conscience, and therefore, the corollary right to refuse to cooperate with another's acts that one has judged to be evil, both arise from the dignity of the human person, who is created to seek the truth in freedom.

As we described in the opening paragraphs of this chapter, there is an ongoing dispute in the United States regarding the apparent conflict between the right of a health-care provider to distance himself from a medical procedure that he finds morally objectionable and the right of a patient to receive all legal medical treatment.[63] The Pontifical Council for Justice and Peace has been resolute in its defense of the conscientious objector:

Unjust laws pose dramatic problems of conscience for morally upright people: *when they are called to cooperate in morally evil acts they must refuse.* Besides being a moral duty, such a refusal is also a basic human right which, precisely as such, civil law itself is obliged to recognize and to protect. "Those who have recourse to conscientious objection must be protected not only from legal penalties but also from any negative effects on the legal, disciplinary, financial and professional plane."[64]

To put it another way, civil laws that force an individual to act in a manner contrary to his conscience are immoral and unjust because they do not respect his dignity as a person, who is created with the freedom to choose the true and the good.

---

62. Declaration on Religious Liberty, *Dignitatis humanae*, no. 3.

63. For an overview of the contemporary legal debate surrounding conscience clauses, see Martha Swartz, "'Conscience Clauses' or 'Unconscionable Clauses': Personal Beliefs versus Professional Responsibilities," *Yale J. Health Policy Law Ethics* 6 (2006): 269–350.

64. Pontifical Council for Justice and Peace, *Compendium of the Social Doctrine of the Church*, no. 399, citing Pope John Paul II, *Evangelium vitae*, no. 73. Cf. *Catechism of the Catholic Church*, no. 2242.

In contrast, critics of the Federal Refusal Rule specifically, and of conscience clauses in medicine more generally, are especially opposed to these laws, because they contend that the health-care providers who are appealing to them were aware that their morally objectionable practices were part of the medical profession when they joined it.[65] For these critics, an individual who has chosen to become a health-care provider has made a professional commitment to provide all medical interventions that are legal, beneficial, and desired by the patient. Therefore, these critics insist that these conscientious objectors should put aside their religious convictions and treat their patients, especially since, according to these critics, religious convictions have no place in the medical profession of a secular society. At least, critics propose, conscientious objectors should be willing to refer their patients to another health-care provider who is willing to provide the controversial medical intervention—a proposal that has been called the conventional compromise[66]—so that every patient can act according to his own conscience just as readily as the professional can. According to their detractors, conscientious objectors should leave the profession if they are unable to at least refer their patients to another individual.

In response, as even John Rawls, the foremost proponent of liberal political theory in the twentieth century, has acknowledged, the freedom to engage in civil disobedience and conscientious refusal is a fundamental pillar of a liberal democracy.[67] It protects the minority against the power of the majority. Especially in light of the medical abuses in government-sponsored research programs in Nazi Germany, health-care providers must be free to object to even legally sanctioned medical procedures. To deny them this liberty is to undermine their autonomy to live and to practice their profession according to the dictates of their consciences, undercutting the very basis of a liberal society. Next, it is unreasonable to expect physicians—most of whom in the United States profess some religious af-

---

65. For representative views, see R. Alta Charo, "The Celestial Fire of Conscience—Refusing to Deliver Medical Care," *N Engl J Med* 352 (2005): 2471–2473; and Julian Savulescu, "Conscientious Objection in Medicine," *BMJ* 332 (2006): 294–297.

66. Dan W. Brock, "Conscientious Refusal by Physicians and Pharmacists: Who Is Obligated to Do What, and Why?" *Theor Med Bioeth* 29 (2008): 187–200.

67. Rawls defines a conscientious refusal as noncompliance with a more or less direct legal injunction or administrative order, where the noncompliance may be based on political, religious, or other principles at variance with the constitutional order. For his defense of civil disobedience and conscientious refusal, see Rawls's seminal work, *Theory of Justice* (Cambridge, Mass.: Harvard University Press, 1971), 363–391.

filiation[68]—to suspend their most deeply held beliefs when they enter the clinic. As physicians Alan E. Hall and Farr Curlin point out, to the extent that religious claims inhere in all meaningful accounts of life, death, health, suffering, and other concepts linked to medicine, strictly secular moral discourse about the practice of health care will never be possible.[69] Finally, it is unacceptable to expect physicians and other health-care providers to be willing to refer their patients for morally objectionable medical practices since, in many cases, this would constitute proximate mediate material cooperation that would make the referring physician complicit in the evil act. Thus, the so-called conventional compromise would, in fact, force the health-care provider to compromise his conscience.

In sum, health-care providers have a right to act, or not to act, in accordance with their consciences. Along with this right, however, they also have a responsibility to minimize the burden of their conscientious refusal on others. For one, they have an obligation to inform potential patients about their moral objections to certain medical procedures, so that these individuals can make a free and informed choice before they enter into the physician-patient relationship. One Canadian physician posted a notice in his waiting room listing all the legally sanctioned medical interventions, including the prescription of birth control pills to unmarried patients, or of Viagra to unmarried men, that he would not offer to his patients.[70] Conscientious objectors should also be willing to discuss all available therapeutic options with their patients, including morally objectionable options, as long as they also mention their moral objections and their refusal, both to perform these procedures and to offer referrals for them. As Patrick Tully has suggested, the goal of this dialogue is not to promote the morally objectionable medical therapies, but precisely to discourage patients from choosing these options.[71] In doing so, the physician fulfills his obligation to inform his patients of their therapeutic options without sacrificing his personal and professional integrity.

68. Farr A. Curlin et al., "Religious Characteristics of U.S. Physicians," *J Gen Intern Med* 20 (2005): 629–634.

69. Daniel E. Hall and Farr A. Curlin, "Can Physicians' Care be Neutral Regarding Religion?" *Academic Medicine* 79 (2004): 677–679.

70. Dr. Stephen Thomas Dawson, "College of Physicians and Surgeons of Ontario: Agreement with Dr. Stephen Thomas Dawson," at http://www.consciencelaws.org/Conscience-Policies-Papers/PPPMedicalOrg04.html.

71. Patrick Tully, "Morally Objectionable Options: Informed Consent and Physician Integrity," *Natl Cathol Bioeth Q* 8 (2008): 491–504.

Finally, the debate over conscientious objection in medicine has raised an interesting question: can an institution like a Catholic hospital have a conscience that should be protected by law? As Daniel Sulmasy, O.F.M., has convincingly argued, health-care institutions seem to qualify as moral agents because they act intentionally according to specific moral commitments.[72] They make decisions for which they may receive praise or blame in order to fulfill their purpose of helping the sick. Therefore, Sulmasy concludes: "The conscience of an institution is rooted in the fact that it professes a set of fundamental moral commitments and it must act in accord with them. The conscience of an institution is exercised in making the moral judgment that a decision that it has made or is considering would violate those fundamental moral commitments."[73] In light of this analysis, the laws that shield individual conscientious objectors from persecution and coercion should also apply to health-care institutions.

Highlighting the Role of Virtue in Bioethics

Which virtue should have pride of place in a pluralistic society composed of moral friends and moral strangers? For Rawls and his liberal friends, that accolade belongs to the virtue of justice, especially justice understood as fairness.[74] First and foremost, the liberal citizen has to be fair. For the Catholic citizen, however, the place of honor should belong to the virtue of charity. Charity is the most excellent of all the virtues (cf. 1 Cor 13:13) because it attains God Himself as its proper object. As we noted in chapter 1, it is the theological virtue that orders our relationship with God by elevating the human agent so that he is capable of divine friendship. It gives us a share in the divine nature and gives us the ability to perform acts that are meritorious in the sight of God. Ultimately, it disposes us to love God for himself in his infinite goodness without any limitation and without any regard to our own personal advantage.

Charity also orders our relationships with the other citizens in a free and democratic society by disposing the citizen of faith to love his neighbors for the love of God. It would allow him to understand that he is an

72. Daniel P. Sulmasy, O.F.M., "What Is Conscience and Why Is Respect for It So Important?" *Theor Med Bioeth* 29 (2008): 135–149.

73. Ibid., 143.

74. John Rawls and Erin Kelly, *Justice as Fairness: A Restatement*, 2nd ed. (Cambridge, Mass.: Harvard University Press, 2001).

adopted son of the Father who is surrounded not by moral friends, nor by moral strangers, but by moral siblings, brothers and sisters in Christ. Therefore, charity should motivate the Catholic citizen to recognize that everyone in society, regardless of his or her particular perspective on bioethics, is seeking the same truth and the same good. This should dispose him not only to give others the benefit of the doubt, but also to try to discern the truth in his moral sibling's worldview. This disposition should facilitate the communication necessary for the healthy functioning of a free and democratic society.

Finally, it is also the common teaching of the theologians that charity is the form of all the other true virtues. As the soul, which is the form of the body, gives it life, so charity, which is the form of the virtues, gives them life by directing them to the human being's final end, who is God himself. This does not mean that charity replaces the other virtues, but that it elevates them to a higher supernatural order, which of themselves they could not attain. For instance, justice disposes the human agent to give to another what is due to him. Informed by charity, justice is elevated so that it disposes the human agent to do the same for the love of God. In the shadow of the Cross, justice involves much more than fairness. It is transformed by charity into mercy.

Appendix: Church Documents on Bioethics

This is an annotated bibliography of Church documents pertaining to bioethics along with links to an online version of the original text when one is available.

Basic Bioethics

DOCUMENT: *Veritatis splendor* ("The Splendor of Truth")

AUTHOR: Pope John Paul II

DATE: August 6, 1993

SUMMARY: *Veritatis splendor* is an encyclical by Blessed John Paul II, that responds to questions raised in fundamental moral theology. It reaffirms the existence of absolute moral truths accessible to all persons that guide the human agent to his perfection in Jesus Christ. The encyclical also defends the role of human reason in discovering and applying the natural law in the moral life.

http://www.vatican.va/holy_father/john_paul_ii/encyclicals/documents/hf_jp-ii_enc_06081993_veritatis-splendor_en.html

DOCUMENT: *Evangelium vitae* ("The Gospel of Life")

AUTHOR: Pope John Paul II

DATE: March 25, 1995

SUMMARY: *Evangelium vitae* is an encyclical by Blessed John Paul II, that reaffirms the Catholic Church's teaching on the dignity and inviolability of human life. It unequivocally condemns both abortion and euthanasia. The pope also argues that the death penalty has become obsolete since contemporary society has other means to defend itself against individuals who threaten the lives of the innocent.

http://www.vatican.va/holy_father/john_paul_ii/encyclicals/documents/hf_jp-ii_enc_25031995_evangelium-vitae_en.html

Bioethics at the Beginning of Life

DOCUMENT: *Humanae vitae* ("Of Human Life")

AUTHOR: Pope Paul VI

DATE: July 25, 1968

SUMMARY: *Humanae vitae* is an encyclical by the Servant of God, Pope Paul VI, that reaffirms the Catholic Church's teaching on the prohibition of contraception. The encyclical asserts the following: "It is necessary that each and every marriage act remain ordered per se to the procreation of human life." This teaching—called the inseparability principle—is "based on the inseparable connection, established by God, which man on his own initiative may not break, between the unitive significance and the procreative significance which are both inherent to the marriage act."

http://www.vatican.va/holy_father/paul_vi/encyclicals/documents/hf_p-vi_enc_25071968_humanae-vitae_en.html

DOCUMENT: *Declaratio de abortu procurato* ("Declaration on Procured Abortion")

AUTHOR: Congregation for the Doctrine of the Faith

DATE: November 18, 1974

SUMMARY: In this declaration, the Congregation for the Doctrine of the Faith traces the history of the Catholic Church's teaching on abortion and reaffirms the Church's constant condemnation of abortion because it is the direct killing of an innocent human being.

http://www.vatican.va/roman_curia/congregations/cfaith/documents/rc_con_cfaith_doc_19741118_declaration-abortion_en.html

DOCUMENT: *Quaecumque sterilizatio* ("Responses on Sterilization in Catholic Hospitals")

AUTHOR: Congregation for the Doctrine of the Faith

DATE: March 13, 1975

SUMMARY: In this response, the Congregation for the Doctrine of the Faith reiterates the constant teaching of the Catholic Church that the deliberate sterilization of an individual is intrinsically evil.

DOCUMENT: *Donum vitae* ("The Gift of Life")

AUTHOR: Congregation for the Doctrine of the Faith

DATE: February 22, 1987

SUMMARY: In this instruction, the Congregation for the Doctrine of the Faith responded to requests from bishops, theologians, and doctors and scientists, concerning biomedical techniques that make it possible to intervene in the initial phase of the life of a human being and in the very processes of procreation and their conformity with the principles of Catholic morality.

http://www.vatican.va/roman_curia/congregations/cfaith/documents/rc_con_cfaith_doc_19870222_respect-for-human-life_en.html

DOCUMENT: *Dignitas personae* ("The Dignity of a Person")

AUTHOR: Congregation for the Doctrine of the Faith

DATE: September 8, 2008

SUMMARY: In this instruction, the Congregation for the Doctrine of the Faith addresses the morality of the following medical interventions: selective reduction of pregnancies, prenatal diagnosis, preimplantation diagnosis, in vitro fertilization, embryo adoption, genetic engineering, and embryo donation.

http://www.vatican.va/roman_curia/congregations/cfaith/documents/rc_con_
cfaith_doc_20081208_dignitas-personae_en.html

Bioethics of Organ Transplantation

DOCUMENT: Address of the Holy Father John Paul II to the 18th International
Congress of the Transplantation Society

AUTHOR: Pope John Paul II

DATE: August 29, 2000

SUMMARY: In this address, Blessed John Paul II summarizes the Catholic Church's
teaching on the morality of organ donation.

http://www.vatican.va/holy_father/john_paul_ii/speeches/2000/jul-sep/
documents/hf_jp-ii_spe_20000829_transplants_en.html

Bioethics at the End of Life

DOCUMENT: *Iura et bona* ("Declaration on Euthanasia")

AUTHOR: Congregation for the Doctrine of the Faith

DATE: May 5, 1980

SUMMARY: In this instruction, the Congregation summarizes the Catholic Church's
teaching regarding medical interventions at the end of life, ruling out the morality
of interventions that deliberately shorten the life of a dying patient.

http://www.vatican.va/roman_curia/congregations/cfaith/documents/rc_con_
cfaith_doc_19800505_euthanasia_en.html

DOCUMENT: Responses to Certain Questions of the United States Conference of
Catholic Bishops Concerning Artificial Nutrition and Hydration

AUTHOR: Congregation for the Doctrine of the Faith

DATE: August 1, 2007

SUMMARY: In this response, the Congregation for the Doctrine of the Faith clari-
fies the Catholic Church's position regarding the care of patients in the persistent
vegetative state. It concludes: "It is therefore obligatory to the extent to which, and
for as long as, it is shown to accomplish its proper finality, which is the hydration
and nourishment of the patient. In this way suffering and death by starvation and
dehydration are prevented."

http://www.vatican.va/roman_curia/congregations/cfaith/documents/rc_con_
cfaith_doc_20070801_risposte-usa_en.html

DOCUMENT: Address of John Paul II to the Participants in the International Congress on "Life-Sustaining Treatments and Vegetative State: Scientific Advances and
Ethical Dilemmas"

AUTHOR: Pope John Paul II

DATE: March 20, 2004

SUMMARY: In this address, Blessed John Paul II addresses the morality of medical interventions in the care of patients who find themselves in the persistent vegetative state. He concludes: "The evaluation of probabilities, founded on waning hopes for recovery when the vegetative state is prolonged beyond a year, cannot ethically justify the cessation or interruption of minimal care for the patient, including nutrition and hydration. Death by starvation or dehydration is, in fact, the only possible outcome as a result of their withdrawal. In this sense it ends up becoming, if done knowingly and willingly, true and proper euthanasia by omission" (no. 4).

http://www.vatican.va/holy_father/john_paul_ii/speeches/2004/march/documents/hf_jp-ii_spe_20040320_congress-fiamc_en.html

Selected Bibliography

This bibliography includes all the works cited in this book except the primary scientific research papers and online websites.

Accattoli, Luigi. *When a Pope Asks for Forgiveness.* Translated by Jordan Aumann, O.P. Boston: Pauline Books and Media, 1998.

Ackerman, Felicia. "Assisted Suicide, Terminal Illness, Severe Disability, and the Double Standard." In *Physician Assisted Suicide: Expanding the Debate,* edited by Margaret P. Battin, Rosamond Rhodes, and Anita Silvers, 149–162. New York: Routledge, 1998.

Akerlof, George. "Men without Children." *Economic Journal* 108 (1998): 287–309.

Akerlof, George, Janet L. Yellen, and Michael L. Katz. "An Analysis of Out-of-Wedlock Childbearing in the United States." *Quarterly Journal of Economics* 111 (1996): 277–317.

Ali Brac De La Perriere, Robert, and Franck Seuret. *Brave New Seeds: The Threat of GM Crops to Farmers.* London: Zed Books, 2001.

Anderson, Fionn, Anna Glasier, Jonathan Ross, and David T. Baird. "Attitudes of Women to Fetal Tissue Research." *J Med Ethics* 20 (1994): 36–40.

Annas, George J., and Michael A. Grodin, eds. *The Nazi Doctors and the Nuremberg Code: Human Rights in Human Experimentatiom.* Oxford: Oxford University Press, 1995.

Anscombe, Elizabeth. *Contraception and Chastity.* London: Catholic Truth Society, 2003.

Aquinas, Thomas. *The Religious State: The Episcopate and the Priestly Office: A Translation of the Minor Work of the Saint, On the Perfection of the Spiritual Life,* edited by John Proctor. Westminster, Md.: Newman Press, 1950.

———. *Summa Theologica.* New York: Benziger Brothers, 1947.

Arieli, Yehoshua. "On the Necessary and Sufficient Conditions for the Emergence of the Doctrine of the Dignity of Man and His Rights." In *The Concept of Human Dignity in Human Rights Discourse,* edited by David Kretzmer and Eckart Klein, 1–17. The Hague: Kluwer Law International, 2002.

Arkes, Hadley, et al. "Production of Pluripotent Stem Cells by Oocyte-Assisted Reprogramming: Joint Statement with Signatories." *Natl Cathol Bioeth Q* 5 (2005): 579–583.

Arras, John D. "The Way We Reason Now: Reflective Equilibrium in Bioethics." In *The Oxford Handbook of Bioethics,* edited by Bonnie Steinbock, 46–71. Oxford: Oxford University Press, 2007.

Ashley, Benedict, O.P. "A Critique of the Theory of Delayed Hominization." In *An Ethical Evaluation of Fetal Experimentation: An Interdisciplinary Study,* edited by Donald

McCarthy, 113–133. St. Louis: Pope John XXIII Medical-Moral Research Center, 1976.

———. "Moral Principles Concerning Infants with Anencephaly: Observations on the Document." *L'Osservatore Romano*, September 23, 1998, 8.

———. *The Way toward Wisdom*. South Bend, Ind.: University of Notre Dame Press, 2006.

Audi, Robert. "The Separation of Church and State and the Obligations of Citizenship." *Philosophy and Public Affairs* 18 (1989): 259–296.

Austriaco, Nicanor Pier Giorgio, O.P. "Debating Embryonic Dignity in a Liberal Society." *Stem Cell Reviews* 1 (2005): 305–308.

———. "How to Navigate Species Boundaries: A Reply to *The American Journal of Bioethics*." *Natl Cathol Bioeth Q* 6 (2006): 61–71.

———. "Immediate Hominization from the Systems Perspective." *Natl Cathol Bioeth Q* 4 (2004): 719–738.

———. "In Defense of the Loss of Bodily Integrity as a Criterion for Death: A Response to the Radical Capacity Argument." *Thomist* 73 (2009): 647–659.

———. "Is Plan B an Abortifacient? A Critical Look at the Scientific Evidence." *Natl Cathol Bioeth Q* 7 (2007): 703–707.

———. "Is the Brain-Dead Patient *Really* Dead?" *Studia Moralia* 41 (2003): 277–308.

———. "On Reshaping Skulls and Unintelligible Intentions." *Nova et Vetera* 3 (2005): 81–99.

———. "On Static Eggs and Dynamic Embryos: A Systems Perspective." *Natl Cathol Bioeth Q* 2 (2002): 659–683.

———. "The Pre-implantation Embryo Revisited: Two-Celled Individual or Two Individual Cells?" *Linacre Q* 70 (2003): 121–126.

———. "Presumed Consent for Organ Procurement: A Violation of the Rule of Informed Consent?" *Natl Cathol Bioeth Q* 9 (2009): 55–62.

———. "The Soul and Its Inclinations: Recovering a Metaphysical Biology with the Systems Perspective." In *The Human Animal: Procreation, Education, and the Foundations of Society*. Proceedings of the X Plenary Session of the Pontifical Academy of St. Thomas Aquinas, June 18–20, 2010, "The Human Animal: Procreation, Education, and the Foundations of Society, 48–63" Vatican City: Pontifical Academy of St. Thomas Aquinas, 2011.

———. "Using Morally Controversial Human Cell Lines after *Dignitas personae*." *Natl Cath Bioeth Q* 10 (2010): 265–272.

Barry, Robert, O.P. "Writing a Pro-life Living Will." *Homiletic and Pastoral Review* 92 (1991): 8–17.

Beauchamp, Tom L., and James F. Childress. *Principles of Biomedical Ethics*. 6th ed. Oxford: Oxford University Press, 2009.

Beauregard, David, O.M.V. "Virtue in Bioethics." In *Catholic Health Care Ethics: A Manual for Practitioners*, 2nd ed., edited by Peter J. Cataldo and Albert S. Moraczewski, O.P., 27–29. Boston, Mass.: National Catholic Bioethics Center, 2001.

Beckwith, Francis J. *Politically Correct Death: Answering Arguments for Abortion Rights*. Grand Rapids, Mich.: Baker Books, 1993.

Bedell, Susanna E., Thomas L. Delbanco, E. Francis Cook, and Franklin H. Epstein. "Survival after Cardiopulmonary Resuscitation in the Hospital." In *Bioethics: An Introduction to the History, Methods, and Practice,* 1st ed., edited by Nancy S. Jecker, Albert R. Jonsen, and Robert A. Pearlman, 202–217. New York: Jones and Bartlett Publishers, 1997.

Beers, Mark H., Robert S. Porter, and Thomas V. Jones, eds. *Merck Manual of Diagnosis and Therapy.* 18th ed. Whitehouse Station, N.J.: Merck Research Laboratories, 2006.

Benedict XVI. *Caritas in veritate.* Vatican City: Libreria Editrice Vaticana, 2009.

Berg, Jessica W., Paul S. Appelbaum, Lisa S. Parker, and Charles W. Lidz, eds. *Informed Consent: Legal Theory and Clinical Practice.* 2nd ed. New York: Oxford University Press, 2001.

Berg, Thomas V., and Edward J. Furton. *Human Embryo Adoption.* Philadelphia: National Catholic Bioethics Center, 2006.

Berkman, John. "Adopting Embryos in America: A Case Study and an Ethical Analysis." *Scottish Journal of Theology* 55 (2002): 438–460.

Berlin, Isaiah. *Four Essays on Liberty.* Oxford: Oxford University Press, 1969.

Bernat, James L. "A Defense of the Whole-Brain Concept of Death." *Hastings Cent Rep* 28 (1998): 14–23.

———. "The Definition, Criterion, and Statute of Death." *Semin Neurol* 4 (1984): 45–51.

———. "The Whole-Brain Concept of Death Remains Optimum Public Policy." *J Law Med Ethics* 34 (2006): 35–43; 41.

Bernat, James L., Charles M. Culver, and Bernard Gert. "On the Definition and Criterion of Death." *Ann Intern Med* 94 (1981): 389–394.

Billings, Evelyn, and Ann Westmore. *The Billings Method: Controlling Fertility without Drugs or Devices.* New York: Random House, 1980.

Blake, Rich. *The Day Donny Herbert Woke Up: A True Story.* Nevada City, Calif.: Harmony Books, 2007.

Bonino, Serge-Thomas, O.P. "To Be a Thomist." *Nova et Vetera* 8 (2010): 763–773.

Boonin, David. *A Defense of Abortion.* Cambridge: Cambridge University Press, 2003.

Bouchard, Charles E., O.P. "Recovering the Gifts of the Holy Spirit in Moral Theology." *Theological Studies* 63 (2002): 539–558.

Bradley, Denis J. M. *Aquinas on the Twofold Human Good.* Washington, D.C.: The Catholic University of America Press, 1997.

Brakman, Sarah Vaughan, and Darlene Fozard Weaver, eds. *The Ethics of Embryo Adoption and the Catholic Tradition.* New York: Springer, 2007.

Brennan, M. Rose Emmanuella. *The Intellectual Virtues according to the Philosophy of St. Thomas.* Palo Alto, Calif.: Pacific Books, 1941.

Brock, Dan W. "Conscientious Refusal by Physicians and Pharmacists: Who Is Obligated to Do What, and Why?" *Theor Med Bioeth* 29 (2008): 187–200.

Brock, Stephen L. "*Veritatis Splendor* §78, St. Thomas, and (Not Merely) Physical Objects of Moral Acts." *Nova et Vetera* 6 (2008): 1–62.

Brown, Mark B. "Three Ways to Politicize Bioethics." *Am J Bioeth* 9.2 (2009): 43–54.

284 Selected Bibliography

Brudney, Daniel. "Are Alcoholics Less Deserving of Liver Transplants?" *Hastings Cent Rep* 37 (2007): 41–47.
Brugger, E. Christian, and William E. May. "John Paul II's Moral Theology on Trial: A Reply to Charles E. Curran." *Thomist* 69 (2005): 279–312.
Buckman, Robert. *How to Break Bad News: A Guide for Health Care Professionals.* Baltimore: Johns Hopkins University Press, 1992.
Budiani-Saberi, Debra A., and Francis L. Delmonico. "Organ Trafficking and Transplant Tourism: A Commentary on the Global Realities." *Am J Transplant* 8 (2008): 925–929.
Burley, Justine, and John Harris, eds. *A Companion to Genethics.* Malden, Mass.: Blackwell Publishers, 2002.
Burnyeat, Myles. "Is an Aristotelian Philosophy of the Mind Still Credible?" In *Essays on Aristotle's De Anima,* edited by Martha Nussbaum and Amelie Oksenberg Rorty, 15–26. Oxford: Clarendon Press, 1995.
Byock, Ira. "The Nature of Suffering and the Nature of Opportunity at the End of Life." *Clin Geriatr Med* 12 (1996): 237–252.
Cahill, Lisa Sowle. "Genetics, Commodification, and Social Justice in the Globalization Era." *Kennedy Inst Ethics J* 11 (2001): 221–238.
Callahan, Daniel. "Bioethics as a Discipline." *Stud Hastings Cent* 1 (1973): 66–73.
———. "Individual Good and the Common Good: A Communitarian Approach to Bioethics." *Perspectives in Biology and Medicine* 46 (2003): 496–507.
———. "Reason, Self-Determination, and Physician-Assisted Suicide." In *The Case against Assisted Suicide: For the Right to End-of-Life Care,* edited by Kathleen Foley and Herbert Hendin, 52–68. Baltimore: Johns Hopkins University Press, 2002.
———. "Religion and the Secularization of Bioethics." *Hastings Cent Rep* 20 (1990): S2–S4.
Campbell, Alastair V., and Teresa Swift. "What Does It Mean to Be a Virtuous Patient? Virtue from the Patient's Perspective." *Scottish Journal of Healthcare Chaplaincy* 5 (2002): 29–35.
Cantor, Norman L. "The Bane of Surrogate Decision-Making: Defining the Best Interests of Never-Competent Persons." *J Leg Med* 26 (2005): 155–205.
Capaldi, Nicholas. "A Catholic Perspective on Organ Sales." *Christ Bioeth* 6 (2000): 139–151.
Caplan, Arthur L., James J. McCarthy, and Dominic A. Sisti, eds. *The Case of Terri Schiavo: Ethics at the End of Life.* New York: Prometheus Books, 2006.
Cassell, Eric. *The Nature of Suffering.* New York: Oxford University Press, 1991.
Cataldo, Peter J. "Pope John Paul II on Nutrition and Hydration: A Change of Catholic Teaching?" *Natl Cathol Bioeth Q* 4 (2005): 513–536.
———"The USCCB and Rape Protocols." *Ethics Medics* 29.4 (2004): 2–4.
A Catechism of Christian Doctrine. Rev. ed. of the Baltimore Catechism, No. 3. Paterson, N.J.: St. Anthony Guild Press, 1949.
Catechism of the Catholic Church. 2nd ed. Vatican City: Libreria Editrice Vaticana, 1997.
Catholic Bishops of Pennsylvania. "Nutrition and Hydration: Moral Considerations." *Origins* 21 (1992): 541–553.

Catholics for Choice. *Truth and Consequence: A Look Behind the Vatican's Ban on Contraception*. Washington, D.C.: Catholics for Choice, 2008.

Catholic Medical Association and the National Catholic Bioethics Center. "Catholic Principles and Guidelines for Clinical Research." *Natl Cathol Bioeth Q* 7 (2007): 153–165.

Cessario, Romanus, O.P. *Introduction to Moral Theology*. Washington, D.C.: The Catholic University of America Press, 2001.

———. *The Moral Virtues and Theological Ethics*. 2nd ed. South Bend, Ind.: University of Notre Dame Press, 2009.

Charo, R. Alta. "The Celestial Fire of Conscience—Refusing to Deliver Medical Care." *N Engl J Med* 352 (2005): 2471–2473.

Cherry, Mark J. "Body Parts and the Market Place: Insights from Thomistic Philosophy." *Christ Bioeth* 6 (2000): 171–193.

Childress, James F., Eric M. Meslin, and Harold T. Shapiro, eds. *Belmont Revisited: Ethical Principles for Research with Human Subjects*. Washington, D.C.: Georgetown University Press, 2005.

Clark, Patrick A. "Methotrexate and Tubal Pregnancies: Direct or Indirect Abortion?" *Linacre Q* 67 (2000): 7–24.

Clarke, Stanley G., and Evan Simpson. *Anti-Theory in Ethics and Moral Conservatism*. Albany: SUNY Press, 1989.

Cobbe, Neville. "Cross-Species Chimeras: Exploring a Possible Christian Perspective." *Zygon* 47 (2007): 599–628.

Cohen-Almagor, Raphael. *Euthanasia in the Netherlands: The Policy and Practice of Mercy Killing*. Dordrecht: Kluwer Academic Publisher, 2004.

Cole, Basil, O.P. "'Prospects for Xenotransplantation': A Brief Overview." *Natl Cathol Bioeth Q* 2 (2002): 391–397.

Coleman, Gerald D. "Is Genetic Engineering the Answer to Hunger?" *America* 192 (2005): 14–17.

Committee on Doctrine, National Conference of Catholic Bishops. "Moral Principles Concerning Infants with Anencephaly." *Origins* 26 (1996): 276.

Condic, Maureen. "When Does Life Begin? A Scientific Perspective." *Natl Cathol Bioeth Q* 9 (2009): 129–149.

Congregation for the Clergy. *The Priest and the Third Christian Millennium: Teacher of the Word, Minister of the Sacraments, and Leader of the Community*. Vatican City: Libreria Editrice Vaticana, 1999.

Congregation for the Doctrine of the Faith. *Declaration on Procured Abortion*. Vatican City: Libreria Editrice Vaticana, 1974.

———. *Dignitas personae*. Vatican City: Libreria Editrice Vaticana, 2008.

———. *Donum veritatis*. Vatican City: Libreria Editrice Vaticana, 1990.

———. "*Donum Veritatis*: Instruction on the Ecclesial Vocation of the Theologian." *Origins* 20 (1990): 117–126.

———. *Donum vitae*. Instruction on Respect for Human Life in its Origin and on the Dignity of Procreation, Replies to Certain Questions of the Day. Vatican City: Libreria Editrice Vaticana, 1987.

————. "Responses to Certain Questions Concerning Artificial Nutrition and Hydration, August 1, 2007." *Origins* 37 (2007): 242–245.

————. *Responses to Questions Proposed Concerning "Uterine Isolation" and Related Matters.* Vatican City: Libreria Editrice Vaticana, 1993.

Conley, Kieran, O.S.B. *A Theology of Wisdom.* Dubuque, Iowa: Priory Press, 1963.

Connery, John R., S.J. *Abortion: The Development of the Roman Catholic Perspective.* Chicago: Loyola University Press, 1977.

Cunningham, Bert, C.M. *The Morality of Organic Transplantation.* Washington, D.C.: The Catholic University of America Press, 1944.

Curran, Charles E. "The Catholic Moral Tradition in Bioethics." In *The Story of Bioethics*, edited by Jennifer K. Walter and Eran P. Klein, 113–130. Washington, D.C.: Georgetown University Press, 2003.

————. *The Moral Theology of Pope John Paul II.* Washington, D.C.: Georgetown University Press, 2005.

Danovitch, Gabriel M., and Francis L. Delmonico. "The Prohibition of Kidney Sales and Organ Markets Should Remain." *Curr Opin Organ Transplant* 13 (2008): 386–394.

Danovitch, Gabriel M., and Alan B. Leichtman. "Kidney Vending: The 'Trojan Horse' of Organ Transplantation." *Clin J Am Soc Nephrol* 1 (2006): 1133–1135.

Davidson, JoAnn L. "A Successful Embryo Adoption." *Natl Cathol Bioeth Q* 1 (2001): 229–233.

De Dios Vial Correa, Juan, and Elio Sgreccia, eds. *The Identity and Status of the Human Embryo.* Vatican City: Libreria Editrice Vaticana, 1999.

De Haro, Ramon Garcia. *Marriage and the Family in the Documents of the Magisterium.* Translated by William E. May. San Francisco: Ignatius Press, 1993.

De Koninck, Charles. "On the Primacy of the Common Good against the Personalists." *Aquinas Review* 4 (1997): 1–71.

De La Soujeole, Benoît-Dominique, O.P. "The Universal Call to Holiness." In *Vatican II: Renewal within Tradition*, edited by Matthew L. Lamb and Matthew Levering, 37–53. Oxford: Oxford University Press, 2008.

Devine, Carol, Carol Rae Hansen, and Ralph Wilde, eds. *Human Rights: The Essential Reference.* Phoenix, Ariz.: Oryz Press, 1999.

Diamond, Eugene F. "Anencephaly and Early Delivery: Can There Ever Be Justification?" *Ethics Medics* 28.10 (2003): 2–3.

————. *The Large Family: A Blessing and a Challenge.* San Francisco: Ignatius Press, 1996.

————. "The Licit Use of Methotrexate." *Ethics Medics* 31.3 (2006): 3.

Dicke, Klaus. "The Founding Function of Human Dignity in the Universal Declaration of Human Rights." In *The Concept of Human Dignity in Human Rights Discourse*, edited by David Kretzmer and Eckart Klein, 111–120. The Hague: Kluwer Law International, 2002.

Donagan, Alan. *A Theory of Morality.* Chicago: University of Chicago Press, 1977.

Donceel, Joseph F., S.J. "Immediate Animation and Delayed Hominization." *Theological Studies* 31 (1970): 76–105.

Dowbiggin, Ian. *A Concise History of Euthanasia: Life, Death, God, and Medicine.* Lanham: Rowman and Littlefield Publishers, 2005.

Drane, James F. *More Humane Medicine: A Liberal Catholic Bioethics.* Edinboro: Edinboro University of Pennsylvania Press, 2003.

Dresser, Rebecca. "Ethical and Legal Issues in Patenting New Animal Life." *Jurimetrics Journal* 28 (1988): 399–435.

DuBois, James. "Avoiding Common Pitfalls in the Determination of Death." *Natl Cathol Bioeth Q* 7 (2007): 545–550.

———. "Non-Heart-Beating Organ Donation: A Defense of the Required Determination of Death." *J Law Med Ethics* 27 (1999): 126–136.

Dulles, Avery, S.J. *Magisterium: Teacher and Guardian of the Faith.* Naples, Fla.: Sapientia Press, 2007.

Dworkin, Ronald. *Life's Dominion.* New York: Alfred A. Knopf, 1993.

Eberl, Jason T. "Extraordinary Care and the Spiritual Goal of Life: A Defense of the View of Kevin O'Rourke, O.P." *Natl Cathol Bioeth Q* 5 (2005): 491–501.

Edelstein, Ludwig. *Hippocratic Oath: Text, Translation and Interpretation.* Baltimore: Johns Hopkins University Press, 1943.

Elliott, George C. "A Brief Guide to Understanding Patentability and the Meaning of Patents." *Acad Med* 77 (2002): 1309–1314.

Engelhardt, H. Tristam, Jr. *The Foundations of Bioethics.* 2nd ed. Oxford: Oxford University Press, 1996.

———. "The Ordination of Bioethicists as Secular Moral Experts." *Social Philosophy and Policy* 19 (2002): 59–82.

———, ed. *Global Bioethics: The Collapse of Consensus.* Salem, Mass.: M&M Scrivener Press, 2006.

English, Veronica. "Is Presumed Consent the Answer to Organ Shortages? Yes." *BMJ* 334 (2007): 1088.

Epstein, Miram. "The Ethics of Poverty and the Poverty of Ethics: The Case of Palestinian Prisoners in Israel Seeking to Sell Their Kidneys in Order to Feed Their Children." *J Med Ethics* 33 (2007): 473–474.

Ethics Committee of the American Society for Reproductive Medicine. "Donating Spare Embryos for Stem Cell Research." *Fertil Steril* 91 (2009): 667–670.

Evans, James P. "Putting Patients before Patents." *Genetics in Medicine* 12 (2010): 204–205.

Farah, Martha J. "Emerging Ethical Issues in Neuroscience." *Nat Neurosci* 5 (2002): 1123–1129.

Feinberg, Joel. *Freedom and Fulfillment, Philosophical Essays.* Princeton, N.J.: Princeton University Press, 1992.

———, ed. *The Problem of Abortion.* 2nd ed. Belmont, Calif.: Wadsworth, 1984.

Feingold, Lawrence. *The Natural Desire to See God according to St. Thomas Aquinas and His Interpreters.* 2nd ed. Naples, Fla.: Sapientia Press, 2010.

Finnis, John. *Moral Absolutes.* Washington, D.C.: The Catholic University of America Press, 1991.

————. "Natural Inclinations and Natural Rights: Deriving 'Ought' from 'Is' according to Aquinas." In *Lex et Libertas: Freedom and Law according to St. Thomas Aquinas,* edited by Leo Elders and Klaus Hedwig, 43–55. Rome: Vatican Press, 1987.

————. *Natural Law and Natural Rights.* Corrected ed. Oxford: Clarendon Press, 1982.

Finnis, John, and Anthony Fisher, O.P. "Theology and the Four Principles of Bioethics: A Roman Catholic View." In *Principles of Health Care Ethics,* edited by Raanan Gillon, 31–44. New York: John Wiley and Sons, 1993.

Fins, Joseph J. *A Palliative Ethic of Care.* Sudbury, Mass.: Jones and Bartlett Publishers, 2006.

————. "Rethinking Disorders of Consciousness: New Research and Its Implications." *Hastings Cent Rep* 35 (2005): 22–24.

Fisher, Anthony, O.P. "Cooperation in Evil: Understanding the Issues." In *Cooperation, Complicity and Conscience,* edited by Helen Watt, 27–64. London: Linacre Center, 2005.

Flannery, Austin, ed. *Vatican Council II: The Conciliar and Post Conciliar Documents.* Northport, N.Y.: Costello Publishing, 1975.

Foley, Kathleen, and Herbert Hendin, eds. *The Case against Assisted Suicide: For the Right to End-of-Life Care.* Baltimore: Johns Hopkins University Press, 2002.

Foot, Phillippa. *Natural Goodness.* Oxford: Oxford University Press, 2003.

Ford, John C., and Germain Grisez. "Contraception and the Infallibility of the Ordinary Magisterium." *Theological Studies* 39 (1978): 258–312.

Ford, Norman, S.D.B. "Early Delivery of a Fetus with Anencephaly." *Ethics Medics* 28.7 (2003): 1–4.

————. "The Human Embryo as Person in Catholic Teaching." *Natl Cathol Bioeth Q* 1 (2001): 155–160, 160.

Forsythe, Don. "The Physician's Vocation." *Ethics Medics* 29.2 (2004): 3–4.

Fox, Renee C. "The Evolution of American Bioethics: A Sociological Perspective." In *Social Science Perspectives on Medical Ethics,* edited by G. Weisz, 201–220. Philadelphia: University of Pennsylvania Press, 1990.

Freedman, Benjamin, Kathleen C. Glass, and Charles Weijer. "Placebo Orthodoxy in Clinical Research. II: Ethical, Legal, and Regulatory Myths." *J Law Med Ethics* 24 (1996): 252–259.

Friedman, Russell, and John W. James. "The Myth of the Stages of Dying, Death and Grief." *Skeptic* 14 (2008): 37–41.

Furton, Edward J. "Embryo Adoption Reconsidered." *Natl Cathol Bioeth Q* 10 (2010): 329–347.

Furton, Edward J., Peter J. Cataldo, and Albert S. Morachewski, eds. *Catholic Health Care Ethics: A Manual for Practitioners.* 2nd ed. Philadelphia: National Catholic Bioethics Center, 2009.

Gallagher, John. "Magisterial Teaching from 1918 to the Present." In Pope John XXIII Medical-Moral Research and Education Center, *Human Sexuality and Personhood: Proceedings of the Workshop for the Hierarchies of the United States and Canada,* 191–210. St. Louis, Mo.: Pope John XXIII Center, 1981.

Garcia, Jorge L. A. "Sin and Suffering in a Catholic Understanding of Medical Ethics." *Christ Bioeth* 12 (2006): 165–186.

George, Robert P., and Christopher Tollefsen. *Embryo: A Defense of Human Life.* New York: Doubleday, 2008.

Gervais, Karen. *Redefining Death.* New Haven, Conn.: Yale University Press, 1986.

Gibbs, David, III. *Fighting for Dear Life.* Bloomington, Minn.: Bethany House Publishers, 2006.

Gill, Michael B., and Robert M. Sade. "Paying for Kidneys: The Case against Prohibition." *Kennedy Inst Ethics J* 12 (2002): 17–45.

Gilson, Etienne. *The Christian Philosophy of St. Thomas Aquinas.* Translated by L. K. Shook, C.S.B. New York: Random House, 1956.

Glannon, Walter. *Defining Right and Wrong in Brain Science: Essential Readings in Neuroethics.* Washington, D.C.: Dana Press, 2007.

Gold, E. Richard, Warren Kaplan, James Orbinski, Sarah Harland-Logan, and Sevil N-Marandi. "Are Patents Impeding Medical Care and Innovation?" *PLoS Med* 7 (2010): e1000208.

Gomez, Fausto B., O.P. "Truth Telling: Bioethical Perspective." *Philippiniana Sacra* 33 (1998): 217–238.

Gondreau, Paul. "The 'Inseparable Connection' between Procreation and Unitive Love (*Humanae vitae*, §12) and Thomistic Hylemorphic Anthropology." *Nova et Vetera* 6 (2008): 731–764.

———. "The Passions and the Moral Life: Appreciating the Originality of Aquinas." *Thomist* 71 (2007): 419–450.

Gormally, Luke. "Marriage and the Prophylactic Use of Condoms." *Natl Cathol Bioeth Q* 5 (2005): 735–749.

Gorsuch, Neil M. *The Future of Assisted Suicide and Euthanasia.* Princeton, N.J.: Princeton University Press, 2006.

Grabowski, John S. *Sex and Virtue: An Introduction to Sexual Ethics.* Washington, D.C.: The Catholic University of America Press, 2003.

Grabowski, John S., and Christopher Gross. "*Dignitas personae* and the Adoption of Frozen Embryos: A New Chill Factor?" *Natl Cathol Bioeth Q* 10 (2010): 307–328.

Gray, Fred D. *The Tuskegee Syphilis Study: The Real Story and Beyond.* Montgomery, Ala.: NewSouth Books, 2002.

Green, Ronald M. *The Human Embryo Research Debates.* Oxford: Oxford University Press, 2001.

Grenz, Stanley J. *A Primer on Postmodernism.* Grand Rapids, Mich.: William B. Eerdmans, 1996.

Griese, Orville N. "The Principle of Material Cooperation." In *Catholic Identity in Health Care: Principles and Practice.* Braintree, Mass.: Pope John Center, 1987.

Grimm, John S. "Living Wills and Health Care Proxies." *Ethics Medics* 26.3 (2001): 3–4.

Grisez, Germain. "Infallibility and Specific Norms: A Review Discussion." *Thomist* 49 (1985): 248–287.

————. *The Way of the Lord Jesus: Christian Moral Principles*. Quincy, Ill.: Franciscan Press, 1983.

————. *The Way of the Lord Jesus*. Vol. 2: *Living a Christian Life*. Quincy, Ill.: Franciscan Press, 1993.

————. *The Way of the Lord Jesus*. Vol. 3: *Difficult Moral Questions*. Quincy, Ill.: Franciscan Press, 1997.

————. "When Do People Begin?" *Proceedings of the American Catholic Philosophical Association* 63 (1989): 27–47.

Grisez, Germain, John Finnis, and Joseph Boyle, Jr. "'Direct' and 'Indirect': A Reply to Critics of Our Action Theory." *Thomist* 65 (2001): 1–44.

Groothuis, Douglas R. *Truth Decay: Defending Christianity against the Challenges of Postmodernism*. Downers Grove, Ill.: InterVarsity Press, 2000.

Guevin, Benedict, O.S.B., and Martin Rhonheimer. "On the Use of Condoms to Prevent Acquired Immune Deficiency Syndrome." *Natl Cathol Bioeth Q* 5 (2005): 37–48.

Haas, John M. "Can You Keep a Secret?" *Ethics Medics* 17.12 (1992): 1–2.

————. "Gift? No!" *Ethics Medics* 18.9 (1993): 1–3.

————. "The Totality and Integrity of the Body." *Ethics Medics* 20.1 (1995): 1–3.

Haldane, John. "Public Reason, Truth, and Human Fellowship: Going beyond Rawls." *Journal of Law, Philosophy and Culture* 1 (2007): 175–190.

Hamel, Ronald P., and Michael R. Panicola. "Embryonic Stem Cell Research: Off Limits? Two Ethicists Discuss a Technological Breakthrough in the Context of Catholic Health Care." *Health Progress* 87.5 (September–October 2006): 23–29.

————. "Emergency Contraception and Sexual Assault: Assessing the Moral Approaches in Catholic Teaching." *Health Progress* 83 (2002): 12–19.

————. "Low Risks of Moral Certitude: A Response to Msgr. Mulligan." *Ethics Medics* 28.12 (2003): 2–4.

Hamel, Ronald P., and James J. Walter, eds. *Artificial Nutrition and Hydration and the Permanently Unconscious Patient: The Catholic Debate*. Washington, D.C.: Georgetown University Press, 2007.

Hamm, Danielle, and Juliet Tizzard. "Presumed Consent for Organ Donation." *BMJ* 336 (2008): 230.

Hanks, Geoffrey, Nathan I. Cherny, Nicholas A. Christakis, Marie Fallon, Stein Kaasa, and Russell K. Portenoy, eds. *Oxford Textbook of Palliative Medicine*. 4th ed. Oxford: Oxford University Press, 2009.

Hanley, Matthew, and Jokin de Irala. *Affirming Love, Avoiding AIDS: What Africa Can Teach the West*. Philadelphia: National Catholic Bioethics Center, 2010.

Hardt, John J., and Kevin O'Rourke, O.P. "Nutrition and Hydration: The CDF Response, In Perspective." *Health Prog* 88 (2007): 44–47.

Hardwig, John. "Is There a Duty to Die?" *Hastings Cent Rep* 27 (1997): 34–42.

Hatcher, Robert A., et al. *Contraceptive Technology*. 19th rev. ed. New York: Ardent Media, 2007.

Hauerwas, Stanley, and C. Pinches, eds. *Christians among the Virtues*. Notre Dame, Ind.: University of Notre Dame Press, 1997.

Hearst, Norman, and Sanny Chen. "Condom Promotion for AIDS Prevention in the Developing World: Is it Working?" *Stud Fam Plann* 35 (2004): 39–47.

Helft, Paul R., Mark Siegler, and John Lantos. "The Rise and Fall of the Futility Movement." *N Engl J Med* 343 (2000): 293–296.

Hendin, Herbert, Chris Rutenfrans, and Zbigniew Zylicz. "Physician-Assisted Suicide and Euthanasia in the Netherlands. Lessons from the Dutch." *JAMA* 277 (1997): 1720–1722.

Henke, Donald E. "A History of Ordinary and Extraordinary Means." *Natl Cathol Bioeth Q* 5 (2005): 555–574.

Henry, Charles W., O.S.B. "The Place of Prudence in Medical Decision Making." *J Relig Health* 32 (1993): 27–37.

Hendin, Herbert. "The Dutch Experience." *Issues Law Med* 17 (2002): 223–246.

———. *Seduced by Death: Doctors, Patients, and the Dutch Cure.* New York: Norton, 1996.

Hibbs, Thomas S. *Virtue's Splendor.* New York: Fordham University Press, 2001.

Hoffenberg, R., et al. "Should Organs from Patients in Permanent Vegetative State Be Used for Transplantation?" *Lancet* 350 (1997): 1320–1321.

Hurlbut, William B., Robert P. George, and Marcus Grompe. "Seeking Consensus: A Clarification and Defense of Altered Nuclear Transfer." *Hastings Cent Rep* 36 (2006): 42–50.

Hyun, Insoo. "Vatican Formalizes Rules on Human Stem-Cell Research." *Nature* 456 (2008): 852.

Jecker, Nancy S., Albert R. Jonsen, and Robert A. Pearlman. *Bioethics: An Introduction to the History, Methods, and Practice.* 2nd ed. Boston: Jones and Bartlett, 2007.

Jennett, Bryan. *The Vegetative State: Medical Facts, Ethical and Legal Dilemmas.* Cambridge: Cambridge University Press, 2002.

Jensen, Steven J. "The Error of the Passions." *Thomist* 73 (2009): 349–379.

———. *Good and Evil Actions.* Washington, D.C.: The Catholic University of America Press, 2010.

Jeub, Chris, and Wendy Jeub. *Love in the House.* Monument, Colo.: Monument Publishing, 2007.

John Paul II. "Address to the First International Congress of the Society for Organ Sharing, June 20, 1991." *L'Osservatore Romano*, English ed. June 24, 1991, 1–2.

———. "Address to the International Congress on Transplants, August 29, 2000." *Natl Cathol Bioeth Q* 1 (2001): 89–92.

———. *Christifideles laici.* Vatican City: Libreria Editrice Vaticana, 1998.

———. "Dangers of Genetic Manipulation: Address to Members of the World Medical Association, October 29, 1983." *L'Osservatore Romano*, English ed. December 5, 1983, 10–11.

———. *Evangelium vitae.* Vatican City: Libreria Editrice Vaticana, 1995.

———. *Familiaris consortio.* Vatican City: Libreria Editrice Vaticana, 1981.

———. *Man and Woman He Created Them: A Theology of the Body.* Boston: Pauline Books and Media, 2006.

———. "Mentally Ill Are Also Made in God's Image." International Conference for Health Care Workers on Illnesses of the Human Mind, November 30, 1996. *L'Osservatore Romano*, December 11, 1996, 9.

——. "On Life-Sustaining Treatments and the Vegetative State: Scientific Advances and Ethical Dilemmas." *Natl Cathol Bioeth Q* 4 (2004): 573–576.

——. *Salvifici doloris.* Vatican City: Libreria Editrice Vaticana, 1984.

——. "To the Participants in the 19th International Conference of the Pontifical Council for Pastoral Health Care, November 12, 2004." *Natl Cathol Bioeth Q* 5 (2005): 153–155.

——. *Veritatis splendor.* Vatican City: Libreria Editrice Vaticana, 1993.

Joint Statement by 16 of the 18 Texas Catholic Bishops and the Texas Conference of Catholic Health Facilities. "On Withdrawing Artificial Nutrition and Hydration." *Origins* 20 (1990): 53–55.

Jones, David Albert. "Sin, Suffering, and the Need for the Theological Virtues." *Christ Bioeth* 12 (2006): 187–198.

——. *The Soul of the Embryo.* London: Continuum, 2004.

Jones, James H. *Bad Blood: The Syphilis Experiment.* Rev. ed. New York: Free Press, 1993.

Jones, R. K., J. E. Darroch, and S. K. Henshaw. "Patterns in the Socioeconomic Characteristics of Women Obtaining Abortions in 2000–2001." *Perspect Sex Reprod Health* 34 (2002): 226–235.

Jones, Robert P. *Liberalism's Troubled Search for Equality: Religion and Cultural Bias in the Oregon Physician-Assisted Suicide Debates.* Notre Dame, Ind.: University of Notre Dame Press, 2007.

Jordan, Mark. "Delayed Hominization: Reflections on Some Recent Catholic Claims for Delayed Hominization." *Theological Studies* 56 (1995): 743–763.

Juengst, Eric T. "Germ-Line Therapy: Back to Basics." *J Med Philos* 16 (1991): 587–592.

Kaczor, Christopher. *The Ethics of Abortion.* New York: Routledge, 2011.

——. "Moral Absolutism and Ectopic Pregnancy." *J Med Philos* 26 (2001): 61–74.

Kambic, R. T., and V. Lamprecht. "Calendar Rhythm Efficacy: A Review." *Adv Contracept* 12 (1996): 123–128.

Kaveny, M. Cathleen. "Appropriation of Evil: Cooperation's Mirror Image." *Theological Studies* 61 (2000): 280–313.

Keenan, James, S.J. "Collaboration and Cooperation in Catholic Health Care." *Australasian Catholic Record* 77 (2000): 163–174.

Kelly, David F. *Contemporary Catholic Health Care Ethics.* Washington, D.C.: Georgetown University Press, 2004.

Kelly, Gerald. "The Morality of Mutilations: Towards a Revision of the Treatise." *Theological Studies* 17 (1956): 322–344.

——. "Pope Pius XII and the Principle of Totality." *Theological Studies* 16 (1955): 373–396.

Keown, John. "Euthanasia in the Netherlands: Sliding Down the Slippery Slope?" In *Euthanasia Examined: Ethical, Clinical and Legal Perspectives,* edited by John Keown, 261–296. Cambridge: Cambridge University Press, 1995.

Kipnis, Kenneth. "A Defense of Unqualified Medical Confidentiality." *Am J Bioeth* 6 (2006): 7–18.

Kippley, John F., and Sheila K. Kippley. *The Art of Natural Family Planning.* 4th ed. Cincinnati: Couple to Couple League International, 1996.

Koenig-Bricker, Woodeene. *Ten Commandments for the Environment: Pope Benedict XVI Speaks Out for Creation and Justice.* Notre Dame, Ind.: Ave Maria Press, 2009.

Kopaczynski, Germain, O.F.M. Conv. "Handling the Truth about HIV/AIDS." *Ethics Medics* 21.7 (1996): 3–4.

———. "Initial Reactions to the Pope's March 20, 2004, Allocution." *Natl Cathol Bioeth Q* 4 (2005): 473–482.

Kubler-Ross, Elisabeth. *On Death and Dying.* New York: Scribner, 1969.

———. *Questions and Answers on Death and Dying.* New York: Touchstone, 1974.

Kuhse, Helga, and Peter Singer. *A Companion to Bioethics.* 2nd ed. New York: Blackwell Publishers, 2009.

Lachs, J. "The Element of Choice in Criteria of Death." In *Death: Beyond Whole-Brain Criteria,* edited by R. M. Zaner, 233–251. Dordrecht: Kluwer Academic Publishers, 1988.

Lamb, Matthew L., and Matthew Levering, eds. *Vatican II: Renewal within Tradition.* Oxford: Oxford University Press, 2008.

Lammers, Stephen. "The Marginalization of Religious Voices in Bioethics." In *Religion and Medical Ethics: Looking Back, Looking Forward,* edited by Allen Verhey, 19–43. Grand Rapids, Mich.: Wm. B. Eerdmans, 1996.

La Puma, John, David Orentlicher, and Robert J. Moss. "Advance Directives on Admission: Clinical Implications and Analysis of the Patient Self-Determination Act of 1990." *JAMA* 266 (1991): 402–405.

Latkovic, Mark S. "The Morality of Tube Feeding PVS Patients: A Critique of the View of Kevin O'Rourke, O.P." *Natl Cathol Bioeth Q* 5 (2005): 503–513.

Lauritzen, Paul. *Pursuing Parenthood: Ethical Issues in Assisted Reproduction.* Bloomington, Ind.: Indiana University Press, 1993.

Lebacqz, Karen. "The Virtuous Patient." In *Virtue and Medicine,* edited by Earl E. Shelp, 275–288. Dordrecht: Kluwer Academic Publishers, 1985.

Lee, Patrick. *Abortion and Unborn Human Life.* 2nd ed. Washington, D.C.: The Catholic University of America Press, 2010.

Lee, Patrick, and Robert George. *Body-Self Dualism in Contemporary Ethics and Politics.* Cambridge: Cambridge University Press, 2007.

Leies, John A. "Advance Directives." *Ethics Medics* 21.8 (1996): 1–2.

Levy, Neil. "Deafness, Culture, and Choice." *J Med Ethics* 28 (2002): 284–285.

———. *Neuroethics: Challenges for the 21st Century.* Cambridge: Cambridge University Press, 2007.

Lichacz, Piotr, O.P. *Did Aquinas Justify the Transition from "Is" to "Ought"?* Warsaw: Instytut Tomistyczny, 2010.

Liguori, Alphonsus. *Opere Ascetiche.* Turin: Marietti, 1845.

Lindemann, Hilde, and Marian Verkerk. "Ending the Life of a Newborn: The Groningen Protocol." *Hastings Cent Rep* 38 (2008): 42–51.

Lombardo, Nicholas E., O.P. *The Logic of Desire: Aquinas on Emotion.* Washington, D.C.: The Catholic University of America, 2011.

London, Alex John. "Clinical Equipoise: Foundational Requirement or Fundamental Error." In *The Oxford Handbook of Bioethics*, edited by Bonnie Steinbock, 571–596. Oxford: Oxford University Press, 2007.

Long, Steven A. "The False Theory Undergirding Condomitic Exceptionalism: A Response to William F. Murphy Jr. and Rev. Martin Rhonheimer." *Natl Cathol Bioeth Q* 8 (2008): 709–732.

———. "Natural Law or Autonomous Practical Reason: Problems for the New Natural Law Theory." In *St. Thomas Aquinas and the Natural Law Tradition: Contemporary Perspectives*, edited by John Goyette, Mark S. Latkovic, and Richard S. Myers, 165–194. Washington, D.C.: The Catholic University of America Press, 2004.

———. *The Teleological Grammar of the Moral Act*. Naples, Fla.: Sapientia Press, 2007.

Luño, Angel Rodriguez. "Ethical Reflections on Vaccines Using Cells from Aborted Fetuses." *Natl Cath Bioeth Q* 6 (2006): 453–459.

Lutz, Christopher Stephen. *Tradition in the Ethics of Alasdair MacIntyre*. Lanham, Md.: Lexington Books, 2004.

Lynne, Diana. *Terri's Story: The Court-Ordered Death of an American Woman*. Nashville, Tenn.: Cumberland House Publishing, 2005.

Lyotard, Jean-François. *The Postmodern Condition: A Report on Knowledge*. Minneapolis: University of Minnesota Press, 1984.

Lysaught, M. Therese. "Vulnerability within the Body of Christ: Anointing of the Sick and Theological Anthropology." In *Health and Human Flourishing*, edited by Carol R. Taylor and Roberto Dell'Oro, 159–182. Washington, D.C.: Georgetown University Press, 2007.

MacIntyre, Alasdair. *Three Rival Versions of Moral Enquiry*. Notre Dame, Ind.: University of Notre Dame Press, 1990.

———. *Whose Justice? Which Rationality?* Notre Dame, Ind.: University of Notre Dame Press, 1988.

Macklin, Ruth. "Dignity Is a Useless Concept." *BMJ* 327 (2003): 1419–1420.

Mall, D., and W. F. Watts, eds. *The Psychological Aspects of Abortion*. Washington, D.C.: University Publications of America, 1979.

Mangan, Joseph T., S.J. "An Historical Analysis of the Principle of Double Effect." *Theological Studies* 10 (1949): 41–61.

Marker, Rita L. "Terri Schiavo and the Catholic Connection." *Natl Cathol Bioeth Q* 4 (2004): 555–569.

Markham, Ian. "Faith and Reason: Reflections on MacIntyre's 'Tradition-Constituted Enquiry.'" *Religious Studies* 27 (1991): 259–262.

Marron-Corwin, Mary-Joan, and Andrew D. Corwin. "When Tenderness Should Replace Technology: The Role of Perinatal Hospice." *NeoReviews* 9 (2008): e348–e352.

Martelet, Gustave, S.J. "A Prophetic Text under Challenge: The Message of *Humanae vitae*." In *Natural Family Planning: Nature's Way/God's Way*, edited by Anthony Zimmerman, S.V.D., 153–167. Collegeville, Minn.: De Rance Inc. and Human Life Center, 1981.

Martin, Douglas K. "Abortion and Fetal Tissue Transplantation." *IRB* 15 (1993): 1–4.

Mattei, Roberto de, ed. *Finis Vitae: Is Brain Death Still Life?* Rome: Consiglio Nazionale delle Rescherche, 2006.

May, William E. *Catholic Bioethics and the Gift of Human Life.* 2nd ed. Huntington, Ind.: Our Sunday Visitor Press, 2008.

———. "Contemporary Perspectives on Thomistic Natural Law." In *St. Thomas Aquinas and the Natural Law Tradition: Contemporary Perspectives,* edited by John Goyette, Mark S. Latkovic, and Richard S. Myers, 113–156. Washington, D.C.: The Catholic University of America Press, 2004.

———. "An End to the Debate?" *Natl Cathol Bioeth Q* 4 (2004): 451–452.

———. "Making Health Care Decisions for Others." *Ethics Medics* 22.6 (1997): 1–3.

———. "Proxy Consent for Nontherapeutic Experimentation." *Natl Cathol Bioeth Q* 7 (2007): 239–248.

———. "Using Condoms to Prevent HIV." *Natl Cathol Bioeth Q* 4 (2004): 667–668.

McCarthy, Donald G. "Gift? Yes!" *Ethics Medics* 18.9 (1993): 3–4.

McConnell, Michael W. "Secular Reason and the Misguided Attempt to Exclude Religious Argument from Democratic Deliberation." *Journal of Law, Philosophy and Culture* 1 (2007): 159–174.

McCormick, Richard, S.J. "Some Early Reactions to *Veritatis splendor.*" *Theological Studies* 55 (1994): 481–506.

———. "The Vatican Document on Bioethics: Two Responses." *America* 156 (1987): 246–248.

McDonaugh, Sean. "Genetic Engineering Is Not the Answer." *America* 192 (2005): 8–10.

McGloughlin, Martina. "Ten Reasons Why Biotechnology Will Be Important to the Developing World." *AgBioForum* 2 (1999): 163–174.

McInerny, Ralph. *Aquinas on Human Action.* Washington, D.C.: The Catholic University of America Press, 1992.

———. *Ethica Thomistica.* Rev. ed. Washington, D.C.: The Catholic University of America Press, 1997.

McMahan, Jeff. "An Alternative to Brain Death." *J Law Med Ethics* 34 (2006): 44–48.

Meilaender, Gilbert. *Neither Beast Nor God: The Dignity of the Human Person.* New York: Encounter Books, 2009.

———. "*Question Disputata:* Ordinary and Extraordinary Treatments: When Does Quality of Life Count?" *Theological Studies* 58 (1997): 527–531.

Merges, Robert P. "Intellectual Property in Higher Life Forms: The Patent System and Controversial Technologies." *Maryland Law Review* 47 (1988): 1051–1075.

Merleau-Ponty, Maurice. *The Phenomenology of Perception.* Translated by Colin Smith. New York: Routledge, 1962.

Merrick, Janna C., and Robert H. Blank. *Contemporary World Issues: Reproductive Issues in America.* Santa Barbara, Calif.: ABC-CLIO, 2003.

Milavec, Aaron. *The Didache: Text, Translation, Analysis, and Commentary.* Collegeville, Minn.: Liturgical Press, 2003.

Miller, Franklin G., and Howard Brody. "A Critique of Clinical Equipoise: Therapeutic Misconception in the Ethics of Clinical Trials." *Hastings Cent Rep* 33 (2003):
19–28.

Miner, Robert. *Thomas Aquinas on the Passions: A Study of Summa Theologiae, 1a2ae 22–48.*
Cambridge: Cambridge University Press, 2009.

Mirkes, Renee, O.S.F. "The Ethics of Uterus Transplantation." *Linacre Q* 75 (2008):
112–131.

Modell, Stephen M. "Approaching Religious Guidelines for Chimera Policymaking." *Zygon* 47 (2007): 629–641.

Molla, Gianna Beretta. *Love Letters to My Husband,* edited by Elio Guerriero. Boston:
Pauline Books and Media, 2002.

Molla, Pietro, Elio Guerriero, and James G. Colbert. *Saint Gianna Molla: Wife, Mother,
Doctor.* San Francisco: Ignatius Press, 2004.

Monks of Solesmes, eds. *The Human Body: Papal Teaching.* Boston: St. Paul Editions,
1960.

Mundy, Liza. *Everything Conceivable: How Assisted Reproduction Is Changing Men, Women, and
the World.* New York: Alfred A. Knopf, 2007.

Murphy, William F., Jr. "Developments in Thomistic Action Theory: Progress toward a Greater Consensus." *Natl Cathol Bioeth Q* 8 (2008): 505–528.

———. "Forty Years Later: Arguments in Support of *Humanae vitae* in Light of *Veritatis splendor.*" *Josephinum Journal of Theology* 14 (2007): 122–167.

Murrell, Kevin J. "Confidentiality." In *Catholic Health Care Ethics: A Manual for Practitioners,* 2nd ed., edited by Edward J. Furton, Peter J. Cataldo, and Albert S. Moraczewski, O.P., 19–23. Philadelphia: National Catholic Bioethics Center, 2009.

Nakamima, Steven T. *Contemporary Guide to Contraception.* Newtown, Pa.: Handbooks
in Health Care, 2006.

National Catholic Bioethics Center. "Cooperating with Non-Catholic Partners."
Ethics Medics 23.11 (1998): 1–5.

National Conference of Catholic Bishops Committee for Pro-Life Activities. "Nutrition and Hydration: Moral and Pastoral Reflections." *Origins* 21 (1992): 705–
712.

Nolan, K. "The Use of Embryo or Fetus in Transplantation: What There Is to
Lose." *Transplant Proc* 22 (1990): 1028–1029.

Nomura, Tatsuji, Takeshi Watanabe, and Sonoku Habu, eds. *Humanized Mice.* Current Topics in Microbiology and Immunology 324. Berlin: Springer, 2008.

Noonan, John T., Jr. *Contraception: A History of Its Treatment by the Catholic Theologians and
Canonists.* Enlarged ed. Cambridge, Mass.: Harvard University Press, 1986.

Nuffield Council on Bioethics. *Genetically Modified Crops: The Ethical and Social Issues.*
London: Nuffield Council on Bioethics, 1999.

Oden, Thomas. "The Death of Modernity and Postmodern Evangelical Spirituality." In *The Challenge of Postmodernism,* 2nd ed., edited by David Dockery, 19–33.
Grand Rapids, Mich.: Baker Book House, 2001.

Oleson, Christopher. "Nature, 'Naturalism,' and the Immorality of Contraception:

A Critique of Fr. Rhonheimer on Condom Use and Contraceptive Intent." *Natl Cathol Bioeth Q* 6 (2006): 719–730.

Olivier, Bernard, O.P. *Christian Hope.* Translated by Paul Barrett, O.F.M. Cap. Westminster: Newman Press, 1963.

O'Neill, Onora. *Autonomy and Trust in Bioethics.* Cambridge: Cambridge University Press, 2002.

O'Rourke, Kevin, O.P. "Ethical Opinions in Regard to the Question of Early Delivery of Anencephalic Infants." *Linacre Q* 63 (1996): 55–59.

———. "Evolution of Church Teaching on Prolonging Life." *Health Prog* 69 (1988): 28–35.

———. "Open Letter to Bishop McHugh: Father Kevin O'Rourke on Hydration and Nutrition." *Origins* 19 (1989): 351–352.

———. "Prolonging Life: A Traditional Interpretation." *Linacre Q* 58 (1991): 12–26.

Outka, Gene, and John P. Reeder, Jr., eds. *Prospects for a Common Morality.* Princeton, N.J.: Princeton University Press, 1993.

Panicola, Michael. "Catholic Teaching on Prolonging Life: Setting the Record Straight." *Hastings Cent Rep* 31 (2001): 14–25.

Parens, Erik, and Adrienne Asch, eds. *Prenatal Testing and Disability Rights.* Washington, D.C.: Georgetown University Press, 2000.

Paterick, Timothy J., et al. "Medical Informed Consent: General Considerations for Physicians." *Mayo Clin Proc* 83 (2008): 313–319.

Paul VI. *Humanae vitae.* Vatican City: Libreria Editrice Vaticana, 1968.

Pellegrino, Edmund D., and David C. Thomasma. *The Christian Virtues in Medical Practice.* Washington, D.C.: Georgetown University Press, 1996.

———. *Helping and Healing: Religious Commitment in Health Care.* Washington, D.C.: Georgetown University Press, 1997.

———. *A Philosophical Basis of Medical Practice: Toward a Philosophy and Ethic of the Healing Professions.* Oxford: Oxford University Press, 1994.

Pernick, M. S. "Back from the Grave: Recurring Controversies over Defining and Diagnosing Death in History." In *Death: Beyond Whole-Brain Criteria,* edited by R. M. Zaner, 17–74. Dordrecht: Kluwer Academic Publishers, 1988.

Perry, Michael J. *The Idea of Human Rights.* Oxford: Oxford University Press, 1993.

Peters, Edward. "Hardt and O'Rourke Err in Minimizing the Scope of CDF Response." *Natl Cathol Bioeth Q* 8 (2008): 14–15.

Petri, J. Thomas, O.P. "Altered Nuclear Transfer, Gift, and Mystery: An Aristotelian-Thomistic Response to David L. Schindler." *Natl Cathol Bioeth Q.* 7 (2007): 729–747.

Pieper, Josef. *Faith, Hope, Love.* San Francisco: Ignatius Press, 1997.

———. *Fortitude and Temperance.* Translated by Daniel F. Coogan. New York: Pantheon Books, 1954.

———. *Four Cardinal Virtues.* South Bend, Ind.: University of Notre Dame Press, 1990.

———. *On Hope.* Translated by Mary Frances McCarthy, S.N.D. San Francisco: Ignatius Press, 1986.

————. *The Silence of St. Thomas.* Translated by J. Murray, S.J., and D. O'Conner. New York: Pantheon Books, 1957.

Pilsner, Joseph. *The Specification of Human Actions in St. Thomas Aquinas.* Oxford: Oxford University Press, 2006.

Pinches, Charles R. *Theology and Action: After Theory in Christian Ethics.* Grand Rapids, Mich.: William B. Eerdmans, 2002.

Pinckaers, Servais, O.P. "Aquinas's Pursuit of Beatitude: From the *Commentary on the Sentences* to the *Summa Theologiae.*" In *The Pinckaers Reader,* edited by John Berkman and Craig Steven Titus, 93–114. Washington, D.C.: The Catholic University of America Press, 2005.

————. "Conscience and Christian Tradition." In *The Pinckaers Reader,* edited by John Berkman and Craig Steven Titus, 321–341. Washington, D.C.: The Catholic University of America Press, 2005.

————. "An Encyclical for the Future: *Veritatis splendor.*" In *Veritatis Splendor and the Renewal of Moral Theology,* edited by J. Augustine DiNoia, O.P., and Romanus Cessario, O.P., 11–71. Huntington, Ind.: Our Sunday Visitor Press, 1999.

————. "A Historical Perspective on Intrinsically Evil Acts." In *The Pinckaers Reader,* edited by John Berkman and Craig Steven Titus, 185–235. Washington, D.C.: The Catholic University of America Press, 2005.

————. "Revisionist Understandings of Actions in the Wake of Vatican II." In *The Pinckaers Reader,* edited by John Berkman and Craig Steven Titus, 236–270. Washington, D.C.: The Catholic University of America Press, 2005.

Pius XII. "Allocution to the Fourth International Congress of Surgeons, May 20, 1948." In *The Human Body: Papal Teaching,* selected and arranged by the Monks of Solesmes, 95–100. Boston: St. Paul Editions, 1960.

————. "Allocution to the Fourth International Congress of Surgeons, May 20, 1948." In *The Human Body: Papal Teaching,* selected and arranged by the Monks of Solesmes, 95–100. Boston: St. Paul Editions, 1960.

————. "Allocution to Delegates at the 26th Congress of Urology, October 8, 1958." In *The Human Body: Papal Teaching,* selected and arranged by the Monks of Solesmes, 277–281. Boston: St. Paul Editions, 1960.

————. "Allocution to Large Families, November 26, 1951." In *The Human Body: Papal Teaching,* selected and arranged by the Monks of Solesmes, 180–182. Boston: St. Paul Editions, 1960.

————. "Allocution to the First International Congress of Histopathology, September 13, 1952." In *The Human Body: Papal Teaching,* selected and arranged by the Monks of Solesmes, 194–208. Boston: St. Paul Editions, 1960.

————. "Allocution to the Italian Medical-biological Union of St. Luke, November 12, 1944." In *The Human Body: Papal Teaching,* selected and arranged by the Monks of Solesmes, 51–65. Boston: St. Paul Editions, 1960.

————. "The Prolongation of Life, November 24, 1957." *The Pope Speaks* 4 (1958): 393–398; 395–396.

Pogge, Thomas. *John Rawls: His Life and Theory of Justice.* Oxford: Oxford University Press, 2007.

Pontifical Academy for Life. "Reflections on Cloning." *Origins* 28 (1998): 14–16.

Pontifical Academy of Sciences. *Papal Addresses to the Pontifical Academy of Sciences 1917–2002 and to the Pontifical Academy of Social Sciences 1994–2002.* Scripta Varia 100. Vatican City: Pontifical Academy of Sciences, 2003.

———. *Working Group on the Artificial Prolongation of Life and the Determination of the Exact Moment of Death, October 19–21, 1985.* Scripta Varia 60. Vatican City: Pontifical Academy of Sciences, 1986.

———. *Working Group on the Determination of Brain Death and Its Relationship to Human Death, December 10–14, 1989.* Scripta Varia 83. Vatican City: Pontifical Academy of Sciences, 1992.

Pontifical Council for Justice and Peace. *Compendium of the Social Doctrine of the Church.* Vatican City: Libreria Editrice Vaticana, 2004.

Pontifical Council for Pastoral Assistance. *Charter for Health Care Workers.* Vatican City: Libreria Editrice Vaticana, 1995.

Pope John XXIII Medical-Moral Research and Education Center. *Human Sexuality and Personhood: Proceedings of the Workshop for the Hierarchies of the United States and Canada.* St. Louis, Mo.: Pope John XXIII Center, 1981.

Pope, Stephen J., ed. *The Ethics of Aquinas.* Washington, D.C.: Georgetown University Press, 2002.

Porter, Jean. "Is the Embryo a Person? Arguing with the Catholic Traditions." *Commonweal,* February 8, 2002, 8–10.

———. *The Recovery of Virtue.* Louisville: Westminster/John Knox Press, 1990.

———. "Tradition in the Recent Work of Alasdair MacIntyre." In *Alasdair MacIntyre,* edited by Mark C. Murphy, 38–69. Cambridge: Cambridge University Press, 2003.

Potts, Malcolm, et al. "Reassessing HIV Prevention." *Science* 320 (2008): 749–750.

President's Commission for the Study of Ethical Problems in Medicine and Biomedical and Behavioral Research. *Defining Death.* Washington, D.C.: Government Printing Office, 1981.

President's Council on Bioethics. *Beyond Therapy: Biotechnology and the Pursuit of Happiness.* Washington, D.C.: President's Council on Bioethics, 2003.

———. *Controversies in the Determination of Death: A White Paper by the President's Council on Bioethics.* Washington, D.C.: President's Council on Bioethics, 2008.

———. *Human Dignity and Bioethics.* Washington, D.C.: President's Council on Bioethics, 2008.

———. *White Paper: Alternative Sources of Pluripotent Stem Cells.* Washington, D.C.: President's Council on Bioethics, 2005.

Provine, William. "Evolution and the Foundation of Ethics." In *Science, Technology, and Social Progress,* edited by Steven L. Goldman, 253–267. Bethlehem, Pa.: Lehigh University Press, 1989.

Pruss, Alexander R. "Complicity, Fetal Tissue, and Vaccines." *Natl Cath Bioeth Q* 6 (2006): 461–470.

———. *The Principle of Sufficient Reason.* Cambridge: Cambridge University Press, 2007.

Quill, Timothy E., and Margaret P. Battin, eds. *Physician-Assisted Dying: The Case for Palliative Care and Patient Choice.* Baltimore: Johns Hopkins University Press, 2004.

Quill, Timothy, Rebecca Dresser, and Dan Brock. "The Rule of Double Effect— A Critique of Its Role in End-of-Life Decision Making." *N Engl J Med* 337 (1997): 1768–1771.

Rachels, James. "Active and Passive Euthanasia." *N Engl J Med* 292 (1975): 78–80.

———. *The End of Life: Euthanasia and Morality.* New York: Oxford University Press, 1986.

Ratzinger, Joseph. *Eschatology: Death and Eternal Life.* Translated by Michael Waldstein and Aidan Nichols, O.P. Washington, D.C.: The Catholic University of America Press, 1988.

———. *On Conscience: Two Essays.* San Francisco: Ignatius Press, 2006.

———. "The Renewal of Moral Theology: Perspectives of Vatican II and *Veritatis splendor.*" *Communio* 32 (2005): 357–368.

Ratzinger, Joseph, and Jürgen Habermas. *The Dialectics of Secularization.* San Francisco: Ignatius Press, 2007.

Rawls, John. *Political Liberalism.* New York: Columbia University Press, 1993.

———. *A Theory of Justice.* Cambridge, Mass.: Harvard University Press, 1971.

Rawls, John, and Erin Kelly. *Justice as Fairness: A Restatement.* 2nd ed. Cambridge, Mass.: Harvard University Press, 2001.

Reardon, David C. *Aborted Women: Silent No More.* Chicago: Loyola University Press, 1987.

Reichberg, Gregory M. "The Intellectual Virtues (Ia IIae, qq. 57–58)." In *The Ethics of Aquinas,* edited by Stephen J. Pope, 131–150. Washington, D.C.: Georgetown University Press, 2002.

Rhonheimer, Martin. "The Contraceptive Choice, Condom Use, and Moral Arguments Based on Nature: A Reply to Christopher Oleson." *Natl Cathol Bioeth Q* 7 (2007): 273–292.

———. "Intentional Actions and the Meaning of Object: A Reply to Richard McCormick." In *Veritatis Splendor and the Renewal of Moral Theology,* edited by J. Augustine Di Noia, O.P., and Romanus Cessario, O.P., 241–268. Huntington, Ind.: Our Sunday Visitor Press, 1999.

———. "The Truth about Condoms." *Tablet* (July 10, 2004): 10–11.

———. "The Use of Contraceptives under Threat of Rape: An Exception?" *Josephinum Journal of Theology* 14 (2007): 168–181.

Rigali, Justin, and William Lori. "On Basic Care for Patients in the 'Vegetative' State: A Response to Dr. Hardt and Fr. O'Rourke." *Health Prog* 89 (2008): 70–72.

Ring-Cassidy, Elizabeth, and Ian Gentles. *Women's Health after Abortion: The Medical and Psychological Evidence.* 2nd ed. Toronto: DeVeber Institute, 2003.

The Rites of the Catholic Church. Vol. 1. Collegeville, Minn.: Liturgical Press, 1990.

Robertson, John A. *Children of Choice.* Princeton, N.J.: Princeton University Press, 1996.

Rollin, Bernard E. "On Chimeras." *Zygon* 47 (2007): 643–647.

Rorty, Richard. *Contingency, Irony, and Solidarity.* Cambridge: Cambridge University Press, 1989.

Rothman, Kenneth J., and Karin B. Michels. "The Continuing Unethical Use of Placebo Controls." *N Engl J Med* 331 (1994): 394–398.

Rozovsky, Fay A. *Consent to Treatment: A Practical Guide.* 4th ed. Frederick, Md.: Aspen Publishers, 2007.

Sanbar, S. Sandy, et al., eds. *Legal Medicine.* 6th ed. Philadelphia: Mosby, 2004.

Savulescu, Julian. "Conscientious Objection in Medicine." *BMJ* 332 (2006): 294–297.

Scheper-Hughes, Nancy. "The Global Traffic in Organs." *Curr Anthropol* 41 (2000): 191–224.

Schmidt, Ulf, and Andreas Frewer, eds. *History and Theory of Human Experimentation: The Declaration of Helsinki and Modern Medical Ethics.* New York: Franz Steiner Publishers, 2007.

Seitz, Mark J. "The Role of the Priest in Bioethical Decision Making." *Natl Cathol Bioeth Q* 4 (2004): 681–689.

Senior, D., et al., eds. *The Catholic Study Bible.* New York: Oxford University Press, 1990.

Seyfer, Tara L. "An Overview of Chimeras and Hybrids." *Natl Cathol Bioeth Q* 6 (2006): 37–49.

Sgreccia, Elio, and Jean Laffitte, eds. *The Human Embryo before Implantation: Scientific Aspects and Bioethical Considerations.* Vatican City: Libreria Editrice Vaticana, 2007.

Shannon, Thomas A. "Cloning, Uniqueness, and Individuality." *Louvain Studies* 19 (1994): 283–306.

Shannon, Thomas A., and James J. Walter. "The PVS Patient and the Forgoing/Withdrawing of Medical Nutrition and Hydration." In *Bioethics,* 4th ed., edited by Thomas A. Shannon. Mahway, N.J.: Paulist Press, 1993.

Shannon, Thomas A., and Allan B. Wolter. "Reflections on the Moral Status of the Pre-embryo." *Theological Studies,* 51 (1990): 603–626.

Shannon, William H. *The Lively Debate: Response to Humanae vitae.* New York: Sheed and Ward, 1970.

Shapiro, Ian, ed. *Abortion: The Supreme Court Decisions.* Indianapolis: Hackett, 2007.

Shelton, James D. "Confessions of a Condom Lover." *Lancet* 368 (2006): 1947–1949.

———. "Ten Myths and One Truth about Generalized HIV Epidemics." *Lancet* 370 (2007): 1809–1811.

Shelton, James D., et al. "Partner Reduction Is Crucial for Balanced 'ABC' Approach to HIV Prevention." *BMJ* 328 (2004): 891–893.

Sherwin, Michael, O.P. "Infused Virtue and the Effects of Acquired Vice: A Test Case for the Thomistic Theory of Infused Cardinal Virtues." *Thomist* 73 (2009): 29–52.

Shewmon, D. Alan. "The Brain and Somatic Integration: Insights into the Standard Biological Rationale for Equating 'Brain Death' with Death." *J Med Philos* 26 (2001): 457–478.

———. "Brain Death: Can It Be Resuscitated?" *Hastings Cent Rep* 39 (2009): 18–24.

———. "'Brainstem Death,' 'Brain Death' and 'Death': A Critical Re-evaluation of the Purported Equivalence." *Issues Law Med* 14 (1998): 125–145.

———. "Chronic 'Brain Death': Meta-analysis and Conceptual Consequences." *Neurology* 51 (1998): 1538–1545.

Shewmon, D. Alan, Alexander M. Capron, Warwick J. Peacock, and Barbara L. Schulman. "The Use of Anencephalic Infants as Organ Sources: A Critique." *JAMA* 261 (1989): 1773–1781.

Shivanadan, Mary. *Crossing the Threshold of Love: A New Vision of Marriage in Light of John Paul II's Anthropology.* Washington, D.C.: The Catholic University of America Press, 1999.

Singer, Peter. *Practical Ethics.* 2nd ed. Cambridge: Cambridge University Press, 1999.

Slade, Francis. "Ends and Purposes." In *Final Causality in Nature and Human Affairs*, edited by Richard Hassing, 83–85. Washington, D.C.: The Catholic University of America Press, 1997.

Smith, David W. "Religion and the Roots of the Bioethics Revival." In *Religion and Medical Ethics: Looking Back, Looking Forward*, edited by Allen Verhey, 9–18. Grand Rapids, Mich.: Wm. B. Eerdmans, 1996.

Smith, Janet E. *The Right to Privacy.* San Francisco: Ignatius Press, 2008.

Smith, Quentin, and William Lane Craig. *Theism, Atheism, and Big Bang Cosmology.* Oxford: Clarendon Press, 1993.

Smith, Russell E. "The Principles of Cooperation and Their Application to the Present State of Health Care Evolution." In *The Splendor of Truth and Health Care*, edited by Russell E. Smith, 217–231. Braintree, Mass.: Pope John Center, 1995.

———. "The Principles of Cooperation in Catholic Thought." In *The Fetal Tissue Issue: Medical and Ethical Aspects*, edited by Peter Cataldo and Albert Moraczewski, O.P., 81–92. Braintree, Mass.: Pope John Center, 1994.

———, ed. *Catholic Conscience: Foundation and Formation.* Braintree, Mass.: Pope John XXIII Center, 1991.

Smith, Wesley J. *Forced Exit: Euthanasia, Assisted Suicide, and the New Duty to Die.* New York: Encounter Books, 2006.

Sokolowski, Robert. "What Is Natural Law? Human Purposes and Natural Ends." *Thomist* 68 (2004): 507–529.

Spar, Debora L. *The Baby Business: How Money, Science, and Politics Drive the Commerce of Conception.* Cambridge, Mass.: Harvard Business School Press, 2006.

Speroff, Leon, and Philip D. Darney. *A Clinical Guide to Contraception.* Philadelphia: Lippincott Williams and Wilkins, 2005.

Staton, Jana, Roger W. Shuy, and Ira Byock. *A Few Months to Live: Different Paths to Life's End.* Washington, D.C.: Georgetown University Press, 2001.

Steinbock, Bonnie. *Life before Birth: The Moral and Legal Status of Embryos and Fetuses.* Oxford: Oxford University Press, 1992.

Stempsey, William E., S.J. "Organ Markets and Human Dignity: On Selling Your Body and Soul." *Christ Bioeth* 6 (2000): 195–204.

Stewart, Felicia H., and James Trussell. "Prevention of Pregnancy Resulting from

Rape: A Neglected Preventive Health Measure." *Am J Prev Med* 19 (2000): 228–229.

Stirrat, G. M., and R. Gill. "Autonomy in Medical Ethics after O'Neill." *J Med Ethics* 31 (2005): 127–130.

Stoneburner, R. L., and D. Low-Beer. "Population-Level HIV Declines and Behavioral Risk Avoidance in Uganda." *Science* 304 (2004): 714–718.

Stout, Jeffrey. *The Flight from Authority: Religion, Morality, and the Quest for Autonomy.* Notre Dame: University of Notre Dame Press, 1981.

Sullivan, Francis, S.J. *Magisterium: Teaching Authority in the Catholic Church.* Dublin: Gill and Macmillan, 1983.

Sulmasy, Daniel P., O.F.M. "Terri Schiavo and the Roman Catholic Tradition of Forgoing Extraordinary Means of Care." *J Law Med Ethics* 33 (2005): 359–362.

———. "What Is Conscience and Why Is Respect for It So Important?" *Theor Med Bioeth* 29 (2008): 135–149.

Suzuki, David, and Peter Knudtson. *Genethics: The Clash between the New Genetics and Human Values.* Cambridge, Mass.: Harvard University Press, 1990.

Swartz, Martha. "'Conscience Clauses' or 'Unconscionable Clauses': Personal Beliefs Versus Professional Responsibilities." *Yale J Health Policy Law Ethics* 6 (2006): 269–350.

Swinburne, Richard. *The Evolution of the Soul.* Rev. ed. Oxford: Oxford University Press, 1997.

Sykes, Nigel, and Andrew Thorns. "Sedative Use in the Last Week of Life and the Implications for End-of-Life Decision Making." *Arch Intern Med* 163 (2003): 341–344.

Taylor, Charles. *A Secular Age.* Cambridge: Harvard University Press, 2007.

Taylor, James S., ed. *Personal Autonomy.* New York: Cambridge University Press, 2005.

Tham, S. Joseph, L.C. "The Secularization of Bioethics." *Natl Cathol Bioeth Q* 8 (2008): 443–453.

Then, Christoph. *The True Cost of Gene Patents: The Economic and Social Consequences of Patenting Genes and Living Organisms, A Greenpeace Document.* Hamburg: Greenpeace, 2004.

Thiel, John E. *Nonfoundationalism.* Minneapolis, Minn.: Fortress Press, 1994.

Titus, Craig Steven. *Resilience and the Virtue of Fortitude.* Washington, D.C.: The Catholic University of America Press, 2006.

Tonelli, Mark R. "Substituted Judgment in Medical Practice: Evidentiary Standards on a Sliding Scale." *J Law Med Ethics* 25 (1997): 22–29.

Tonti-Filippini, Nicholas, John I. Fleming, Gregory K. Pike, and Ray Campbell. "Ethics and Human-Animal Transgenesis." *Natl Cathol Bioethics Q* 6 (2006): 689–704.

Truog, Robert D. "Brain Death—Too Flawed to Endure, Too Ingrained to Abandon." *J Law Med Ethics* 35 (2007): 273–281.

Truog, Robert D., and John C. Fletcher. "Anencephalic Newborns: Can Organs Be Transplanted before Brain Death?" *N Engl J Med* 321 (1989): 388–391.

Truog, Robert D., and Franklin G. Miller. "The Dead Donor Rule and Organ Transplantation." *N Engl J Med* 359 (2008): 674–675.

Tucker, Kathryn L., and Fred B. Steele. "Patient Choice at the End of Life: Getting the Language Right." *J Leg Med* 28 (2007): 305–325.

Tully, Patrick. "Morally Objectionable Options: Informed Consent and Physician Integrity." *Natl Cath Bioeth Q* 8 (2008): 491–504.

Twycross, Robert G. "Where There Is Hope, There Is Life: A View from the Hospice." In *Euthanasia Examined: Ethical, Clinical, and Legal Perspectives*, edited by John Keown, 141–168. Cambridge: Cambridge University Press, 1995.

Ulrich, Lawrence P. *The Patient Self-Determination Act: Meeting the Challenges in Patient Care.* Washington, D.C.: Georgetown University Press, 2001.

United States Conference of Catholic Bishops. *Critical Decisions: Genetic Testing and its Implications.* Washington, D.C.: United States Conference of Catholic Bishops, 1996.

———. *Ethical and Religious Directives for Catholic Health Care Services.* 5th ed. Washington, D.C.: United States Conference of Catholic Bishops, 2009.

———. *For I Was Hungry and You Gave Me Food.* Washington, D.C.: United States Conference of Catholic Bishops, 2003.

Valko, Nancy. "The Case against Premature Induction." *Ethics Medics* 29.5 (2004): 1–3.

Veatch, Robert M. "The Impending Collapse of the Whole-Brain Definition of Death." *Hastings Cent Rep* 23 (1993): 18–24.

———. *A Theory of Medical Ethics.* New York: Basic Books, 1981.

Verhagen, Eduard, and Pieter J. J. Sauer. "End-of-Life Decisions in Newborns: An Approach from the Netherlands." *Pediatrics* 116 (2005): 736–739.

———. "The Groningen Protocol: Euthanasia in Severely Ill Newborn." *N Engl J Med.* 352 (2005): 959–962.

Waldstein, Michael. "The Common Good in St. Thomas and John Paul II." *Nova et Vetera* 3 (2005): 569–578.

Walter, James J. "Human Germline Therapy: Proper Human Responsibility or Playing God?" In *Design and Destiny*, edited by Ronald Cole-Turner, 119–143. Cambridge, Mass.: MIT Press, 2008.

Watt, Helen. "The Origin of Persons." In *The Identity and Status of the Human Embryo*, edited by Juan de Dios Vial Correa and Elio Sgreccia, 343–364. Vatican City: Libreria Editrice Vaticana, 1999.

Weller, Susan C., and Karen Davis-Beaty. "Condom Effectiveness in Reducing Heterosexual HIV Transmission (Cochrane Review)." In *Cochrane Library*, issue 4. Chichester, UK: John Wiley and Sons, 2003.

Weschler, Toni. *Taking Charge of Your Fertility, 10th Anniversary Edition: The Definitive Guide to Natural Birth Control, Pregnancy Achievement, and Reproductive Health.* New York: Harper Collins, 2006.

West, Christopher. *Theology of the Body Explained: A Commentary on John Paul II's "Gospel of the Body."* Rev. ed. Boston: Pauline Books, 2007.

Westberg, Daniel. *Right Practical Reason: Aristotle, Action, and Prudence in Aquinas.* Oxford: Clarendon Press, 1994.

Wilcox, W. Bradford. "The Facts of Life and Marriage: Social Science and the Vindication of Christian Moral Teaching." *Touchstone* 18 (2005): 38–44.

Wildes, Kevin, S.J. *Moral Acquaintances: Methodology in Bioethics.* Washington, D.C.: Georgetown University Press, 2000.

―――. "Ordinary and Extraordinary Means and the Quality of Life." *Theological Studies* 57 (1996): 500–512.

Wilson, Mercedes Arzu. "The Practice of Natural Family Planning versus the Use of Artificial Birth Control: Family, Sexual, and Moral Issues." *Catholic Social Science Review* 7 (2002): 1–20.

Wojtyla, Karol. *Love and Responsibility.* Translated by H. T. Willetts. New York: Farrar, Straus and Giroux, Inc., 1981.

Wolf, S. M. , et al. "Sources of Concern about the Patient Self-Determination Act." *N Engl J Med* 325 (1991): 1666–1671.

Wolfe, Christopher, and John Hittinger, eds. *Liberalism at the Crossroads.* Lanham, Md.: Rowan and Littlefield Publishers, Inc., 1994.

Wolpe, Paul Root. "The Triumph of Autonomy in American Medical Ethics: A Sociological View." In *Bioethics and Society: Constructing the Ethical Enterprise,* edited by Raymond DeVries and Janardan Subedi, 38–59. New York: Prentice Hall, 1998.

Woodward, P. A., ed. *The Doctrine of Double Effect.* Notre Dame, Ind.: University of Notre Dame Press, 2001.

Wright, Linda. "Is Presumed Consent the Answer to Organ Shortages? No." *BMJ* 334 (2007): 1089.

Youngner, Stuart J., and Edward T. Bartlett. "Human Death and High Technology: The Failure of the Whole-Brain Formulations." *Ann Inter Med* 99 (1983): 252–258.

Zylicz, Zbigniew. "Palliative Care and Euthanasia in the Netherlands." In *The Case against Assisted Suicide: For the Right to End-of-Life Care,* edited by Kathleen Foley and Herbert Hendin, 122–143. Baltimore: Johns Hopkins University Press, 2002.

Scripture Index

Books are arranged by order of occurrence in the Bible.

Old Testament

Genesis, 75
1:27, 45
1:28, 226
3:16-19, 21
30:1, 97

Exodus
20:13, 46

Deuteronomy
5:17, 46

Job, 21

Proverbs
27:17, 260n41

Isaiah
11:2-3, 19

New Testament

Matthew
5:48, 32
7:16-17, 89
16:18-19, 22
19:16, 9, 126
19:21, 10
25:34, 168
25:36, 115
28:19-20, 257

Luke
17:1-2, 266
29:38, 136

John
2:20, 88
2:27, 88

3:3-8, 137
8:32, 22
10:10, 115
11:11, 137
15:12-13, 175
16:13, 19
21:15-17, 22

Acts
2:24, 137

Romans
2:14-15, 35—36
5:12, 137
5:19-21, 137
6:23, 136
8:24, 168

11:17-24, 242
14:9, 137
15:13, 169

1 Corinthians
13:13, 274
15:21, 136

2 Corinthians
5:8, 137

Ephesians
1:12, 10

Philippians
1:21, 137

Colossians
1:24, 21

1 Timothy
3:15, 22

2 Timothy
1:10, 137

Hebrews
2:14, 137
5:1, 128
9:27, 136
10:23, 169

Subject Index

abortion, Catholic Church's teachings on, 2, 7, 23, 41–42, 44, 47–72; on abortifacient use, 95–96; as act of killing, 58–59; bodily rights argument against, 57–59; Catholic health-care institutions not permitted to perform, 267; common arguments against, 50–70; delayed hominization argument against, 59–60; direct *vs.* indirect, 62–63, 65, 66, 67, 90, 94; for ectopic pregnancies, 64–65; effects on mothers, 49–50; ensoulment question, 69–70; for fetal abnormalities, 65–67, 220; nonpersonhood argument against, 55–57; physicians' refusals to perform, 247; post-conception beginning of life argument against, 50–54; procuring organs through, 179–84; after rape, 60–61; for selective reduction of multiple fetuses, 73, 99–100, 101; statistics on, 43–44; time of conception argument against, 50–54; virtues applied to, 70–72; women's reasons for having, 70–71

abstinence, virtue of, 93, 111

Ackerman, Felicia: on euthanasia and physician-assisted suicide, 154

acts, human: capacity for, 59–60; circumstances of, 27–28; evaluation of, 36, 37–38; evil, 16, 20–21, 27, 29, 31–32, 36, 37, 38, 40–41; good, 16, 19–20, 27–29, 32, 38, 80, 113, 127–28, 268, 274; healing, 39, 50, 107, 115–16, 118; heroic, 18, 19, 269; morality of, 8–11, 17, 24–42, 87, 139–41, 175n16, 271; natural inclinations and, 11–13; objects of, 24–27, 28, 31–32, 38, 39; obstacles to, 13–14; of omission, 144,

146, 156–57; pursuit of beatitude and, 8–11; pursuit of perfection through, 2, 18; structure of, 11–13, 26n48, 40n70; virtues' role in, 5–6, 10–11, 15, 29, 41. *See also* choices; conjugal acts; cooperation in evil acts; decision making; deliberation; double effect, principle of; execution, in human acts; human agents; intention(s); mental acts

Adderol, 222

adultery, 25n46, 152

adult stem cells (AS), 234; Church's support of research on, 4, 235, 236, 238; pluripotent stem cells from, 240–41, 246

advanced health-care directives (AHCDs), 112, 128–30, 131, 145

agnosticism, 250

agribiotech industry, 226, 229

Akerloff, George: on contraceptive methods, 83–84

alcoholics: organ transplant allocations for, 190

almsgiving, 27, 28, 31

alpha-fetoprotein (AFP): use for prenatal testing, 66

Alphonsus Ligouri, Saint, 7, 19; on cooperation with evil acts, 266–67

altered nuclear transfer-oocyte assisted reproduction (ANT-OAR), 240

Alzheimer's disease treatments, 223

Amatas, Arthur J.: on regulated sale of kidneys, 188

Ambien: effects on PVS patients, 158n62

American College of Physicians and the Infectious Diseases: on confidentiality, 122

Sherwin, Michael: on virtues, 15

Shewmon, D. Alan: on whole-brain death criteria, 195–96, 198, 199, 200, 201

simony, object of, 25n47

sin, 137, 143, 168, 267; original, 21, 36

Singer, Peter: utilitarian theories of, 251n11

6-mercaptopurine (immunosuppressant), 171

skepticism, 250

sleeping individuals: personhood of, 55, 56

Smith, Quentin: on principle of sufficient reason, 258n32

Snowflakes Program (embryo adoption), 108

society: democratic, 275; liberal, 5, 253n18, 255–56, 262–63; pluralistic, 45n12, 247–75; postmodern, 249–53, 259–60; right ordering of, 121; secular, 253–54, 272

Society for Assisted Reproductive Technology (SART), 107–8

solidarity, human, 46, 151, 229; of organ donation, 173, 186

Solomon (Old Testament), 260n41

somatic cell gene therapy, 216, 217

somatic cell nuclear transfer (SCNT), 103. See also cloning

soul, the, 19, 35, 115, 173; preparation for death, 153–54; unity of body and, 173, 194–95, 200–201, 275; virtues' assistance to, 15–16. See also ensoulment

Spain: embryonic stem cell research in, 237n94

Spence, Canterbury v., 124–25

sperm: defects in, 97, 99, 216; post-rape protocols on, 94–95; role in conception, 51n29, 52, 60, 82; in vitro fertilization and, 73, 101, 103

Spe salvi (Saved in Hope, Benedict XVI, 2007), 168

stem cells: pluripotent, 234, 238–41, 246; research on, 4, 232–41, 243, 246, 269; somatic, 217; used for organ transplantations, 185. See also adult stem cells (AS); embryonic stem cells (ES)

sterilization: Church's teachings on, 176, 247, 267; direct, 80, 82

Stout, Jeffrey: on secular worldviews, 253

suffering: alleviation of, 138n7, 139, 153–54, 160, 234, 236, 238; of animals, 225–26, 242; of infertile couples, 97–98, 107; patients', 114, 116; pursuit of beatitude and, 18, 20–21

sufficient reason, principle of, 257–58

suicides, 49, 202. See also euthanasia and physician-assisted suicide

Sullivan, Francis: on infallibility of Magisterium, 85n37

Sulmasy, Daniel P.: on conscientious objections by health-care institutions, 274

sure-knowledge (scientia), intellectual virtue of, 14, 243–44. See also God, knowledge of; knowledge

surgeries, prophylactic, 220–21

surrogates: for incompetent patients, 123–25, 128–31, 142n21, 143, 146, 166, 214; for infertility treatments, 73, 101–3

sympto-thermal method of NFP, 81

T. K. (brain-dead patient), survival of, 195, 200

Tarasoff v. Regents of the University of California (California Supreme Court), 122

telos. See anthropology, teleological; ends, human

temperance, moral virtue of, 16, 17, 111

testicles: donation of, 176n18; prophylactic removal of, 89, 90; stem cells from, 234

Texas Conference of Bishops: on provision of food and water to dying patients, 161–62, 163, 164

thanksgiving. See gratitude, virtue of

theft: commandment against, 121n15

theology. See body, the, theology of; moral theology

therapeutic privilege: as exception to informed consent, 132

Thomas Aquinas, Saint, 7; on abortion, 47–48; on beginning of life, 59; on

Biomedicine and Beatitude: An Introduction to Catholic Bioethics was designed and typeset in Centaur by Kachergis Book Design of Pittsboro, North Carolina. It was printed on 60-pound House Natural Smooth and bound by Sheridan Books of Ann Arbor, Michigan.